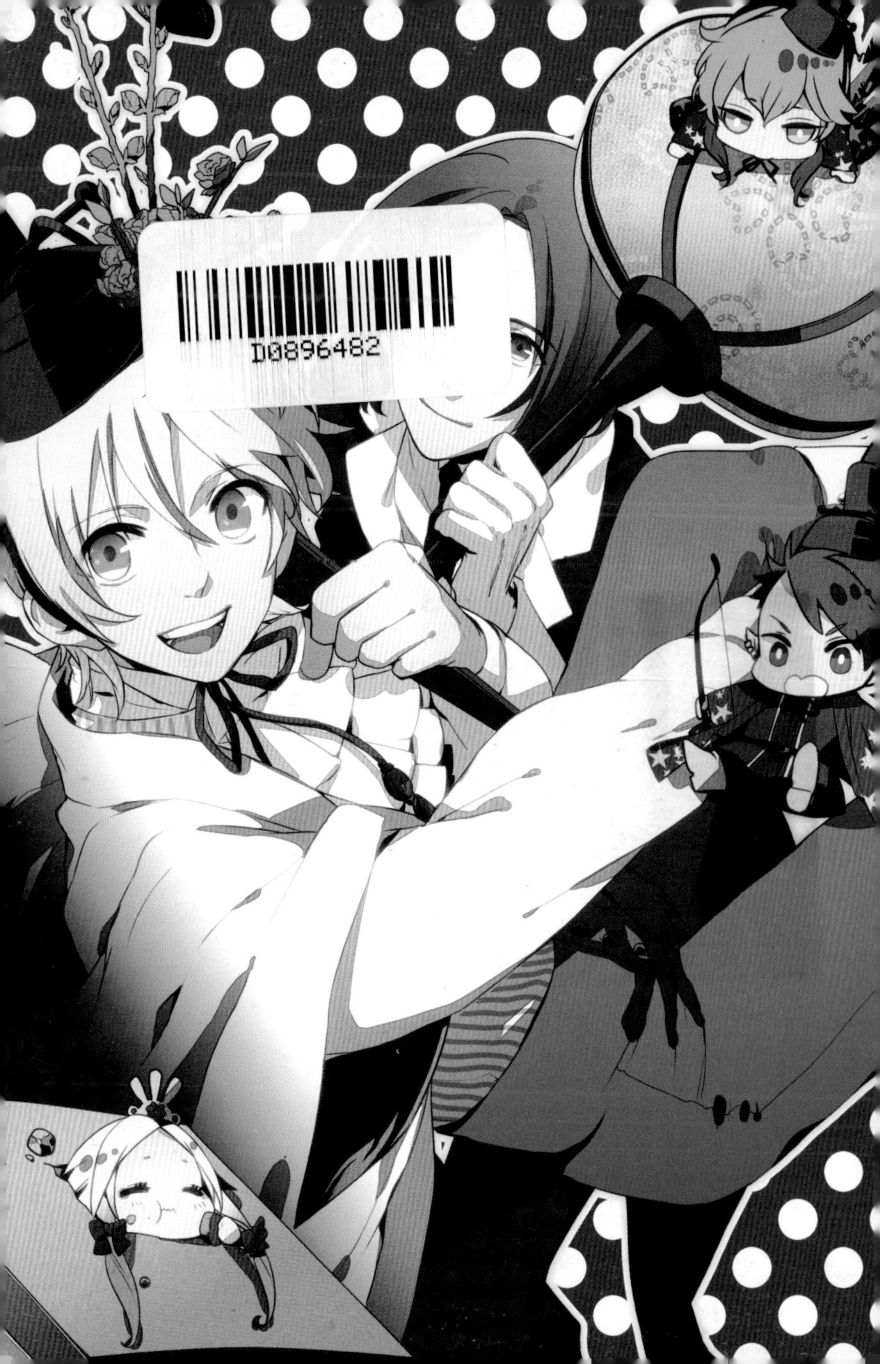

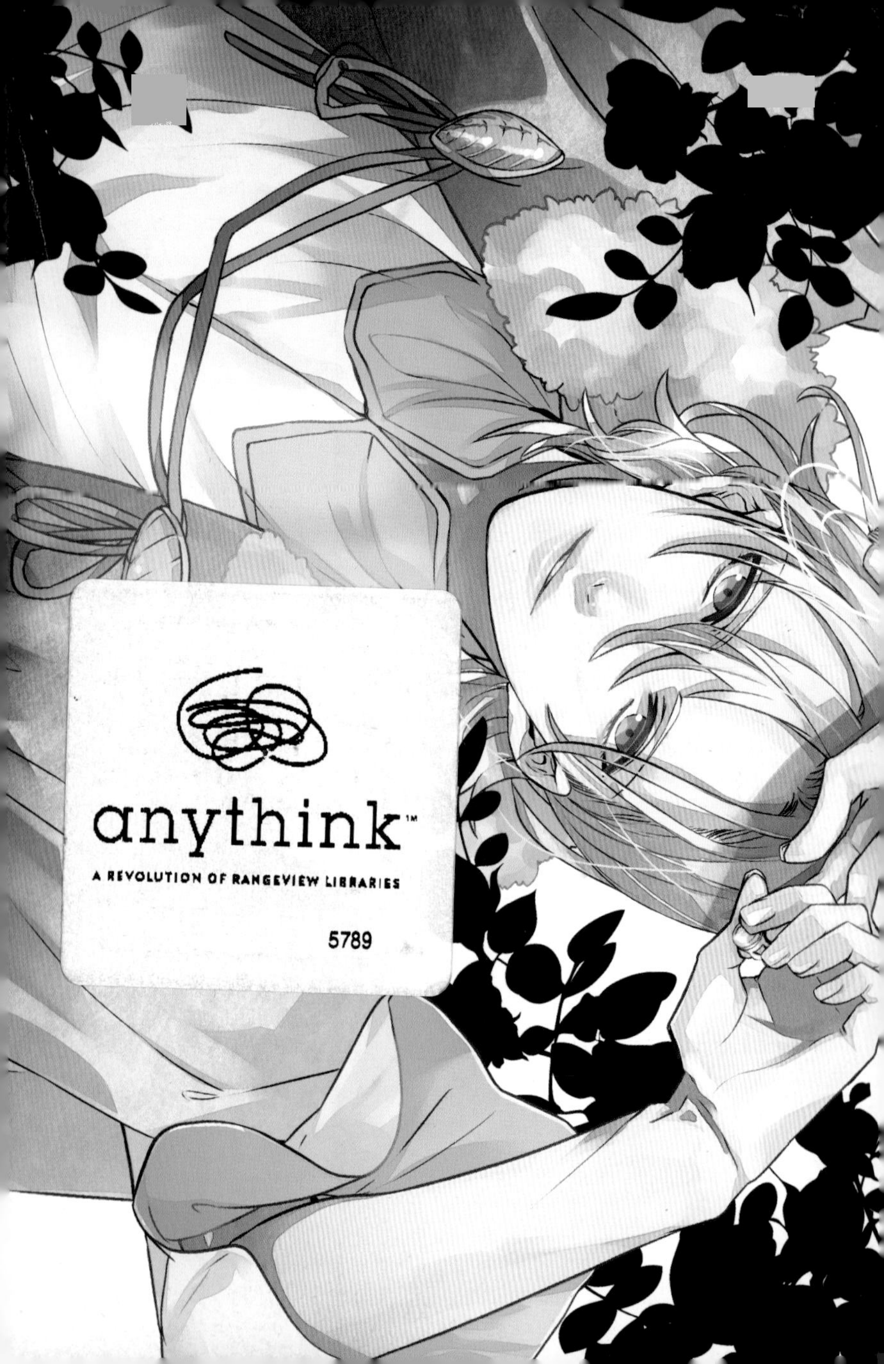

Devils and Realist

vol. 5

story by **Madoka Takadono**
art by **Utako Yukihiro**

Cast of Characters

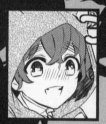

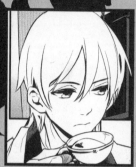

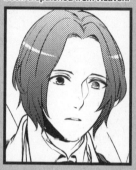

Kevin

William's capable yet gambling-addicted butler, who is also a pastor at the academy. In truth, he is the angel Uriel, who has been dispatched from Heaven.

William

A brilliant realist from a famous noble family. As the descendant of King Solomon, he is the Elector with the authority to choose the representative of the king of Hell although he is in denial of this fact.

Isaac

William's classmate who is obsessed with supernatural phenomena.

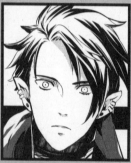

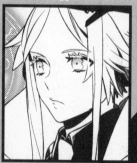

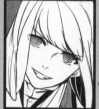

Michael

Vicious archangel who is planning to take William to Heaven. He visits Kevin to administer a kick from time to time.

Sytry

Twelfth Pillar of Hell, who leads 60 armies. Sytry is Prince of Hell and a candidate to represent the king. He is treated like a princess at school because of his beautiful appearance.

Dantalion

Seventy-first Pillar of Hell, who commands its leading 36 armies. He is Grand Duke of the Underworld and a candidate to represent the king. At school, students rely on him during sporting events.

The Story So Far

Two demons, Dantalion and Sytry, appear suddenly before the impoverished noble William and inform him that he is the Elector with the power to select the representative king of Hell. The two demons masquerade as students at Stradford School, and William's life becomes more and more entangled in Hell's affairs. On top of all this, a series of events complicates William's life even more: his butler Kevin is appointed to be pastor, it turns out that even the school representative is a demon, and finally, the archangel Michael possesses a classmate in an attempt to get closer to William. Further, William harbors doubts when he finds his father's ring, a family heirloom, in Kevin's room! Meanwhile, Lucifer's would-be successors decide that they must bring William to Hell...

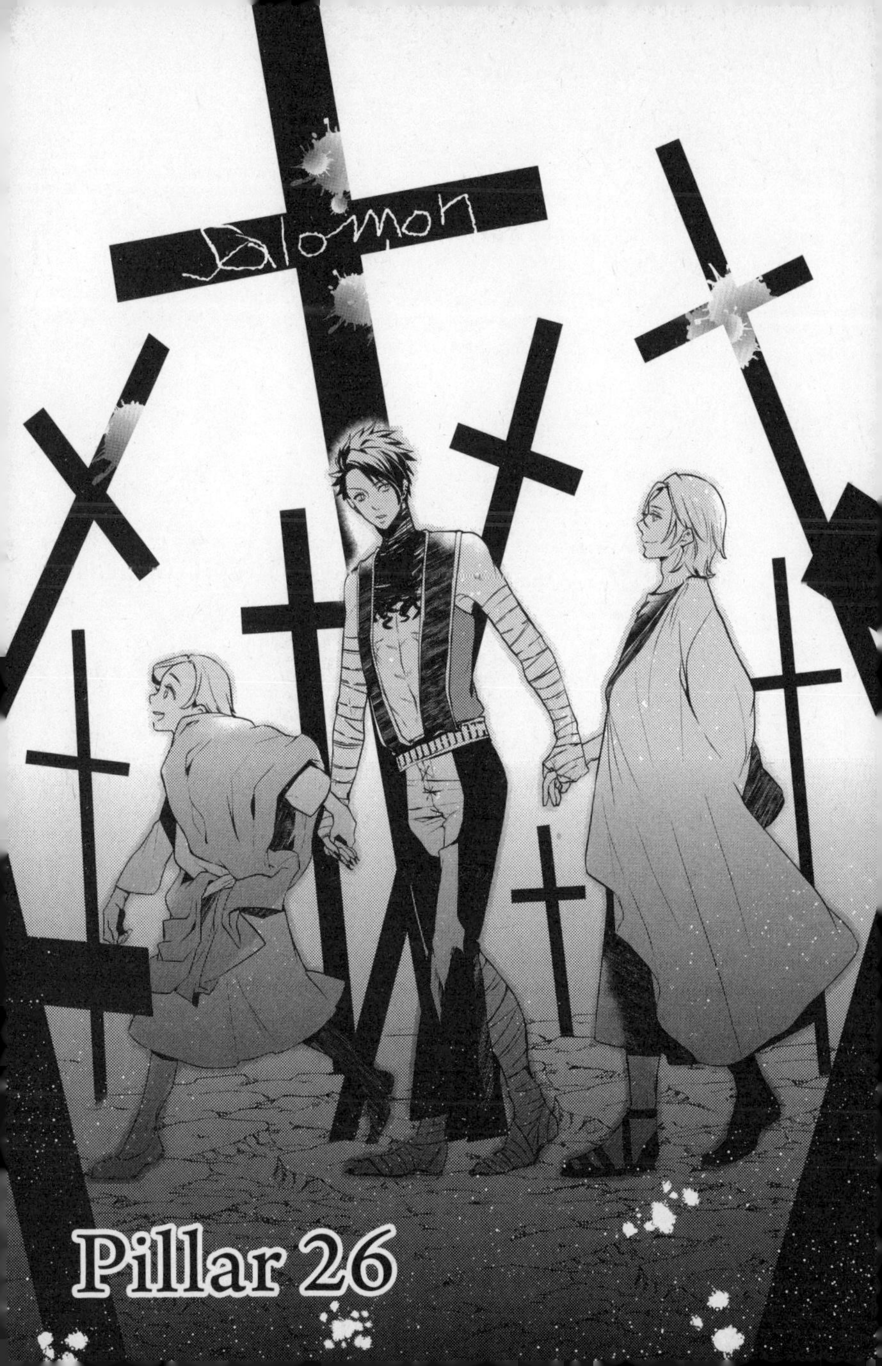
Salomon
Pillar 26

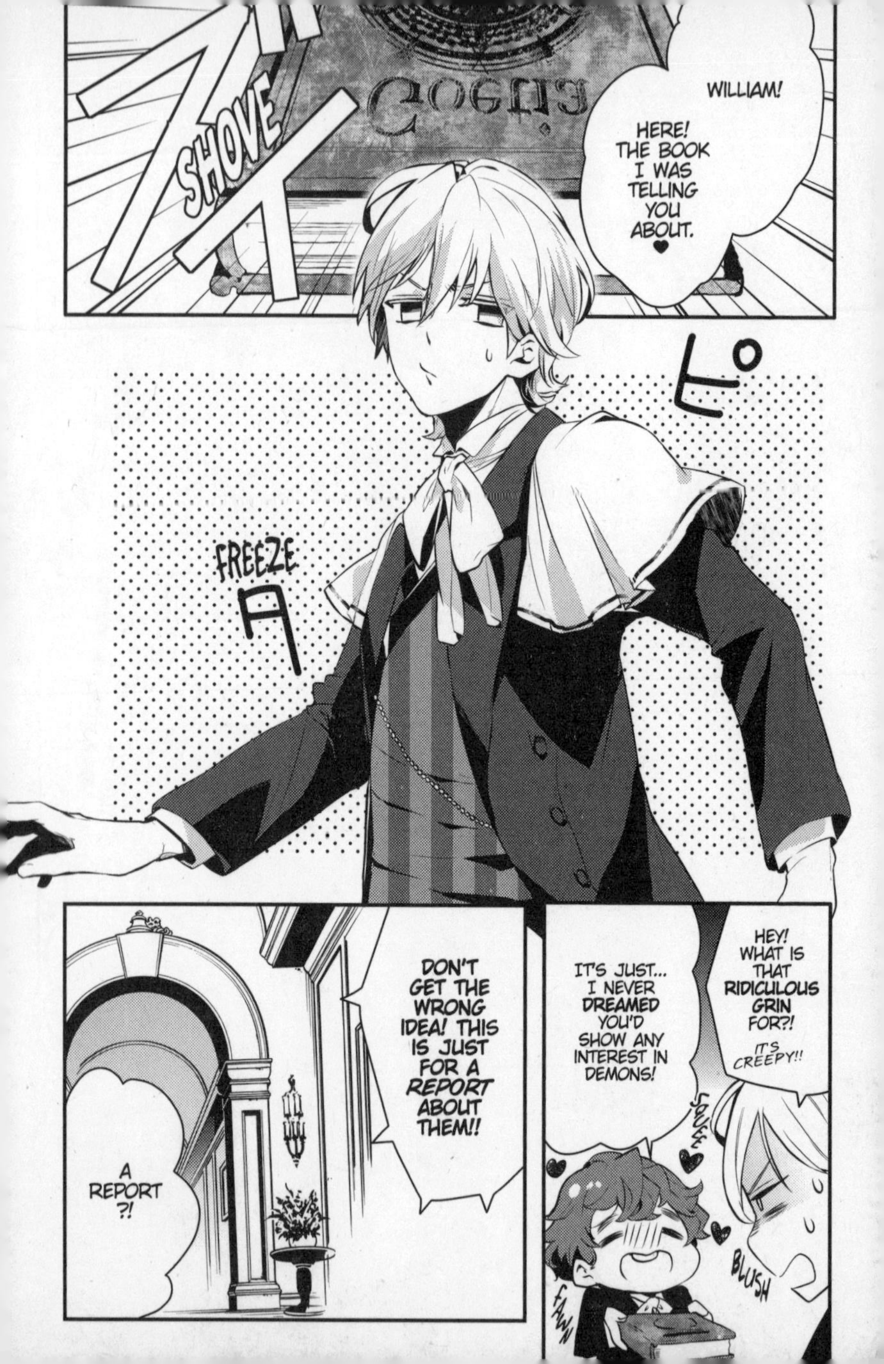
WILLIAM!
HERE! THE BOOK I WAS TELLING YOU ABOUT. ♥
SHOVE
FREEZE
HEY! WHAT IS THAT RIDICULOUS GRIN FOR?!
IT'S CREEPY!!
IT'S JUST... I NEVER DREAMED YOU'D SHOW ANY INTEREST IN DEMONS!
SQUEE
BLUSH
FAWN
DON'T GET THE WRONG IDEA! THIS IS JUST FOR A REPORT ABOUT THEM!!
A REPORT ?!

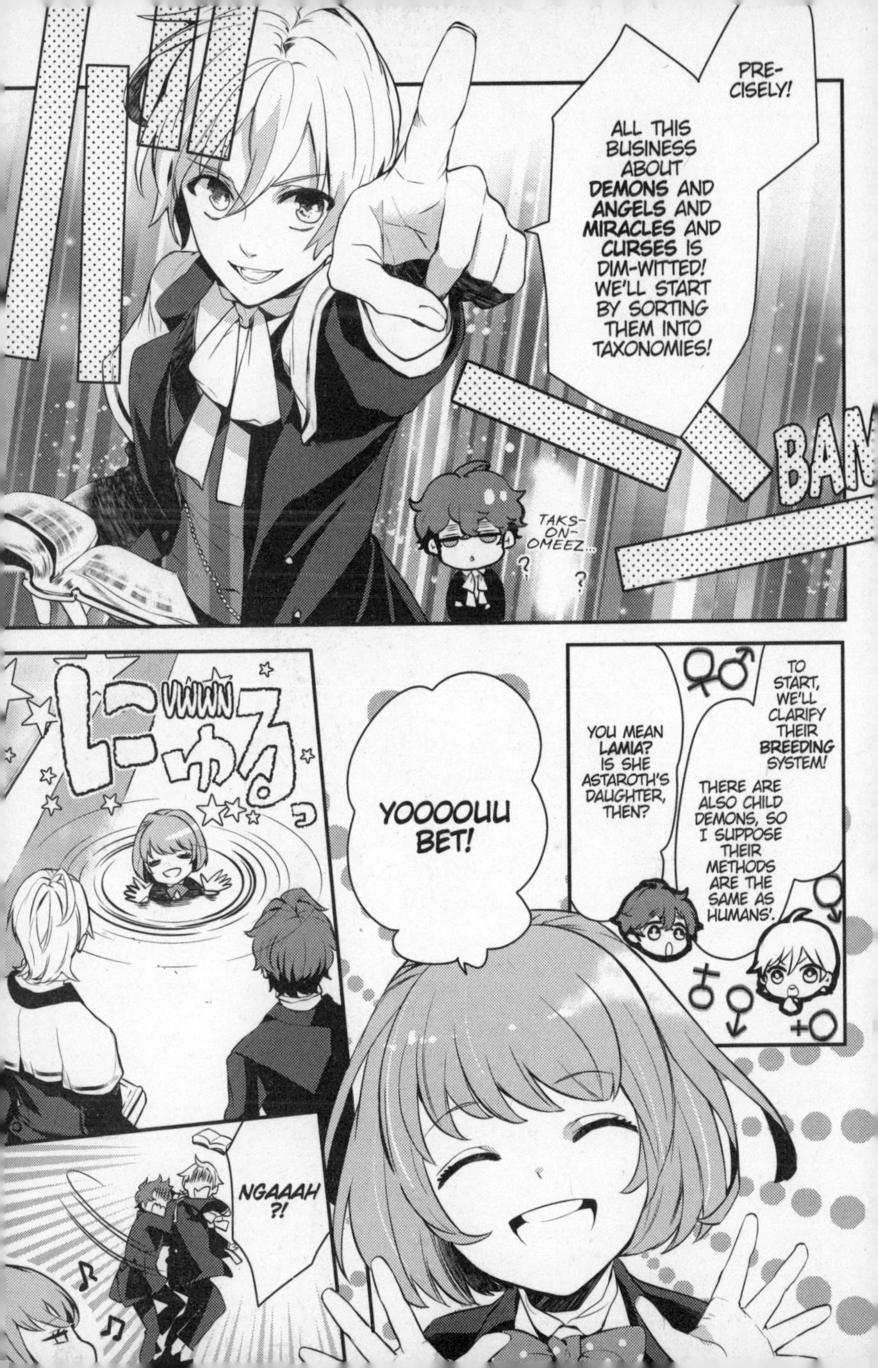
PRE-CISELY!
ALL THIS BUSINESS ABOUT DEMONS AND ANGELS AND MIRACLES AND CURSES IS DIM-WITTED! WE'LL START BY SORTING THEM INTO TAXONOMIES!
BAM
TAKS-ON-OMEEZ...
?
?
TO START, WE'LL CLARIFY THEIR BREEDING SYSTEM!
THERE ARE ALSO CHILD DEMONS, SO I SUPPOSE THEIR METHODS ARE THE SAME AS HUMANS'.
YOU MEAN LAMIA? IS SHE ASTAROTH'S DAUGHTER, THEN?
YOOOOUU BET!
VWWN
NGAAAH?!

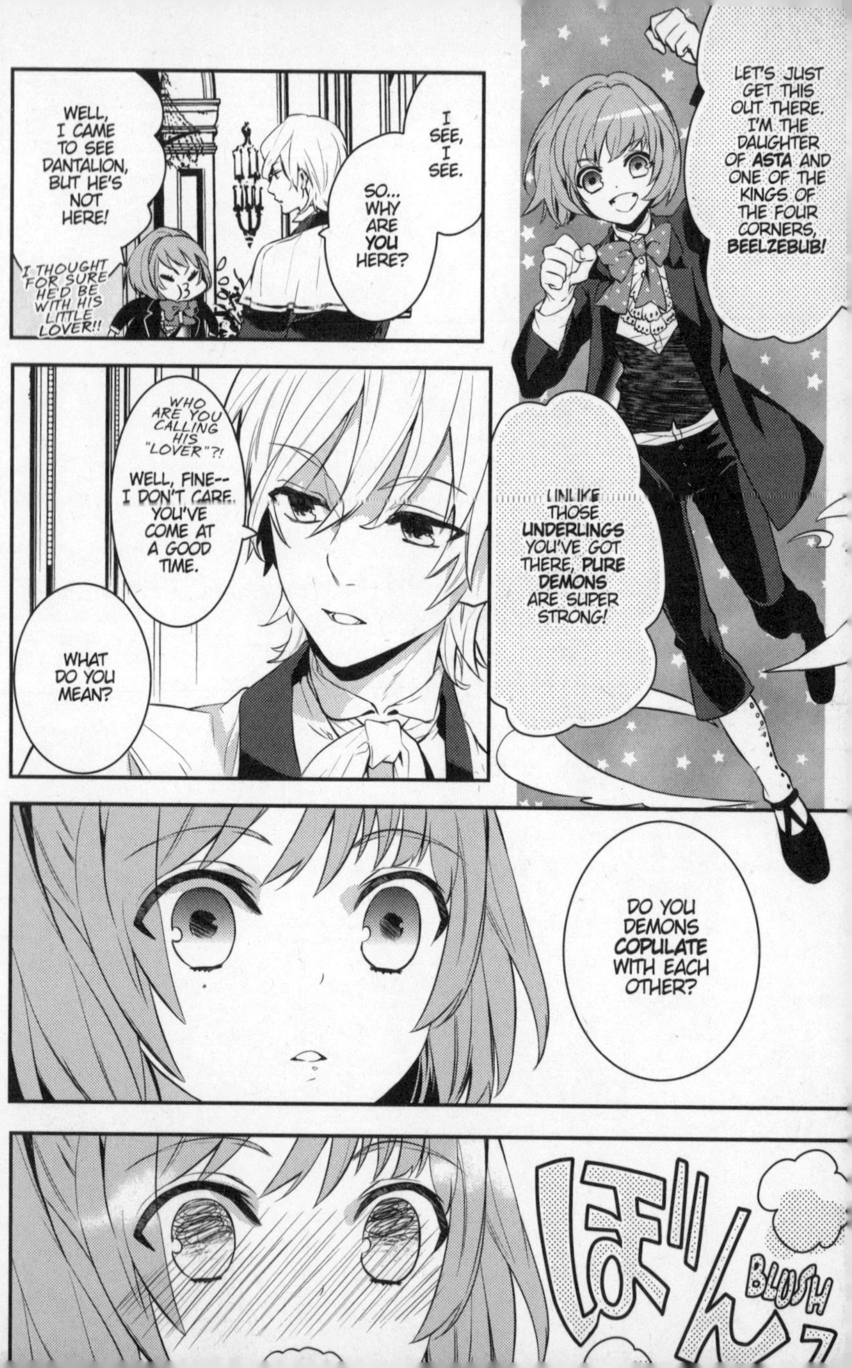
LET'S JUST GET THIS OUT THERE. I'M THE DAUGHTER OF ASTA AND ONE OF THE KINGS OF THE FOUR CORNERS, BEELZEBUB!
UNLIKE THOSE UNDERLINGS YOU'VE GOT THERE, PURE DEMONS ARE SUPER STRONG!
I SEE, I SEE.
SO... WHY ARE YOU HERE?
WELL, I CAME TO SEE DANTALION, BUT HE'S NOT HERE!
I THOUGHT FOR SURE HE'D BE WITH HIS LITTLE LOVER!!
WHO ARE YOU CALLING HIS "LOVER"?!
WELL, FINE-- I DON'T CARE. YOU'VE COME AT A GOOD TIME.
WHAT DO YOU MEAN?
DO YOU DEMONS COPULATE WITH EACH OTHER?
ぼん
BLUSH

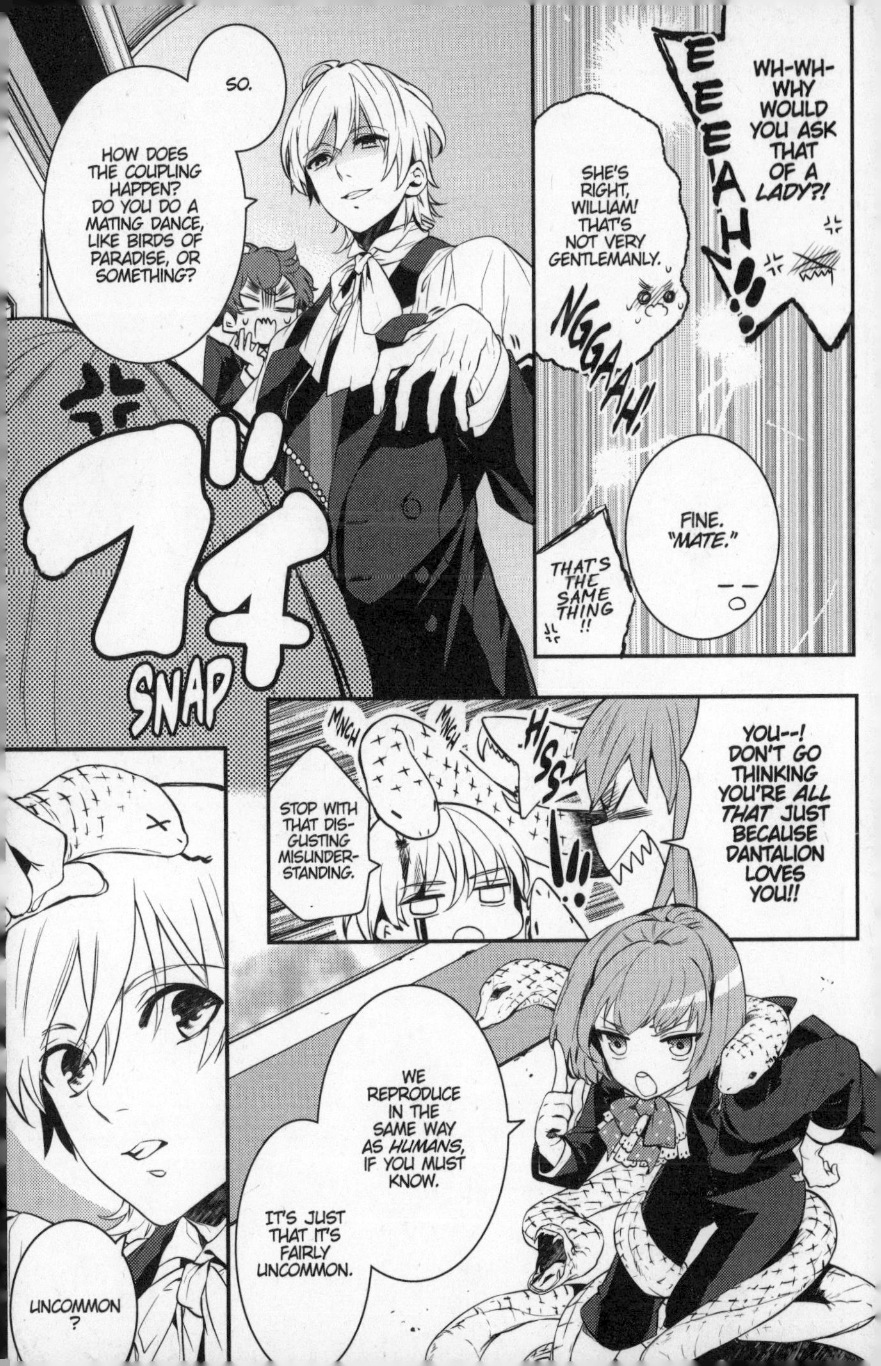
WH-WH-WHY WOULD YOU ASK THAT OF A LADY?!
EEEAH!!
SHE'S RIGHT, WILLIAM! THAT'S NOT VERY GENTLEMANLY.
NGGAAH!
FINE. "MATE."
THAT'S THE SAME THING!!
SO.
HOW DOES THE COUPLING HAPPEN? DO YOU DO A MATING DANCE, LIKE BIRDS OF PARADISE, OR SOMETHING?
SNAP
YOU--! DON'T GO THINKING YOU'RE ALL THAT JUST BECAUSE DANTALION LOVES YOU!!
HISS
MNCH
MNCH
STOP WITH THAT DIS-GUSTING MISUNDER-STANDING.
WE REPRODUCE IN THE SAME WAY AS HUMANS, IF YOU MUST KNOW.
IT'S JUST THAT IT'S FAIRLY UNCOMMON.
UNCOMMON ?

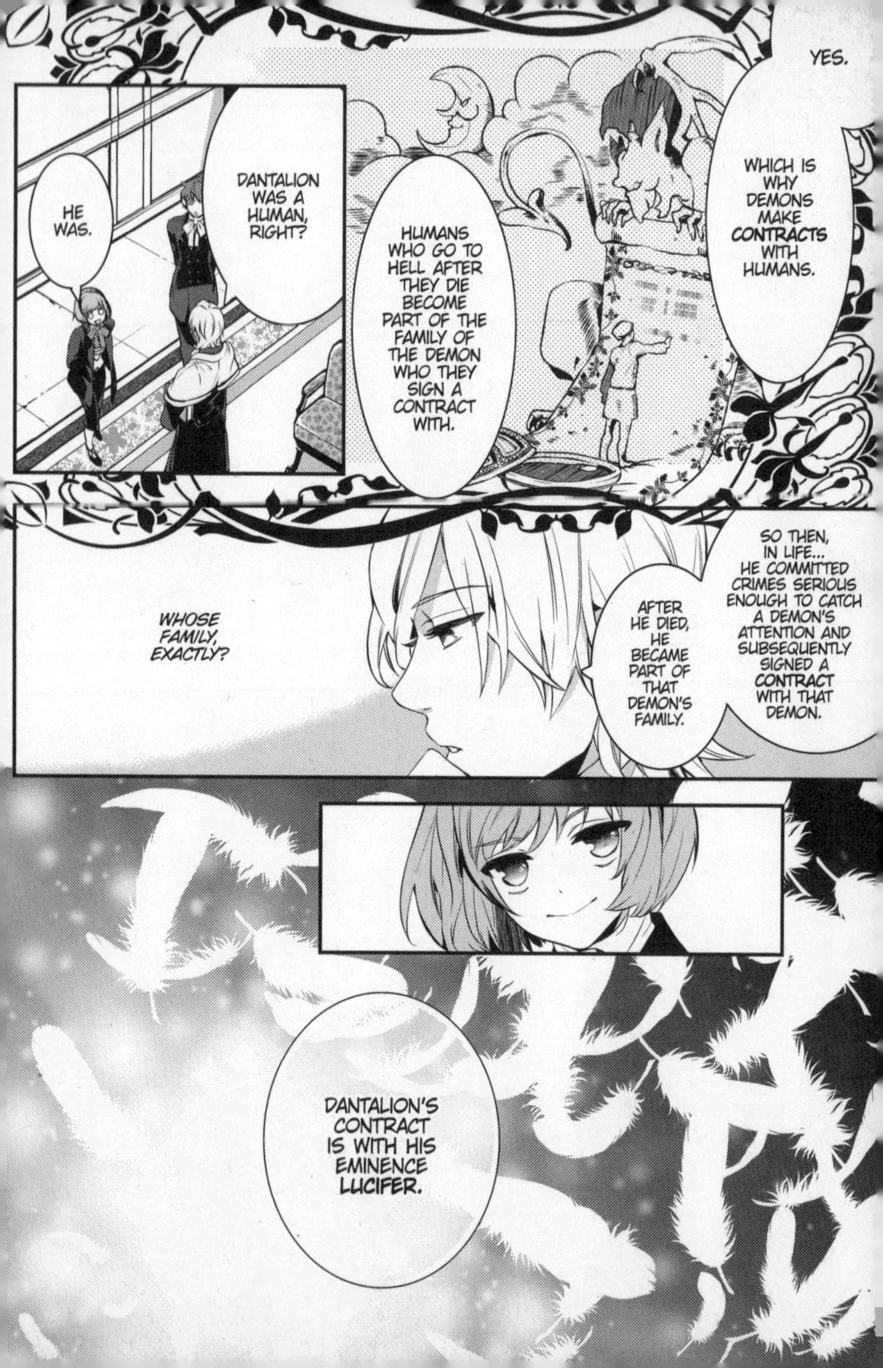
YES.
WHICH IS WHY DEMONS MAKE CONTRACTS WITH HUMANS.
HUMANS WHO GO TO HELL AFTER THEY DIE BECOME PART OF THE FAMILY OF THE DEMON WHO THEY SIGN A CONTRACT WITH.
DANTALION WAS A HUMAN, RIGHT?
HE WAS.
SO THEN, IN LIFE... HE COMMITTED CRIMES SERIOUS ENOUGH TO CATCH A DEMON'S ATTENTION AND SUBSEQUENTLY SIGNED A CONTRACT WITH THAT DEMON.
AFTER HE DIED, HE BECAME PART OF THAT DEMON'S FAMILY.
WHOSE FAMILY, EXACTLY?
DANTALION'S CONTRACT IS WITH HIS EMINENCE LUCIFER.

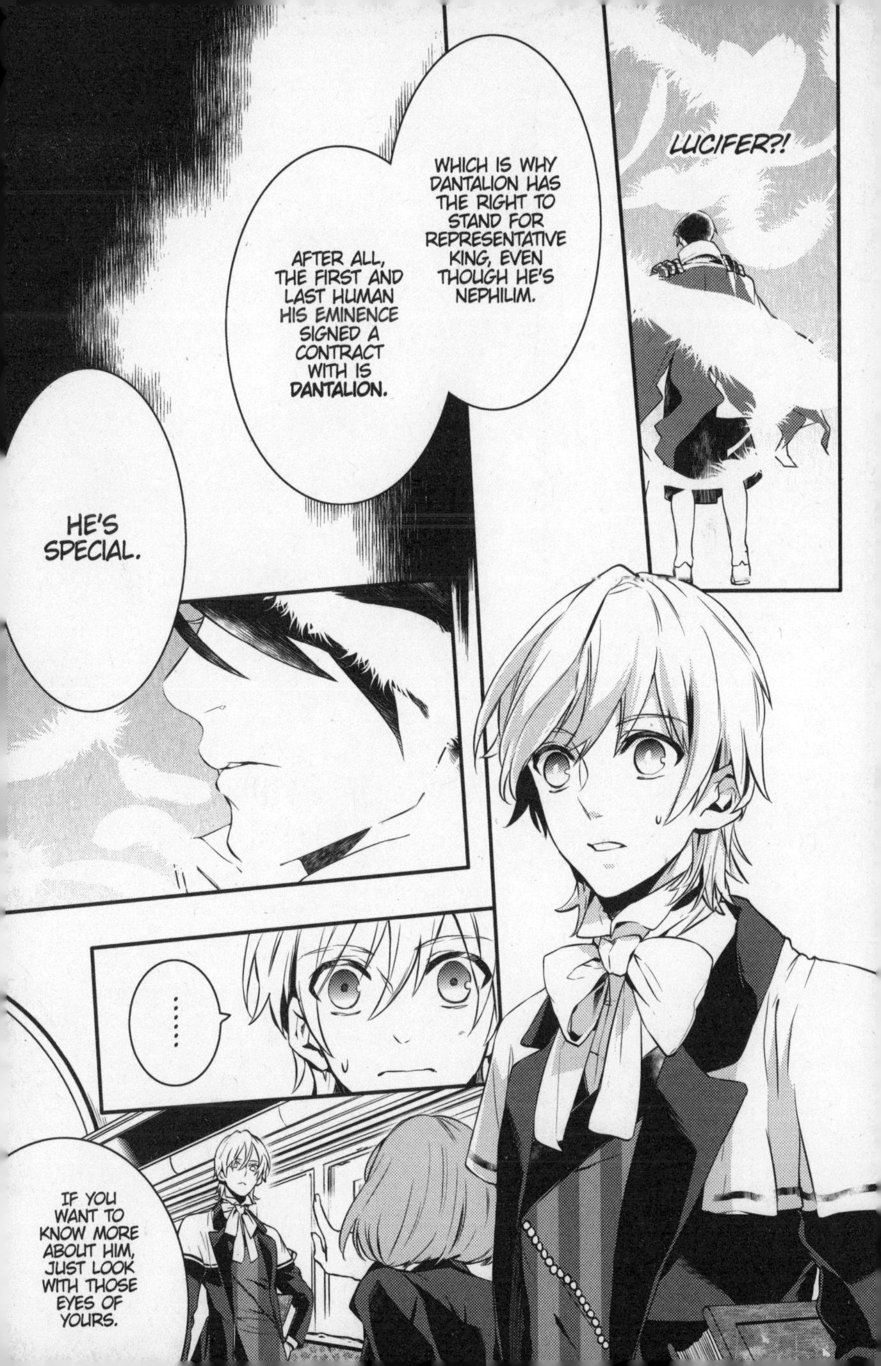
LUCIFER?!
HE'S SPECIAL.
AFTER ALL, THE FIRST AND LAST HUMAN HIS EMINENCE SIGNED A CONTRACT WITH IS DANTALION.
WHICH IS WHY DANTALION HAS THE RIGHT TO STAND FOR REPRESENTATIVE KING, EVEN THOUGH HE'S NEPHILIM.
......
IF YOU WANT TO KNOW MORE ABOUT HIM, JUST LOOK WITH THOSE EYES OF YOURS.

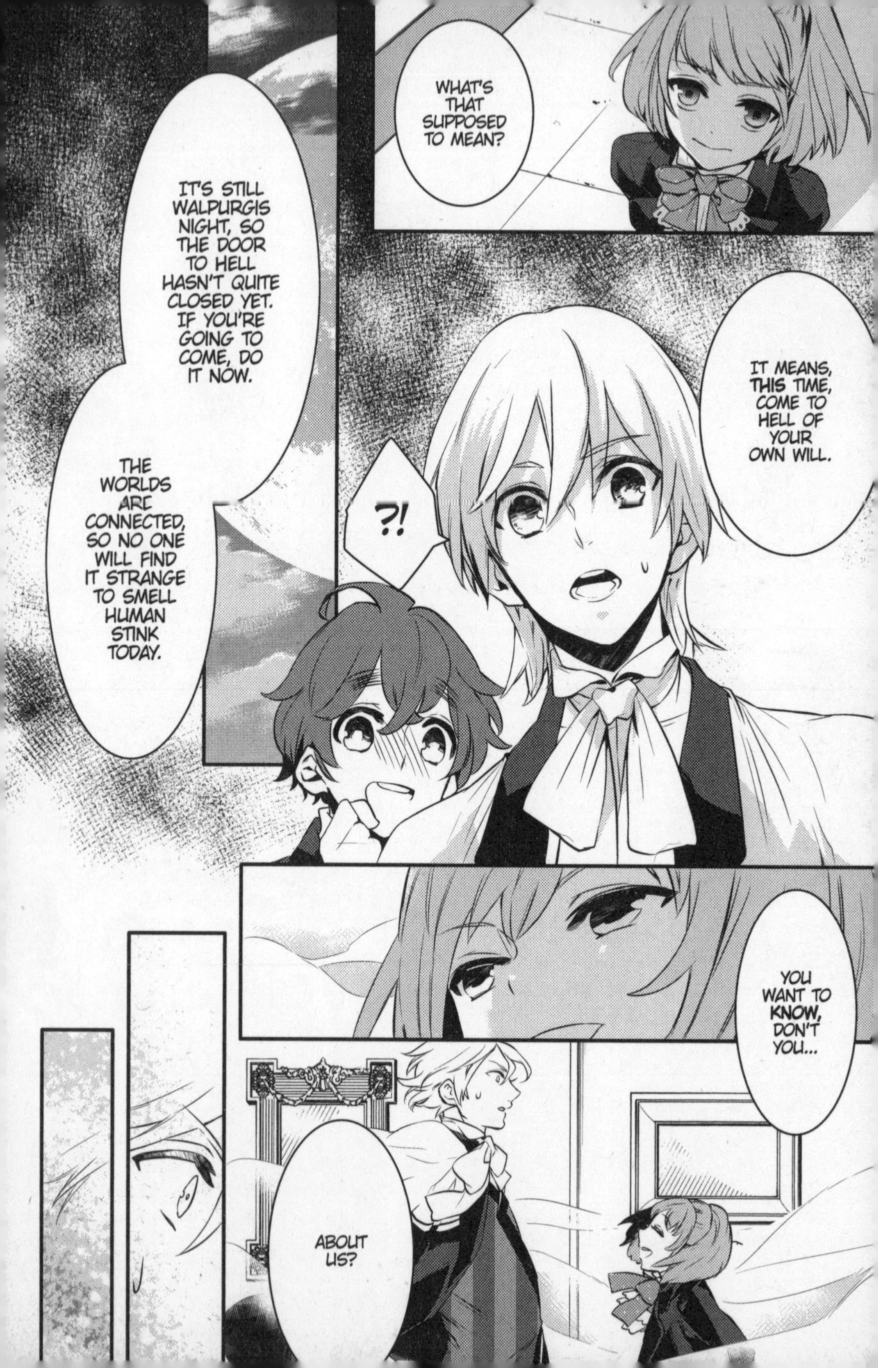
WHAT'S THAT SUPPOSED TO MEAN?
IT MEANS, THIS TIME, COME TO HELL OF YOUR OWN WILL.
?!
IT'S STILL WALPURGIS NIGHT, SO THE DOOR TO HELL HASN'T QUITE CLOSED YET. IF YOU'RE GOING TO COME, DO IT NOW.
THE WORLDS ARE CONNECTED, SO NO ONE WILL FIND IT STRANGE TO SMELL HUMAN STINK TODAY.
YOU WANT TO KNOW, DON'T YOU...
ABOUT US?

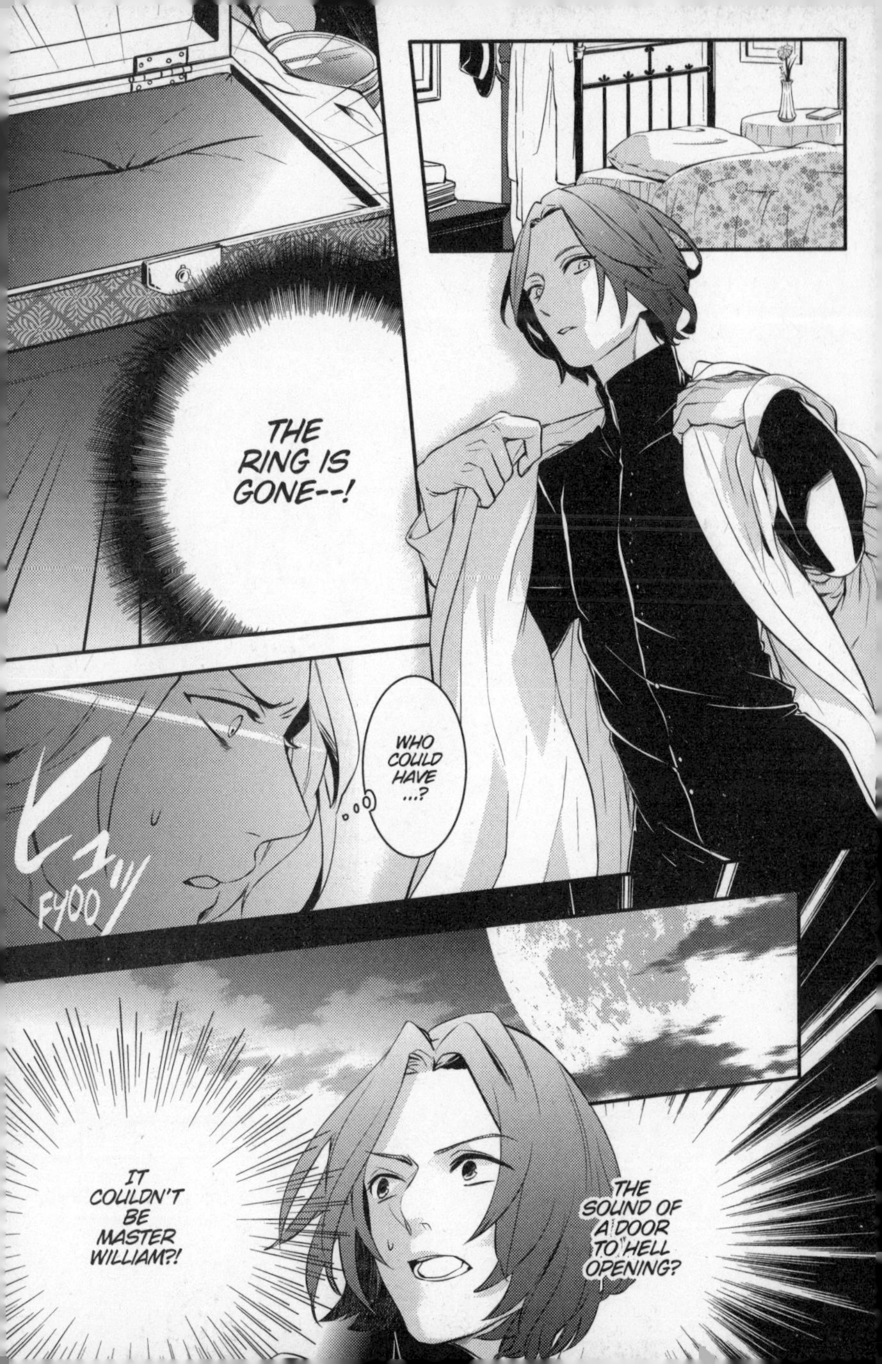
THE RING IS GONE--!
WHO COULD HAVE ...?
ヒュッ
FYOO
THE SOUND OF A DOOR TO HELL OPENING?
IT COULDN'T BE MASTER WILLIAM?!

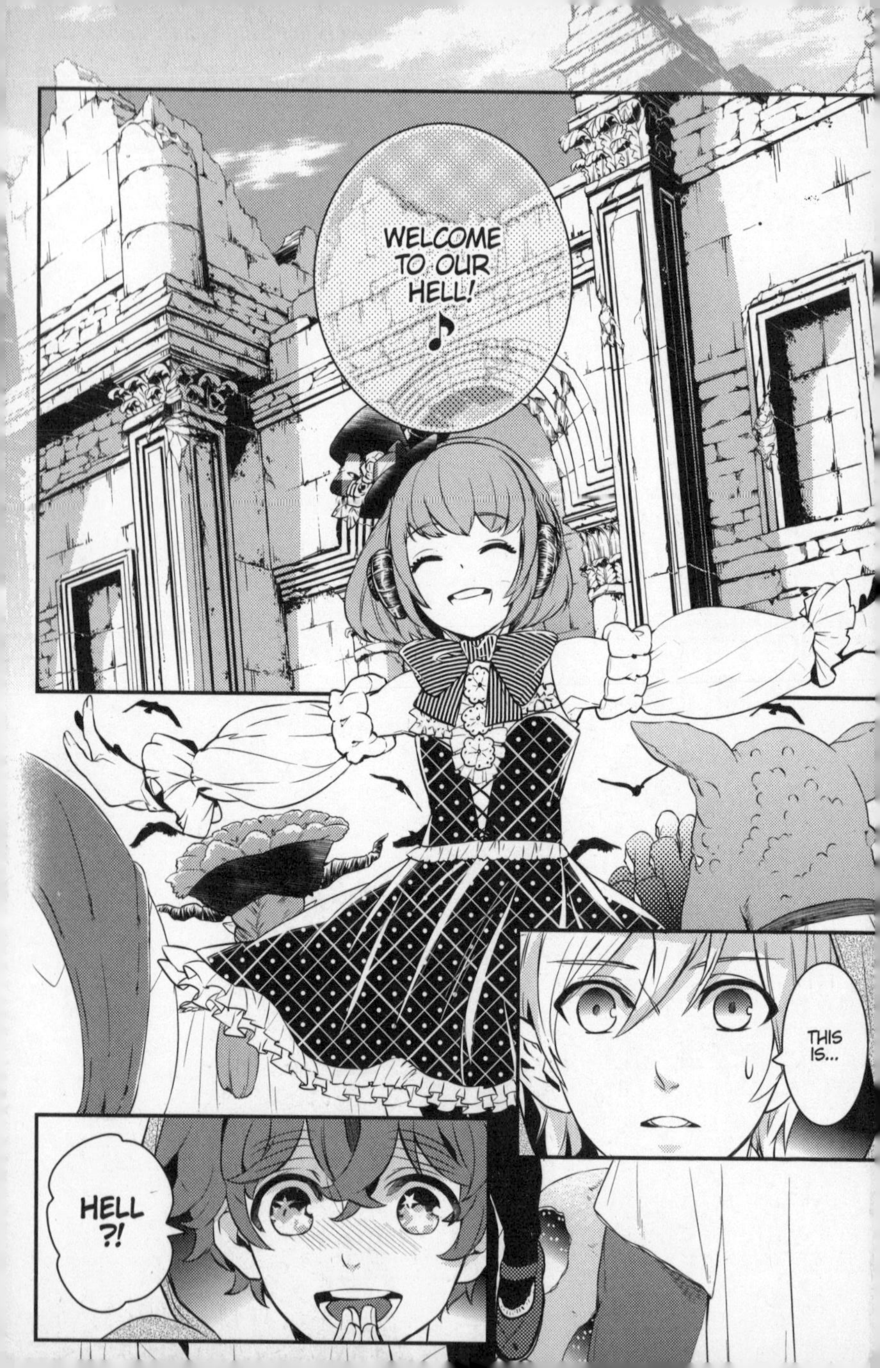
WELCOME TO OUR HELL! ♪
THIS IS...
HELL ?!

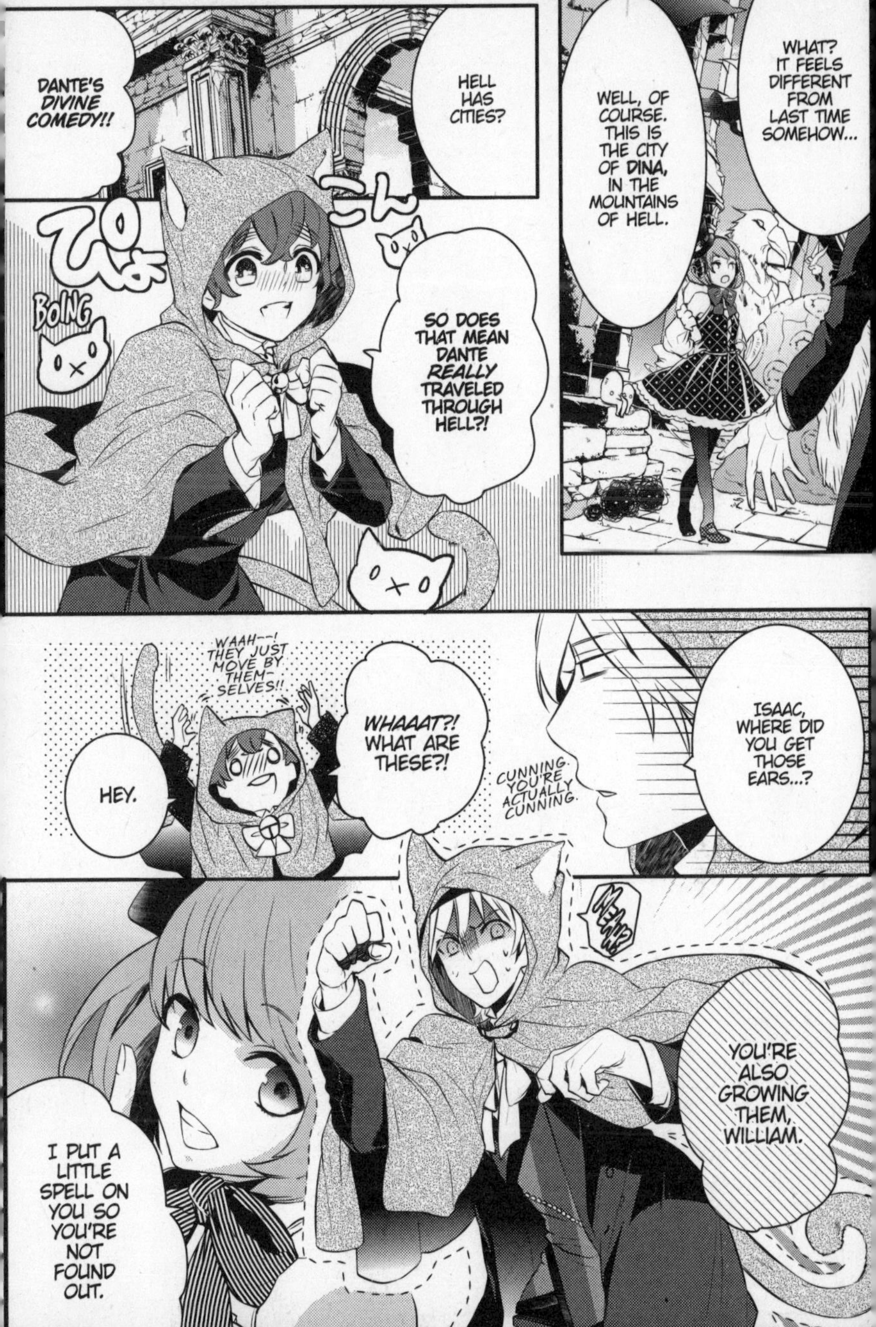
WHAT? IT FEELS DIFFERENT FROM LAST TIME SOMEHOW...
WELL, OF COURSE. THIS IS THE CITY OF DINA, IN THE MOUNTAINS OF HELL.
HELL HAS CITIES?
DANTE'S DIVINE COMEDY!!
こん
ぴょ
BOING
SO DOES THAT MEAN DANTE REALLY TRAVELED THROUGH HELL?!
ISAAC, WHERE DID YOU GET THOSE EARS...?
CUNNING. YOU'RE ACTUALLY CUNNING.
WHAAAT?! WHAT ARE THESE?!
WAAH--! THEY JUST MOVE BY THEM-SELVES!!
HEY.
YOU'RE ALSO GROWING THEM, WILLIAM.
MEW?!
I PUT A LITTLE SPELL ON YOU SO YOU'RE NOT FOUND OUT.

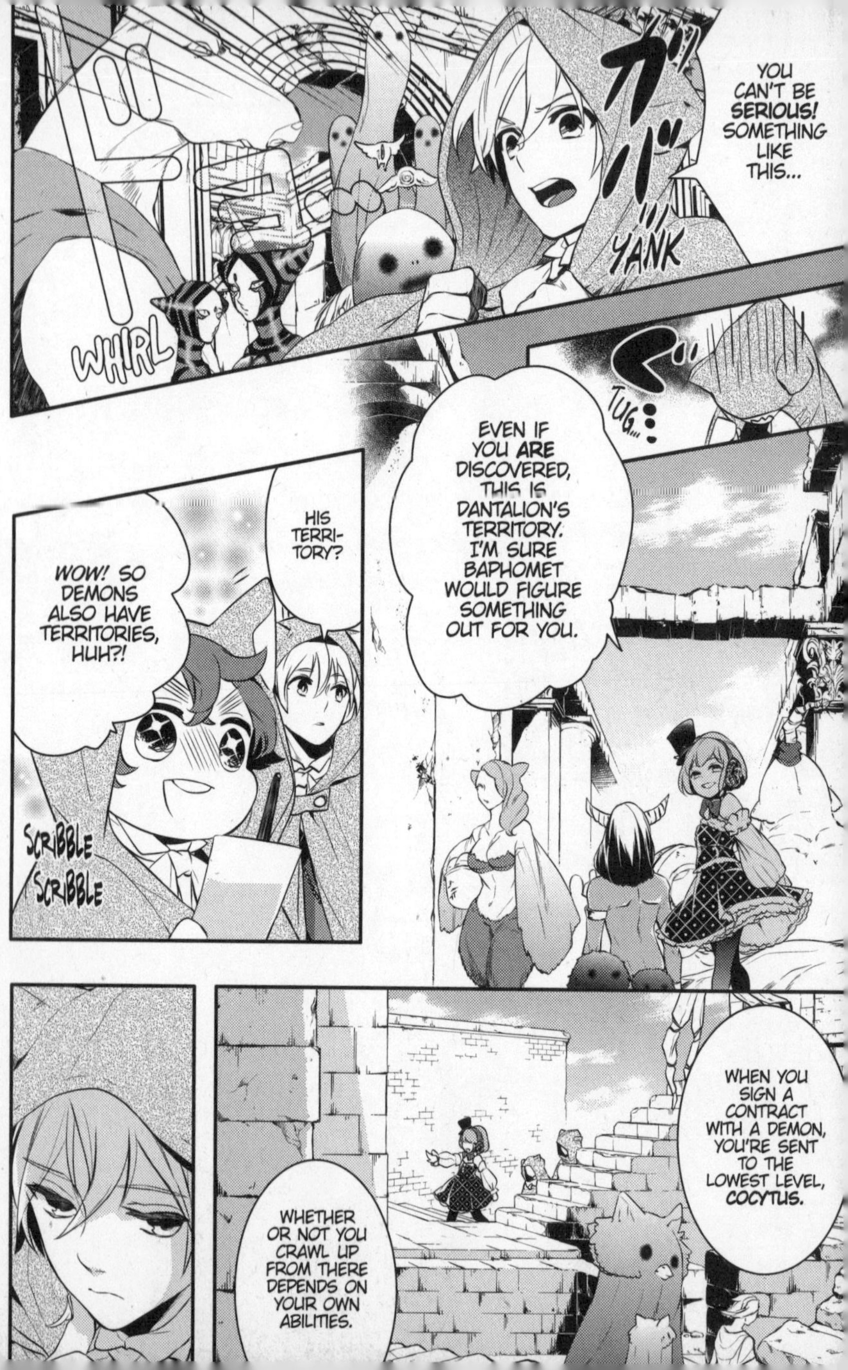
YOU CAN'T BE SERIOUS! SOMETHING LIKE THIS...
YANK
WHIRL
TUG...
EVEN IF YOU ARE DISCOVERED, THIS IS DANTALION'S TERRITORY. I'M SURE BAPHOMET WOULD FIGURE SOMETHING OUT FOR YOU.
HIS TERRITORY?
WOW! SO DEMONS ALSO HAVE TERRITORIES, HUH?!
SCRIBBLE SCRIBBLE
WHEN YOU SIGN A CONTRACT WITH A DEMON, YOU'RE SENT TO THE LOWEST LEVEL, COCYTUS.
WHETHER OR NOT YOU CRAWL UP FROM THERE DEPENDS ON YOUR OWN ABILITIES.

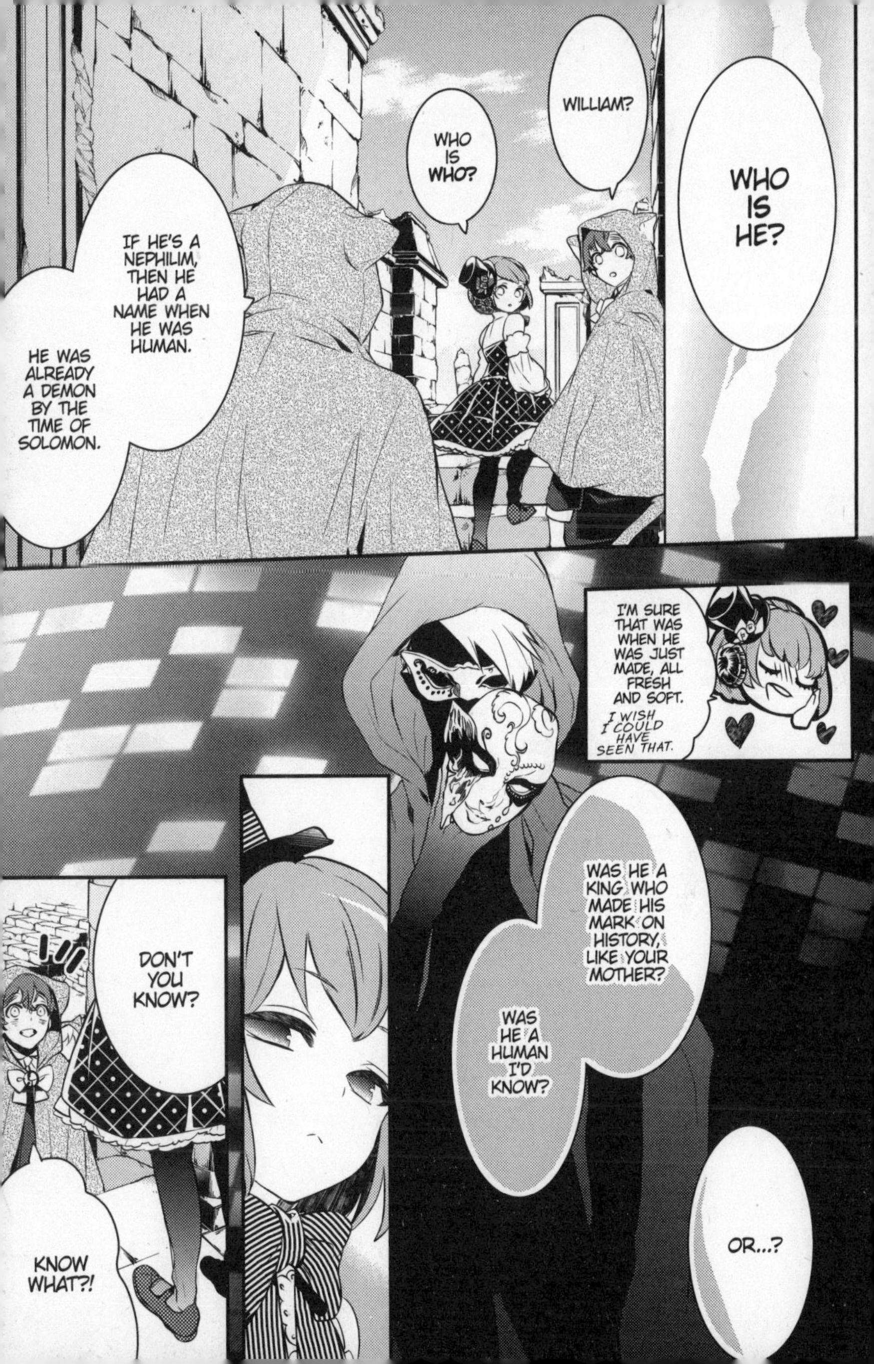
WHO IS HE?
WILLIAM?
WHO IS WHO?
IF HE'S A NEPHILIM, THEN HE HAD A NAME WHEN HE WAS HUMAN.
HE WAS ALREADY A DEMON BY THE TIME OF SOLOMON.
I'M SURE THAT WAS WHEN HE WAS JUST MADE, ALL FRESH AND SOFT.
I WISH I COULD HAVE SEEN THAT.
WAS HE A KING WHO MADE HIS MARK ON HISTORY, LIKE YOUR MOTHER?
WAS HE A HUMAN I'D KNOW?
OR...?
DON'T YOU KNOW?
KNOW WHAT?!

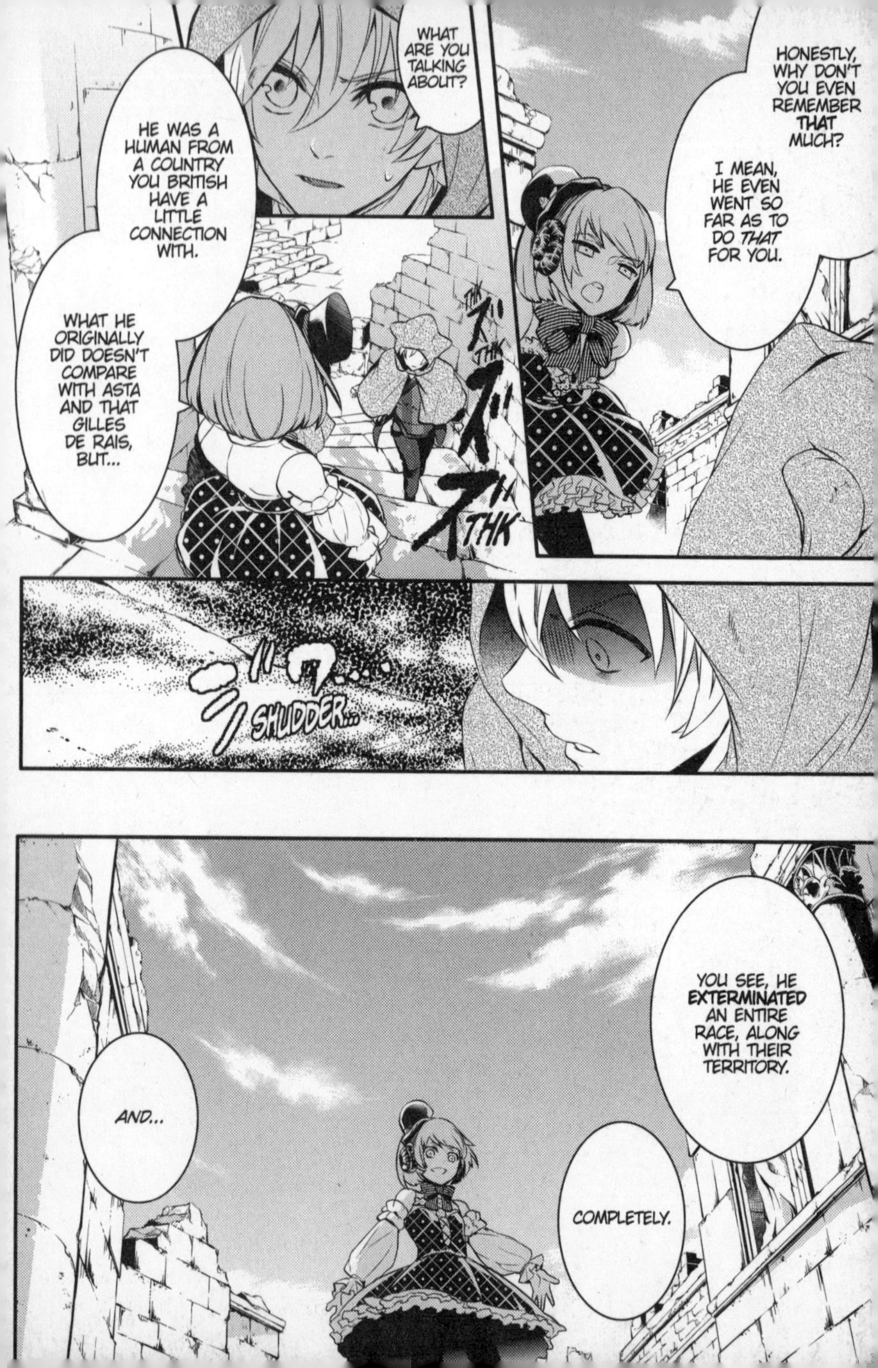
HONESTLY, WHY DON'T YOU EVEN REMEMBER THAT MUCH?
I MEAN, HE EVEN WENT SO FAR AS TO DO THAT FOR YOU.
WHAT ARE YOU TALKING ABOUT?
HE WAS A HUMAN FROM A COUNTRY YOU BRITISH HAVE A LITTLE CONNECTION WITH.
WHAT HE ORIGINALLY DID DOESN'T COMPARE WITH ASTA AND THAT GILLES DE RAIS, BUT...
THK THK THK
SHUDDER...
YOU SEE, HE EXTERMINATED AN ENTIRE RACE, ALONG WITH THEIR TERRITORY.
AND...
COMPLETELY.

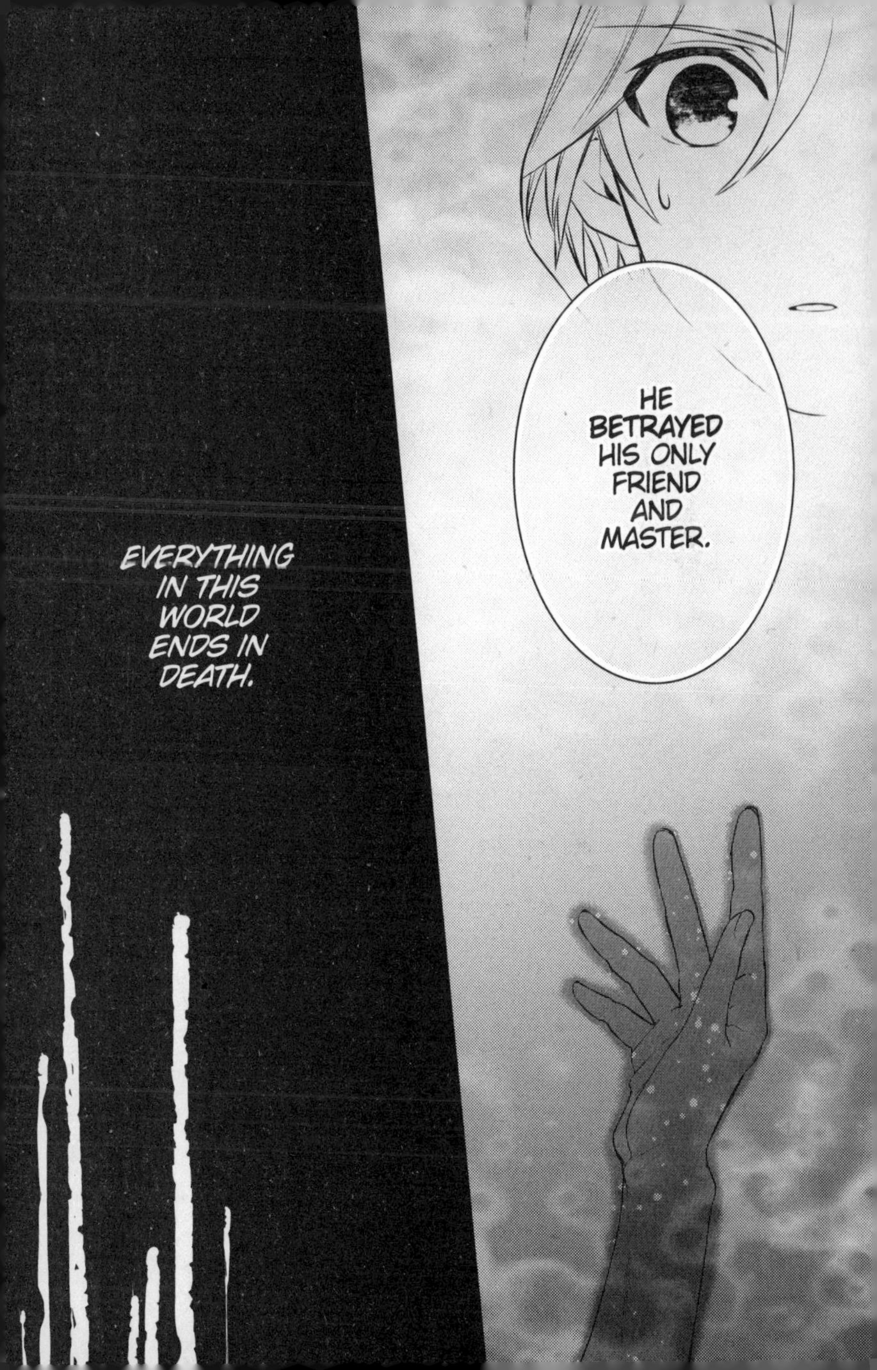
HE BETRAYED HIS ONLY FRIEND AND MASTER.
EVERYTHING IN THIS WORLD ENDS IN DEATH.

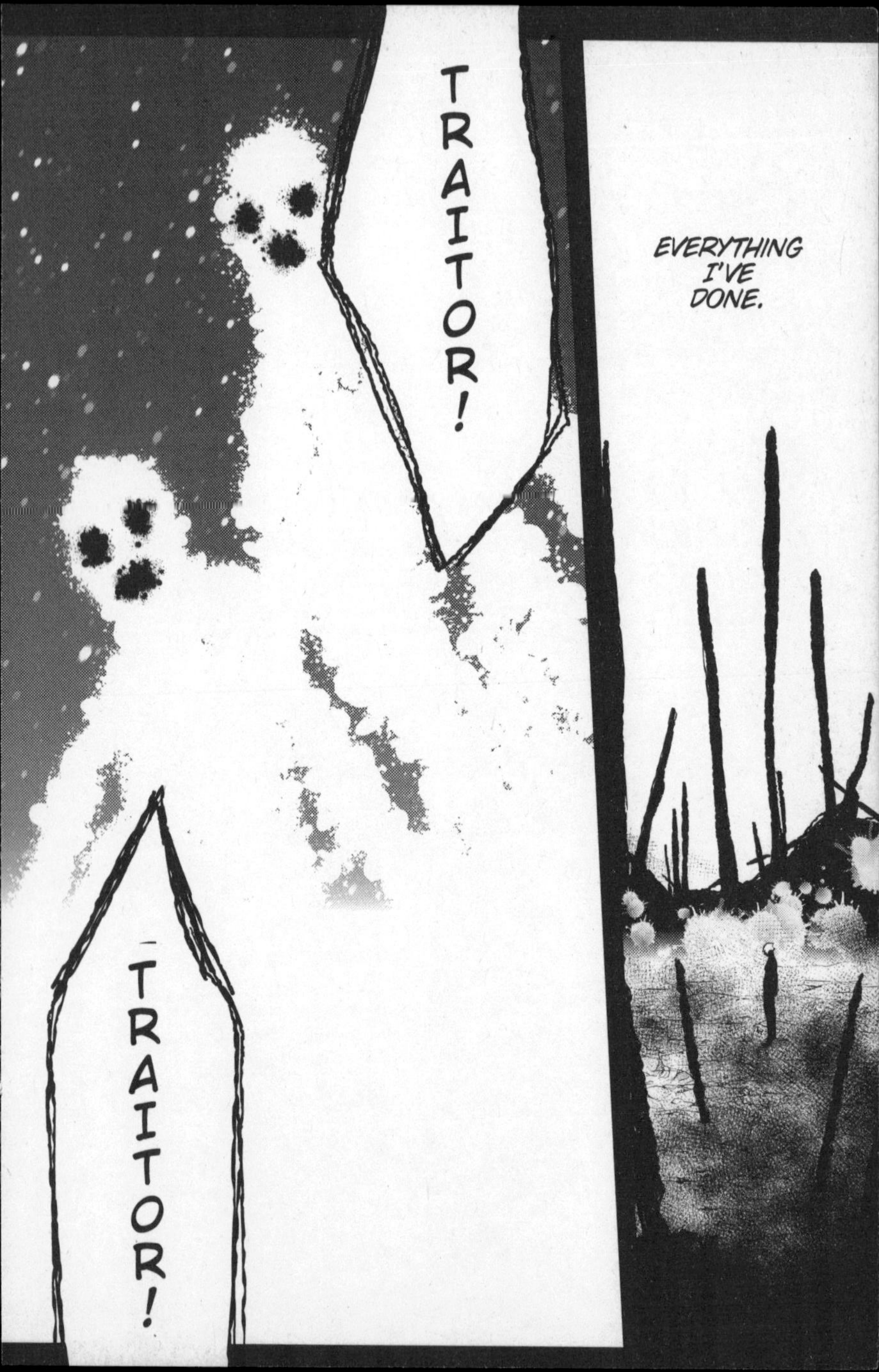
EVERYTHING I'VE DONE.
TRAITOR!
TRAITOR!

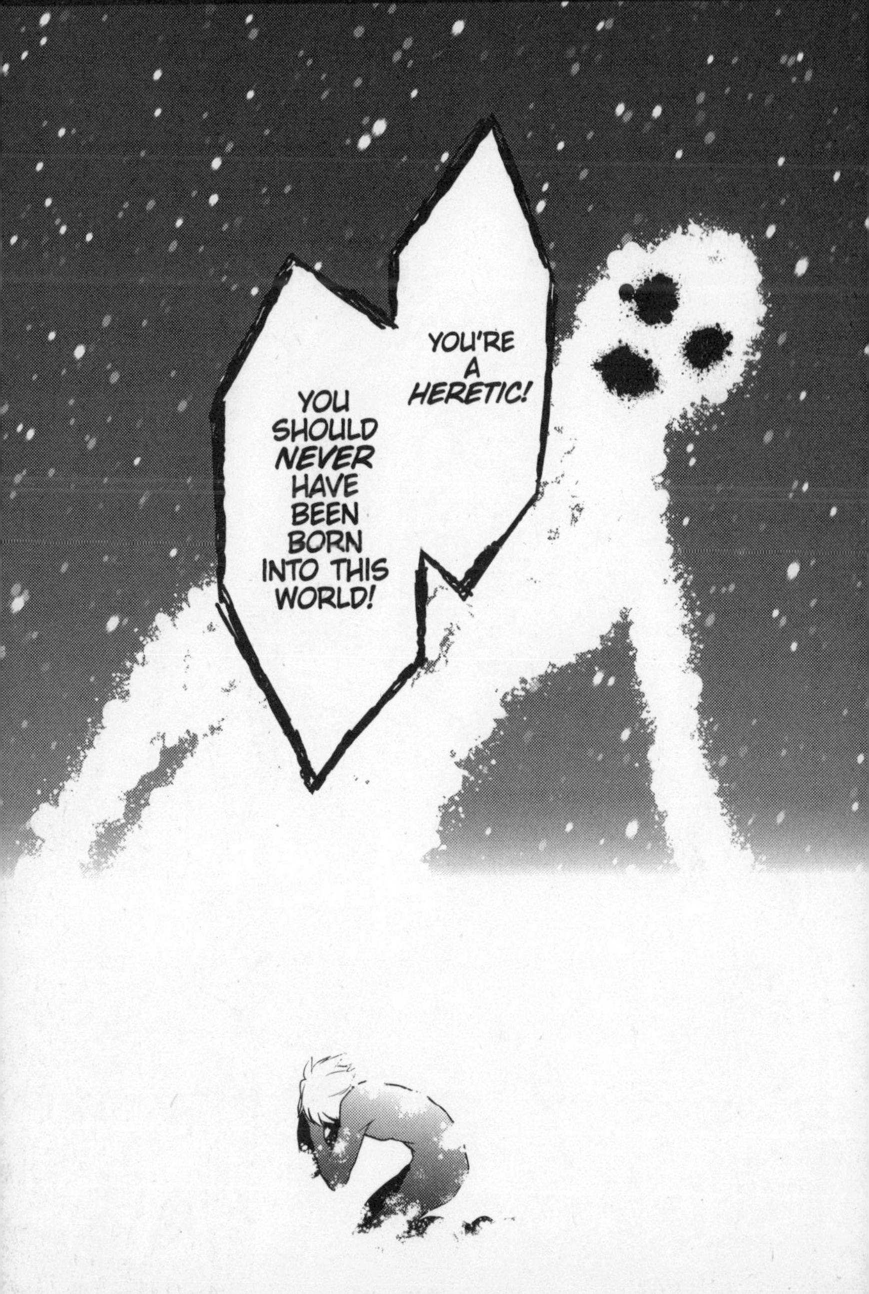
YOU'RE A HERETIC!
YOU SHOULD NEVER HAVE BEEN BORN INTO THIS WORLD!

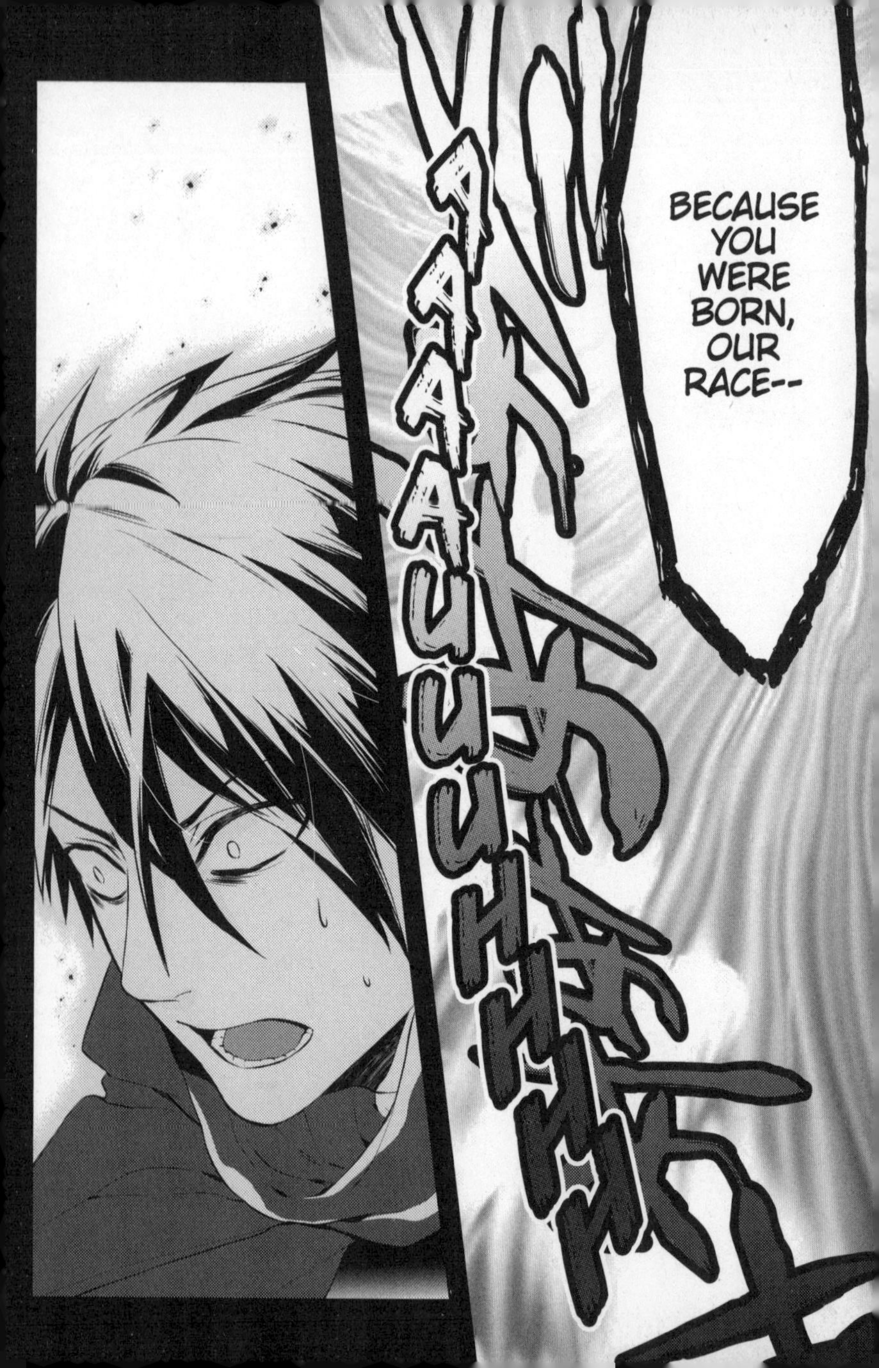
BECAUSE YOU WERE BORN, OUR RACE--
AAAAUUUUHHHH!

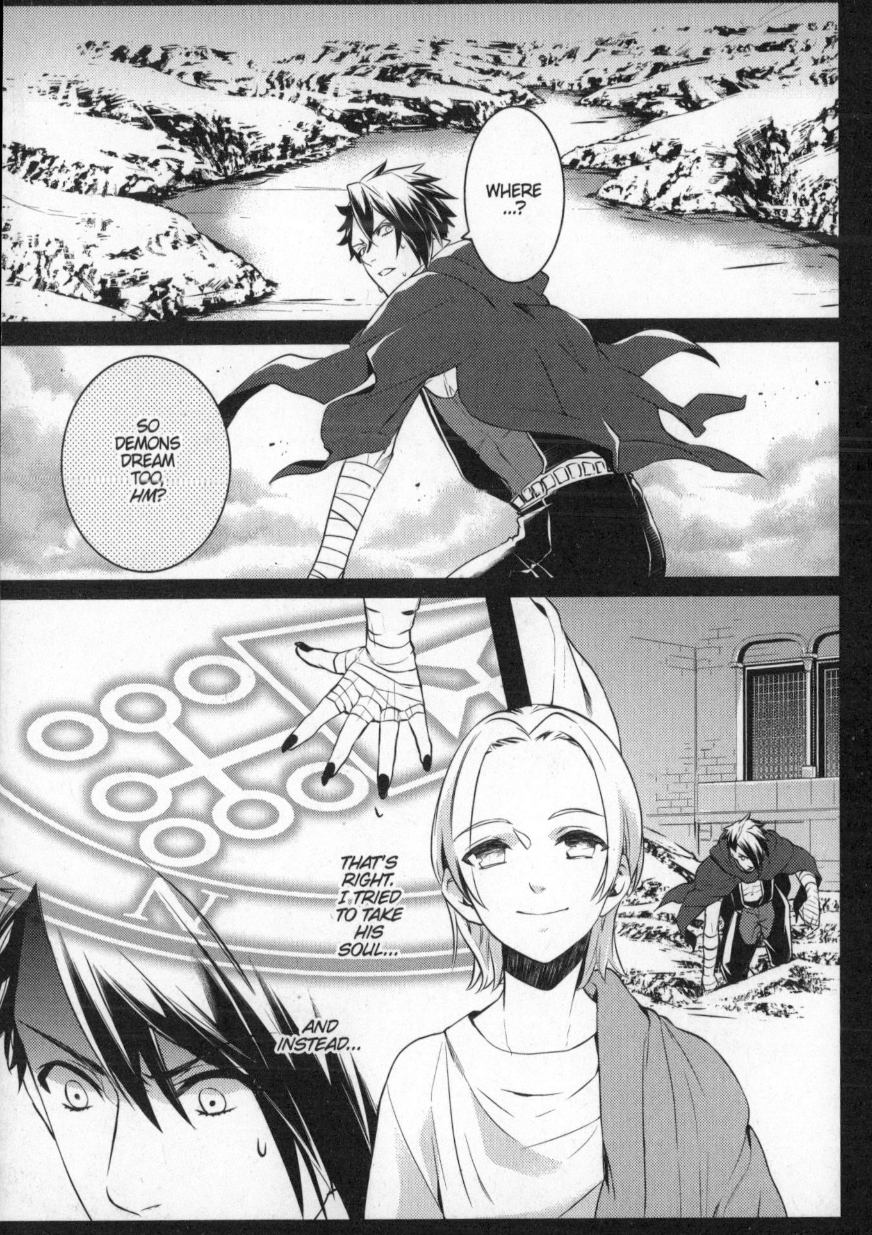
WHERE ...?
SO DEMONS DREAM TOO, HM?
THAT'S RIGHT. I TRIED TO TAKE HIS SOUL...
AND INSTEAD...

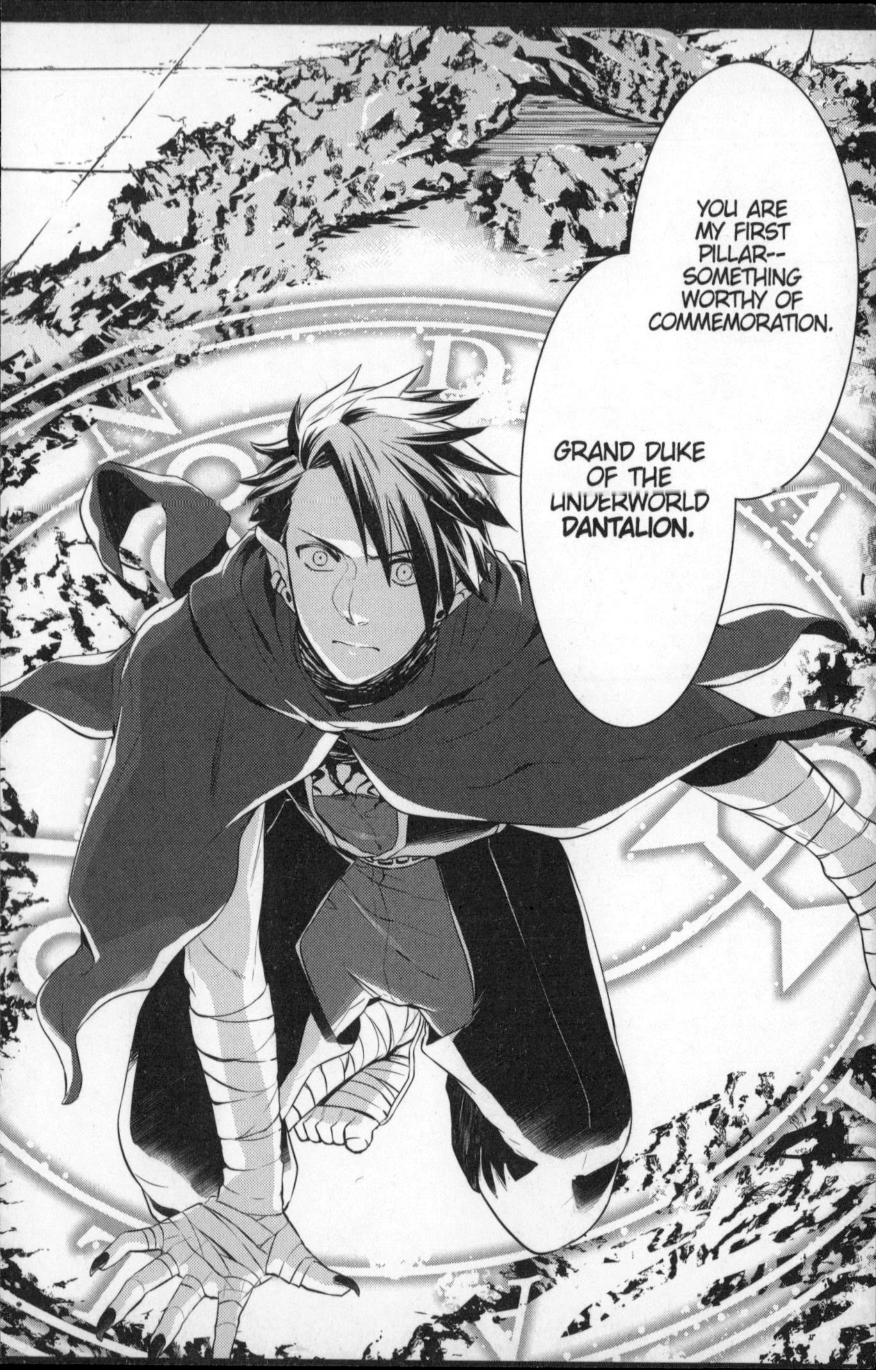
YOU ARE MY FIRST PILLAR--SOMETHING WORTHY OF COMMEMORATION.
GRAND DUKE OF THE UNDERWORLD DANTALION.

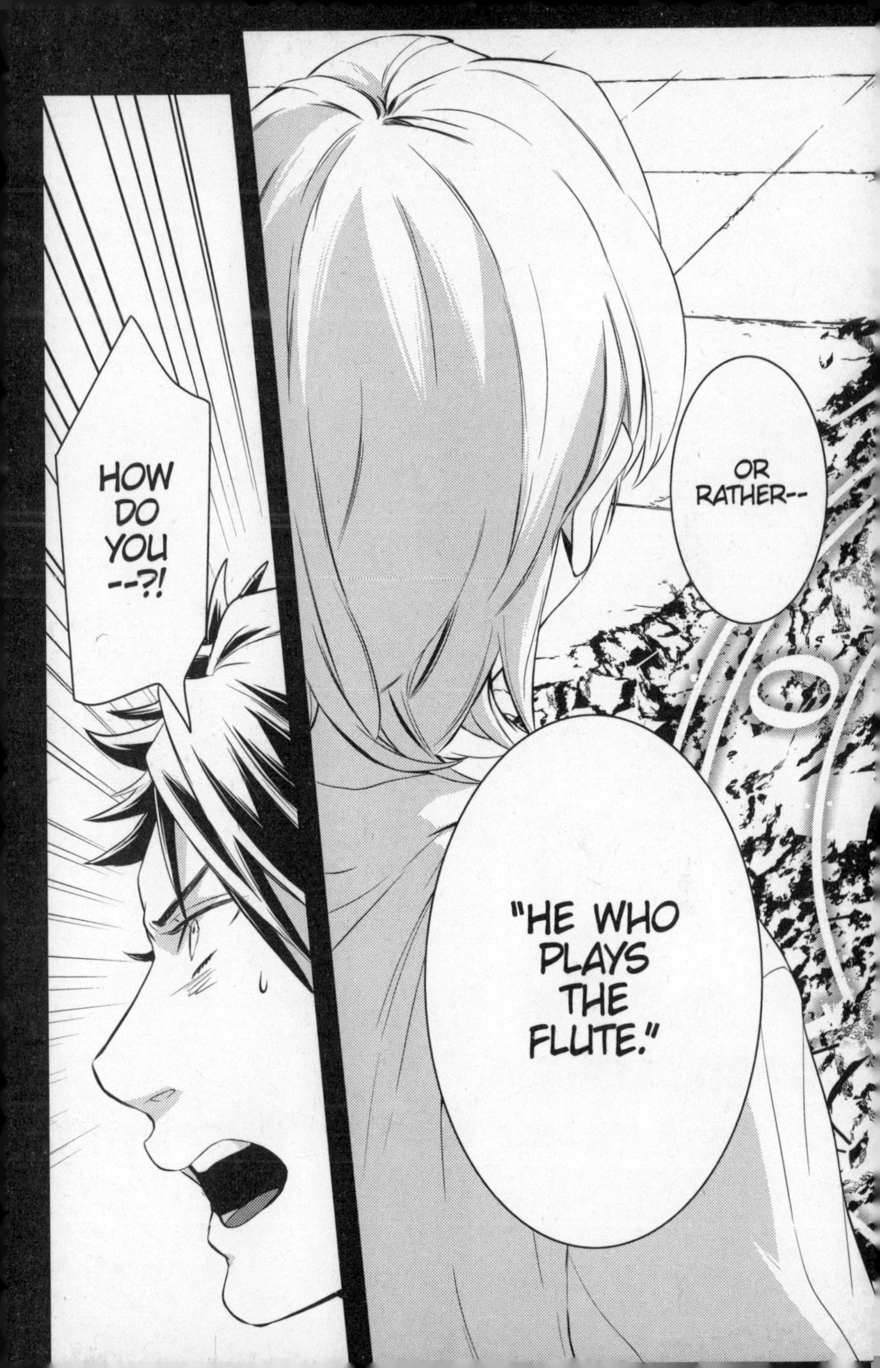
OR RATHER--
"HE WHO PLAYS THE FLUTE."
HOW DO YOU --?!

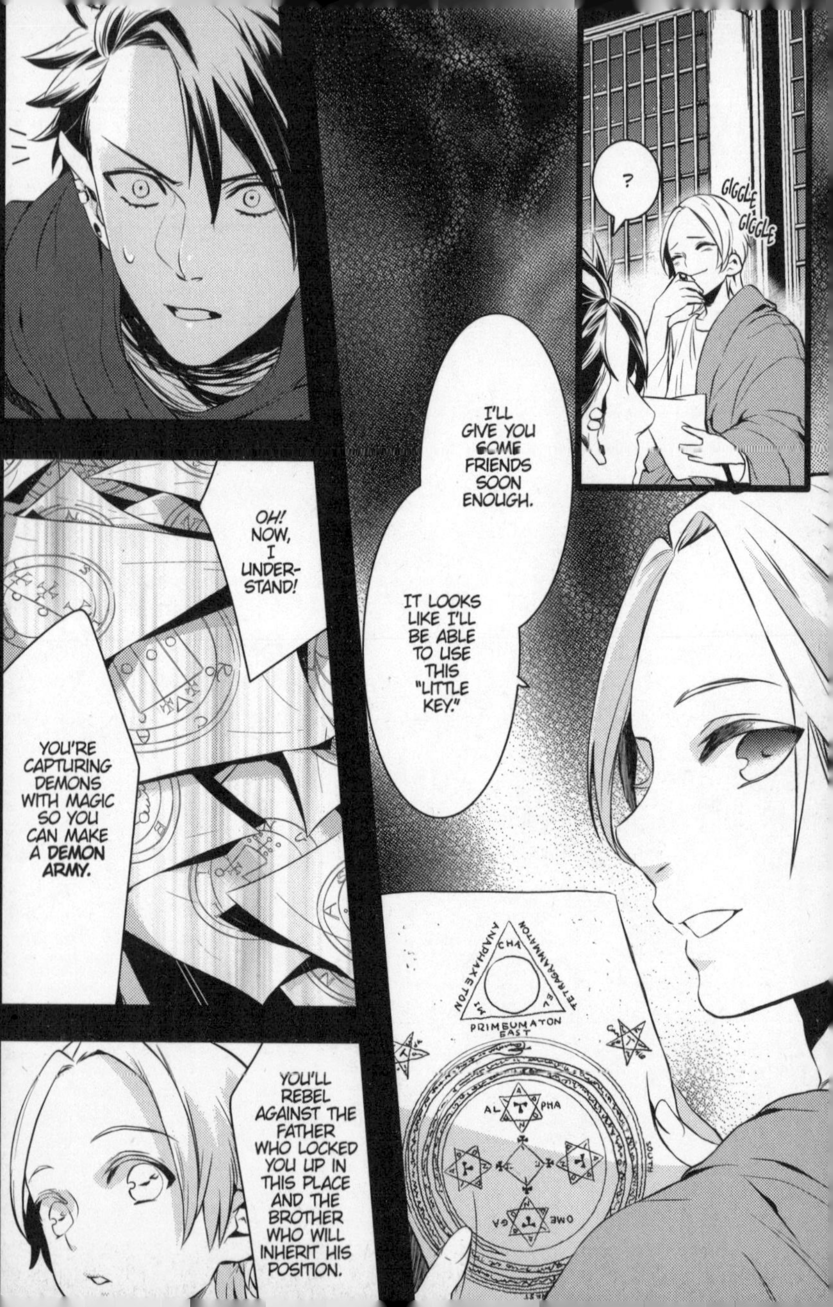
?
GIGGLE GIGGLE
I'LL GIVE YOU SOME FRIENDS SOON ENOUGH.
IT LOOKS LIKE I'LL BE ABLE TO USE THIS "LITTLE KEY."
ANAPHAXETON
TETRAGAMMATON
CHA
EL
IM
PRIMSUMATON
EAST
AL PHA
OME GA
SOUTH
OH! NOW, I UNDER-STAND!
YOU'RE CAPTURING DEMONS WITH MAGIC SO YOU CAN MAKE A **DEMON ARMY.**
YOU'LL REBEL AGAINST THE FATHER WHO LOCKED YOU UP IN THIS PLACE AND THE BROTHER WHO WILL INHERIT HIS POSITION.

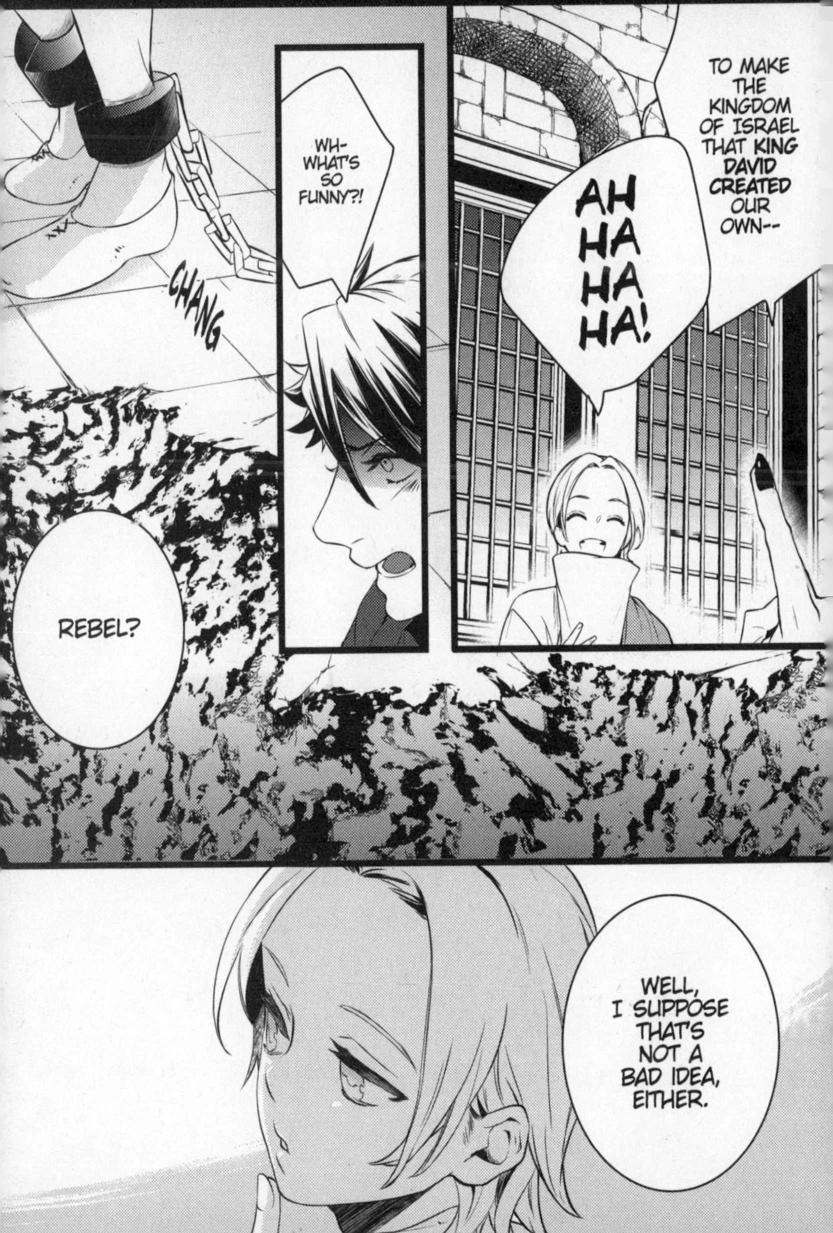
TO MAKE THE KINGDOM OF ISRAEL THAT KING DAVID CREATED OUR OWN--
AH HA HA HA!
WH- WHAT'S SO FUNNY?!
CHANG
REBEL?
WELL, I SUPPOSE THAT'S NOT A BAD IDEA, EITHER.

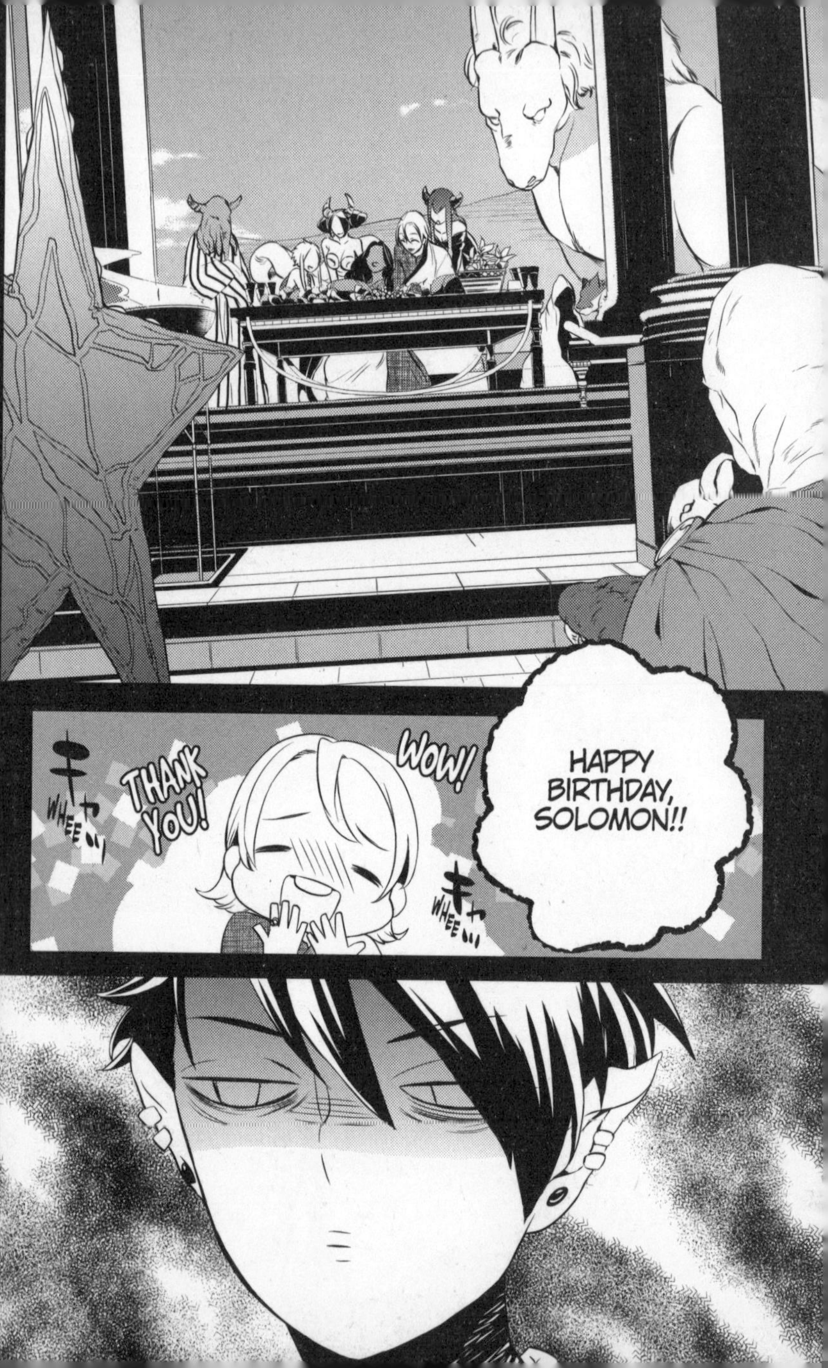
HAPPY BIRTHDAY, SOLOMON!!
WHEE…
WOW!
THANK YOU!
WHEE…

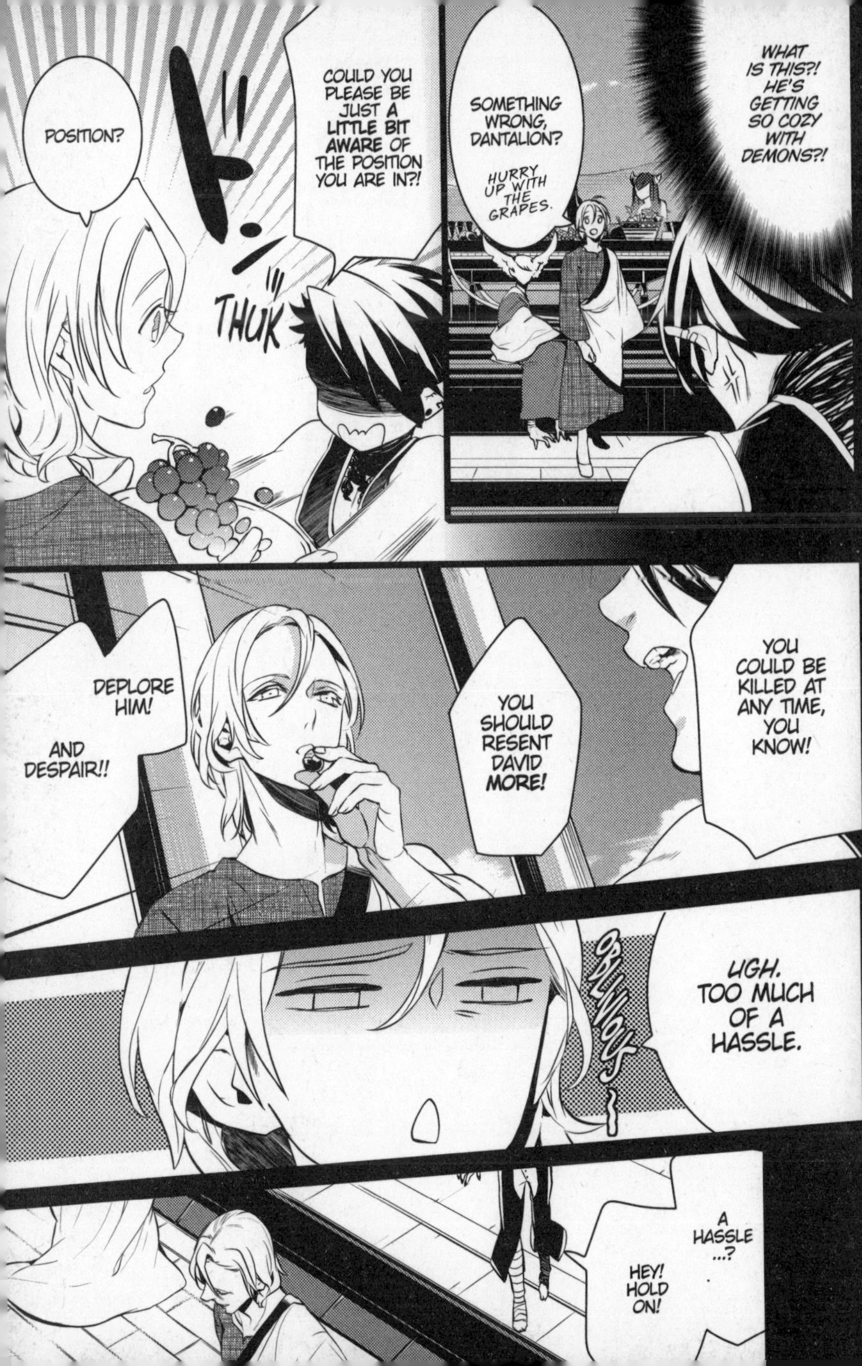
WHAT IS THIS?! HE'S GETTING SO COZY WITH DEMONS?!
SOMETHING WRONG, DANTALION?
HURRY UP WITH THE GRAPES.
COULD YOU PLEASE BE JUST A LITTLE BIT AWARE OF THE POSITION YOU ARE IN?!
THUK
POSITION?
YOU COULD BE KILLED AT ANY TIME, YOU KNOW!
YOU SHOULD RESENT DAVID MORE!
DEPLORE HIM!
AND DESPAIR!!
UGH. TOO MUCH OF A HASSLE.
OBLIVIOUS~
A HASSLE...?
HEY! HOLD ON!

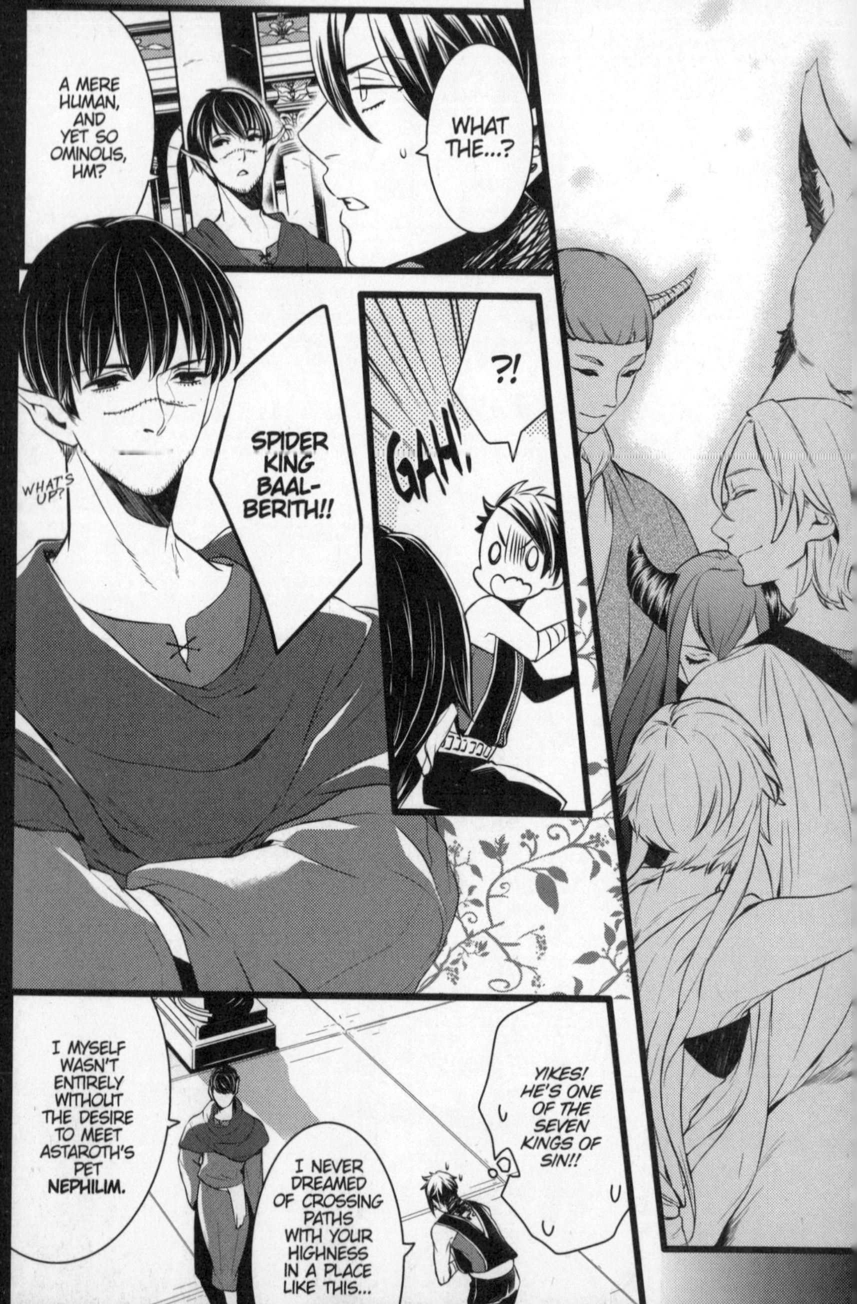
WHAT THE...?
A MERE HUMAN, AND YET SO OMINOUS, HM?
?!
GAH!
SPIDER KING BAAL-BERITH!!
WHAT'S UP?
YIKES! HE'S ONE OF THE SEVEN KINGS OF SIN!!
I NEVER DREAMED OF CROSSING PATHS WITH YOUR HIGHNESS IN A PLACE LIKE THIS...
I MYSELF WASN'T ENTIRELY WITHOUT THE DESIRE TO MEET ASTAROTH'S PET NEPHILIM.

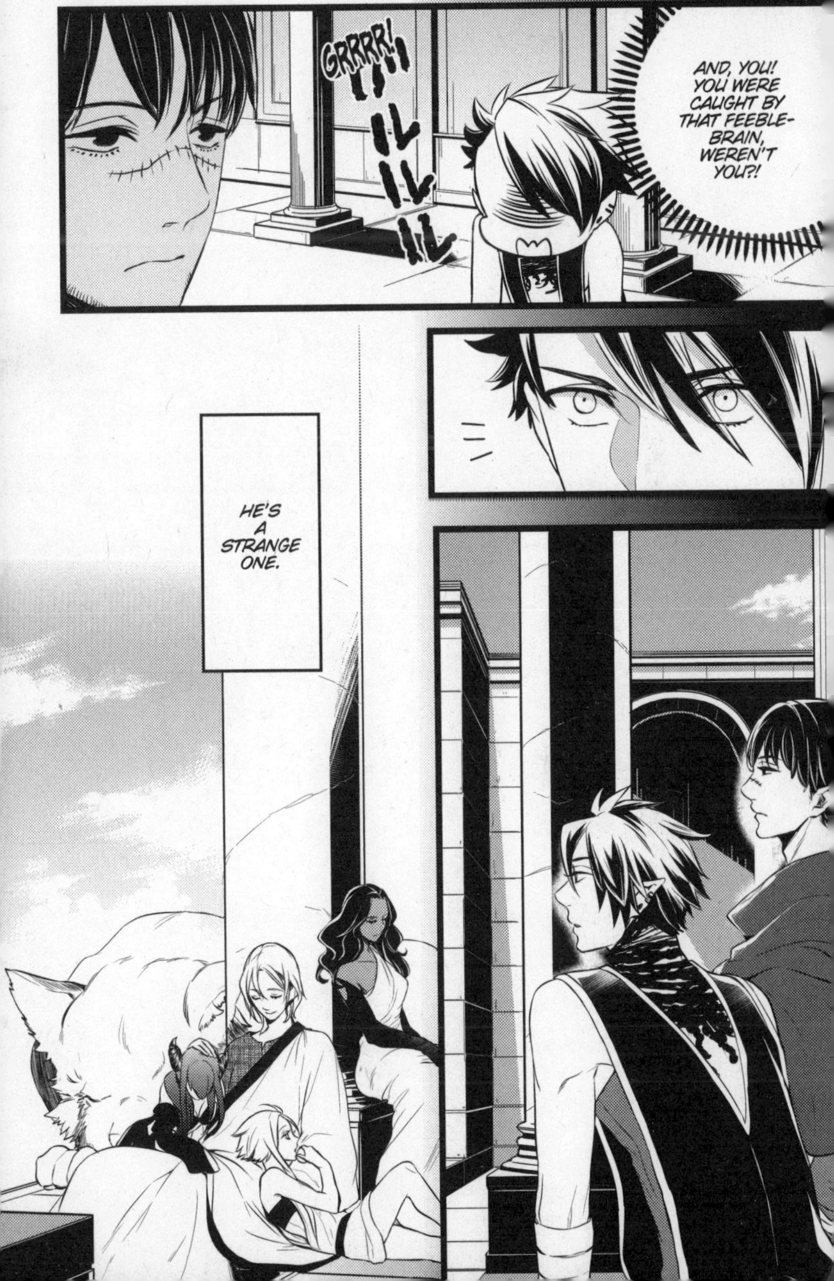
AND, YOU! YOU WERE CAUGHT BY THAT FEEBLE-BRAIN, WEREN'T YOU?!
GRRRR!
HE'S A STRANGE ONE.

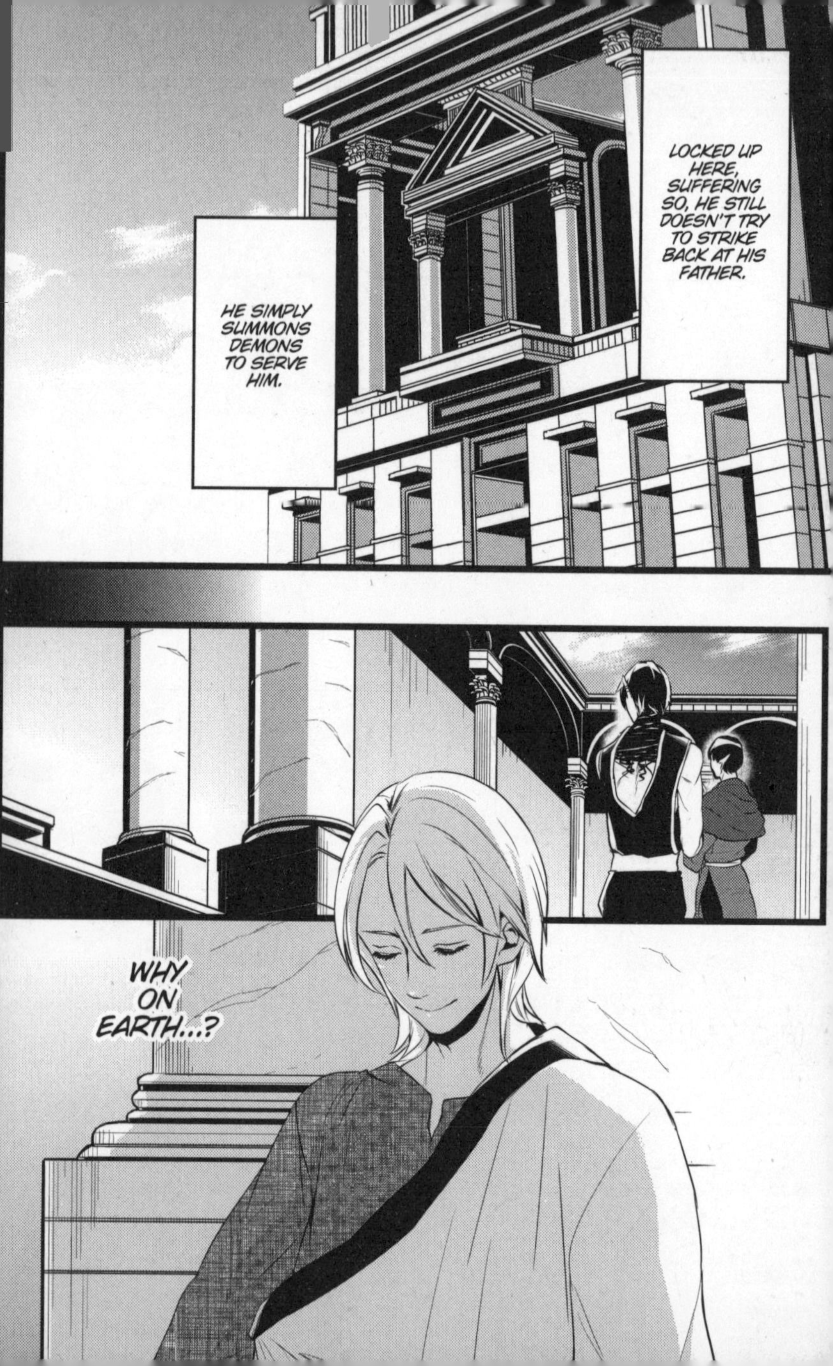
LOCKED UP HERE, SUFFERING SO, HE STILL DOESN'T TRY TO STRIKE BACK AT HIS FATHER.
HE SIMPLY SUMMONS DEMONS TO SERVE HIM.
WHY ON EARTH...?

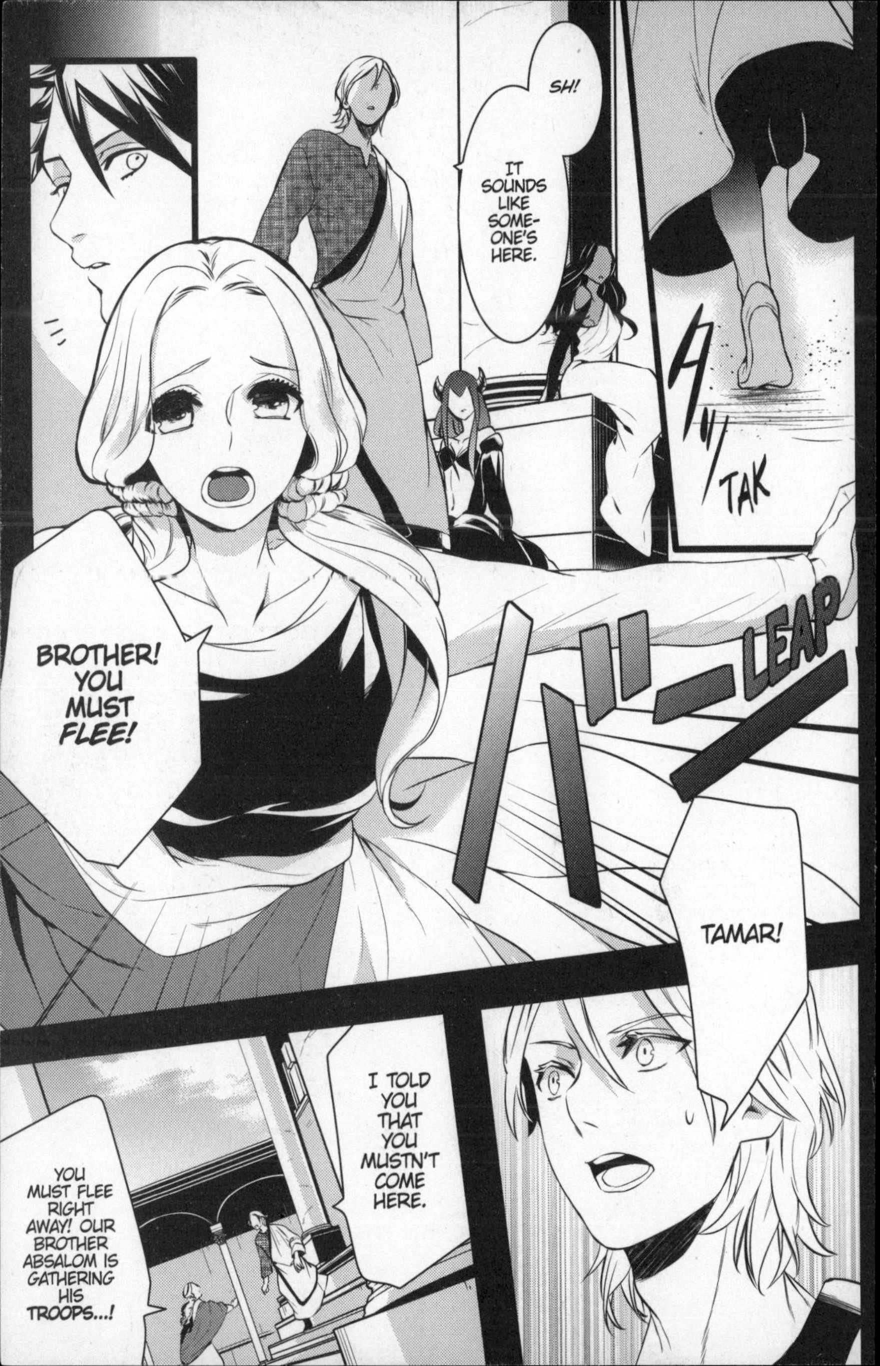
TAK
SH!
IT SOUNDS LIKE SOME-ONE'S HERE.
LEAP
BROTHER! YOU MUST FLEE!
TAMAR!
I TOLD YOU THAT YOU MUSTN'T COME HERE.
YOU MUST FLEE RIGHT AWAY! OUR BROTHER ABSALOM IS GATHERING HIS TROOPS...!

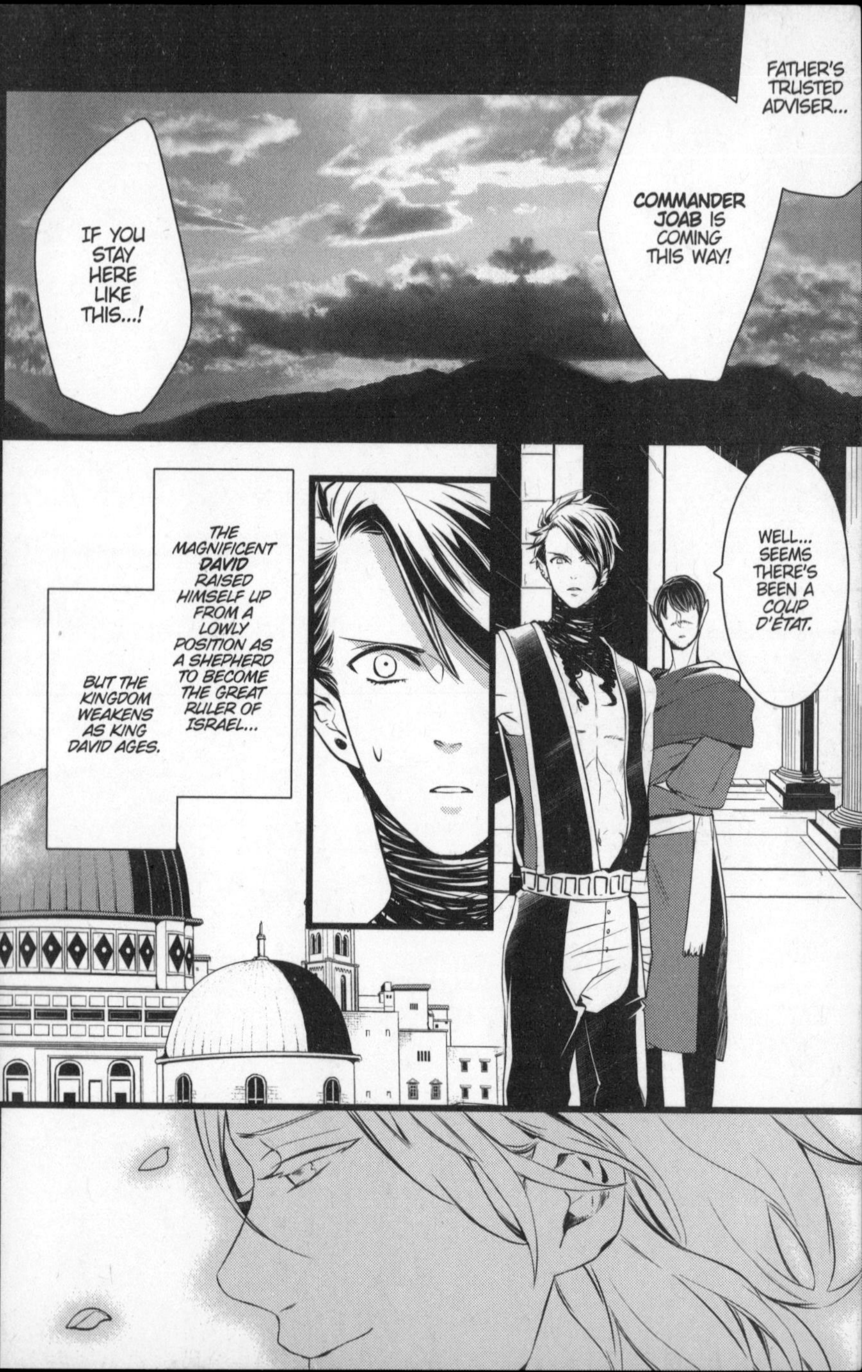
FATHER'S TRUSTED ADVISER...
COMMANDER JOAB IS COMING THIS WAY!
IF YOU STAY HERE LIKE THIS...!
WELL... SEEMS THERE'S BEEN A COUP D'ÉTAT.
THE MAGNIFICENT DAVID RAISED HIMSELF UP FROM A LOWLY POSITION AS A SHEPHERD TO BECOME THE GREAT RULER OF ISRAEL...
BUT THE KINGDOM WEAKENS AS KING DAVID AGES.

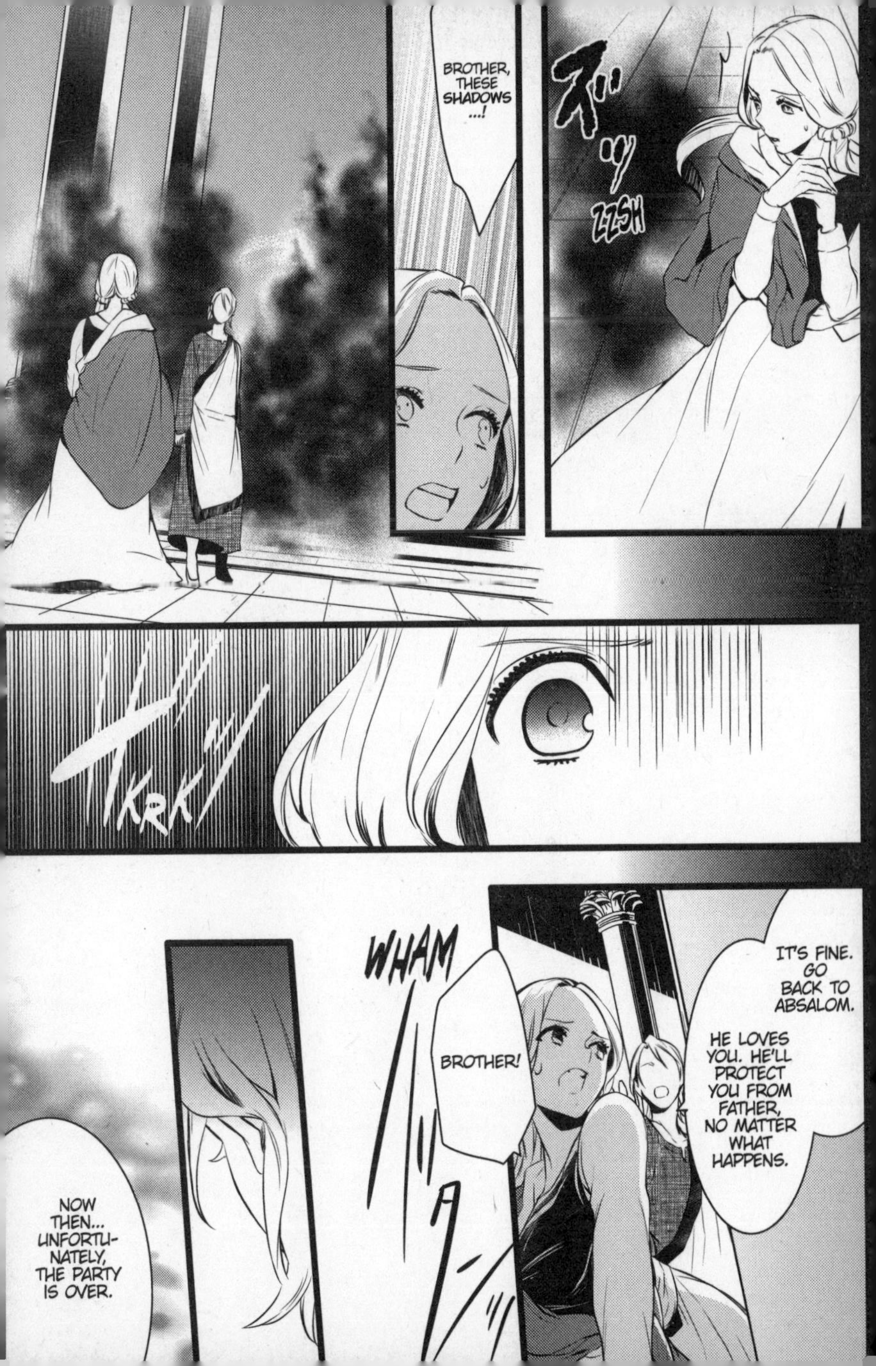
ZZSH
BROTHER, THESE SHADOWS ...!
KRK
IT'S FINE. GO BACK TO ABSALOM.
HE LOVES YOU. HE'LL PROTECT YOU FROM FATHER, NO MATTER WHAT HAPPENS.
WHAM
BROTHER!
NOW THEN... UNFORTUNATELY, THE PARTY IS OVER.

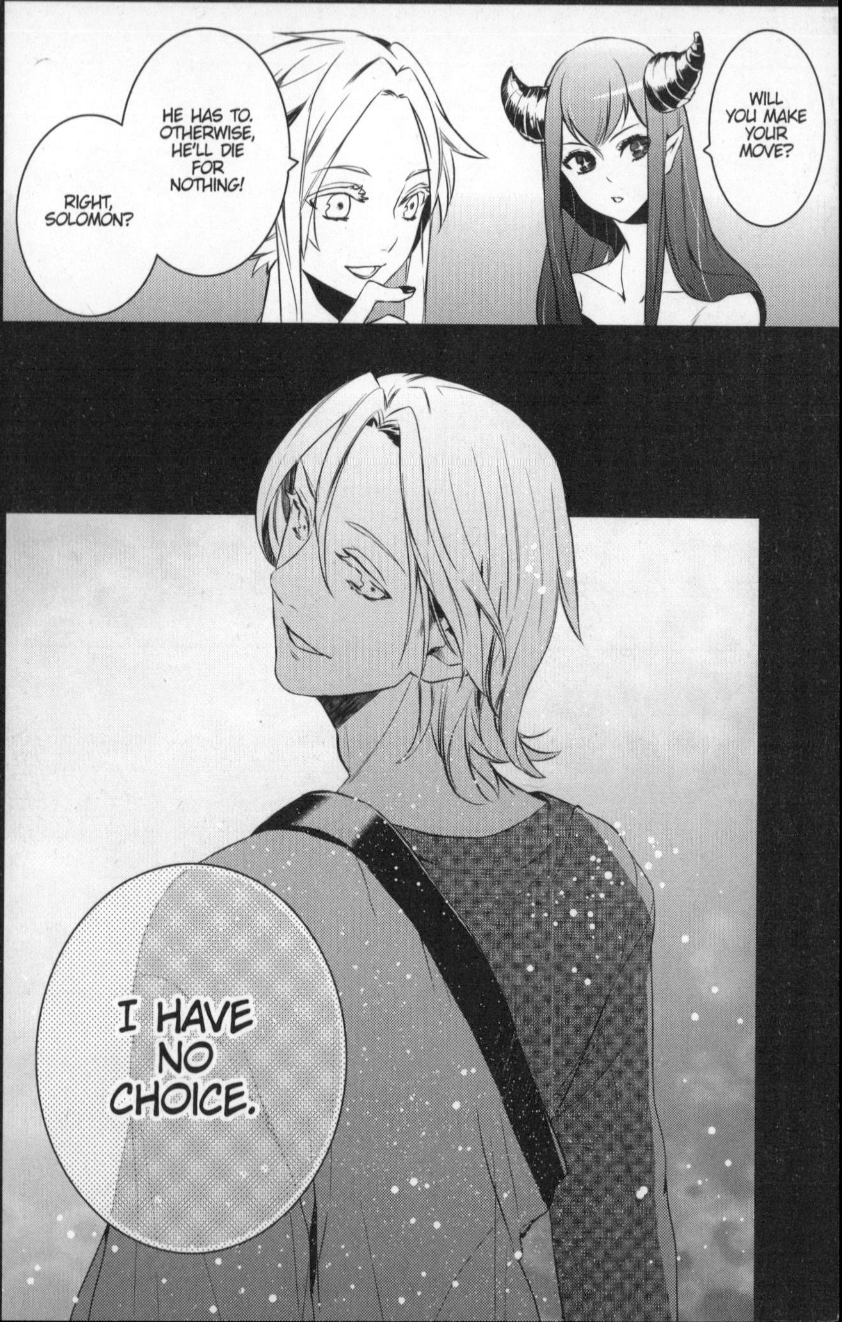
WILL YOU MAKE YOUR MOVE?
HE HAS TO. OTHERWISE, HE'LL DIE FOR NOTHING!
RIGHT, SOLOMON?
I HAVE NO CHOICE.

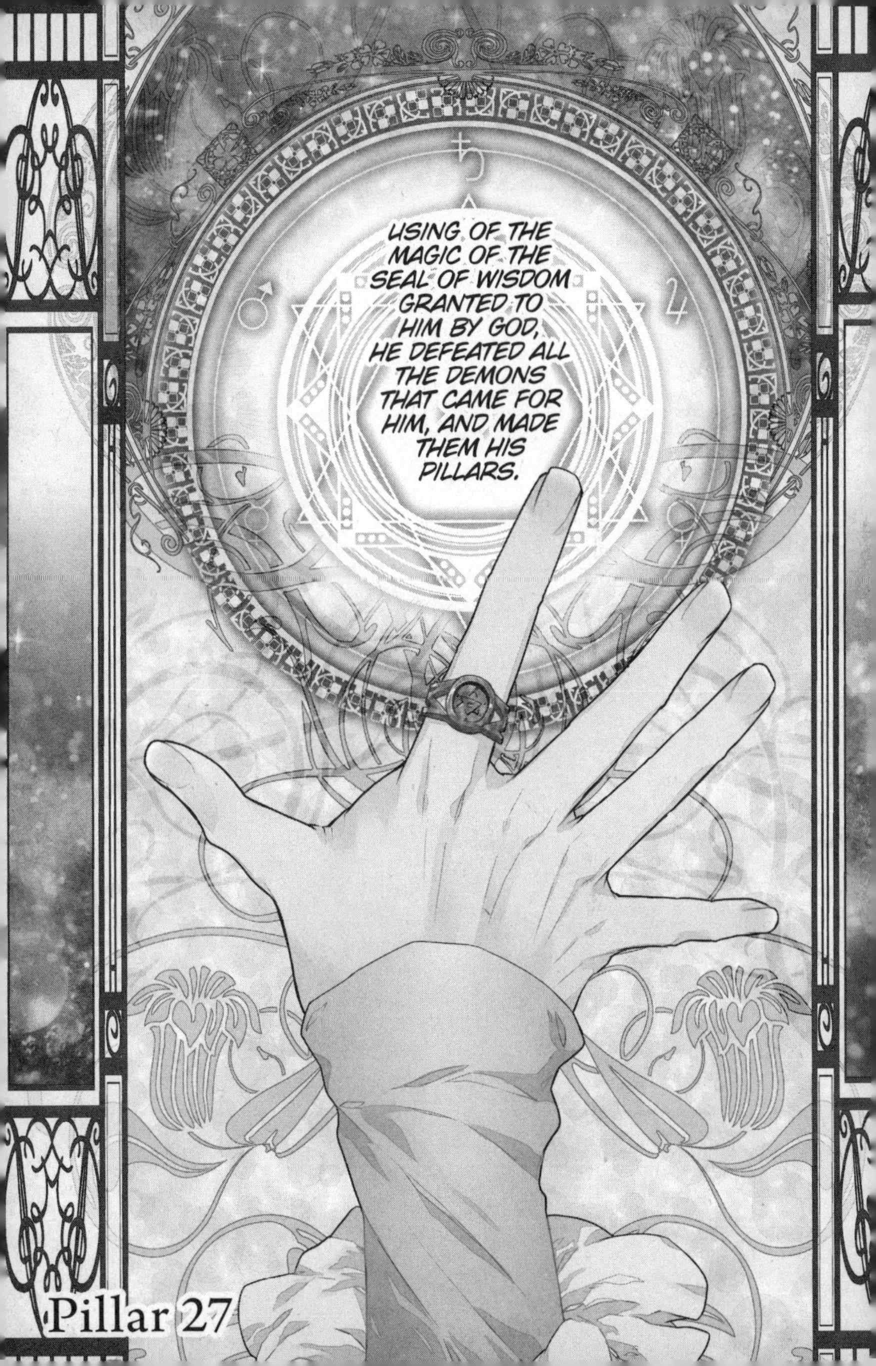
USING OF THE MAGIC OF THE SEAL OF WISDOM GRANTED TO HIM BY GOD, HE DEFEATED ALL THE DEMONS THAT CAME FOR HIM, AND MADE THEM HIS PILLARS.
Pillar 27

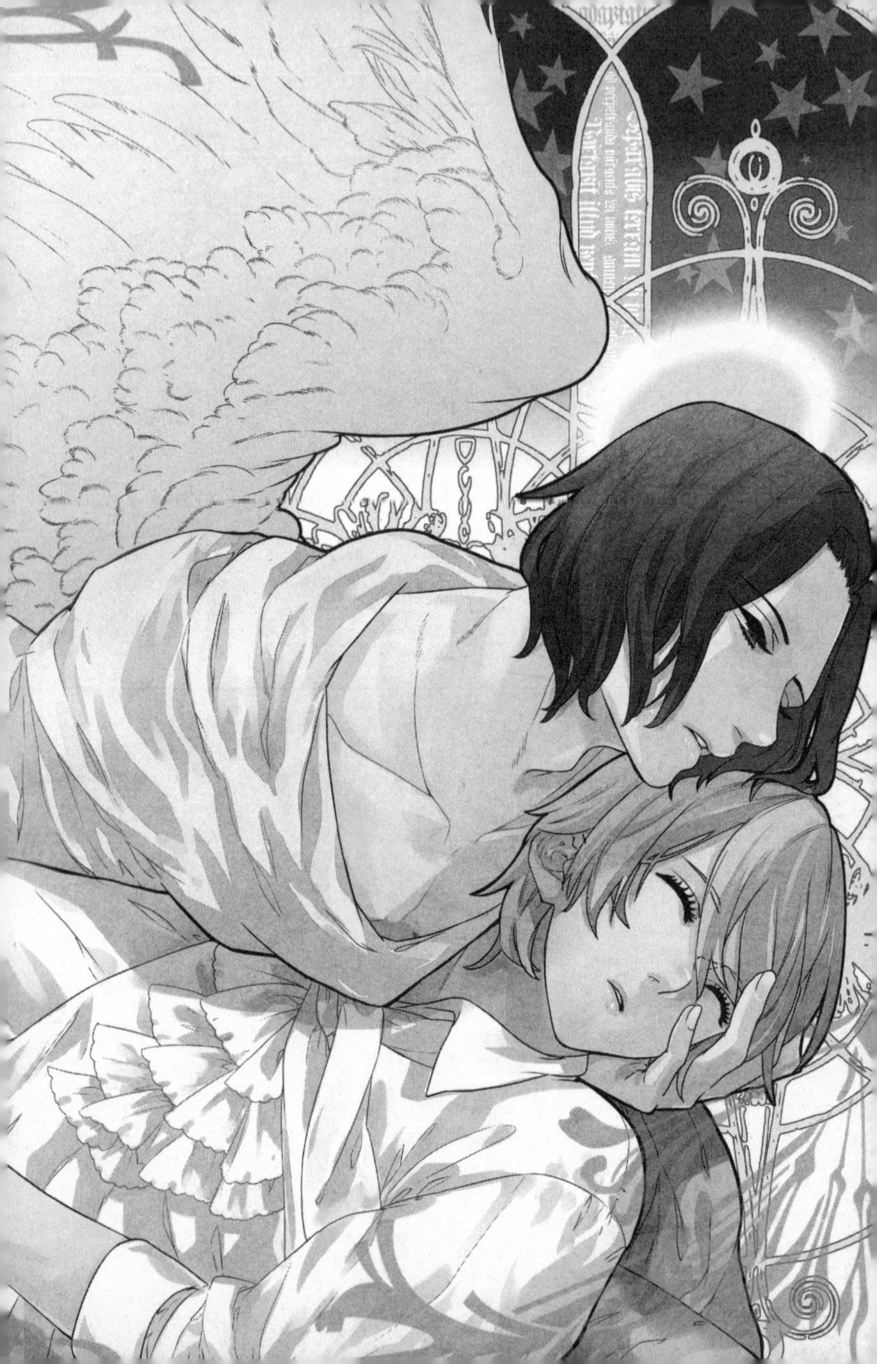

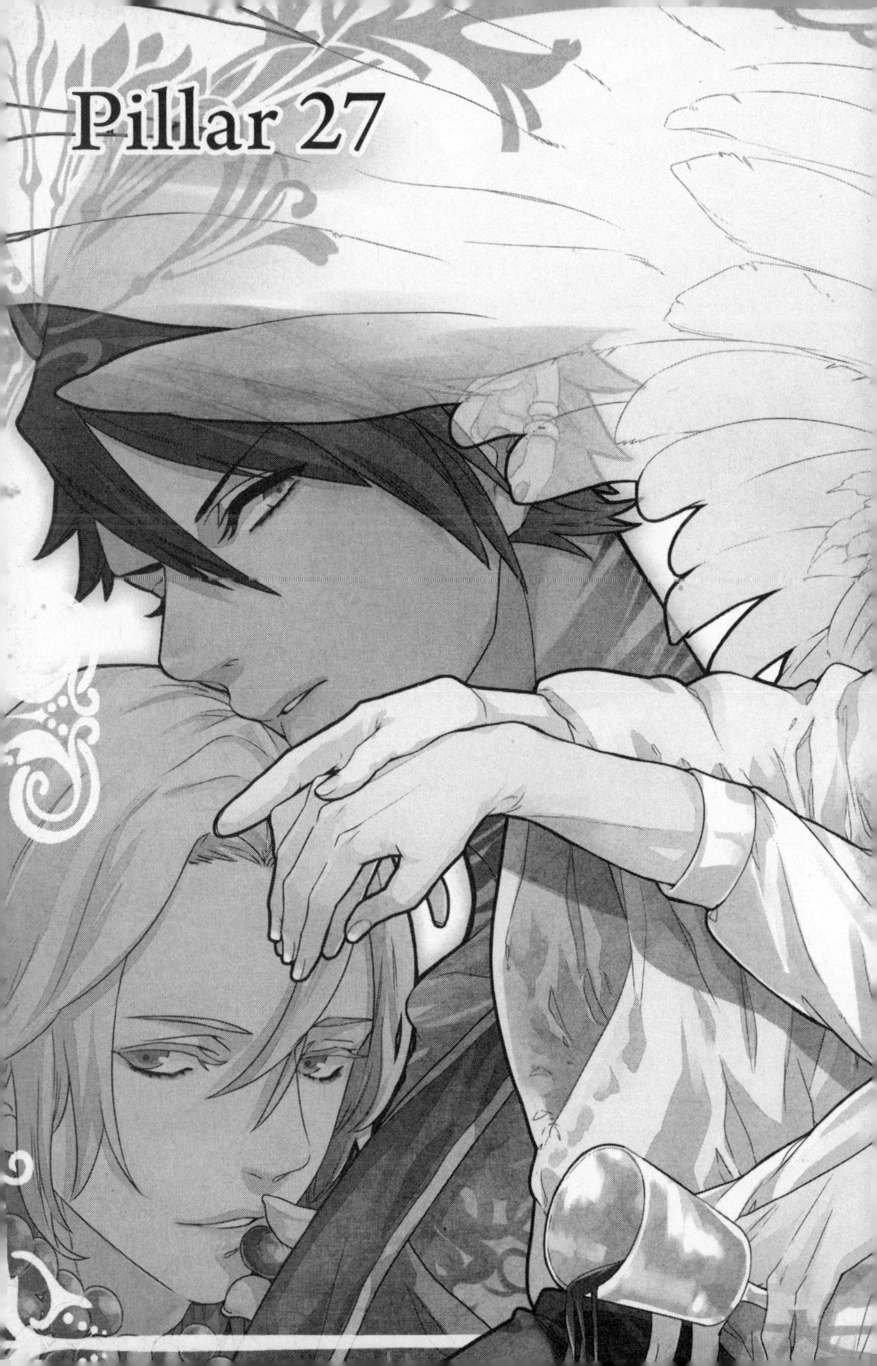
Pillar 27

EEEAAUGH!!
AAAAH!

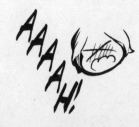

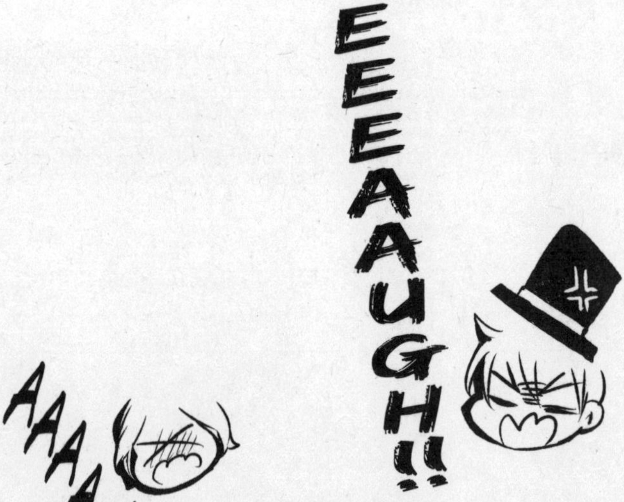

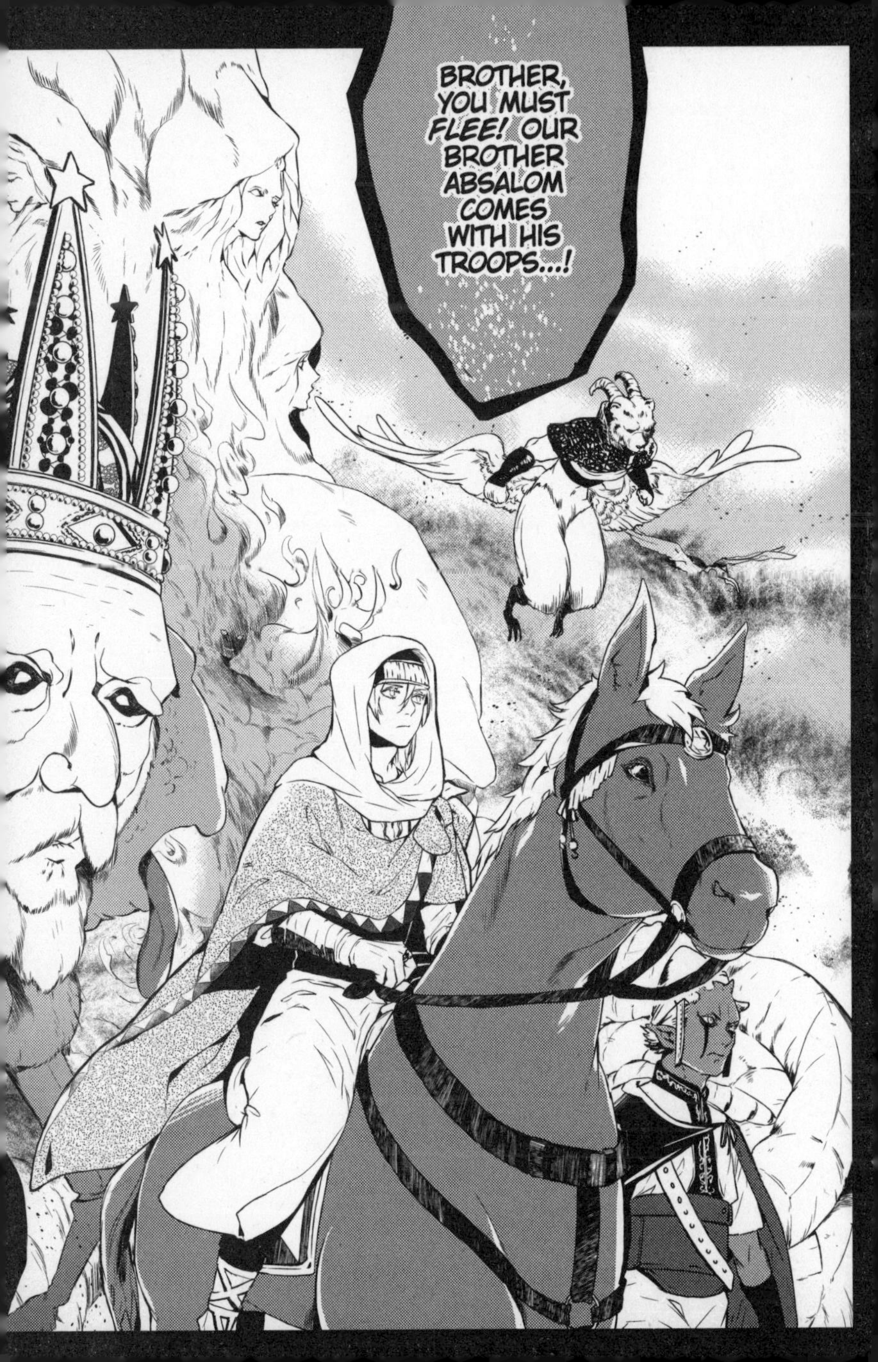
BROTHER, YOU MUST FLEE! OUR BROTHER ABSALOM COMES WITH HIS TROOPS...!

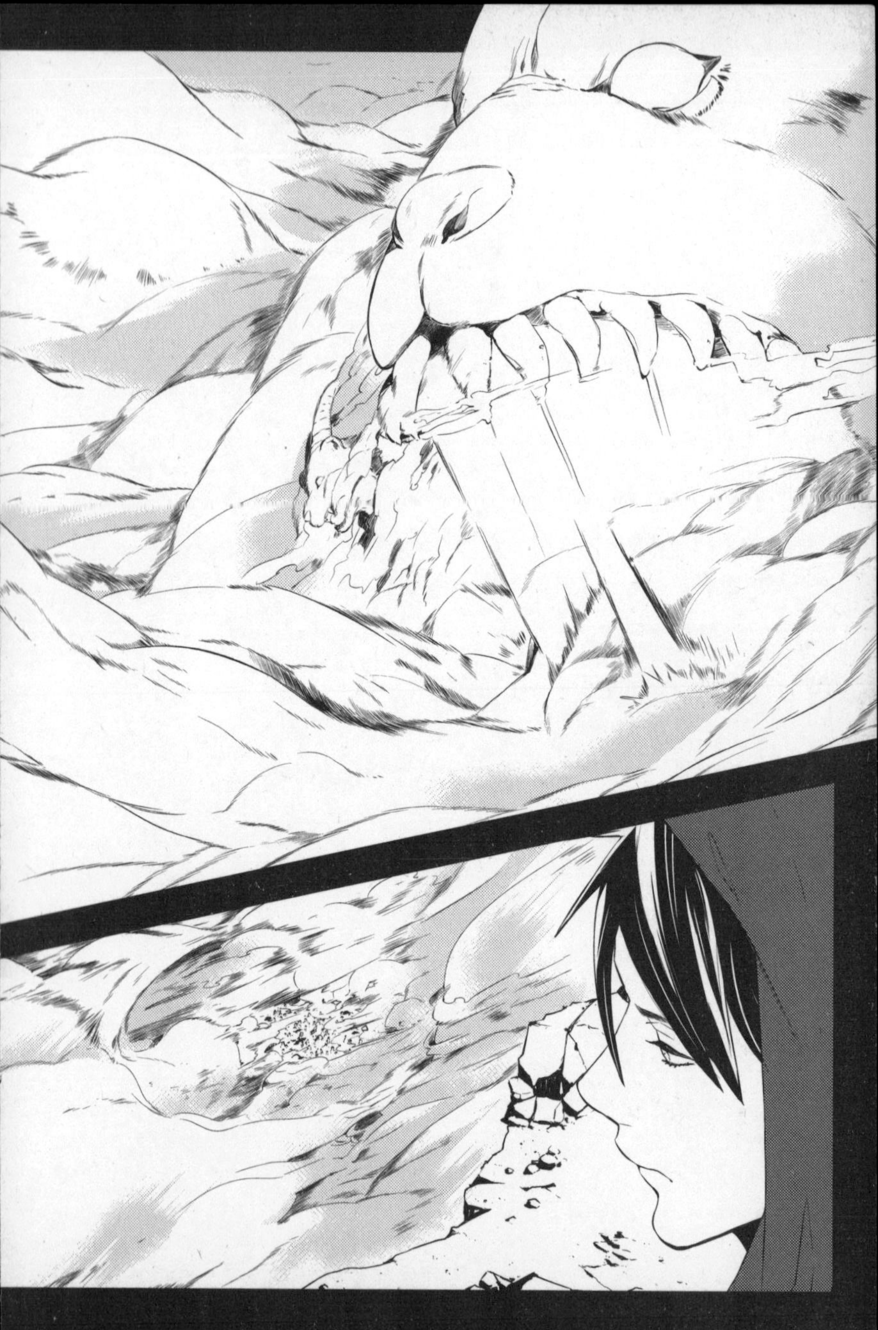

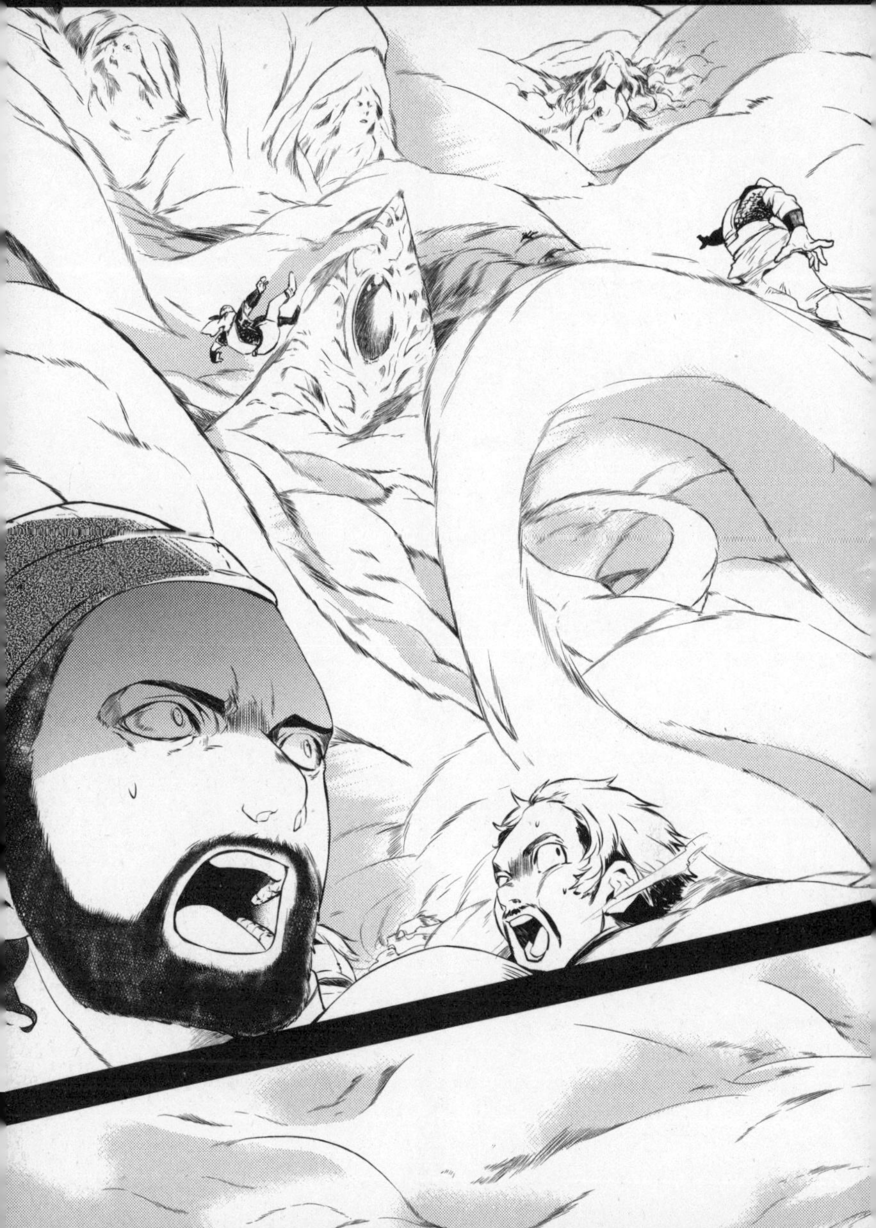

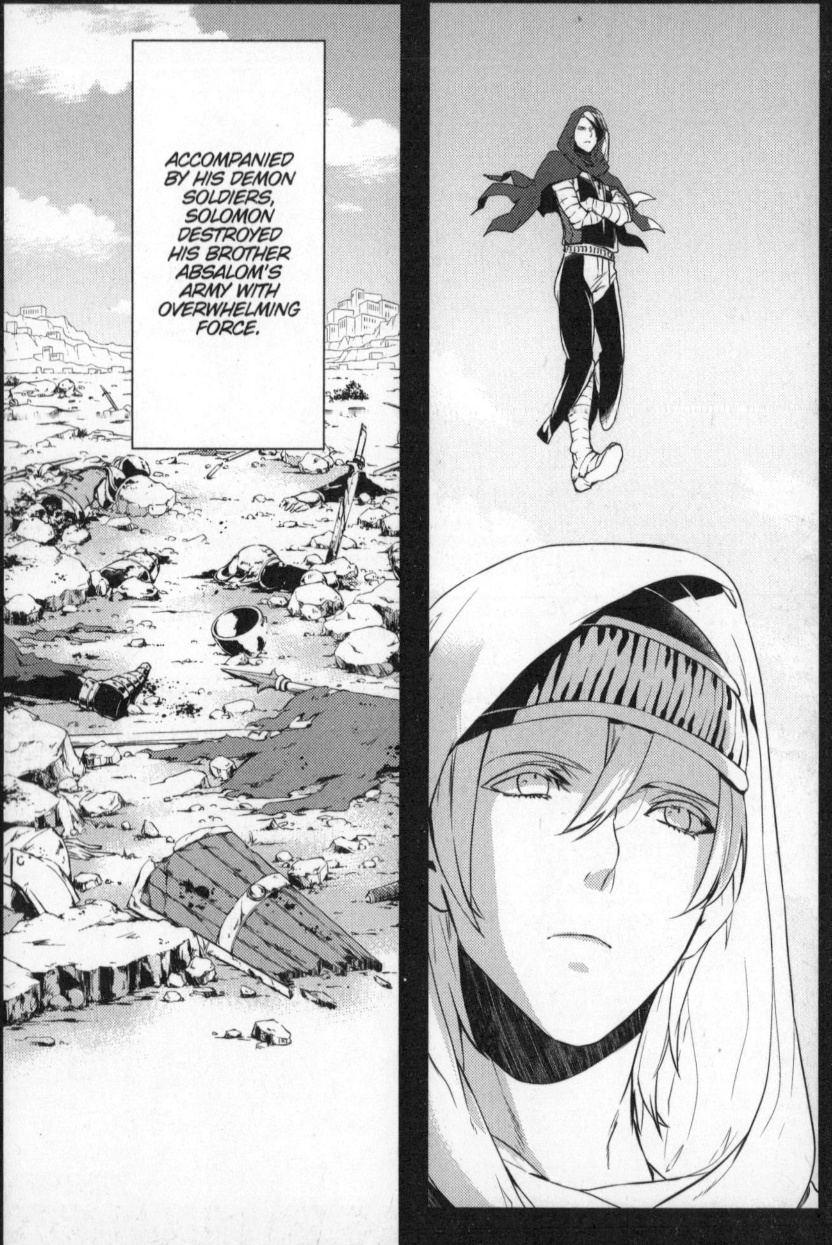
ACCOMPANIED BY HIS DEMON SOLDIERS, SOLOMON DESTROYED HIS BROTHER ABSALOM'S ARMY WITH OVERWHELMING FORCE.

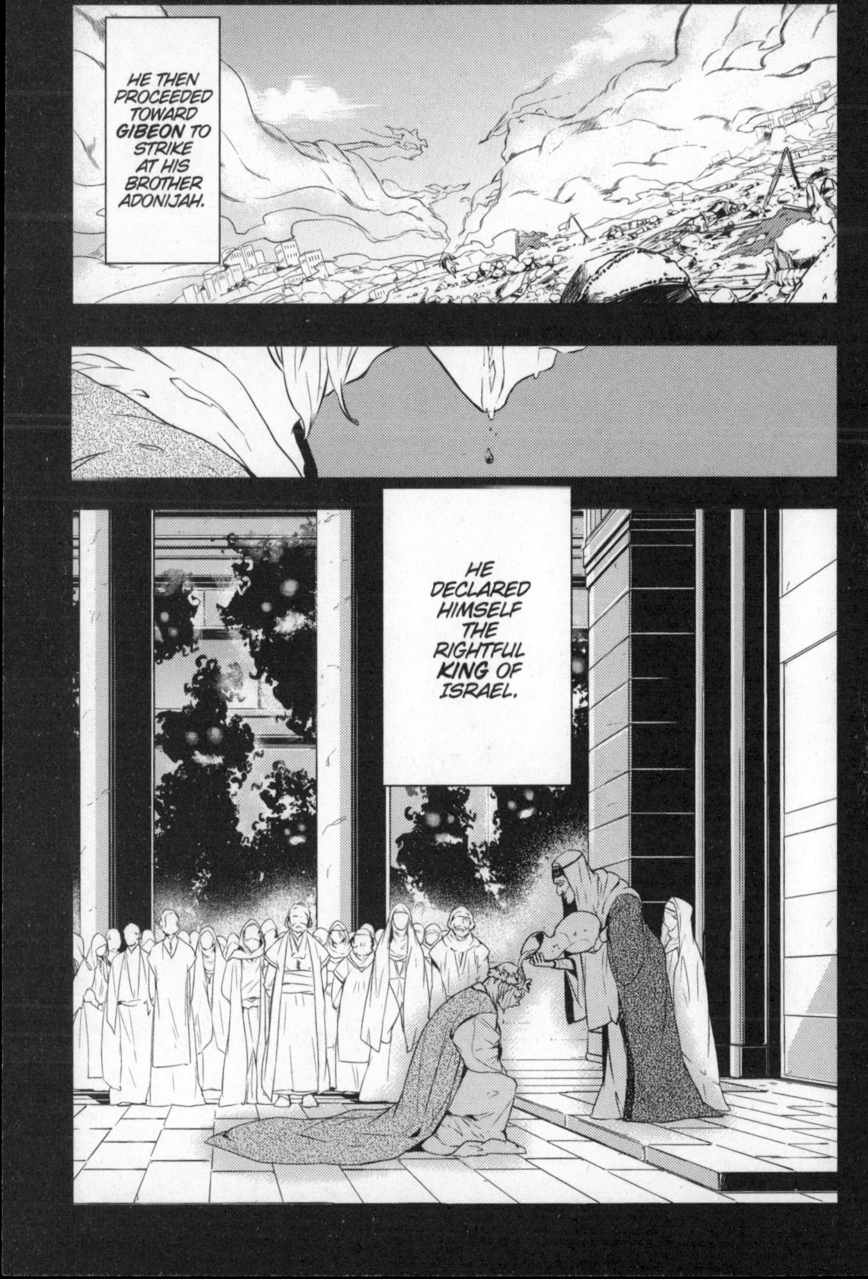
HE THEN PROCEEDED TOWARD GIBEON TO STRIKE AT HIS BROTHER ADONIJAH.
HE DECLARED HIMSELF THE RIGHTFUL KING OF ISRAEL.

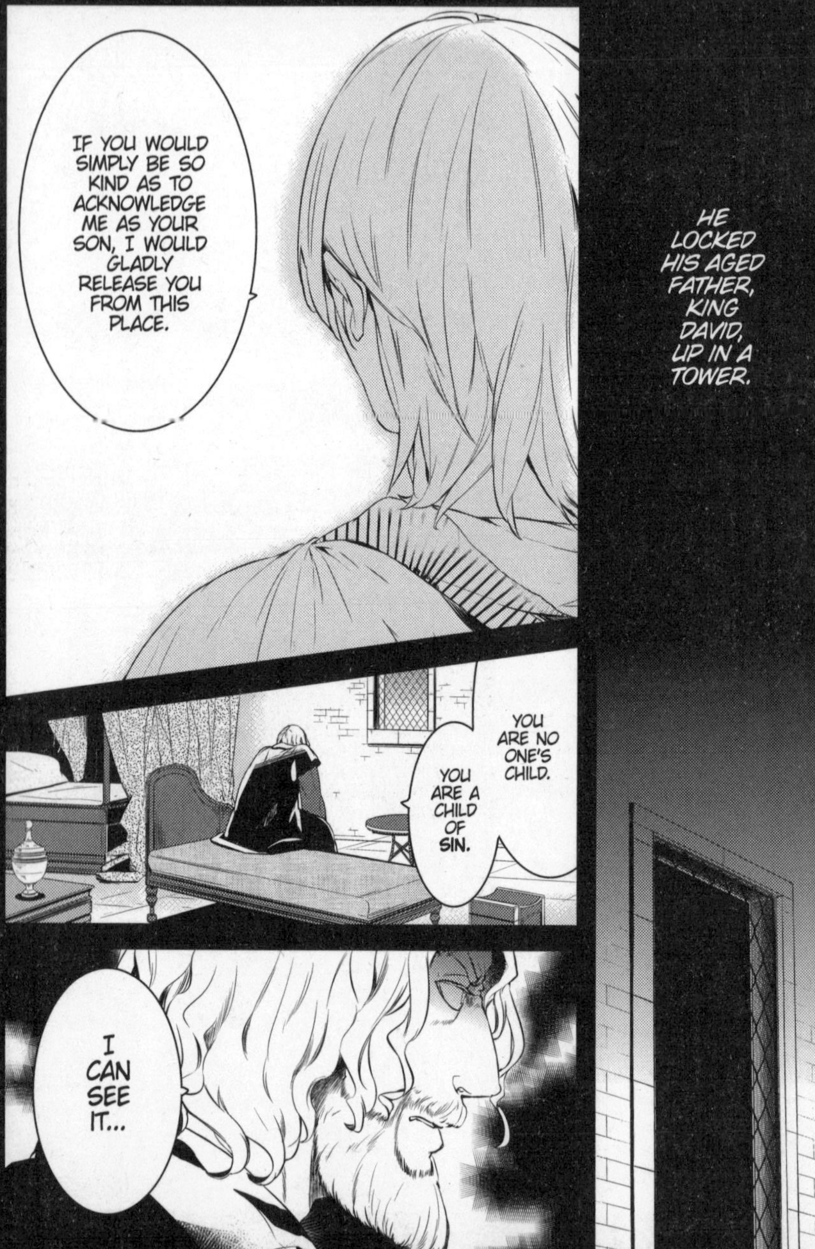
HE LOCKED HIS AGED FATHER, KING DAVID, UP IN A TOWER.
IF YOU WOULD SIMPLY BE SO KIND AS TO ACKNOWLEDGE ME AS YOUR SON, I WOULD GLADLY RELEASE YOU FROM THIS PLACE.
YOU ARE NO ONE'S CHILD.
YOU ARE A CHILD OF SIN.
I CAN SEE IT...

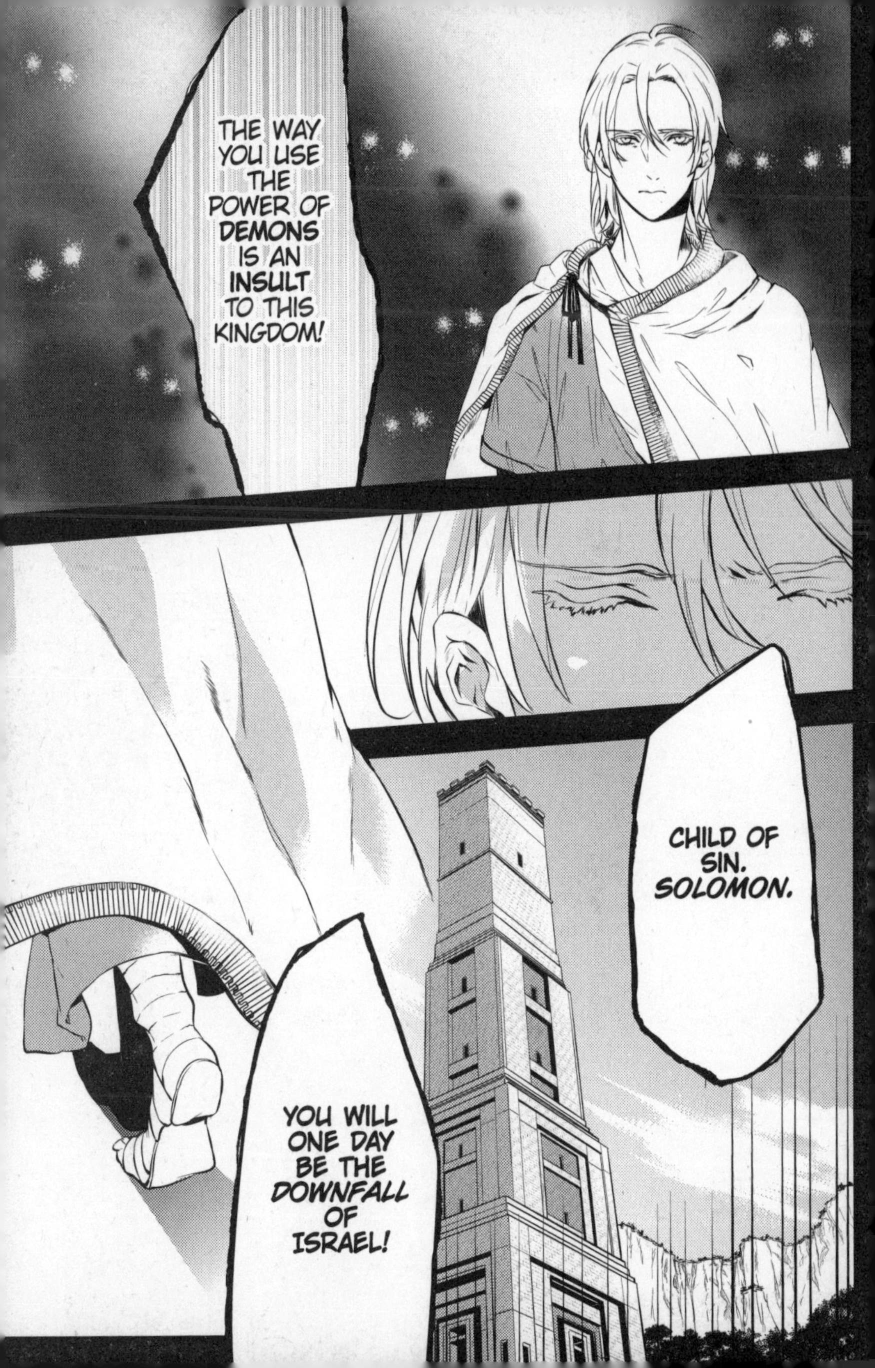
THE WAY YOU USE THE POWER OF DEMONS IS AN INSULT TO THIS KINGDOM!
CHILD OF SIN. SOLOMON.
YOU WILL ONE DAY BE THE DOWNFALL OF ISRAEL!

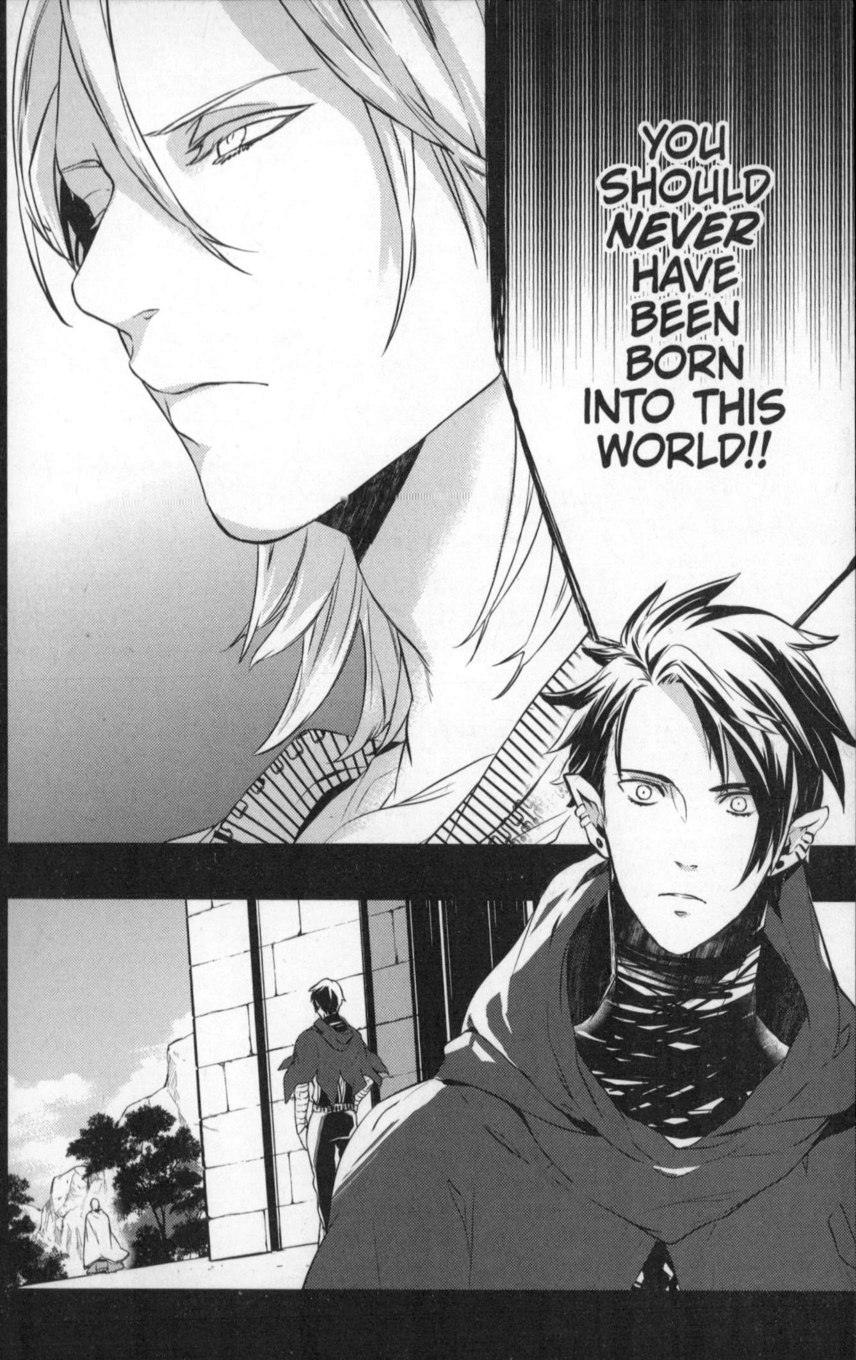
YOU SHOULD NEVER HAVE BEEN BORN INTO THIS WORLD!!

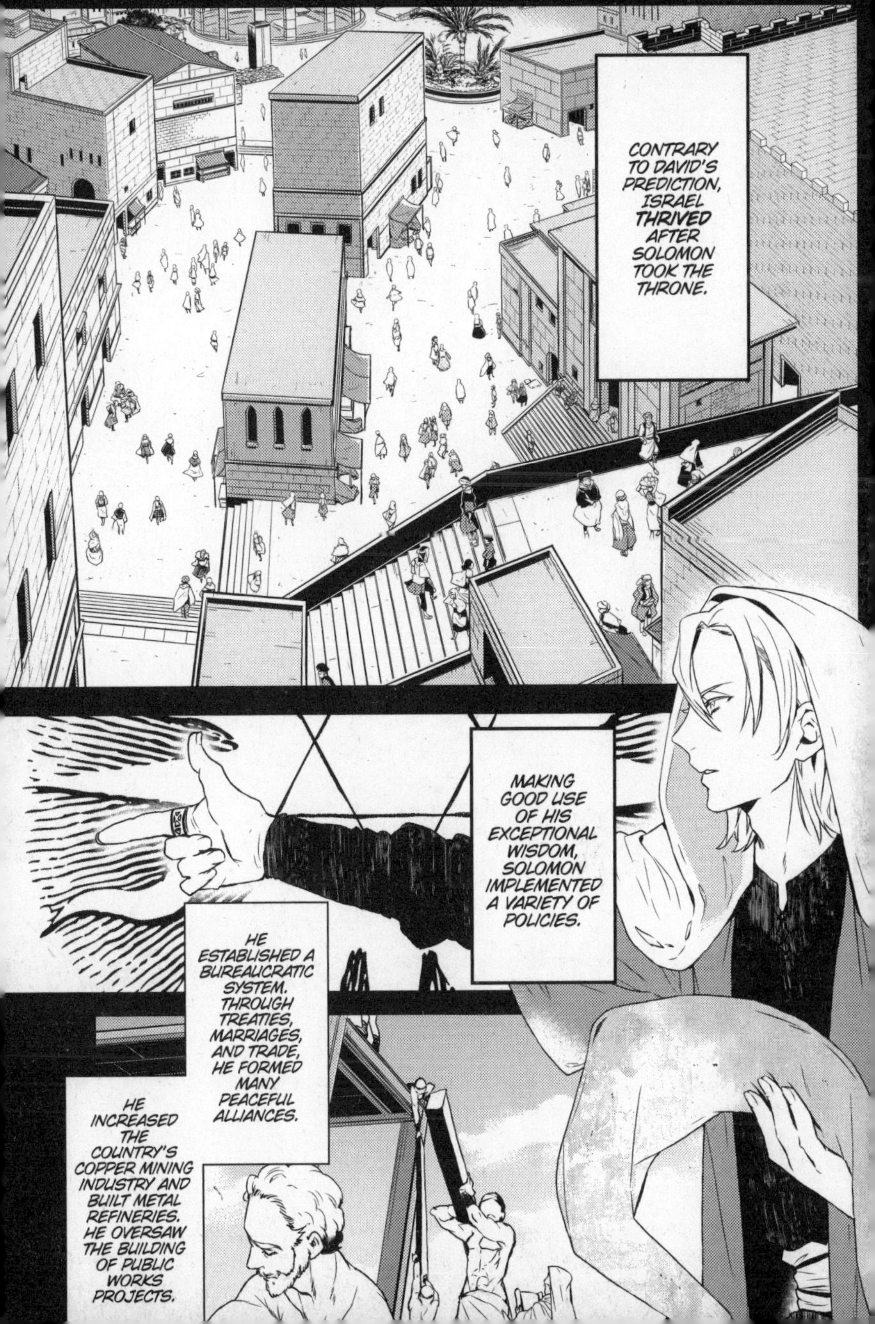
CONTRARY TO DAVID'S PREDICTION, ISRAEL **THRIVED** AFTER SOLOMON TOOK THE THRONE.
MAKING GOOD USE OF HIS EXCEPTIONAL WISDOM, SOLOMON IMPLEMENTED A VARIETY OF POLICIES.
HE ESTABLISHED A BUREAUCRATIC SYSTEM. THROUGH TREATIES, MARRIAGES, AND TRADE, HE FORMED MANY PEACEFUL ALLIANCES.
HE INCREASED THE COUNTRY'S COPPER MINING INDUSTRY AND BUILT METAL REFINERIES. HE OVERSAW THE BUILDING OF PUBLIC WORKS PROJECTS.

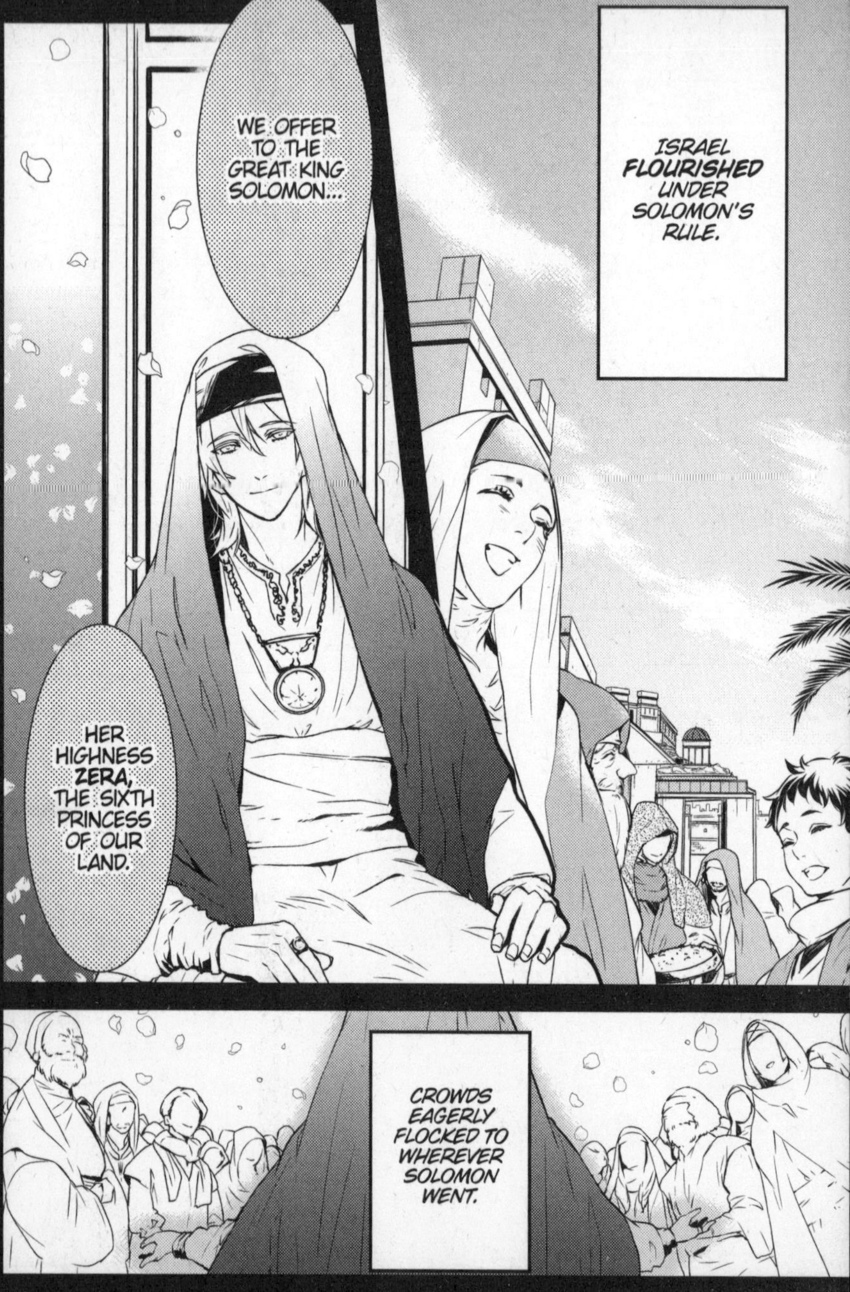
ISRAEL FLOURISHED UNDER SOLOMON'S RULE.
WE OFFER TO THE GREAT KING SOLOMON...
HER HIGHNESS ZERA, THE SIXTH PRINCESS OF OUR LAND.
CROWDS EAGERLY FLOCKED TO WHEREVER SOLOMON WENT.

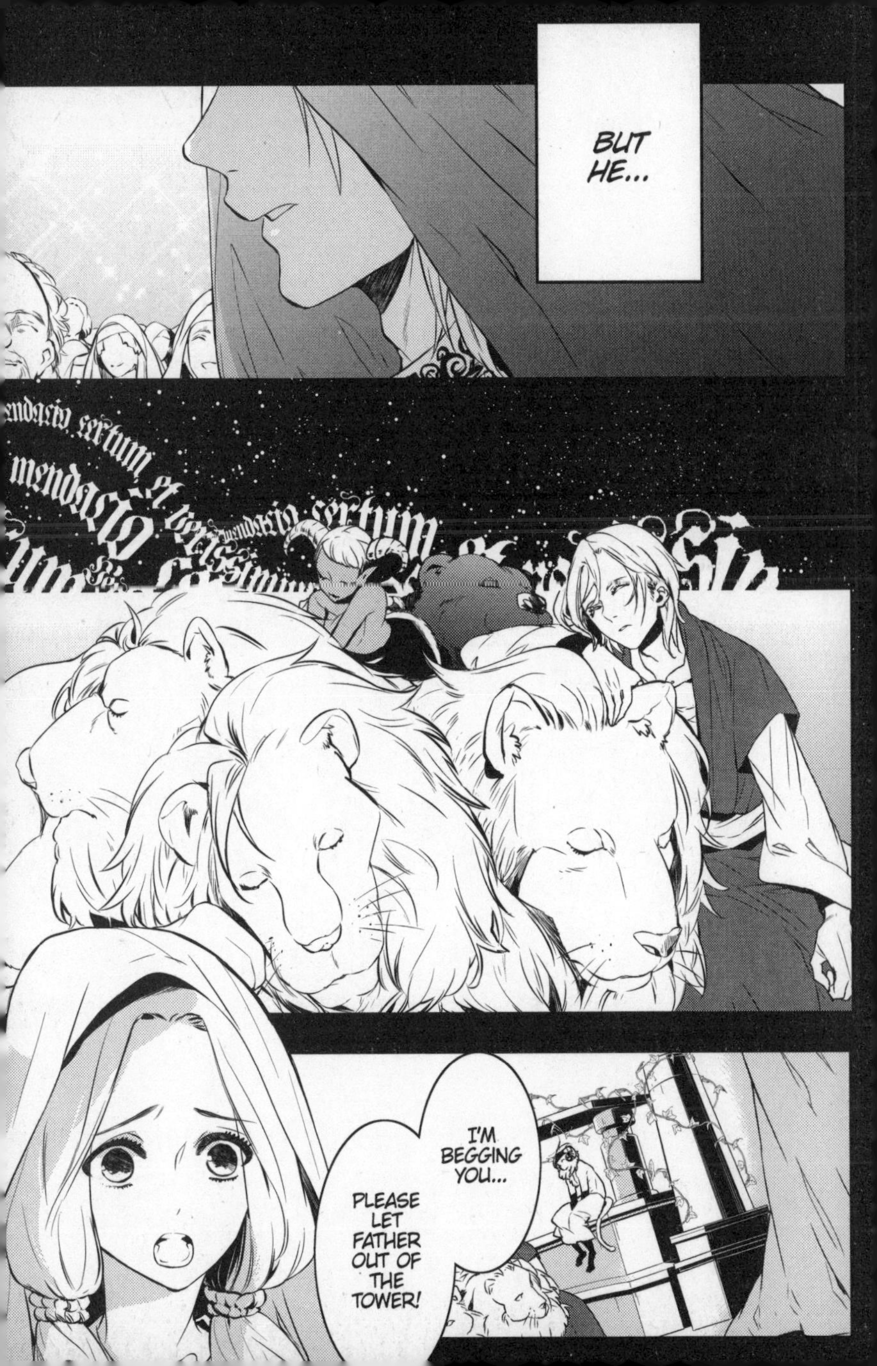
BUT HE...
mendacio certum
I'M BEGGING YOU...
PLEASE LET FATHER OUT OF THE TOWER!

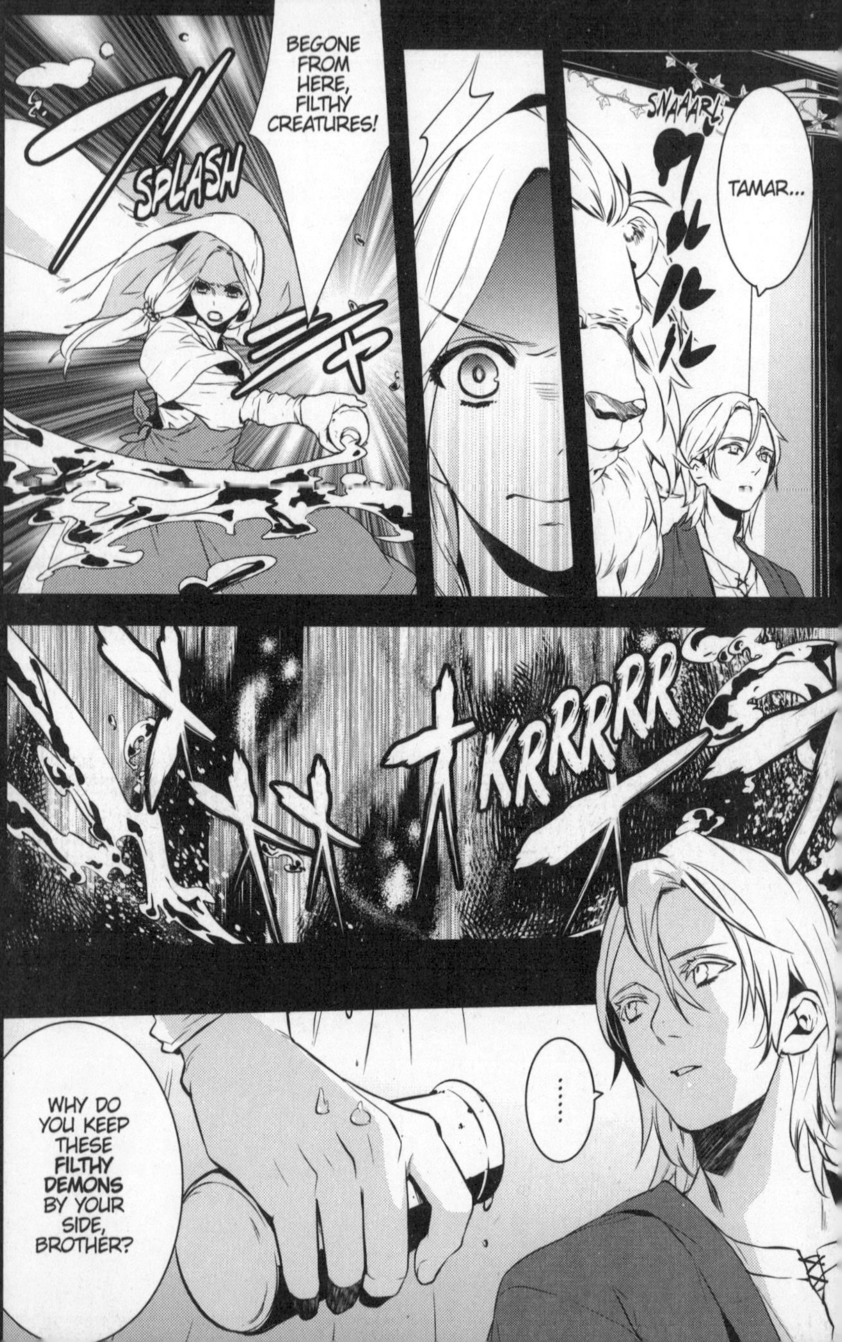
SNAAARL
TAMAR...
BEGONE FROM HERE, FILTHY CREATURES!
SPLASH
KRRRRRR
......
WHY DO YOU KEEP THESE FILTHY DEMONS BY YOUR SIDE, BROTHER?

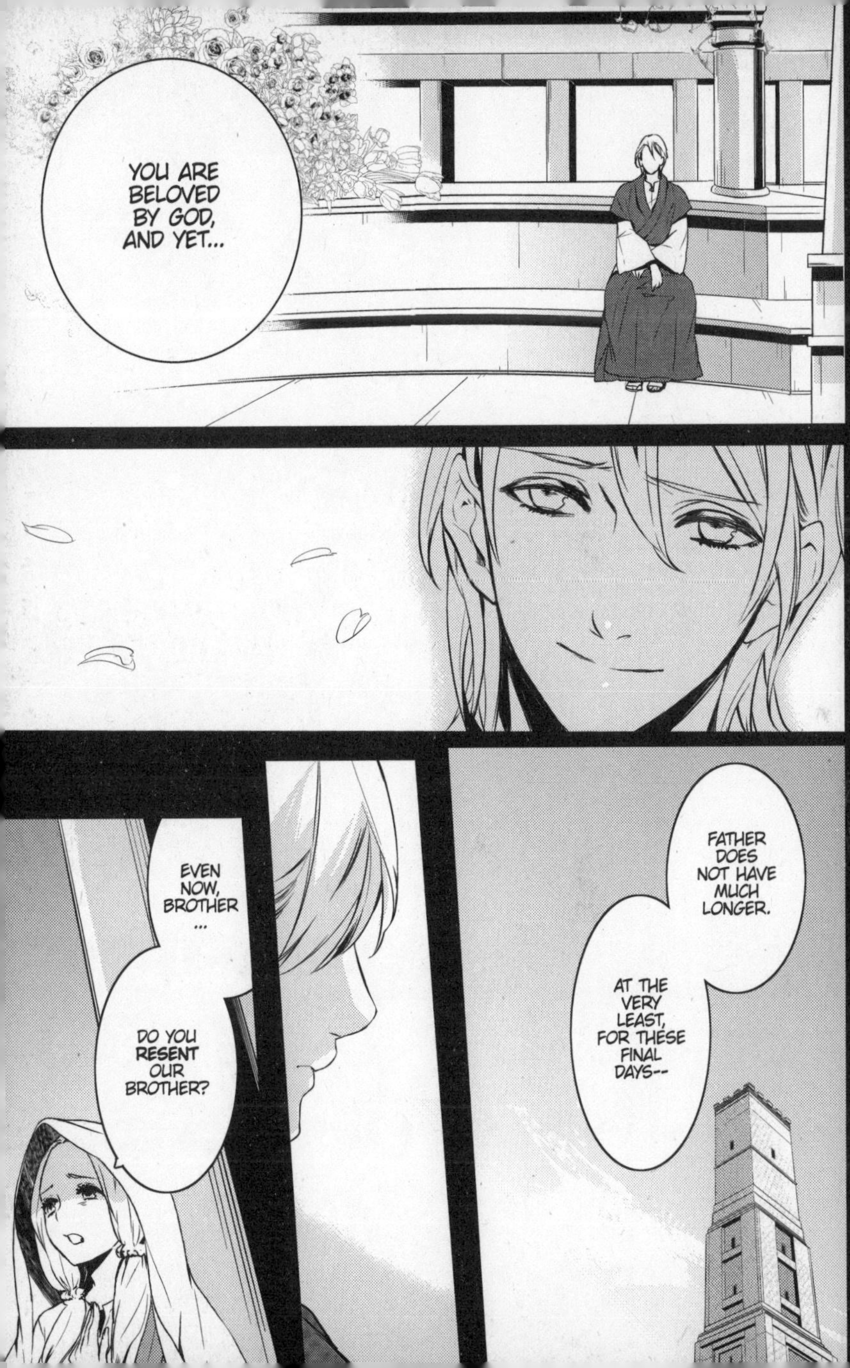
YOU ARE BELOVED BY GOD, AND YET...
FATHER DOES NOT HAVE MUCH LONGER.
AT THE VERY LEAST, FOR THESE FINAL DAYS--
EVEN NOW, BROTHER ...
DO YOU RESENT OUR BROTHER?

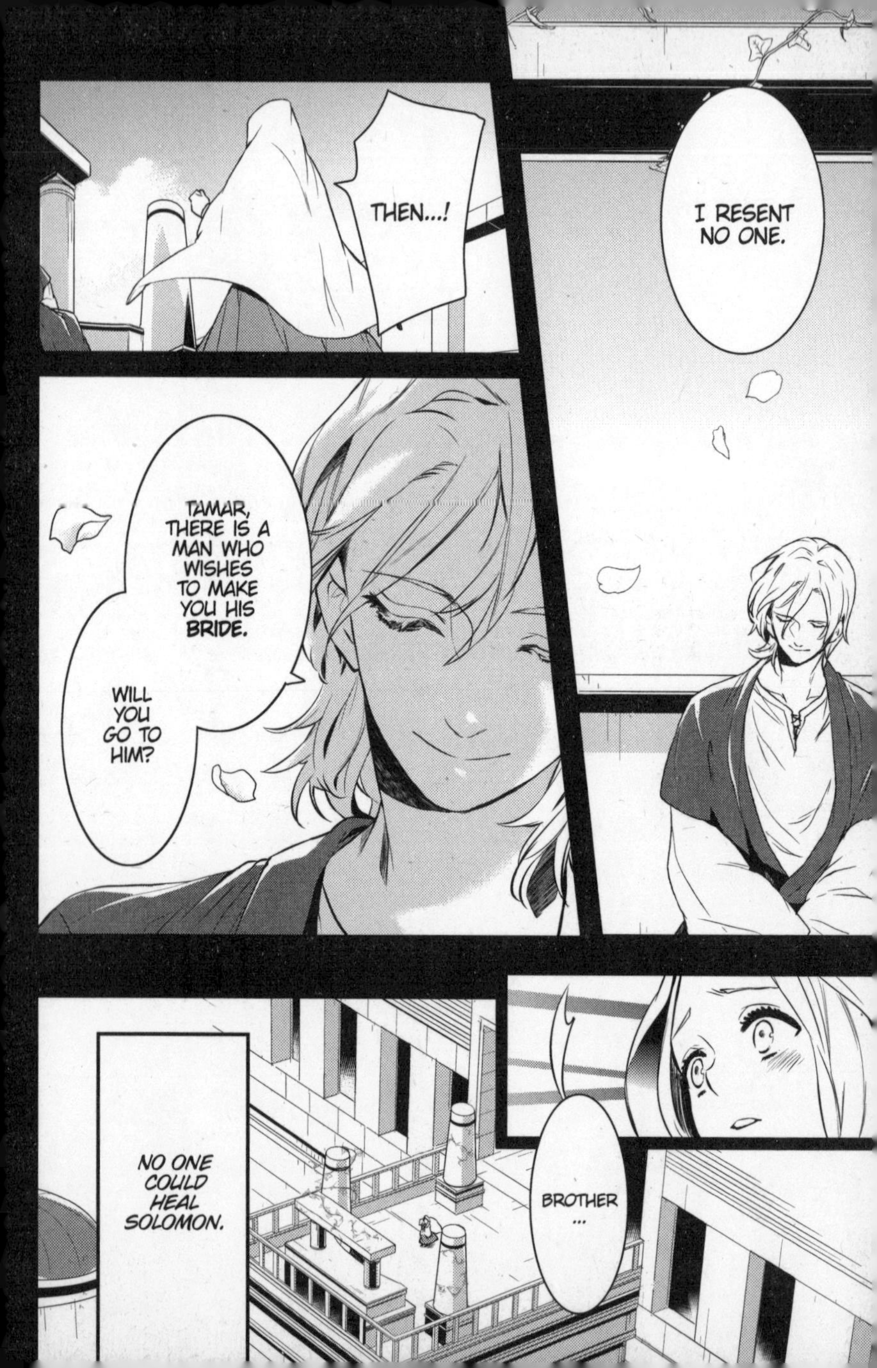

I RESENT NO ONE.
THEN...!
TAMAR, THERE IS A MAN WHO WISHES TO MAKE YOU HIS BRIDE.
WILL YOU GO TO HIM?
BROTHER ...
NO ONE COULD HEAL SOLOMON.

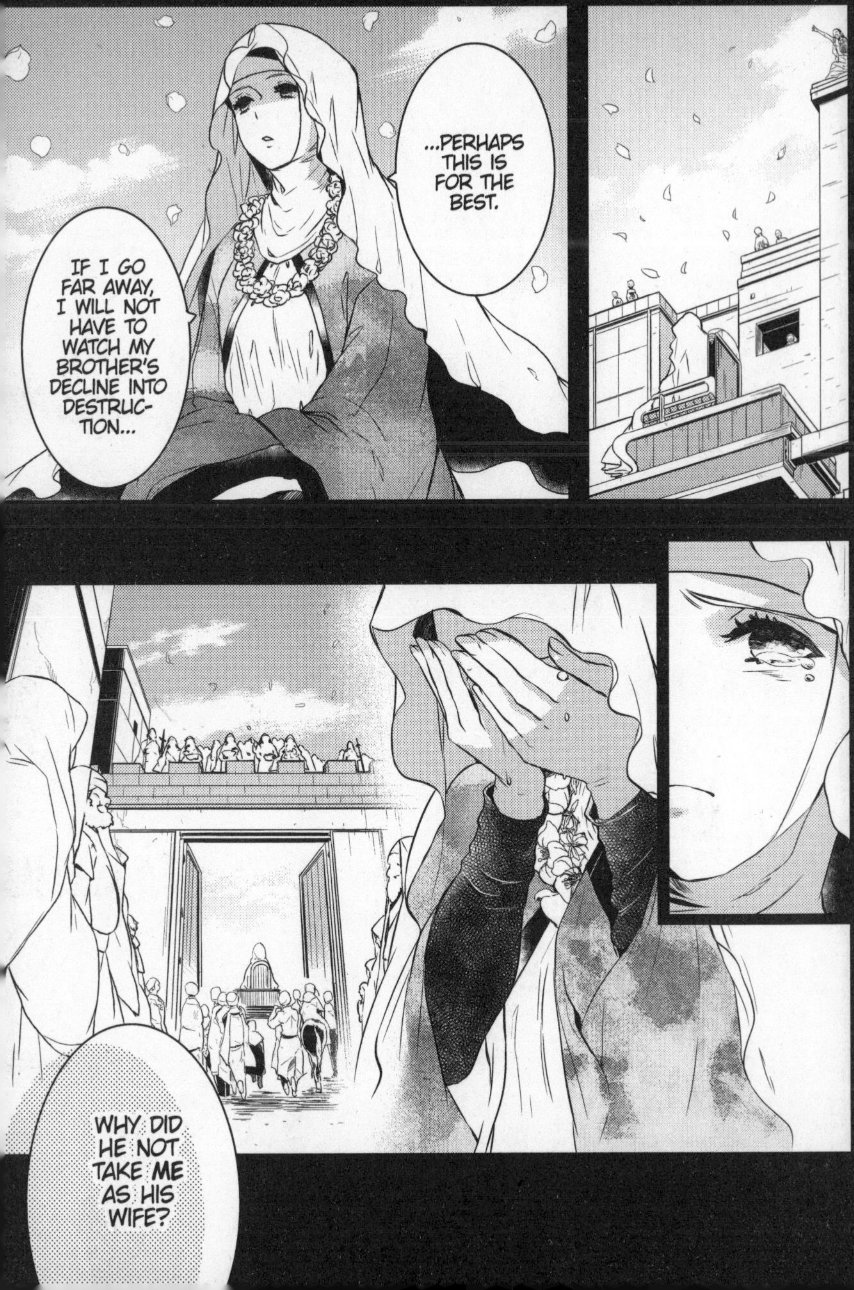
...PERHAPS THIS IS FOR THE BEST.
IF I GO FAR AWAY, I WILL NOT HAVE TO WATCH MY BROTHER'S DECLINE INTO DESTRUC-TION...
WHY DID HE NOT TAKE ME AS HIS WIFE?

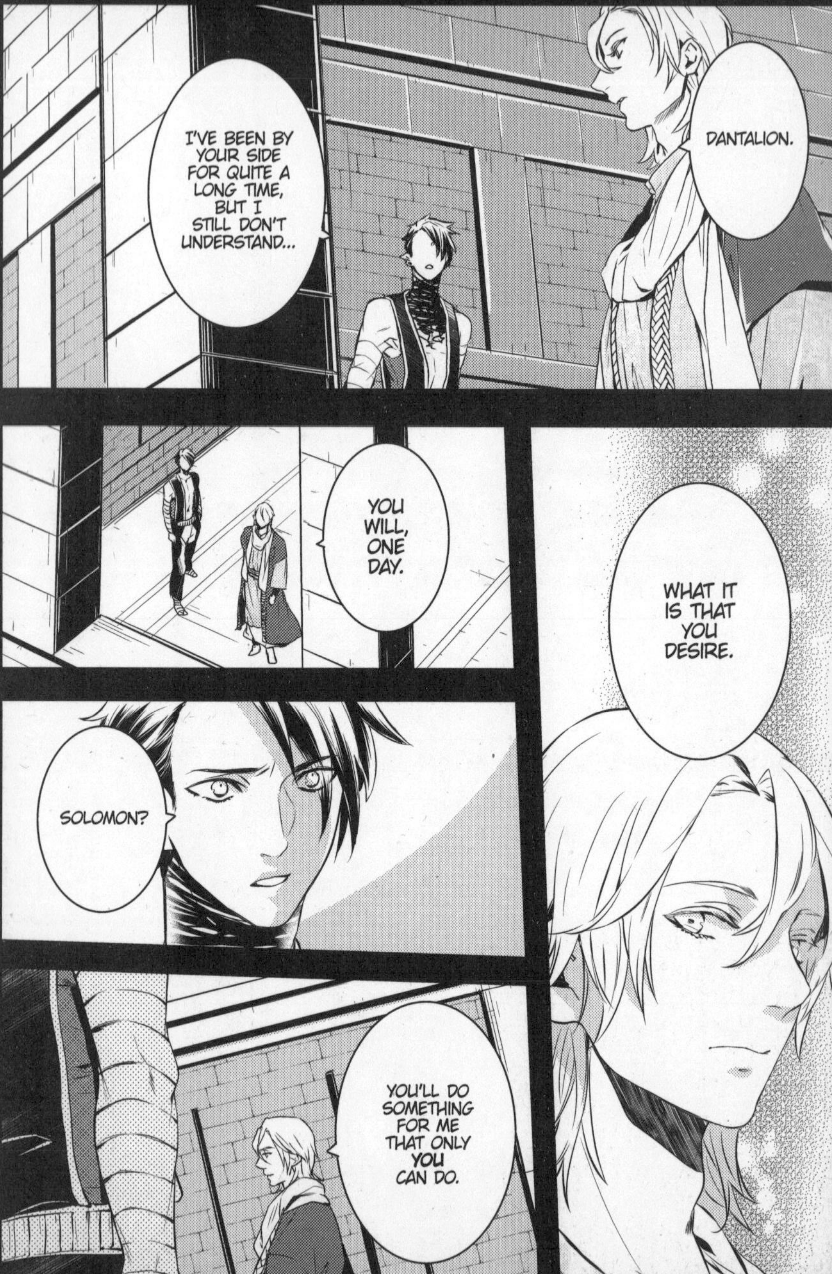
DANTALION.
I'VE BEEN BY YOUR SIDE FOR QUITE A LONG TIME, BUT I STILL DON'T UNDERSTAND...
WHAT IT IS THAT YOU DESIRE.
YOU WILL, ONE DAY.
SOLOMON?
YOU'LL DO SOMETHING FOR ME THAT ONLY YOU CAN DO.

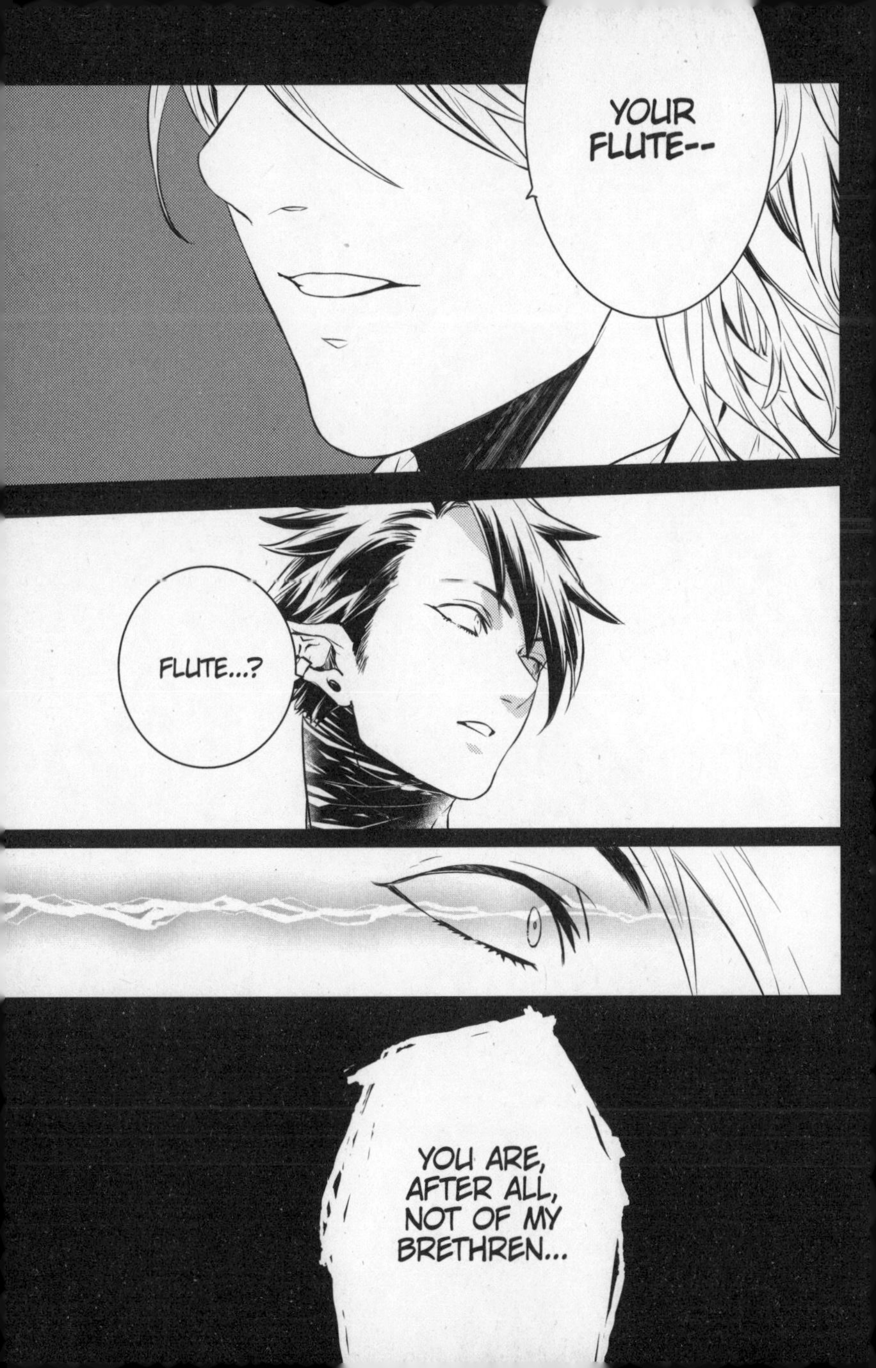
YOUR FLUTE--
FLUTE...?
YOU ARE, AFTER ALL, NOT OF MY BRETHREN...

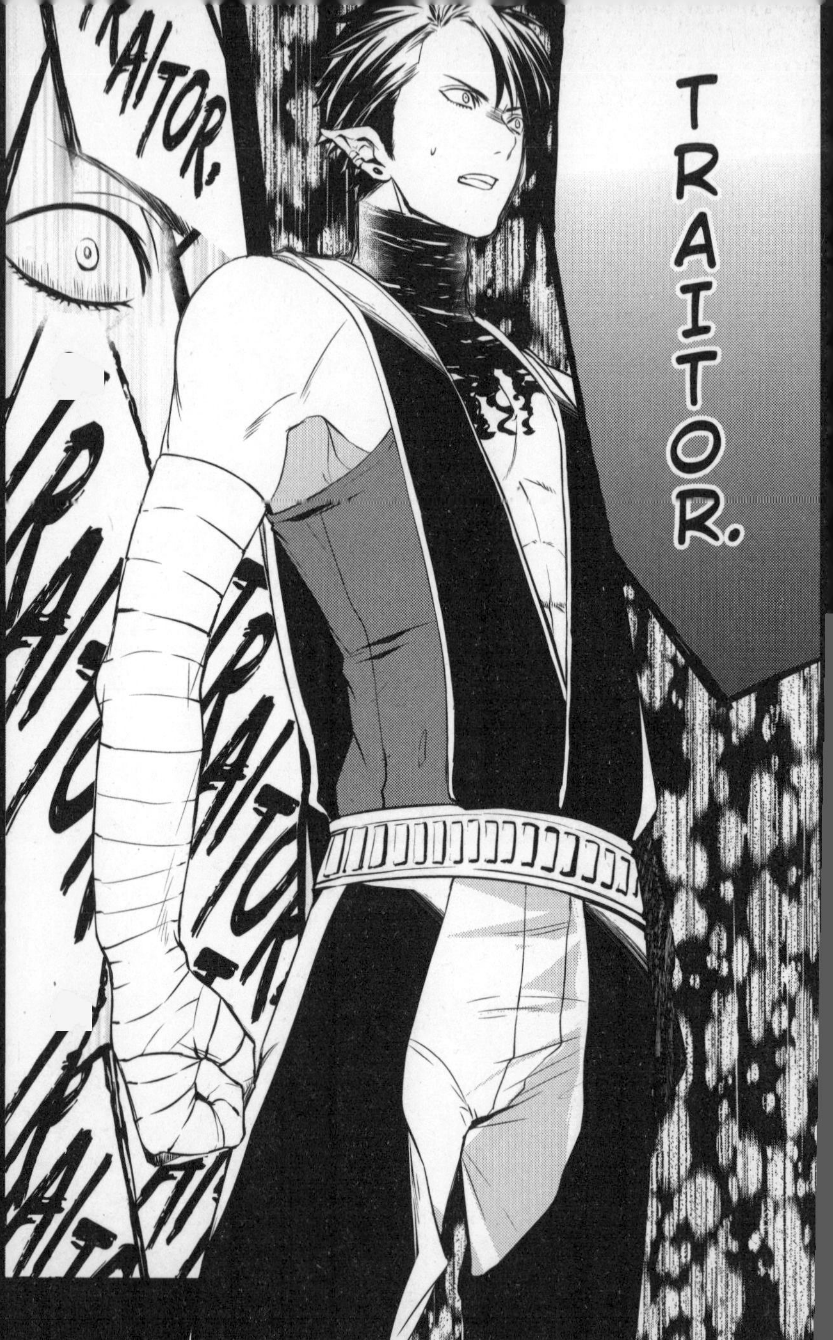
TRAITOR.
TRAITOR.

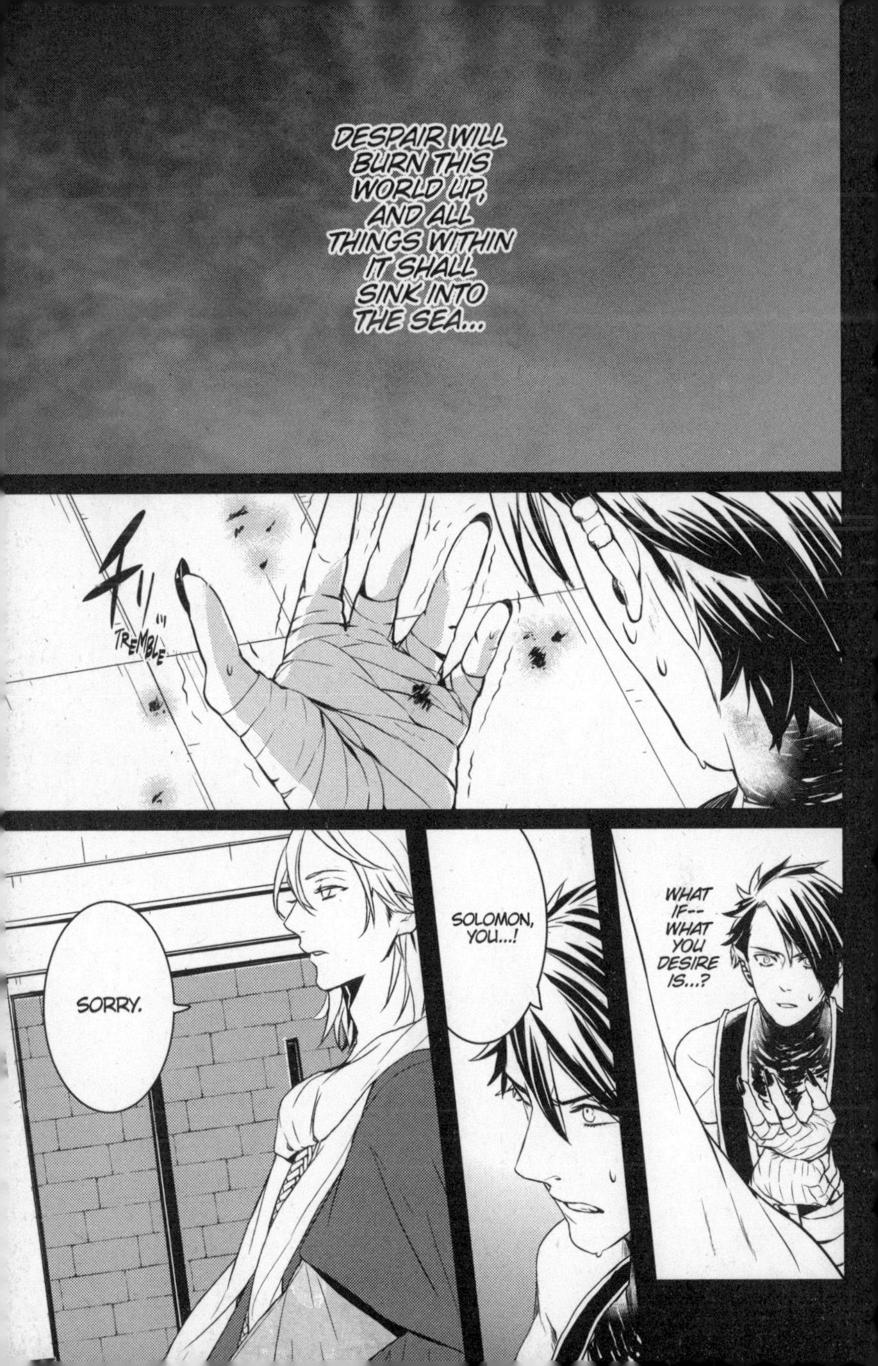
DESPAIR WILL BURN THIS WORLD UP, AND ALL THINGS WITHIN IT SHALL SINK INTO THE SEA...
TREMBLE
WHAT IF-- WHAT YOU DESIRE IS...?
SOLOMON, YOU...!
SORRY.

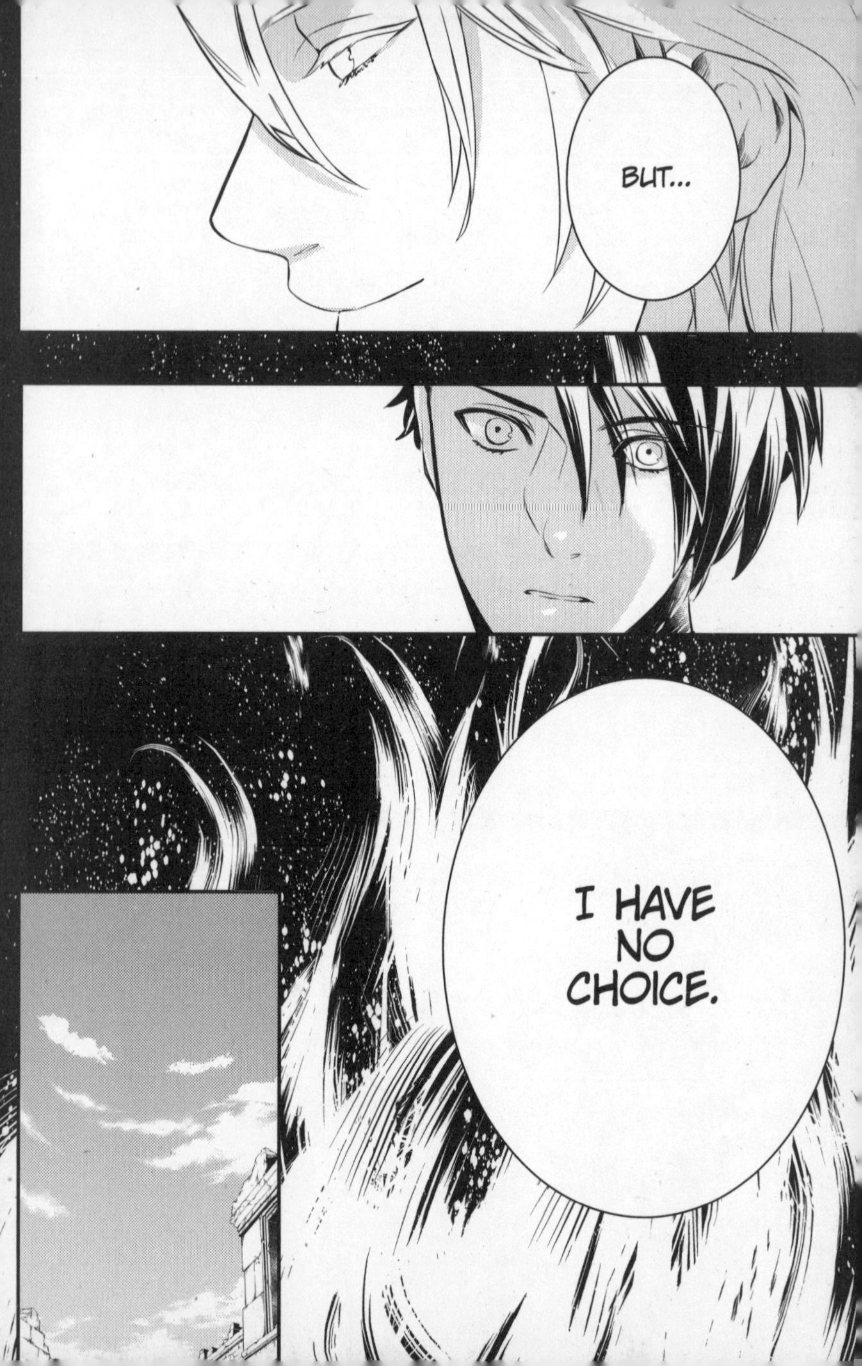
BUT...
I HAVE NO CHOICE.

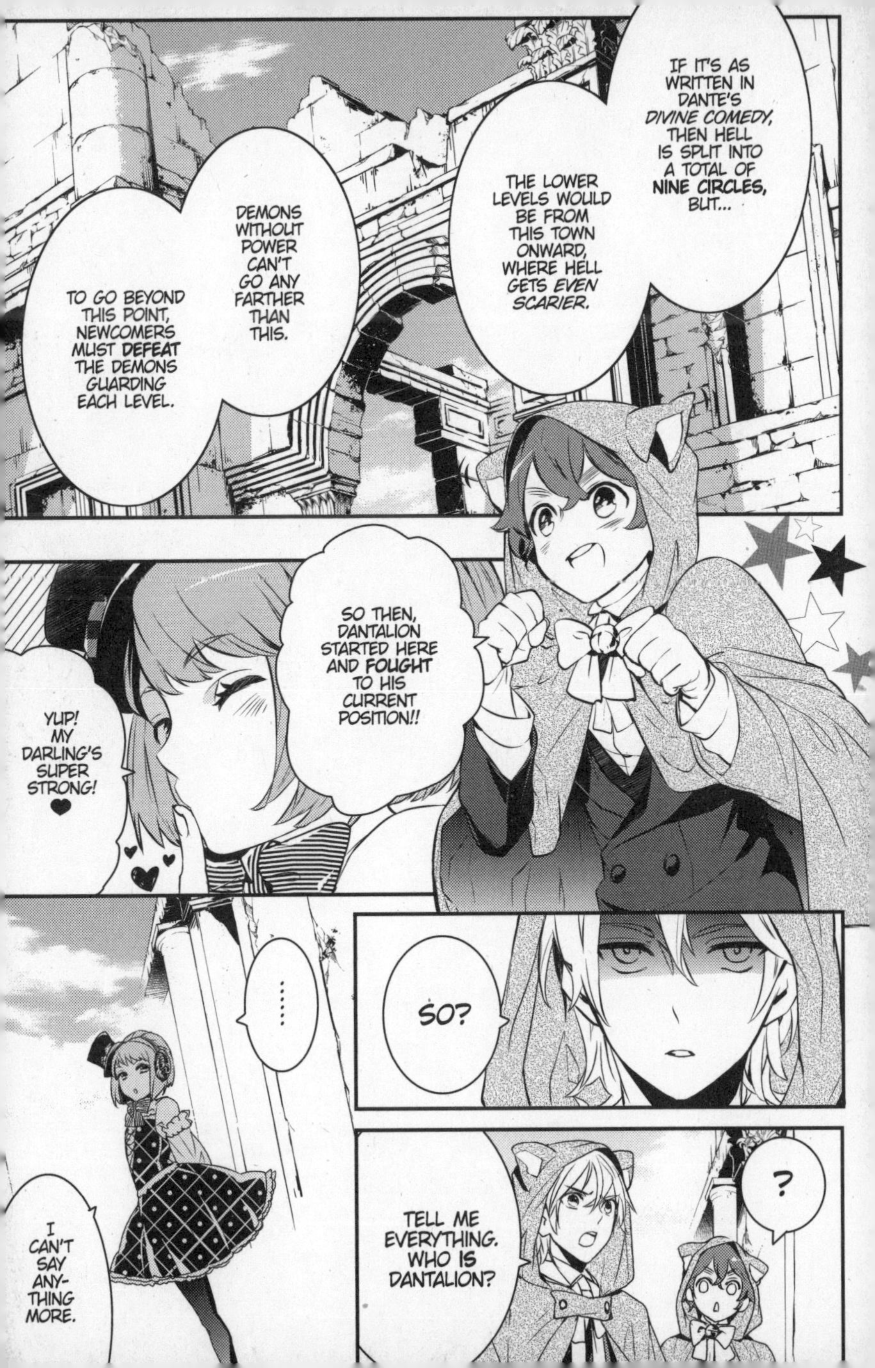
IF IT'S AS WRITTEN IN DANTE'S *DIVINE COMEDY,* THEN HELL IS SPLIT INTO A TOTAL OF **NINE CIRCLES,** BUT...
THE LOWER LEVELS WOULD BE FROM THIS TOWN ONWARD, WHERE HELL GETS *EVEN SCARIER.*
DEMONS WITHOUT POWER CAN'T GO ANY FARTHER THAN THIS.
TO GO BEYOND THIS POINT, NEWCOMERS MUST **DEFEAT** THE DEMONS GUARDING EACH LEVEL.
SO THEN, DANTALION STARTED HERE AND **FOUGHT** TO HIS CURRENT POSITION!!
YUP! MY DARLING'S SUPER STRONG! ♥
SO?
?
TELL ME EVERYTHING. WHO IS DANTALION?
......
I CAN'T SAY ANY-THING MORE.

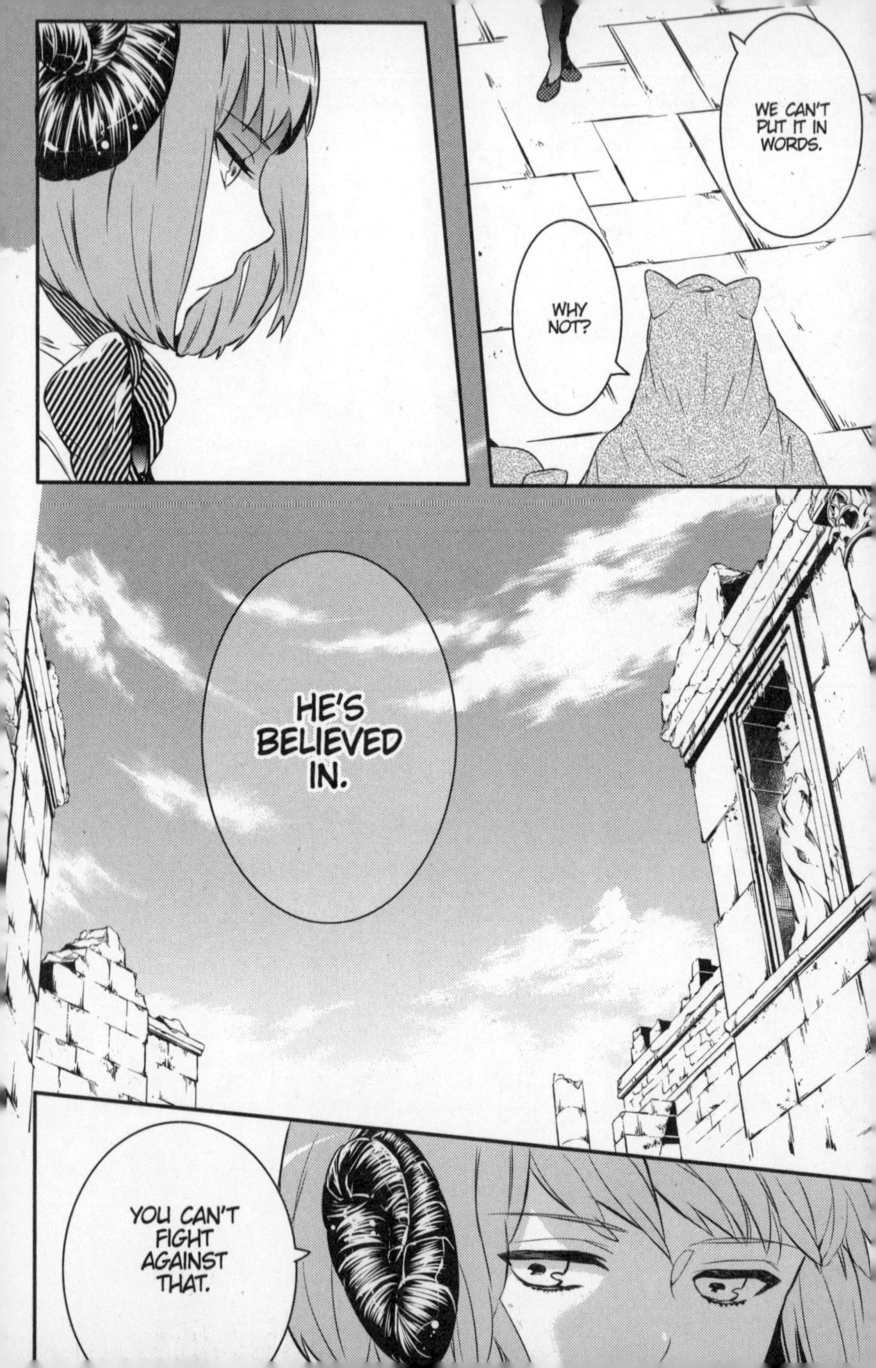
WE CAN'T PUT IT IN WORDS.
WHY NOT?
HE'S BELIEVED IN.
YOU CAN'T FIGHT AGAINST THAT.

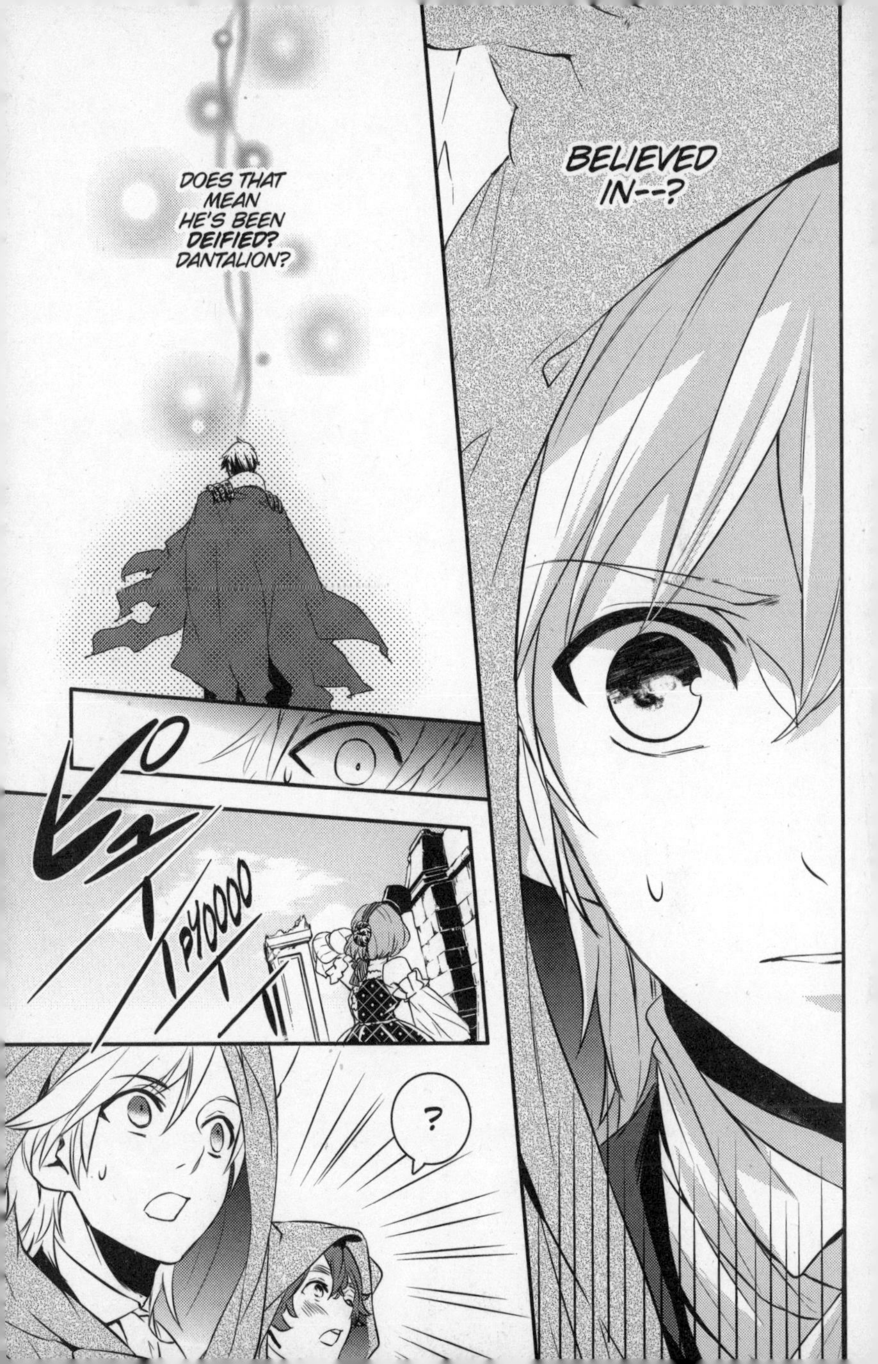
BELIEVED IN--?
DOES THAT MEAN HE'S BEEN DEIFIED? DANTALION?
PYOOOO
?

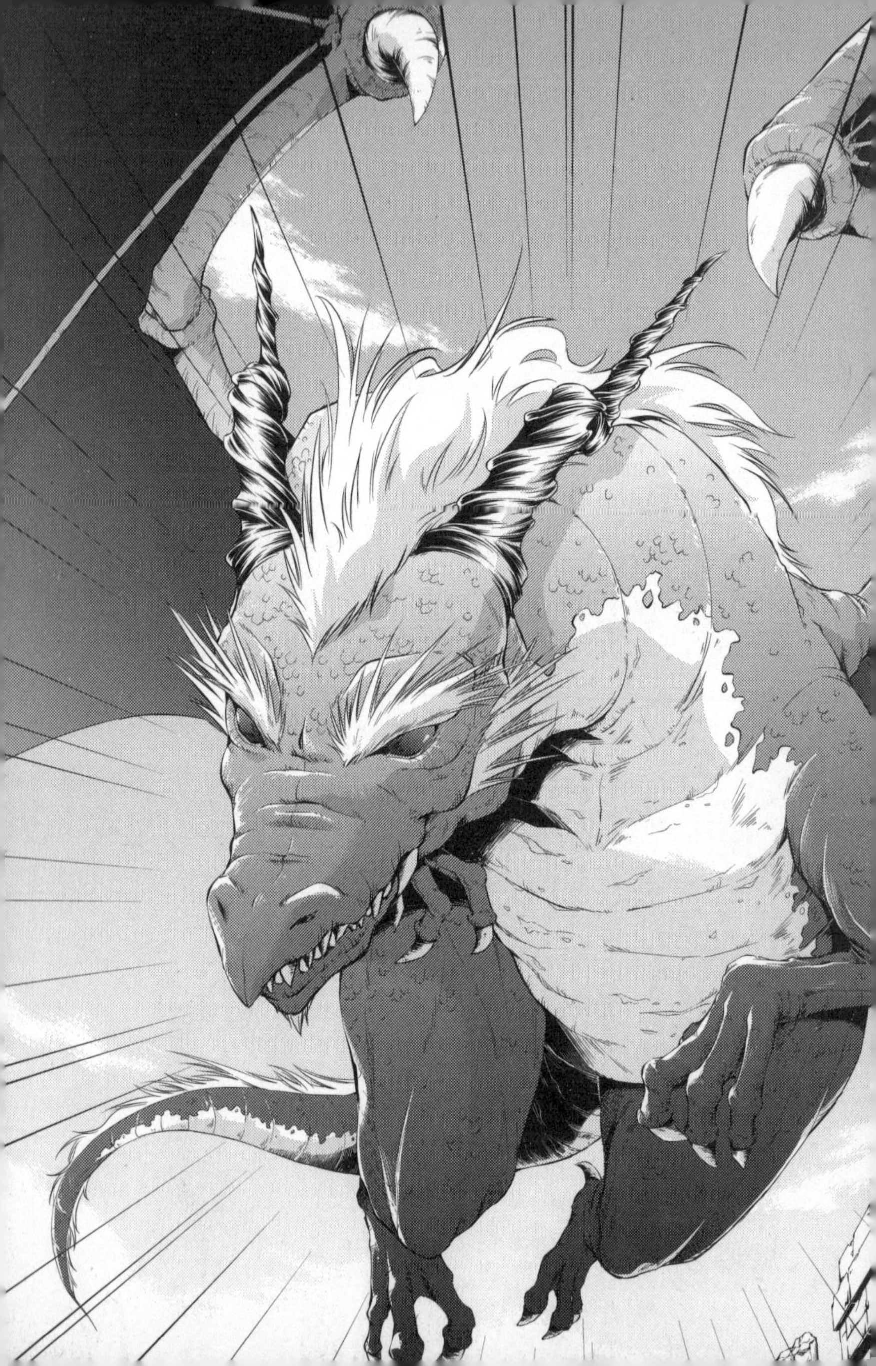

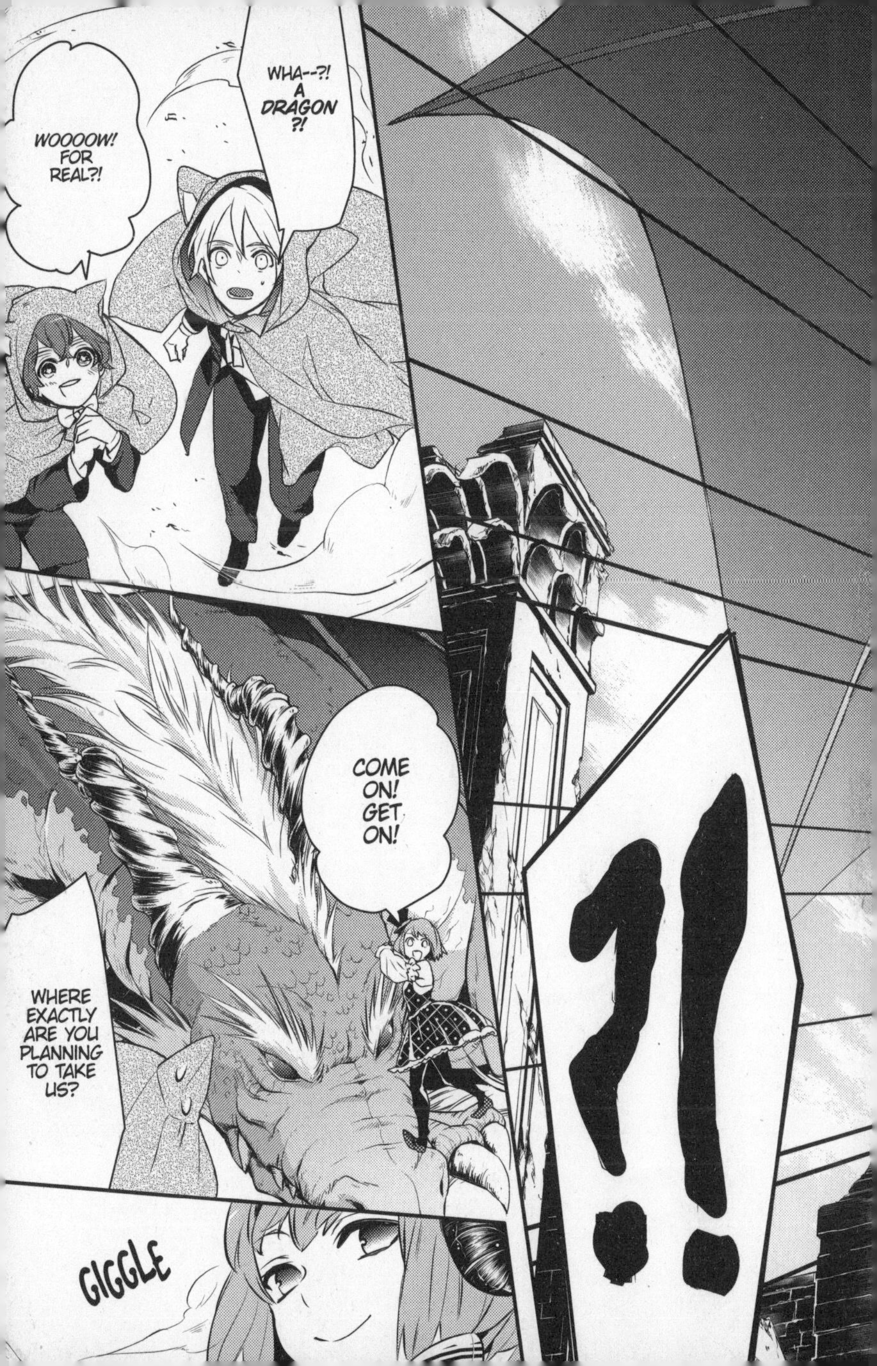
WHA--?! A DRAGON ?!
WOOOOW! FOR REAL?!
?!
COME ON! GET ON!
WHERE EXACTLY ARE YOU PLANNING TO TAKE US?
GIGGLE

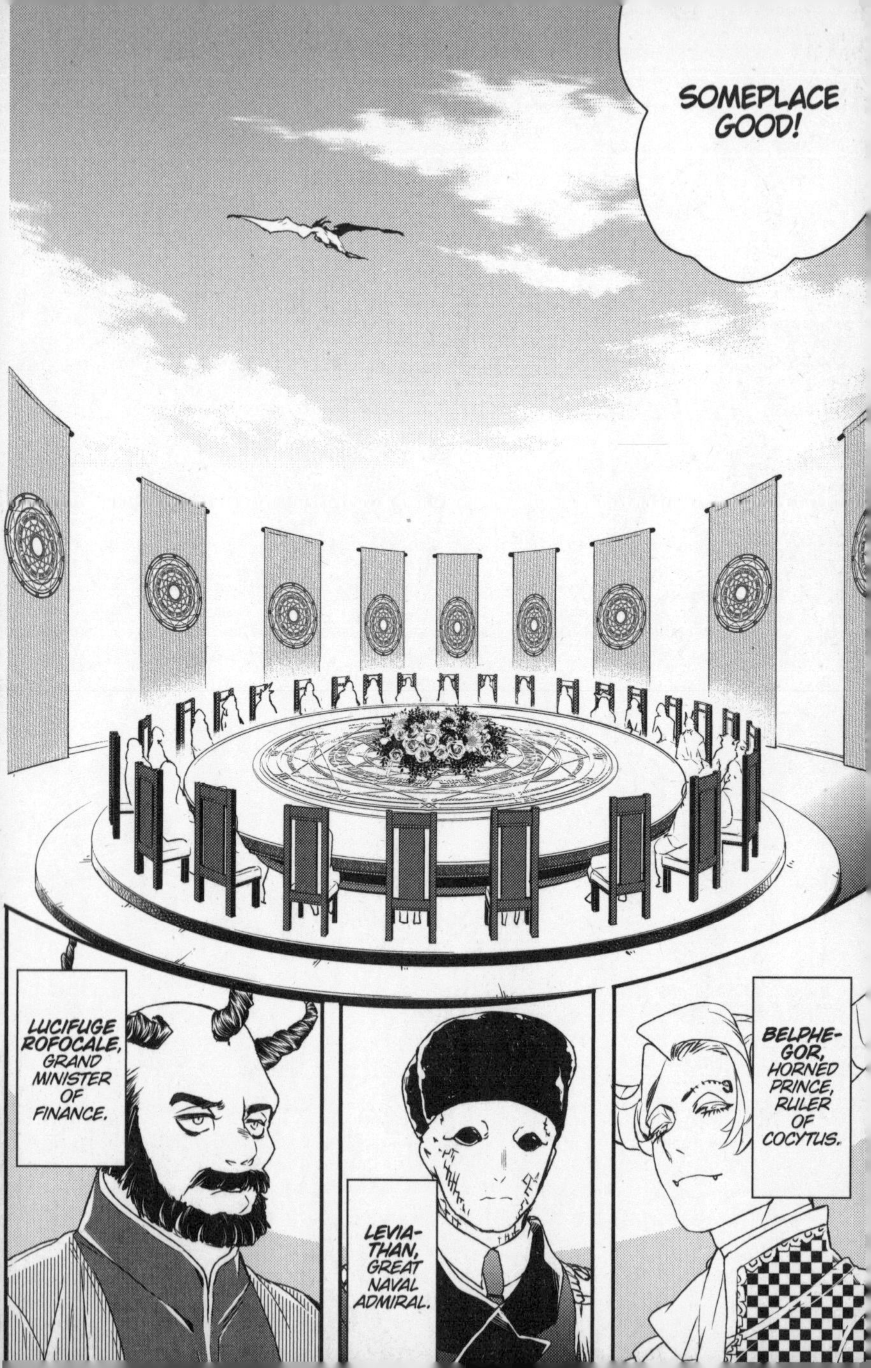
SOMEPLACE GOOD!
BELPHEGOR, HORNED PRINCE, RULER OF COCYTUS.
LEVIATHAN, GREAT NAVAL ADMIRAL.
LUCIFUGE ROFOCALE, GRAND MINISTER OF FINANCE.

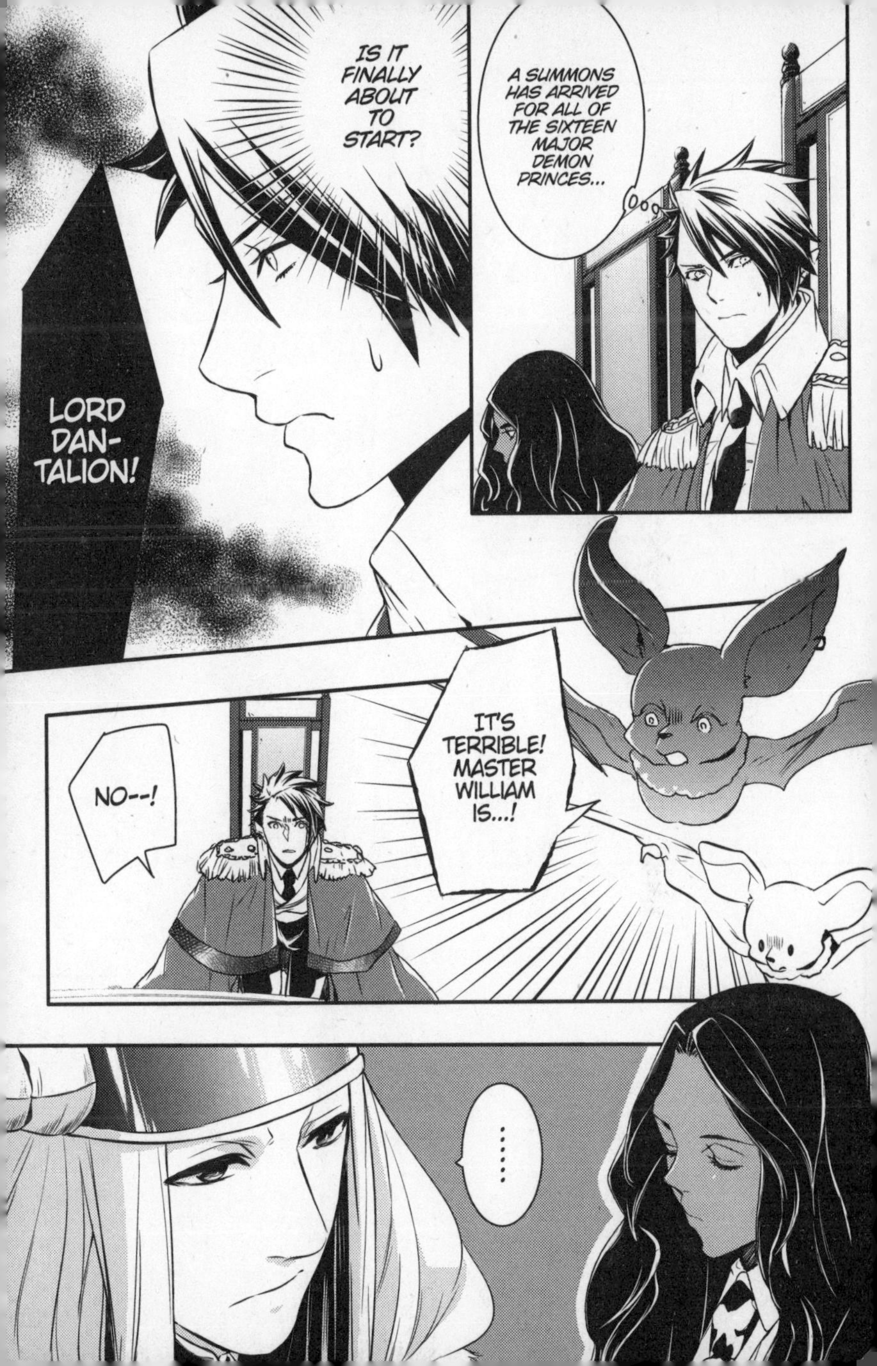
A SUMMONS HAS ARRIVED FOR ALL OF THE SIXTEEN MAJOR DEMON PRINCES...
IS IT FINALLY ABOUT TO START?
LORD DAN-TALION!
IT'S TERRIBLE! MASTER WILLIAM IS...!
NO--!
......

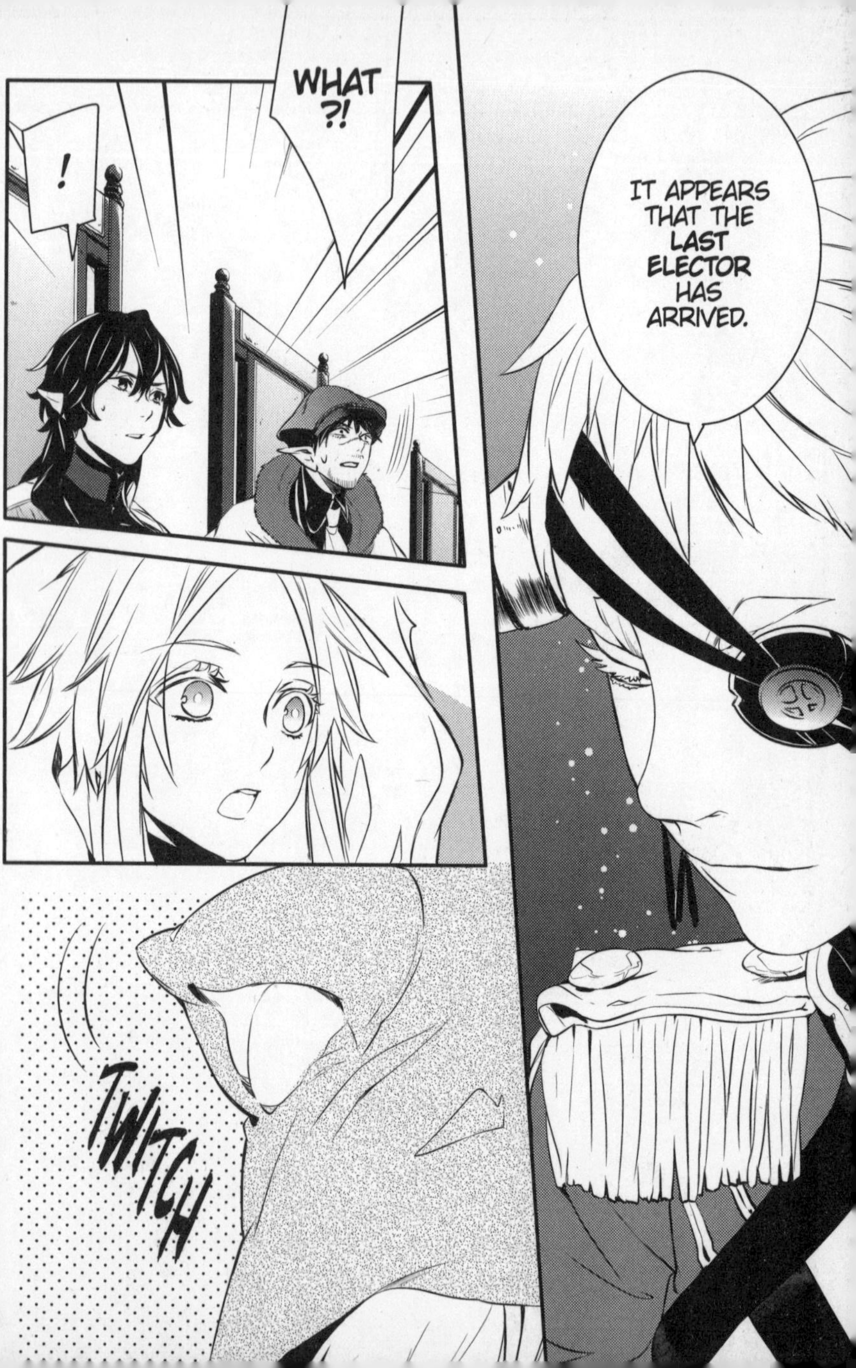
IT APPEARS THAT THE LAST ELECTOR HAS ARRIVED.
WHAT?!
!
TWITCH

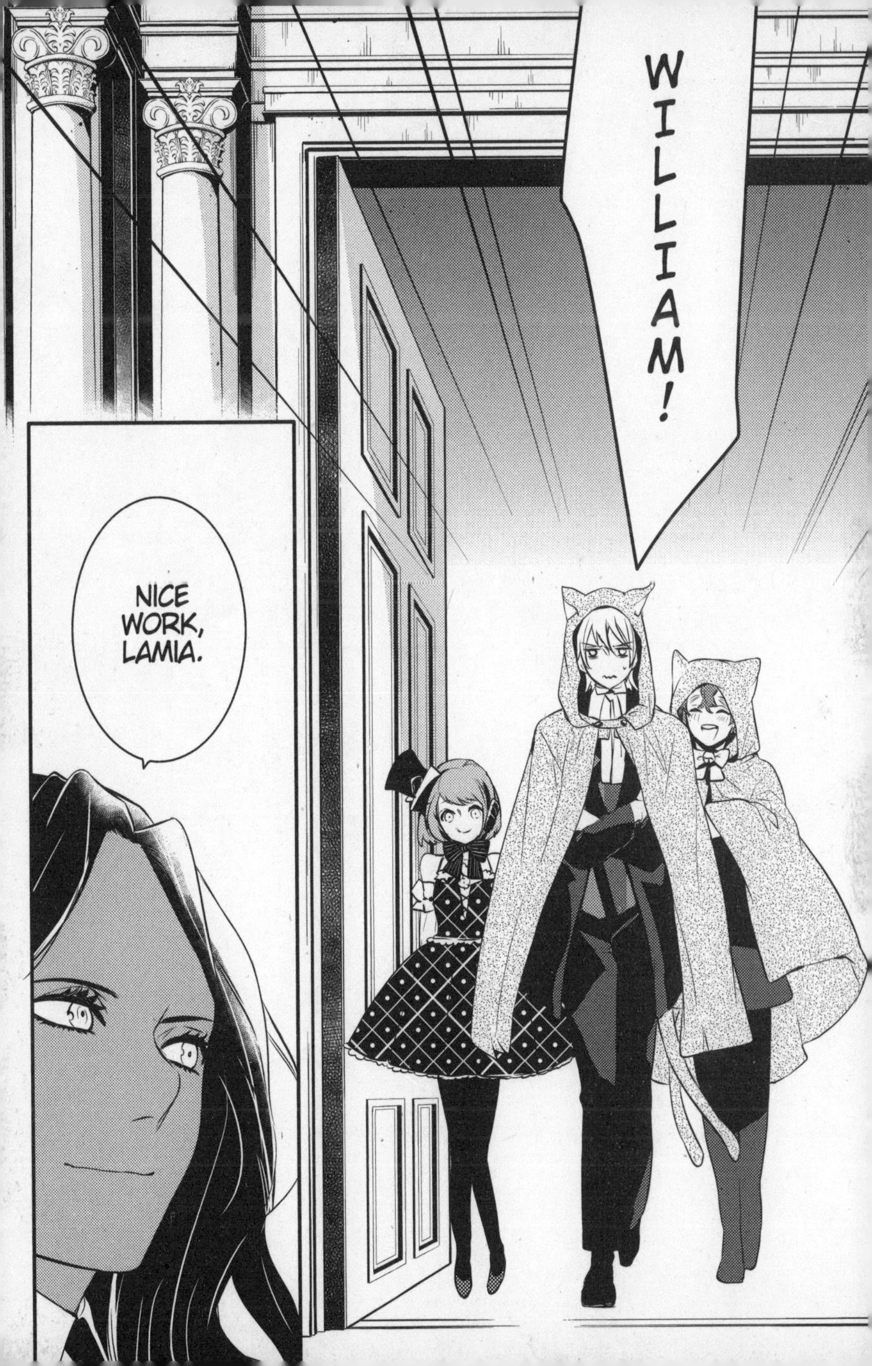
WILLIAM!
NICE WORK, LAMIA.

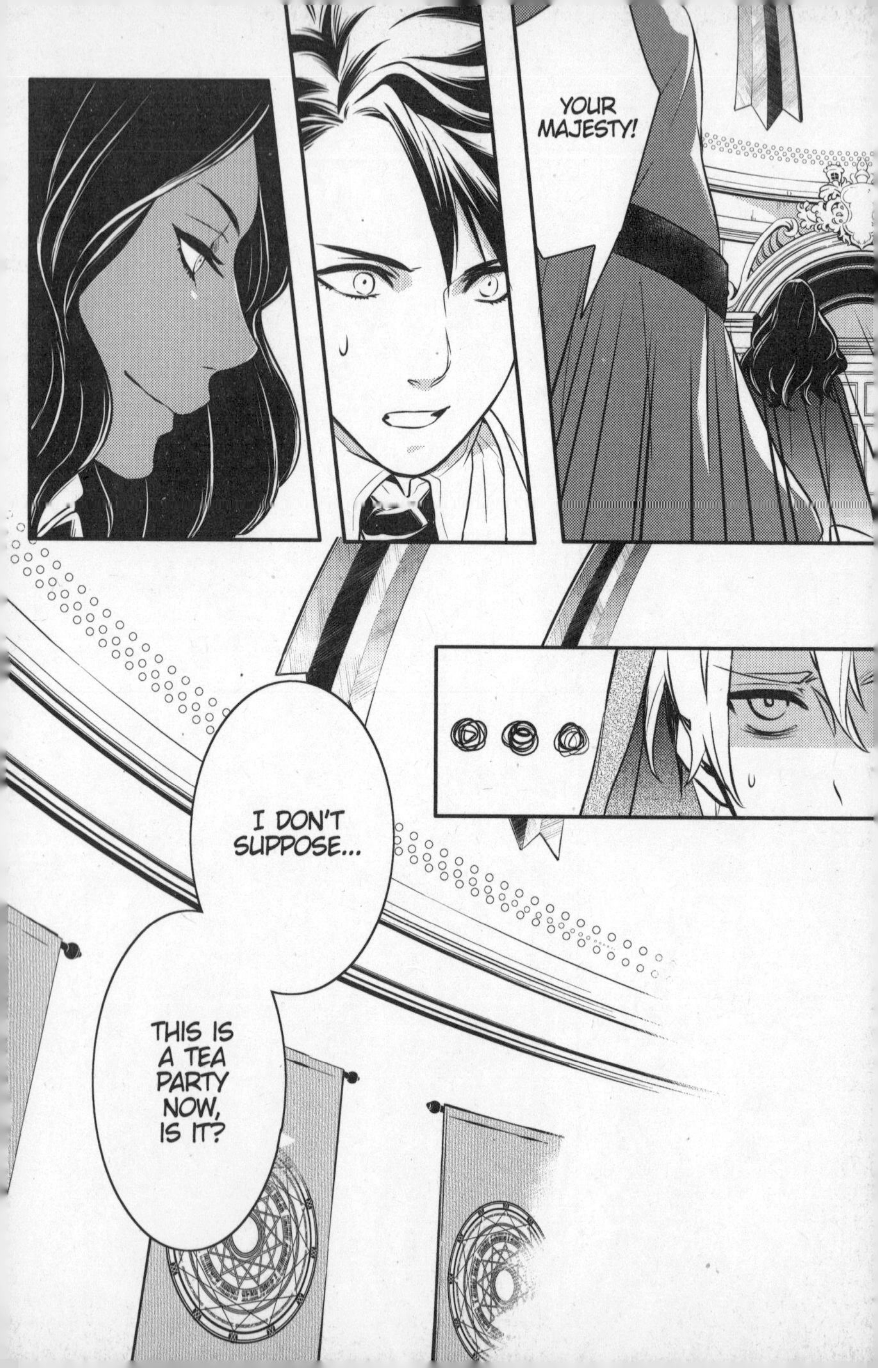
YOUR MAJESTY!
I DON'T SUPPOSE...
THIS IS A TEA PARTY NOW, IS IT?

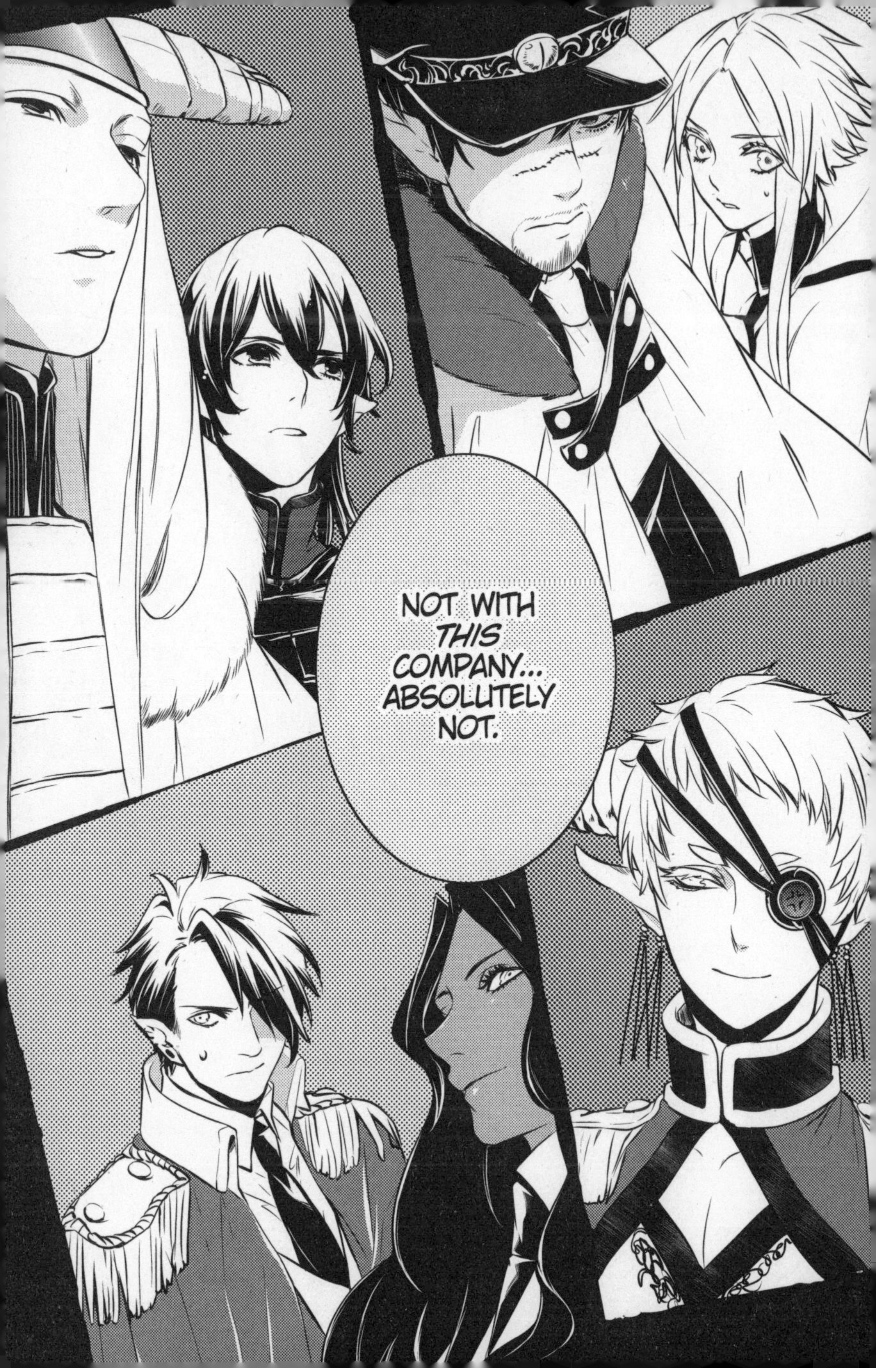
NOT WITH *THIS* COMPANY... ABSOLUTELY NOT.

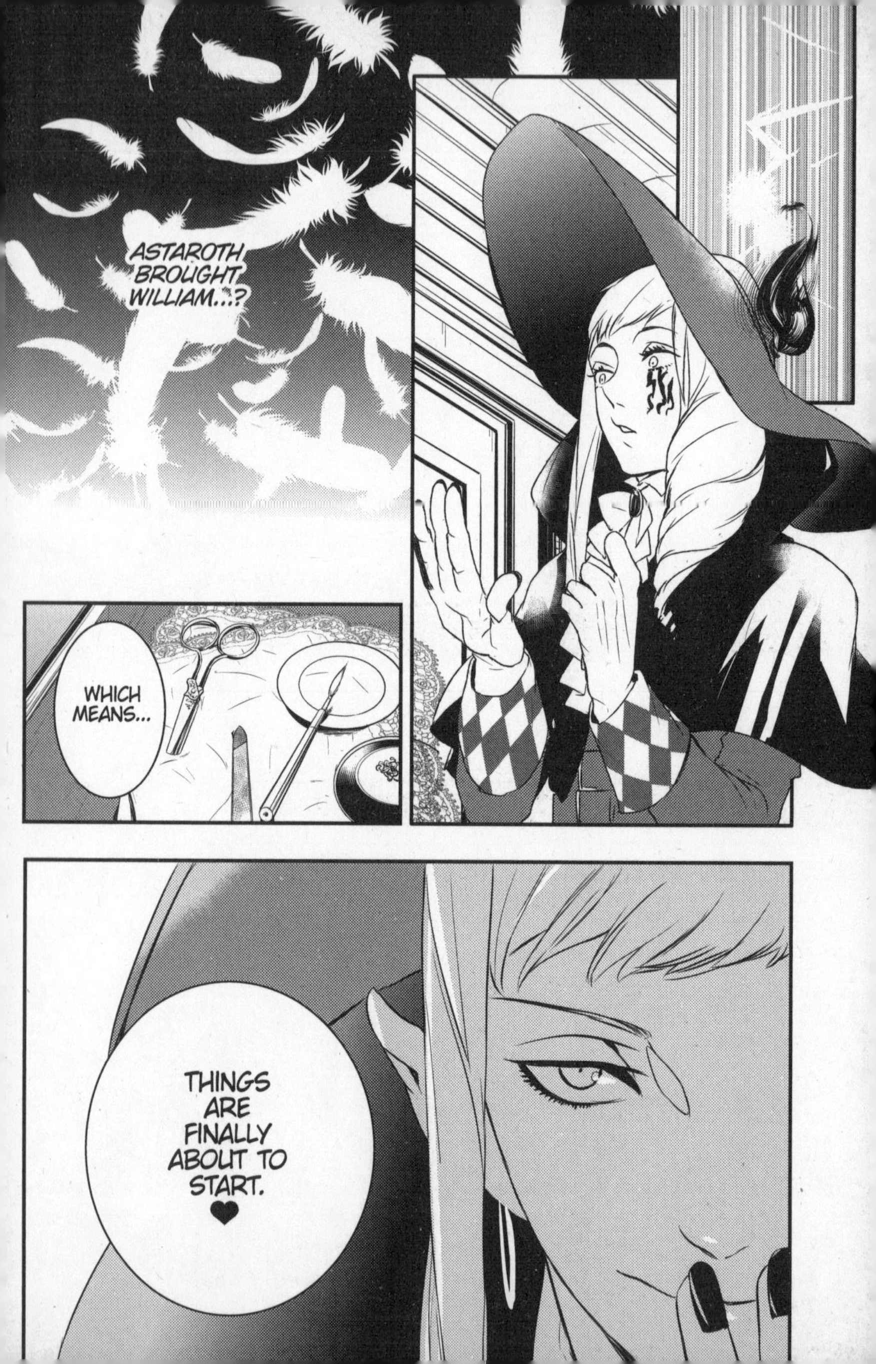
ASTAROTH BROUGHT WILLIAM...?
WHICH MEANS...
THINGS ARE FINALLY ABOUT TO START. ♥

Pillar 28

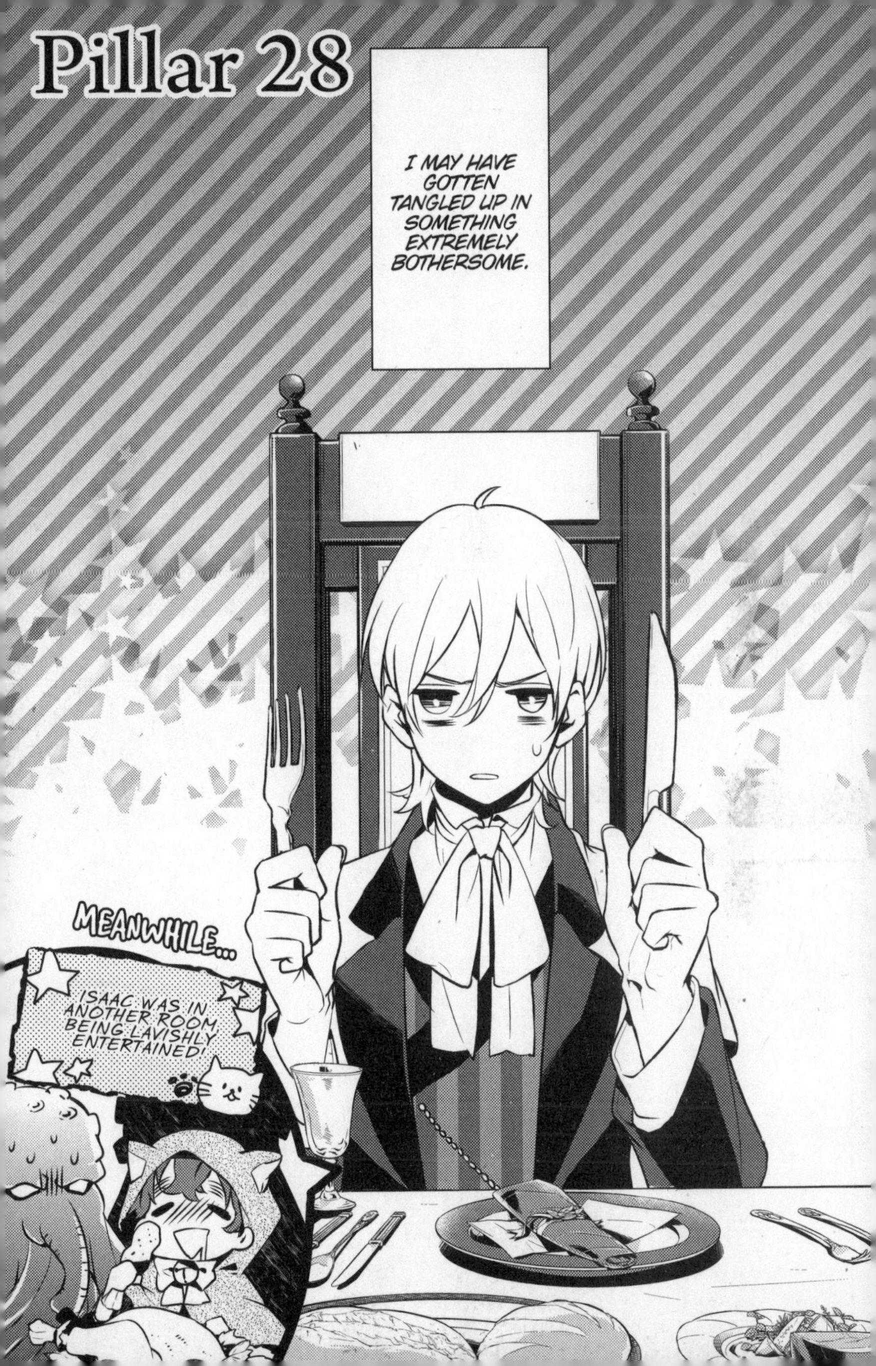
I MAY HAVE GOTTEN TANGLED UP IN SOMETHING EXTREMELY BOTHERSOME.
MEANWHILE...
ISAAC WAS IN ANOTHER ROOM BEING LAVISHLY ENTERTAINED!

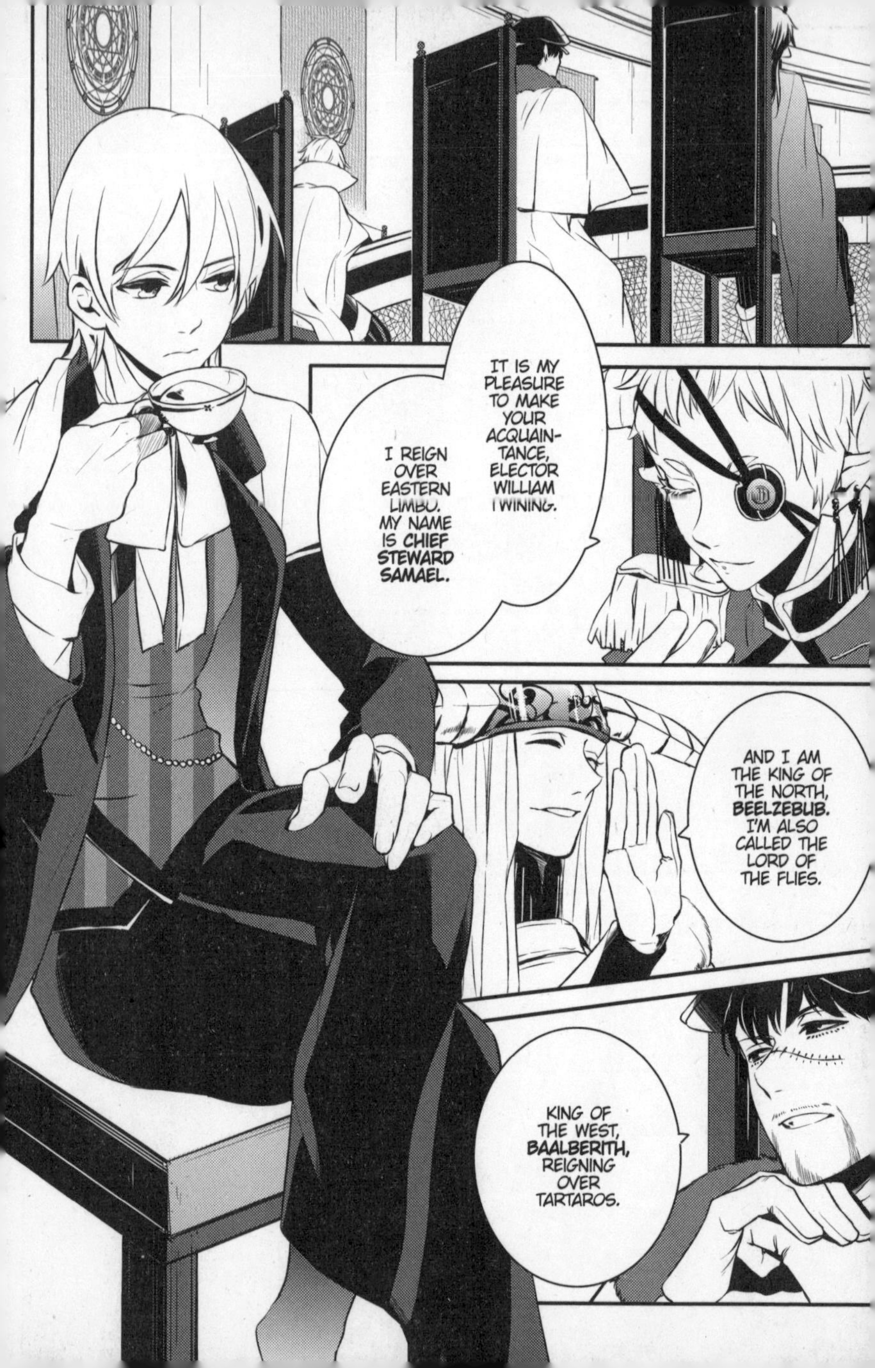
IT IS MY PLEASURE TO MAKE YOUR ACQUAINTANCE, ELECTOR WILLIAM TWINING.
I REIGN OVER EASTERN LIMBO. MY NAME IS CHIEF STEWARD **SAMAEL.**
AND I AM THE KING OF THE NORTH, **BEELZEBUB.** I'M ALSO CALLED THE LORD OF THE FLIES.
KING OF THE WEST, **BAALBERITH,** REIGNING OVER TARTAROS.

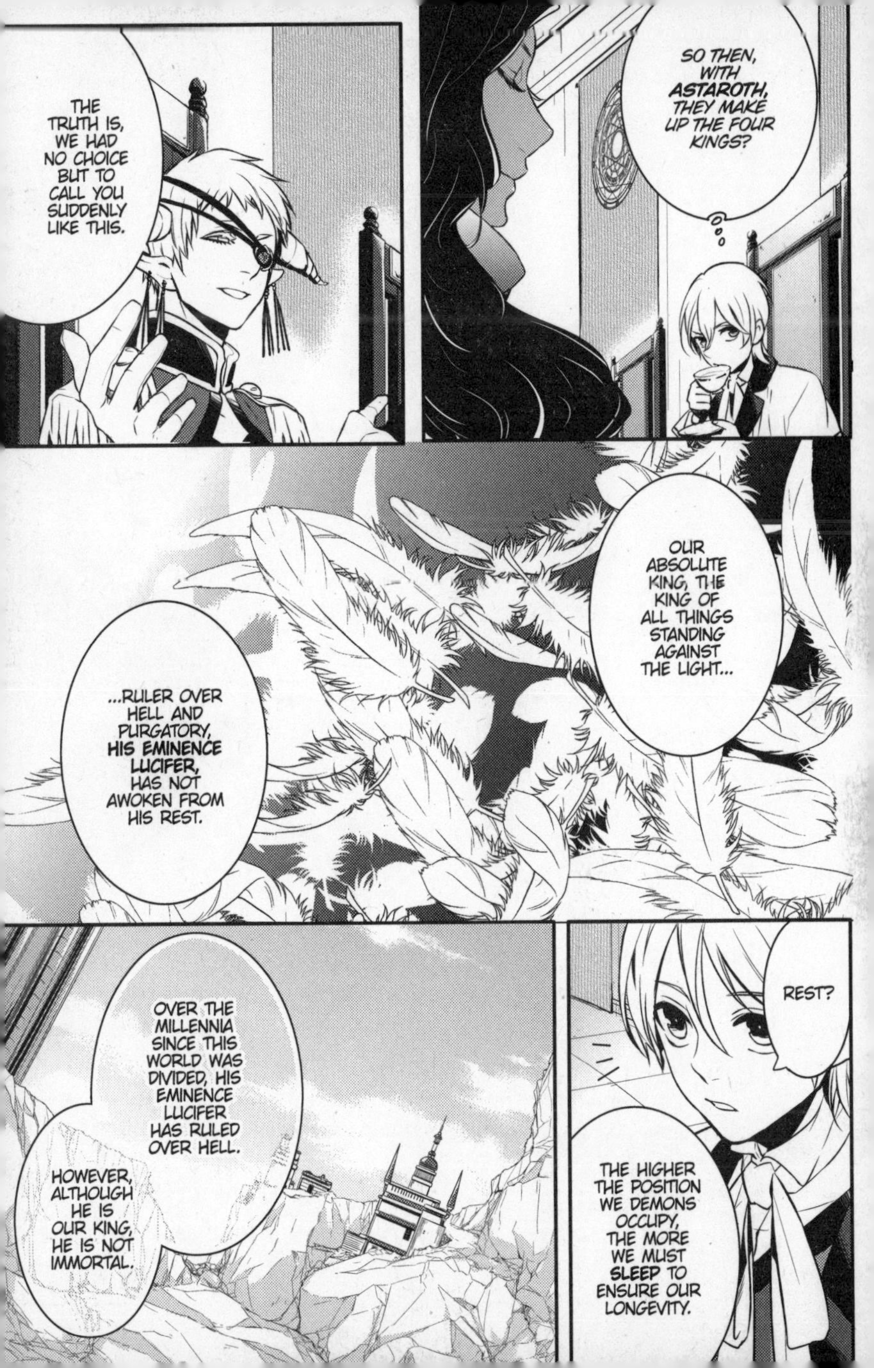
SO THEN, WITH **ASTAROTH,** THEY MAKE UP THE FOUR KINGS?
THE TRUTH IS, WE HAD NO CHOICE BUT TO CALL YOU SUDDENLY LIKE THIS.
OUR ABSOLUTE KING, THE KING OF ALL THINGS STANDING AGAINST THE LIGHT...
...RULER OVER HELL AND PURGATORY, **HIS EMINENCE LUCIFER,** HAS NOT AWOKEN FROM HIS REST.
REST?
THE HIGHER THE POSITION WE DEMONS OCCUPY, THE MORE WE MUST **SLEEP** TO ENSURE OUR LONGEVITY.
OVER THE MILLENNIA SINCE THIS WORLD WAS DIVIDED, HIS EMINENCE LUCIFER HAS RULED OVER HELL.
HOWEVER, ALTHOUGH HE IS OUR KING, HE IS NOT IMMORTAL.

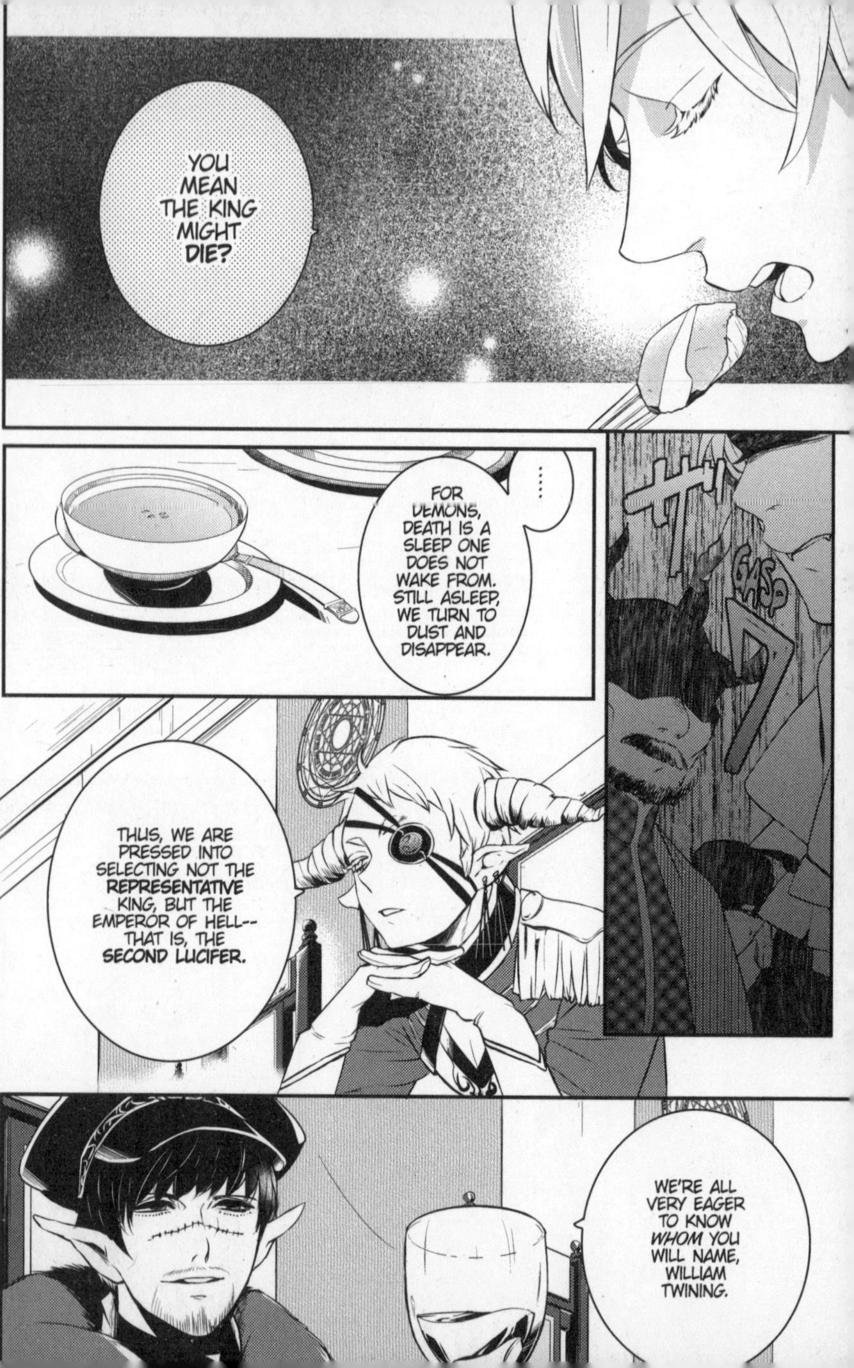
YOU MEAN THE KING MIGHT DIE?
GASP
.....
FOR DEMONS, DEATH IS A SLEEP ONE DOES NOT WAKE FROM. STILL ASLEEP, WE TURN TO DUST AND DISAPPEAR.
THUS, WE ARE PRESSED INTO SELECTING NOT THE REPRESENTATIVE KING, BUT THE EMPEROR OF HELL--THAT IS, THE SECOND LUCIFER.
WE'RE ALL VERY EAGER TO KNOW WHOM YOU WILL NAME, WILLIAM TWINING.

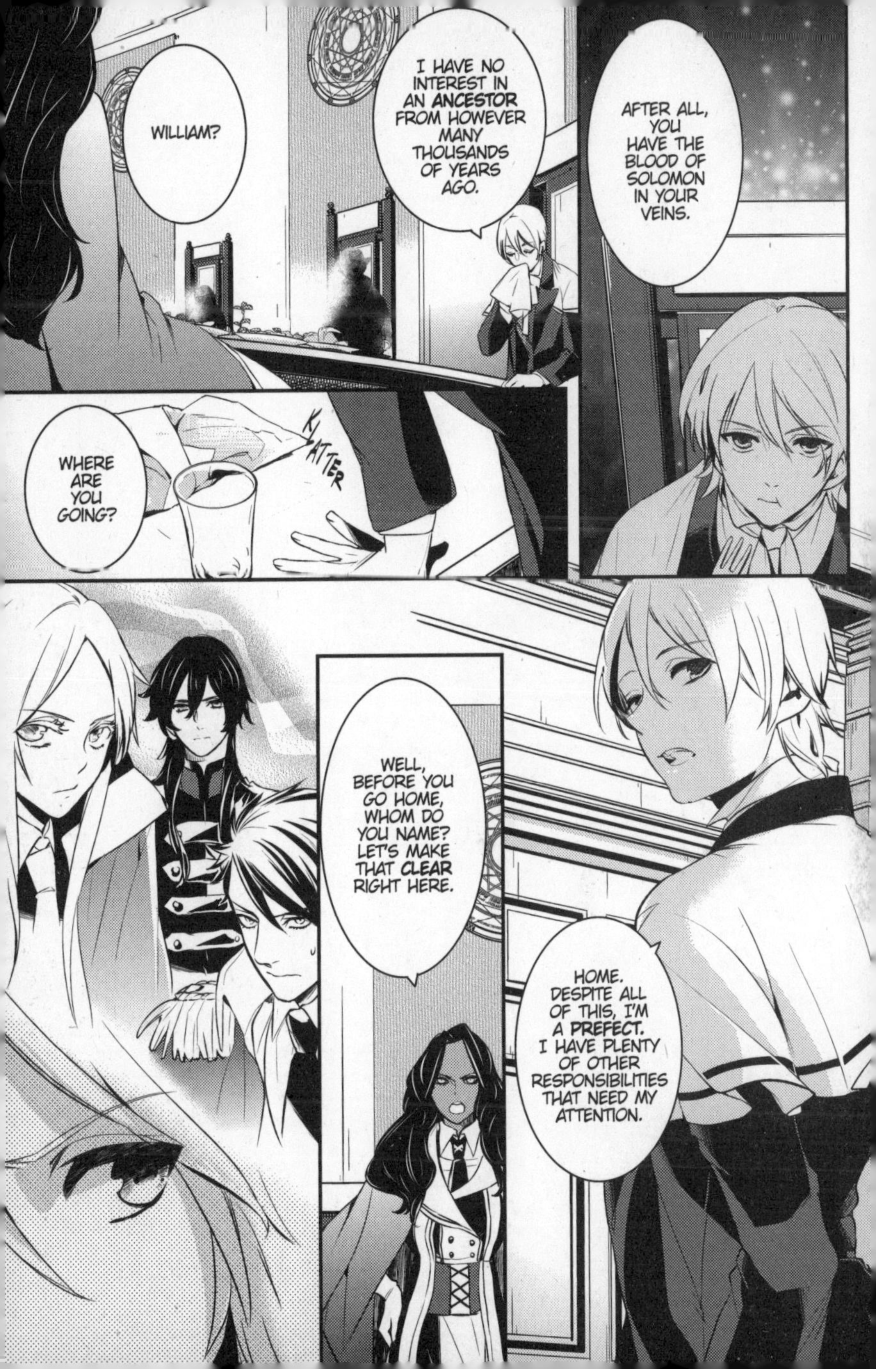
AFTER ALL, YOU HAVE THE BLOOD OF SOLOMON IN YOUR VEINS.
I HAVE NO INTEREST IN AN **ANCESTOR** FROM HOWEVER MANY THOUSANDS OF YEARS AGO.
WILLIAM?
KLATTER
WHERE ARE YOU GOING?
WELL, BEFORE YOU GO HOME, WHOM DO YOU NAME? LET'S MAKE THAT **CLEAR** RIGHT HERE.
HOME. DESPITE ALL OF THIS, I'M A **PREFECT**. I HAVE PLENTY OF OTHER RESPONSIBILITIES THAT NEED MY ATTENTION.

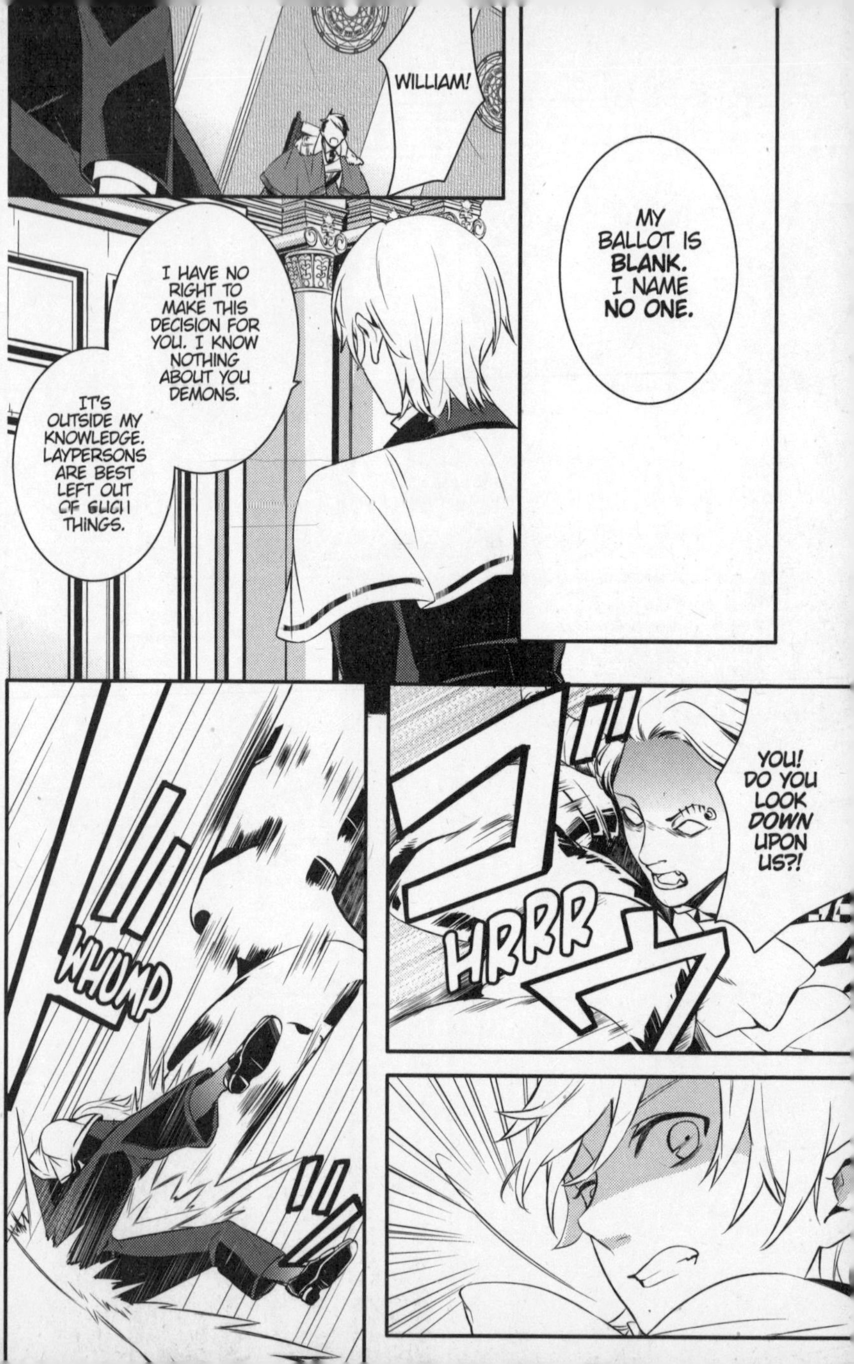
MY BALLOT IS BLANK. I NAME NO ONE.
WILLIAM!
I HAVE NO RIGHT TO MAKE THIS DECISION FOR YOU. I KNOW NOTHING ABOUT YOU DEMONS.
IT'S OUTSIDE MY KNOWLEDGE. LAYPERSONS ARE BEST LEFT OUT OF SUCH THINGS.
YOU! DO YOU LOOK DOWN UPON US?!
HRRR
WHUMP

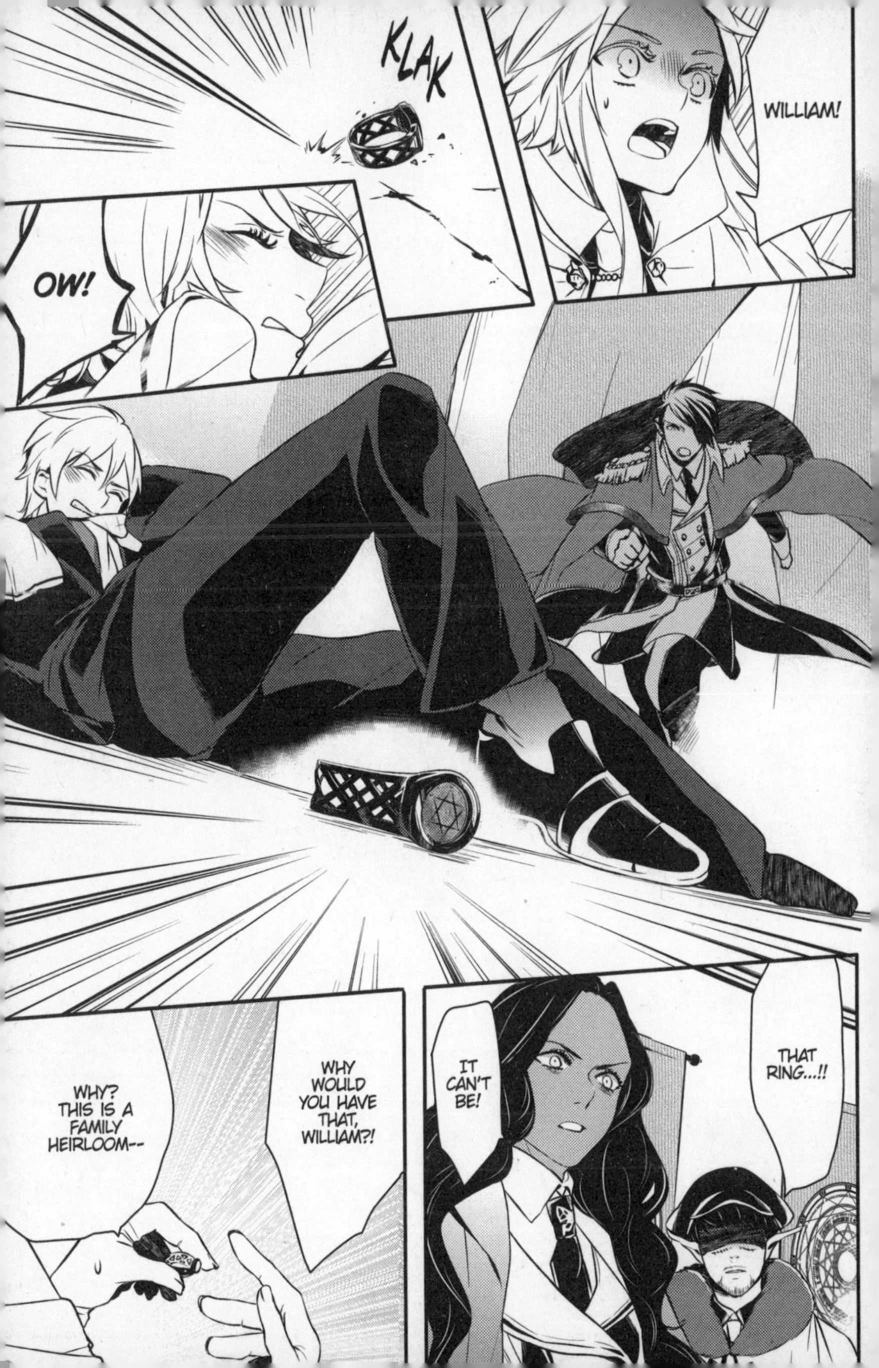
WILLIAM!
KLAK
OW!
THAT RING...!!
IT CAN'T BE!
WHY WOULD YOU HAVE THAT, WILLIAM?!
WHY? THIS IS A FAMILY HEIRLOOM--

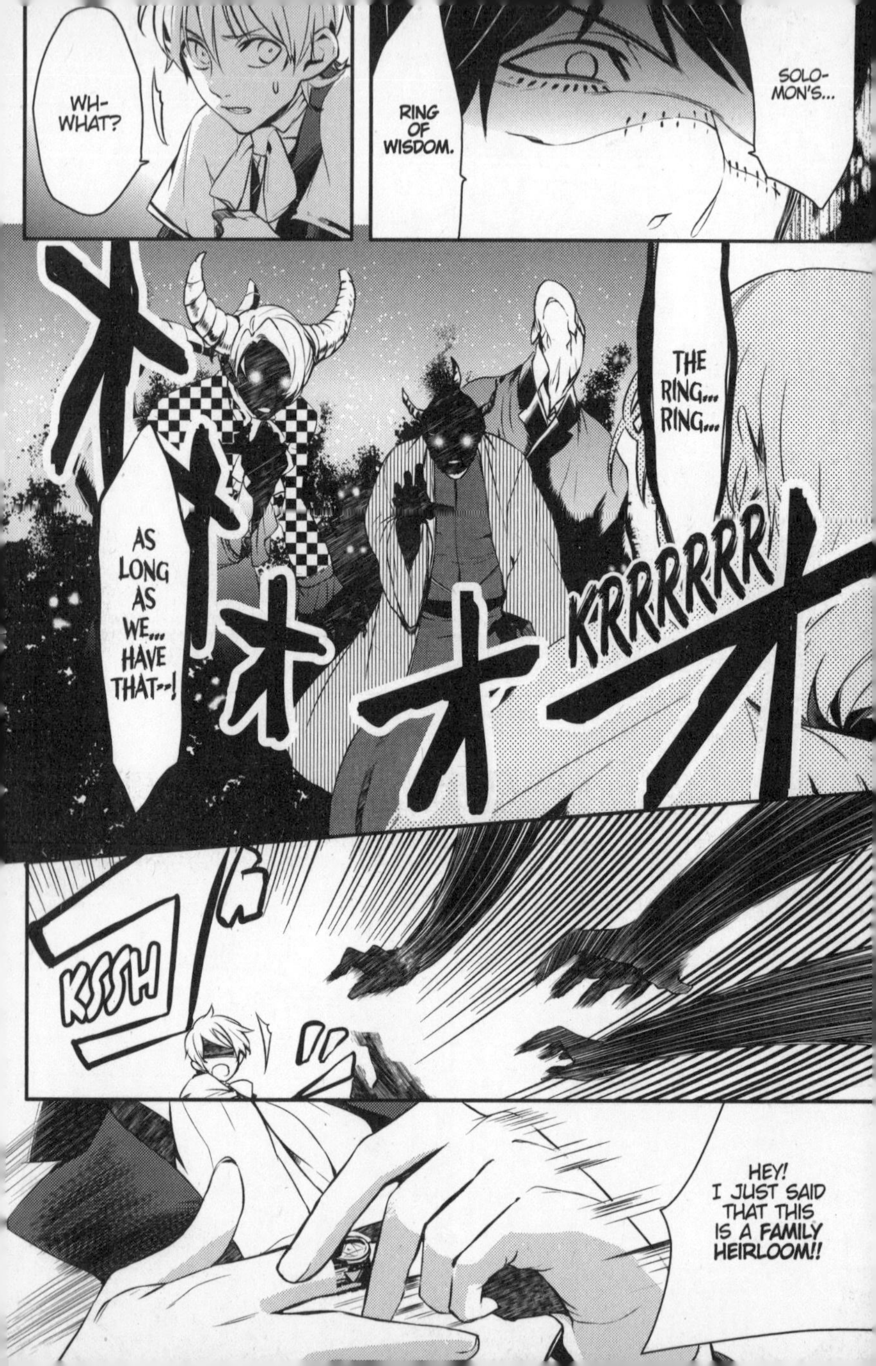
SOLO-MON'S...
RING OF WISDOM.
WH-WHAT?
THE RING... RING...
KRRRRRR
AS LONG AS WE... HAVE THAT--!
KSSH
HEY! I JUST SAID THAT THIS IS A FAMILY HEIRLOOM!!

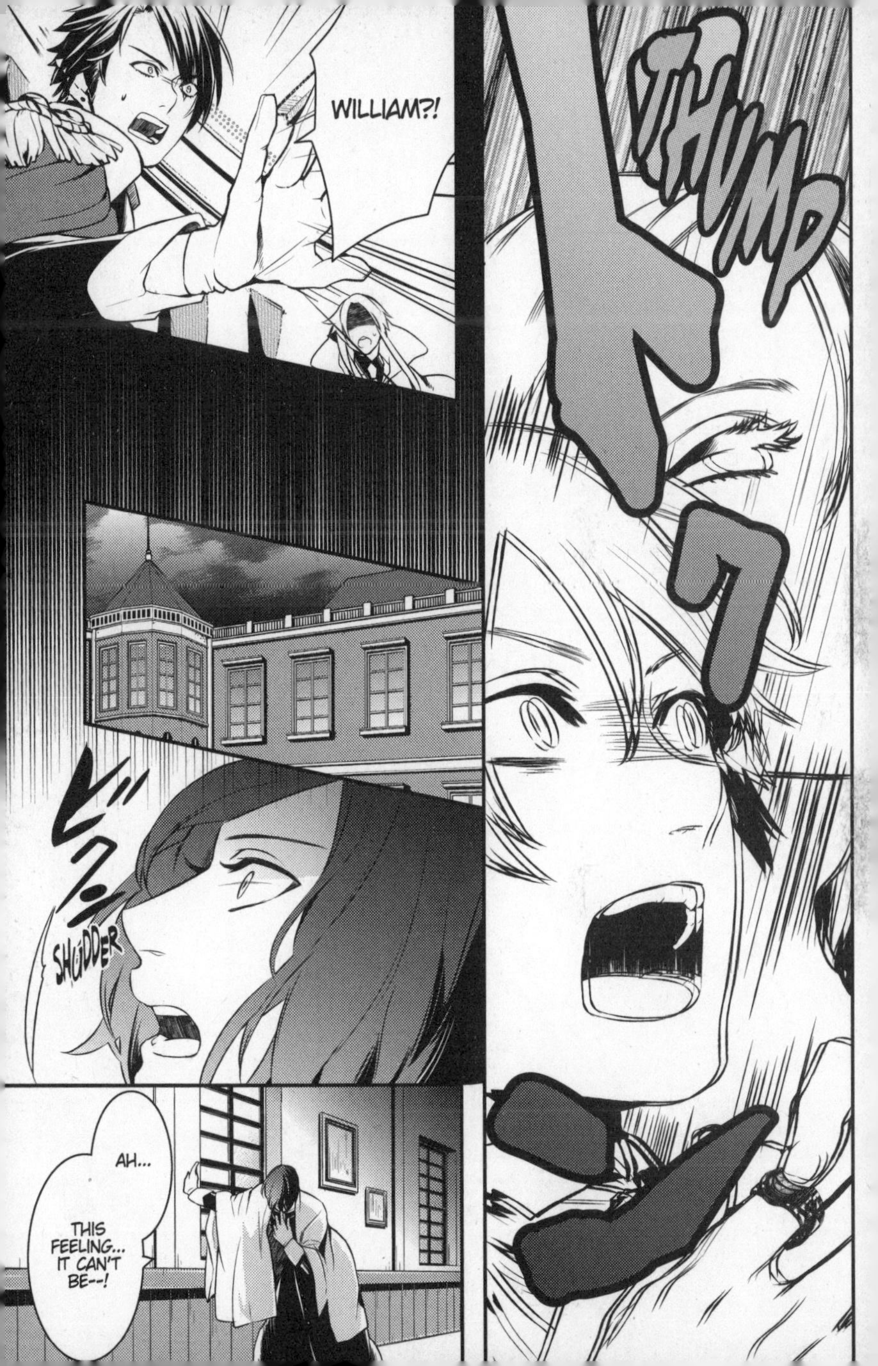
THUMP
WILLIAM?!
SHUDDER
AH...
THIS FEELING... IT CAN'T BE--!

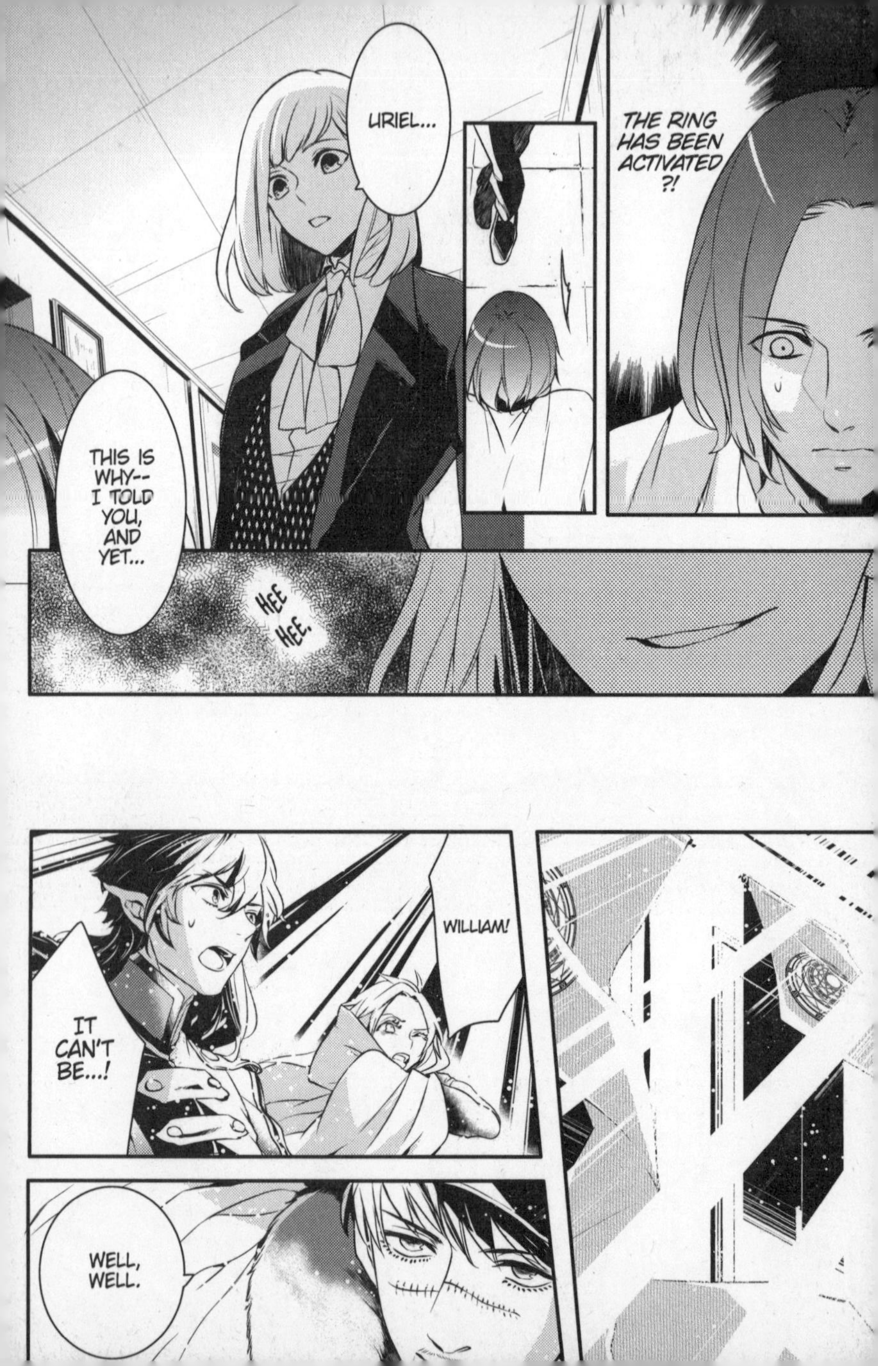
THE RING HAS BEEN ACTIVATED ?!
URIEL...
THIS IS WHY-- I TOLD YOU, AND YET...
HEE HEE.
WILLIAM!
IT CAN'T BE...!
WELL, WELL.

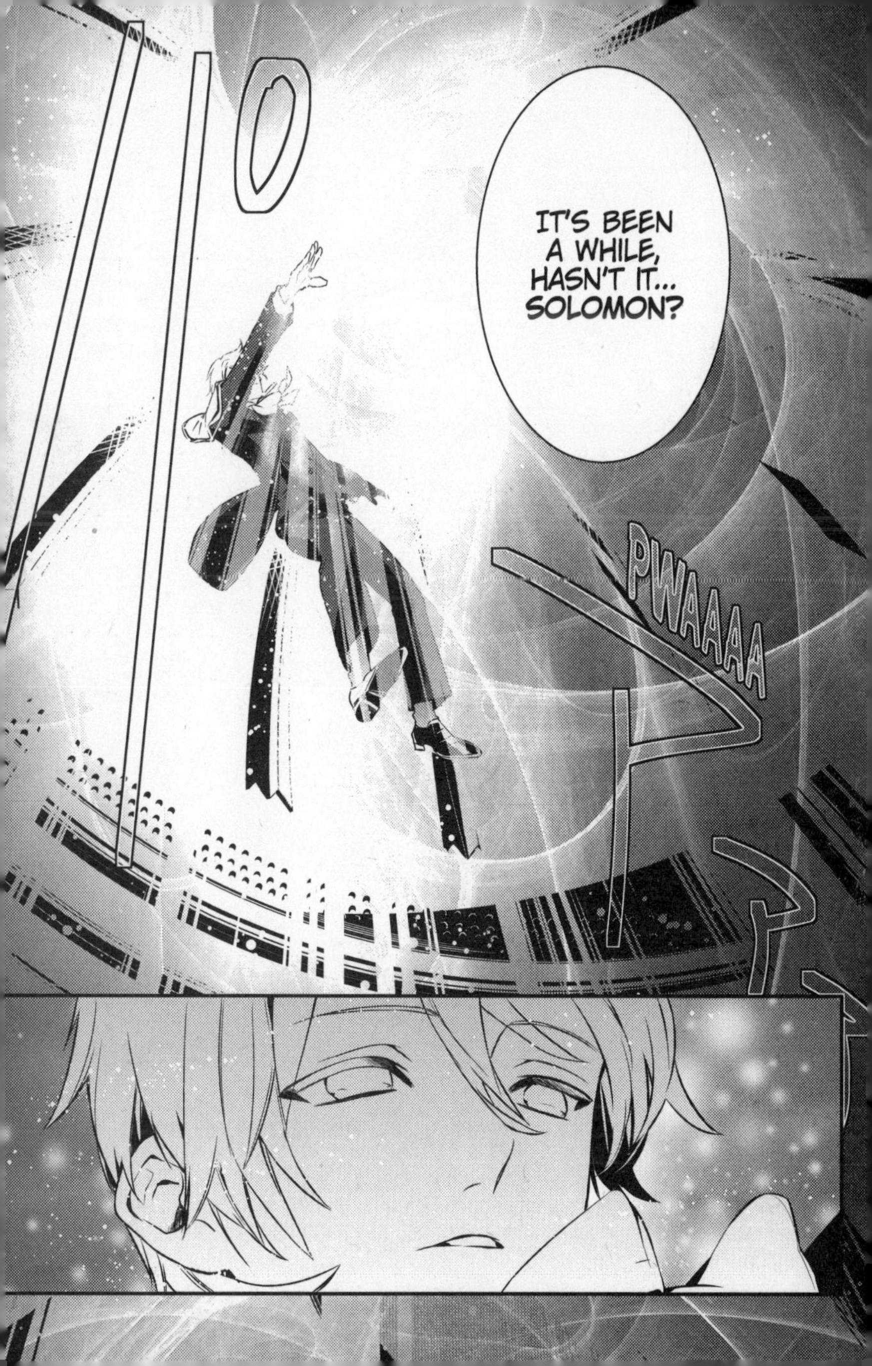
IT'S BEEN A WHILE, HASN'T IT... SOLOMON?
PWAAAA

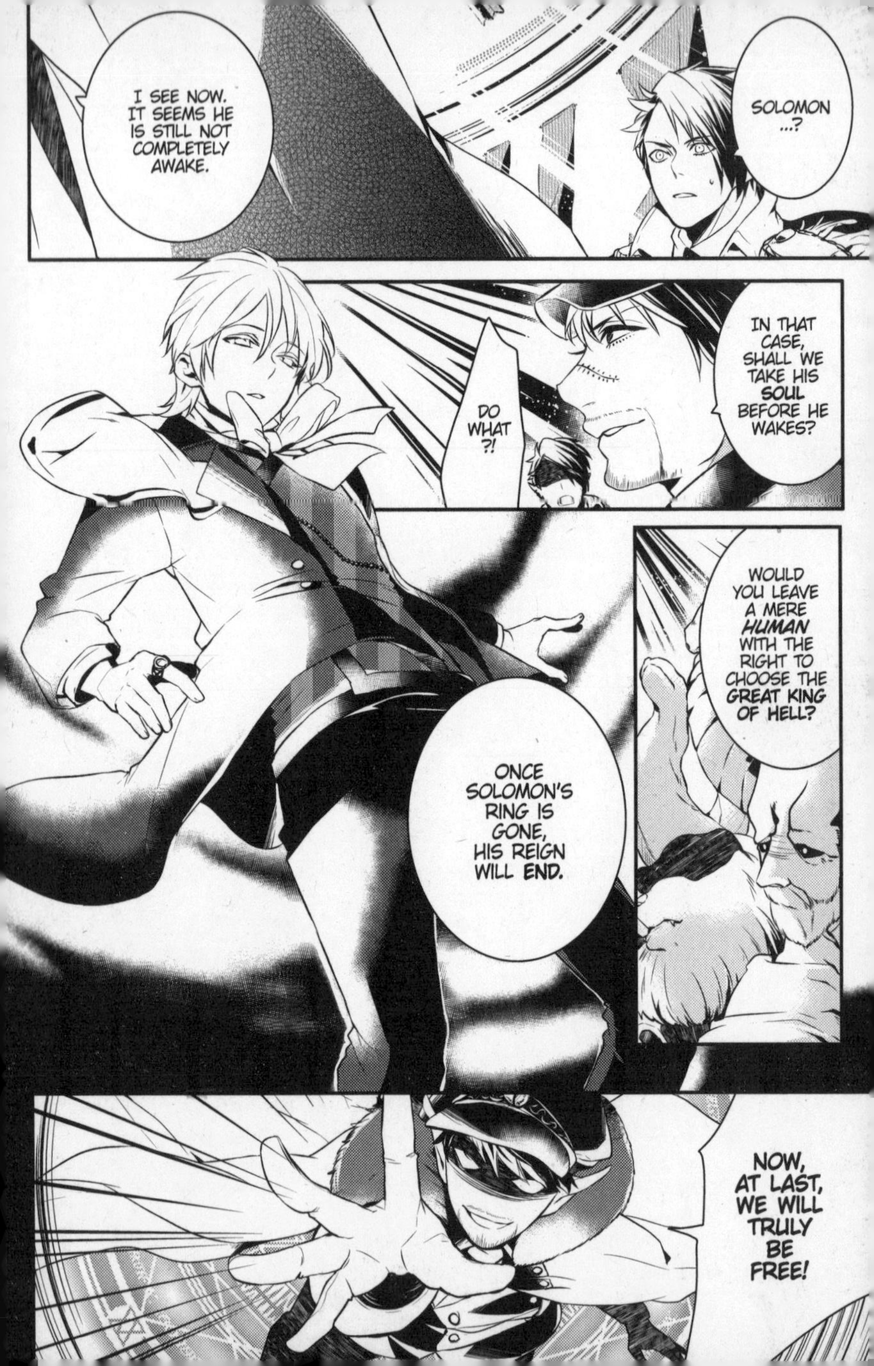
SOLOMON ...?
I SEE NOW. IT SEEMS HE IS STILL NOT COMPLETELY AWAKE.
IN THAT CASE, SHALL WE TAKE HIS SOUL BEFORE HE WAKES?
DO WHAT ?!
WOULD YOU LEAVE A MERE HUMAN WITH THE RIGHT TO CHOOSE THE GREAT KING OF HELL?
ONCE SOLOMON'S RING IS GONE, HIS REIGN WILL END.
NOW, AT LAST, WE WILL TRULY BE FREE!

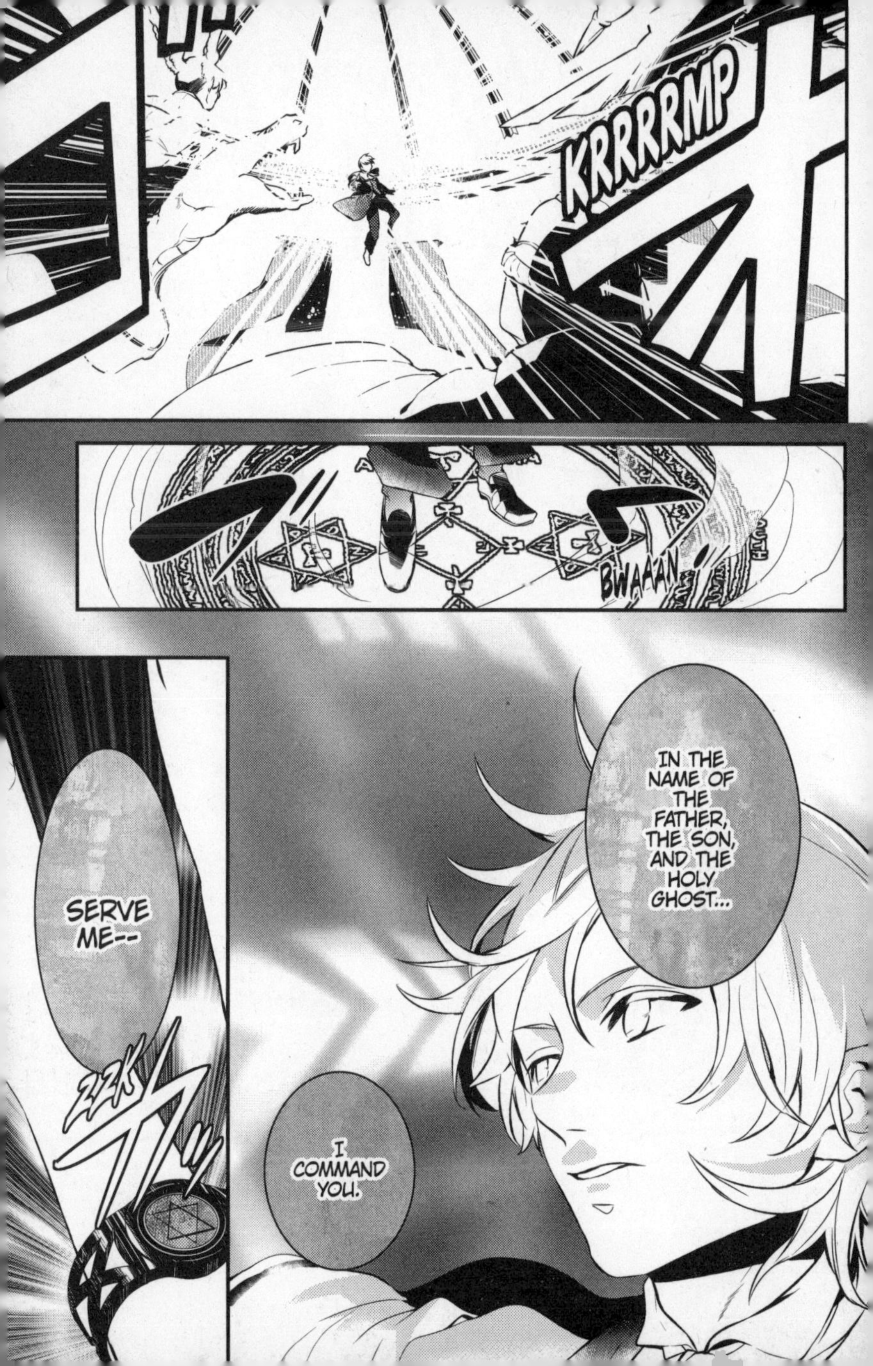
KRRRRMP
BWAAAN
IN THE NAME OF THE FATHER, THE SON, AND THE HOLY GHOST...
I COMMAND YOU.
SERVE ME--

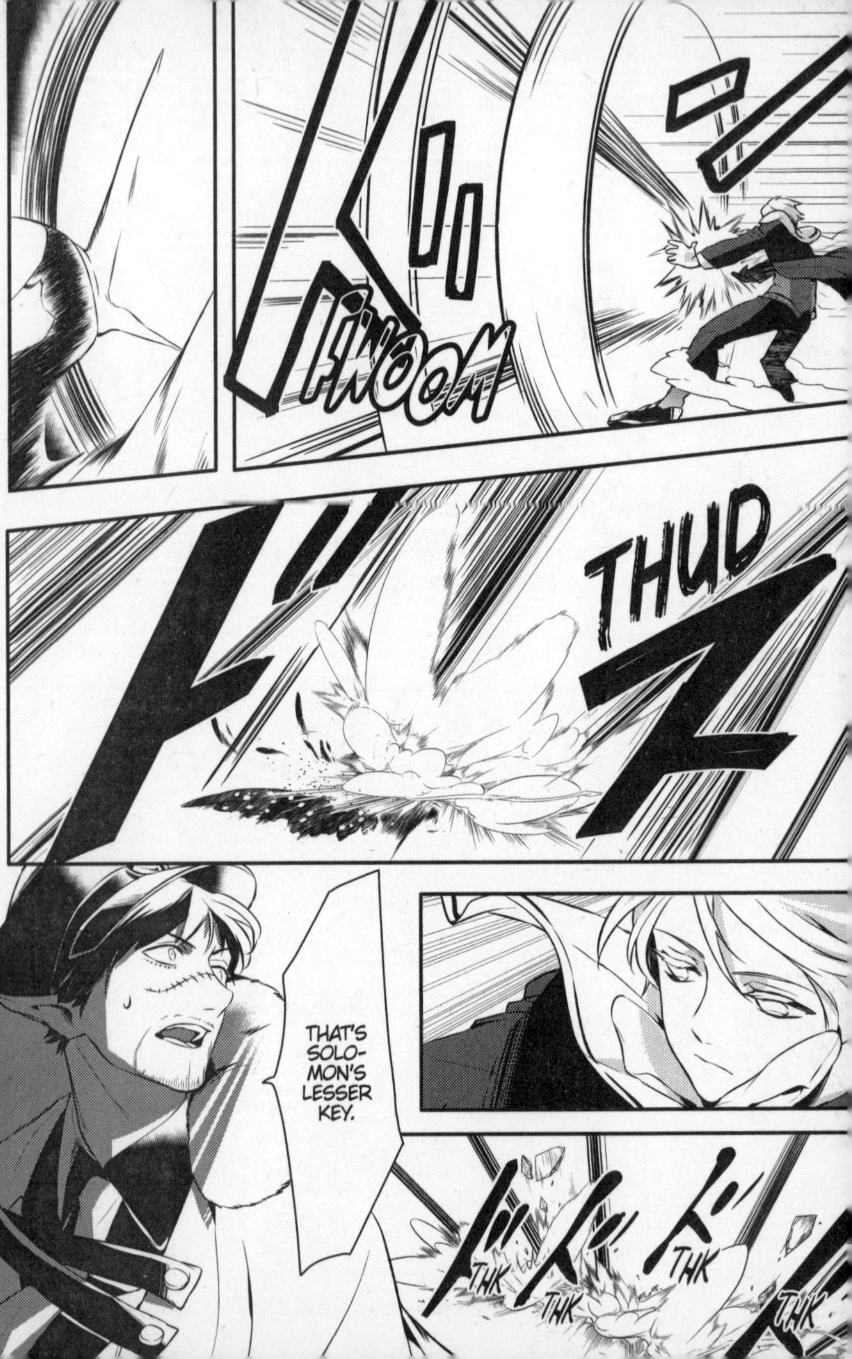
FWOOM
THUD
THK
THK
THK
THK
THAT'S SOLO-MON'S LESSER KEY.

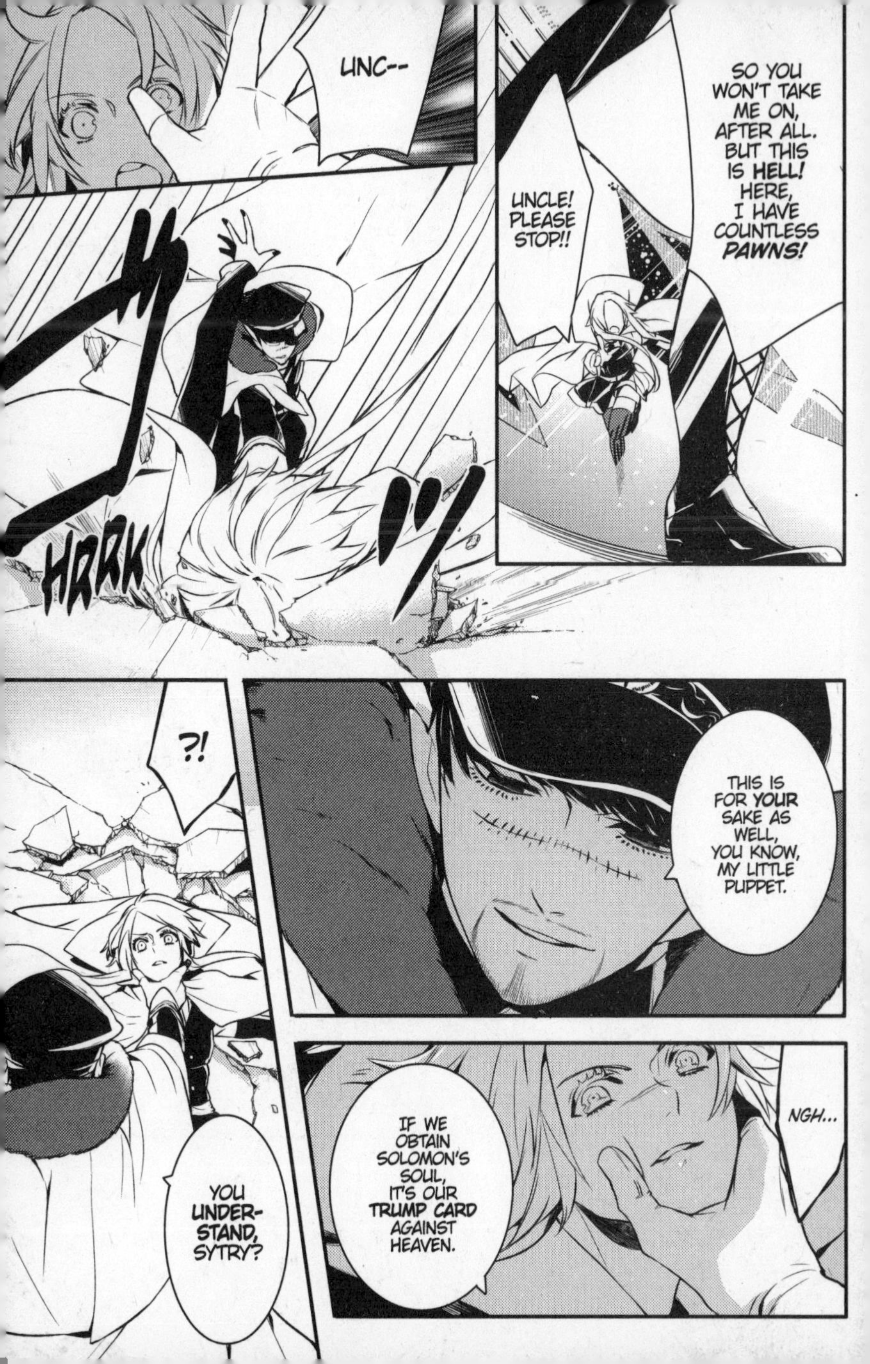
SO YOU WON'T TAKE ME ON, AFTER ALL. BUT THIS IS HELL! HERE, I HAVE COUNTLESS PAWNS!
UNCLE! PLEASE STOP!!
UNC--
HRRK
THIS IS FOR YOUR SAKE AS WELL, YOU KNOW, MY LITTLE PUPPET.
NGH...
IF WE OBTAIN SOLOMON'S SOUL, IT'S OUR TRUMP CARD AGAINST HEAVEN.
?!
YOU UNDER-STAND, SYTRY?

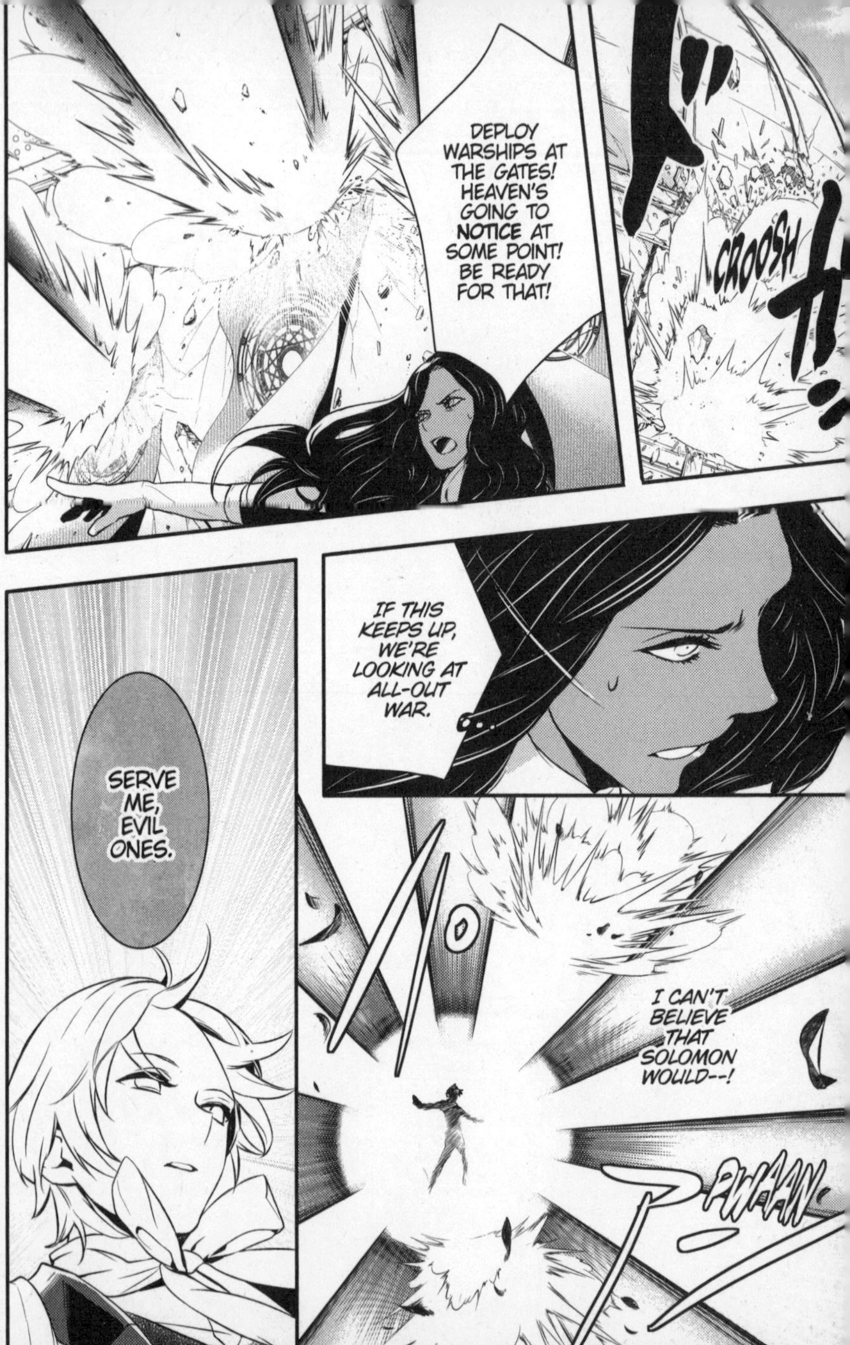
CROOSH
DEPLOY WARSHIPS AT THE GATES! HEAVEN'S GOING TO NOTICE AT SOME POINT! BE READY FOR THAT!
IF THIS KEEPS UP, WE'RE LOOKING AT ALL-OUT WAR.
I CAN'T BELIEVE THAT SOLOMON WOULD--!
PWAAN
SERVE ME, EVIL ONES.

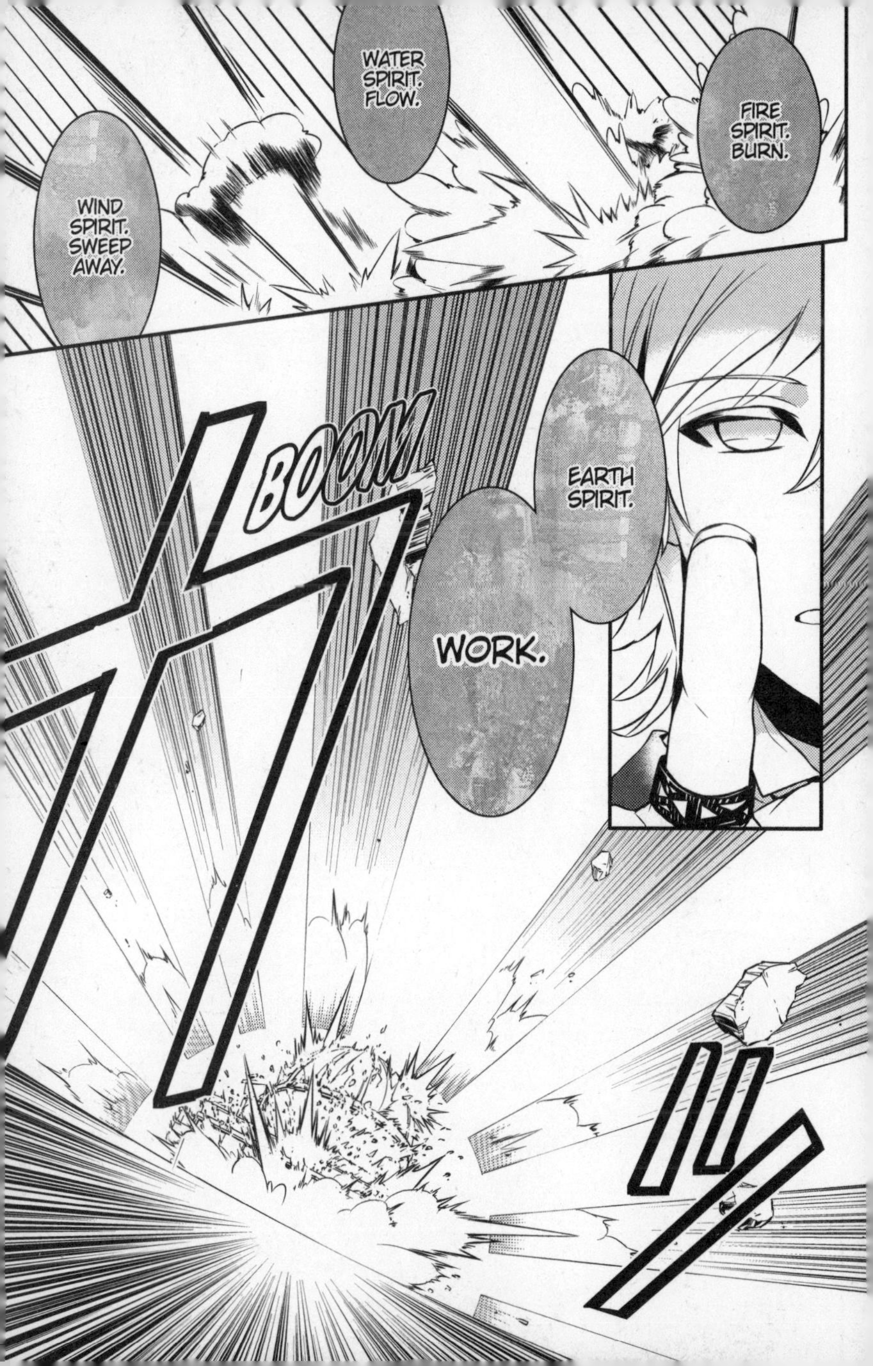
FIRE SPIRIT. BURN.
WATER SPIRIT. FLOW.
WIND SPIRIT. SWEEP AWAY.
EARTH SPIRIT.
WORK.
BOOM

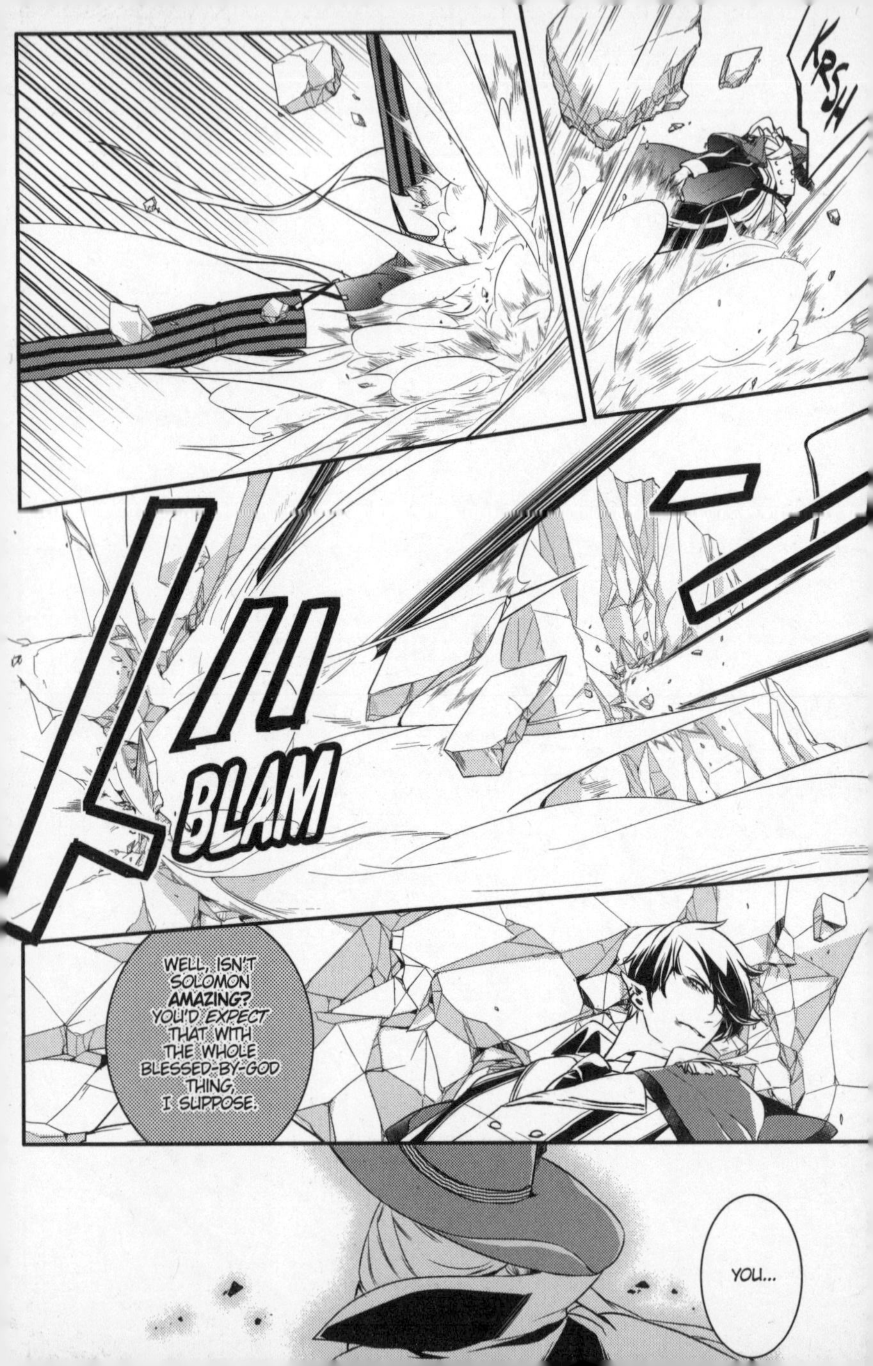
KRSH
BLAM
WELL, ISN'T SOLOMON AMAZING? YOU'D EXPECT THAT WITH THE WHOLE BLESSED-BY-GOD THING, I SUPPOSE.
YOU...

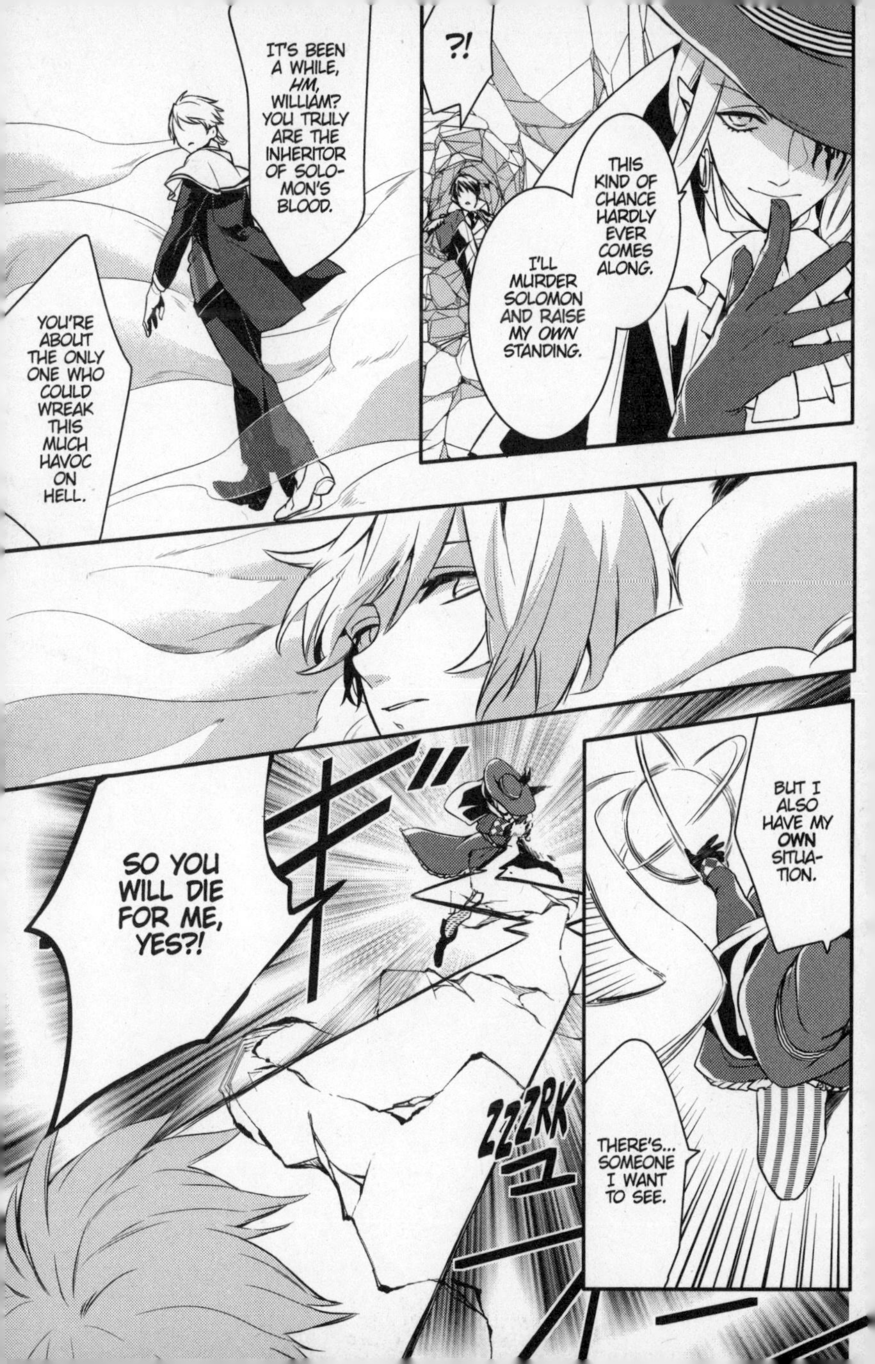
?!
THIS KIND OF CHANCE HARDLY EVER COMES ALONG.
I'LL MURDER SOLOMON AND RAISE MY *OWN* STANDING.
IT'S BEEN A WHILE, *HM*, WILLIAM? YOU TRULY ARE THE INHERITOR OF SOLO-MON'S BLOOD.
YOU'RE ABOUT THE ONLY ONE WHO COULD WREAK THIS MUCH HAVOC ON HELL.
BUT I ALSO HAVE MY *OWN* SITUA-TION.
THERE'S... SOMEONE I WANT TO SEE.
SO YOU WILL DIE FOR ME, YES?!
ZZZRK

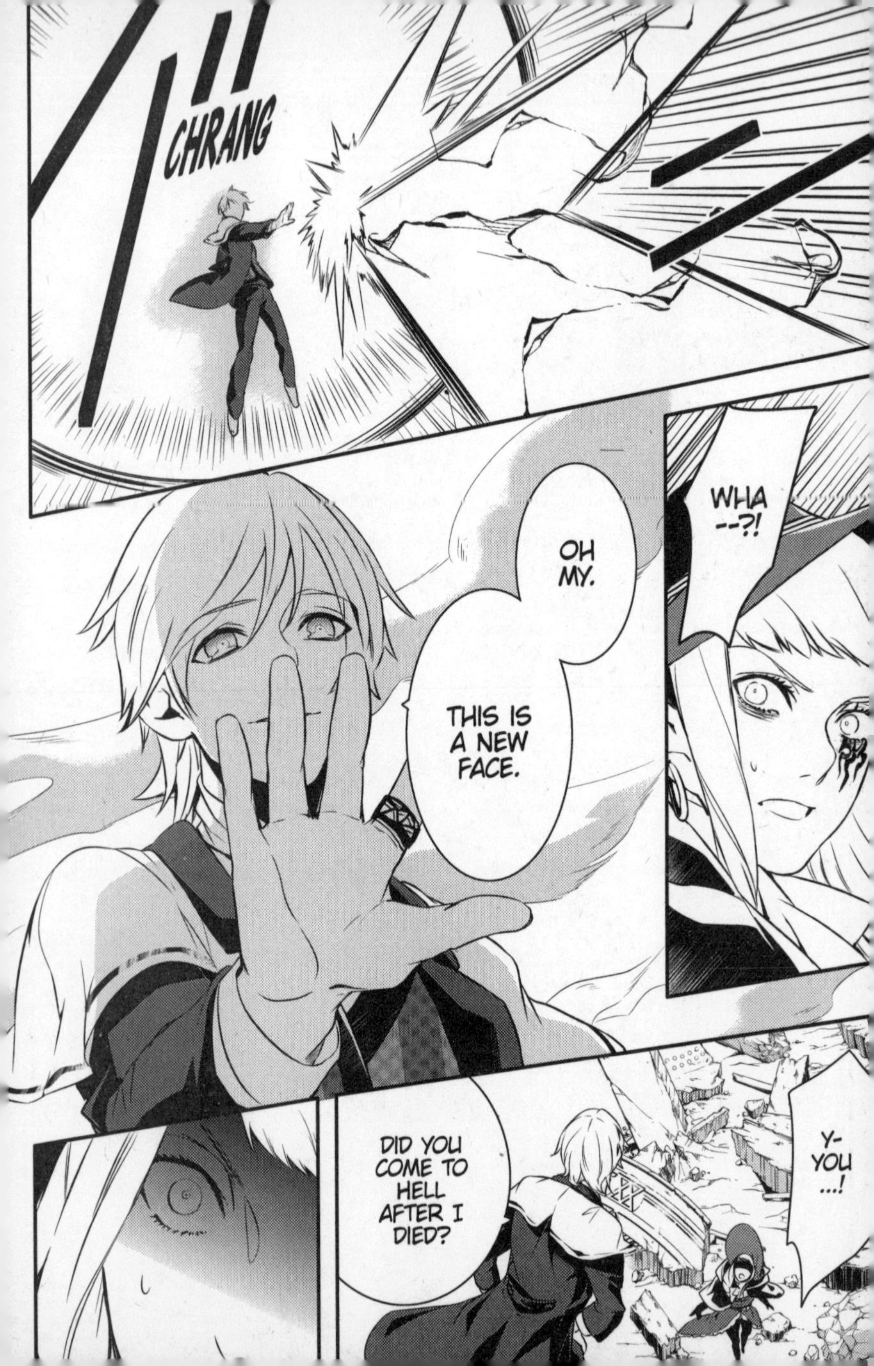
CHRANG
WHA--?!
OH MY.
THIS IS A NEW FACE.
Y-YOU...!
DID YOU COME TO HELL AFTER I DIED?

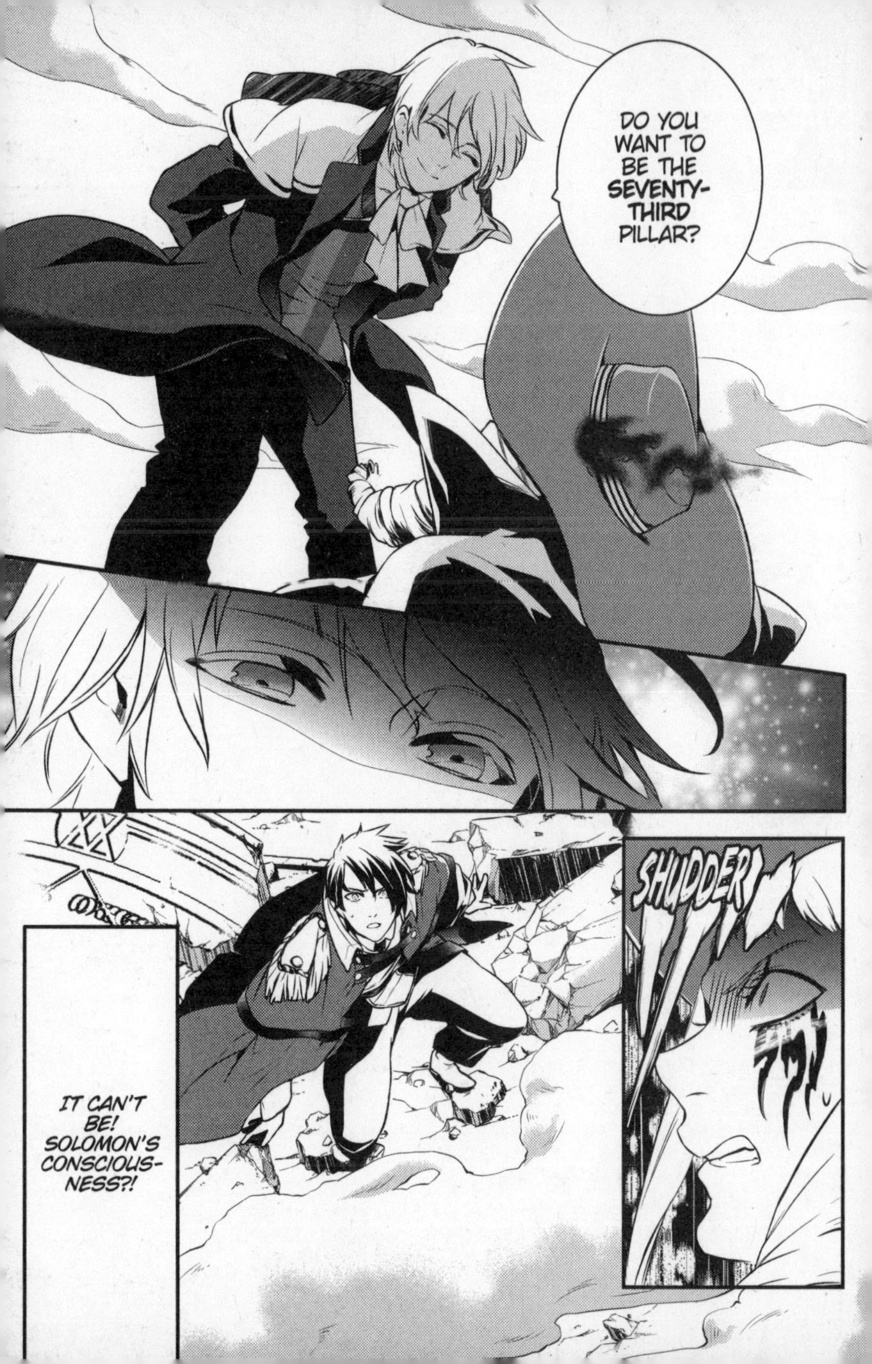
DO YOU WANT TO BE THE SEVENTY-THIRD PILLAR?
SHUDDER!
IT CAN'T BE! SOLOMON'S CONSCIOUS-NESS?!

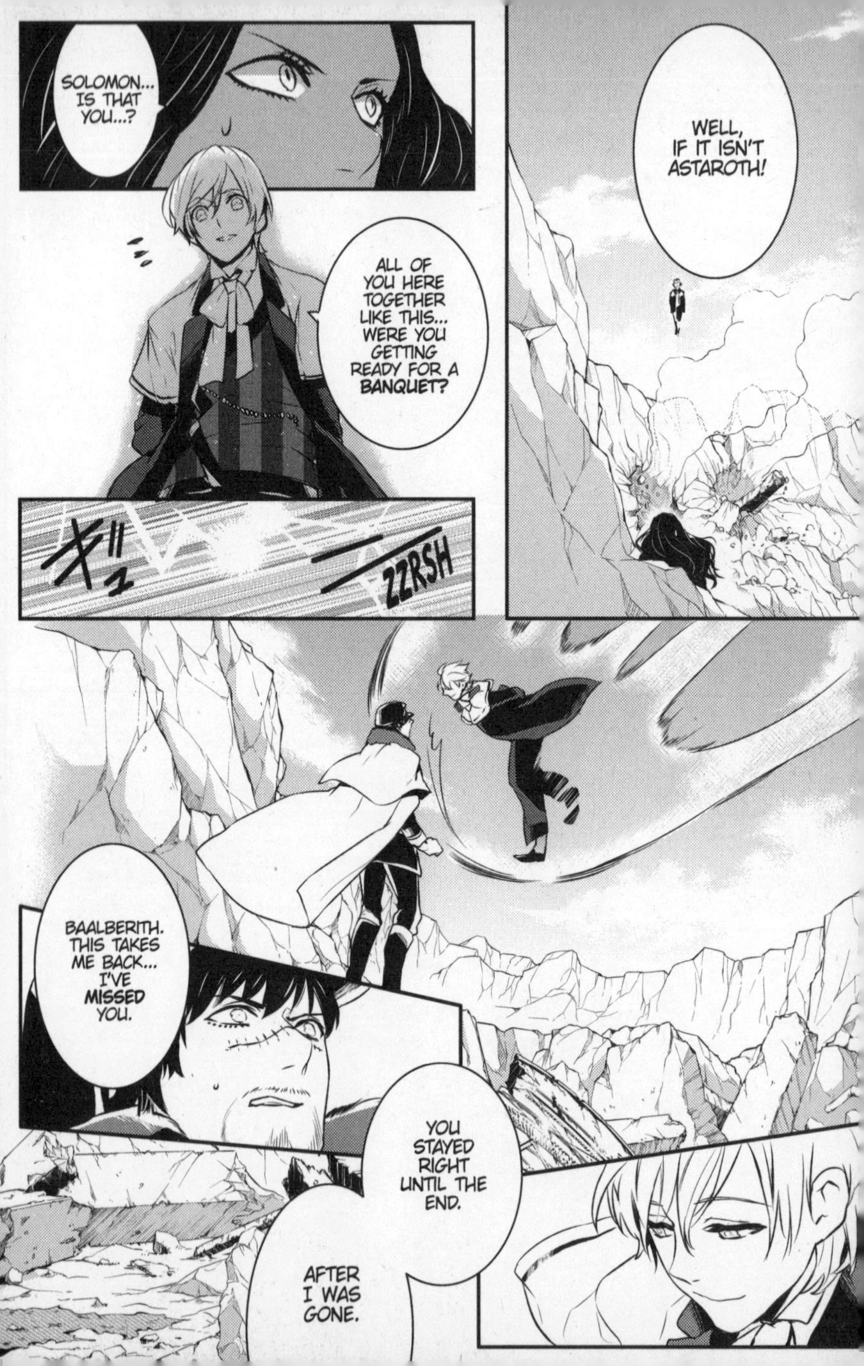
WELL, IF IT ISN'T ASTAROTH!
SOLOMON... IS THAT YOU...?
ALL OF YOU HERE TOGETHER LIKE THIS... WERE YOU GETTING READY FOR A BANQUET?
ZZRSH
BAALBERITH. THIS TAKES ME BACK... I'VE MISSED YOU.
YOU STAYED RIGHT UNTIL THE END.
AFTER I WAS GONE.

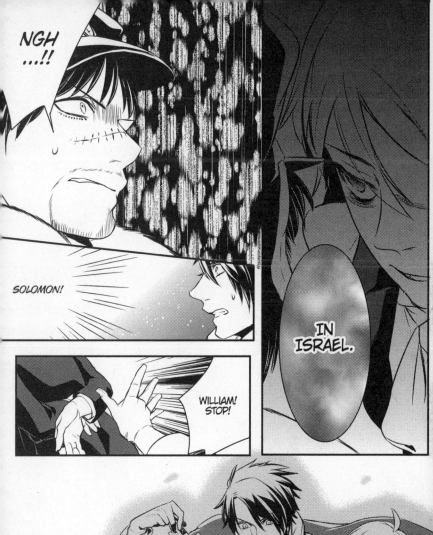

NGH ...!!

SOLOMON!

IN ISRAEL.

WILLIAM! STOP!

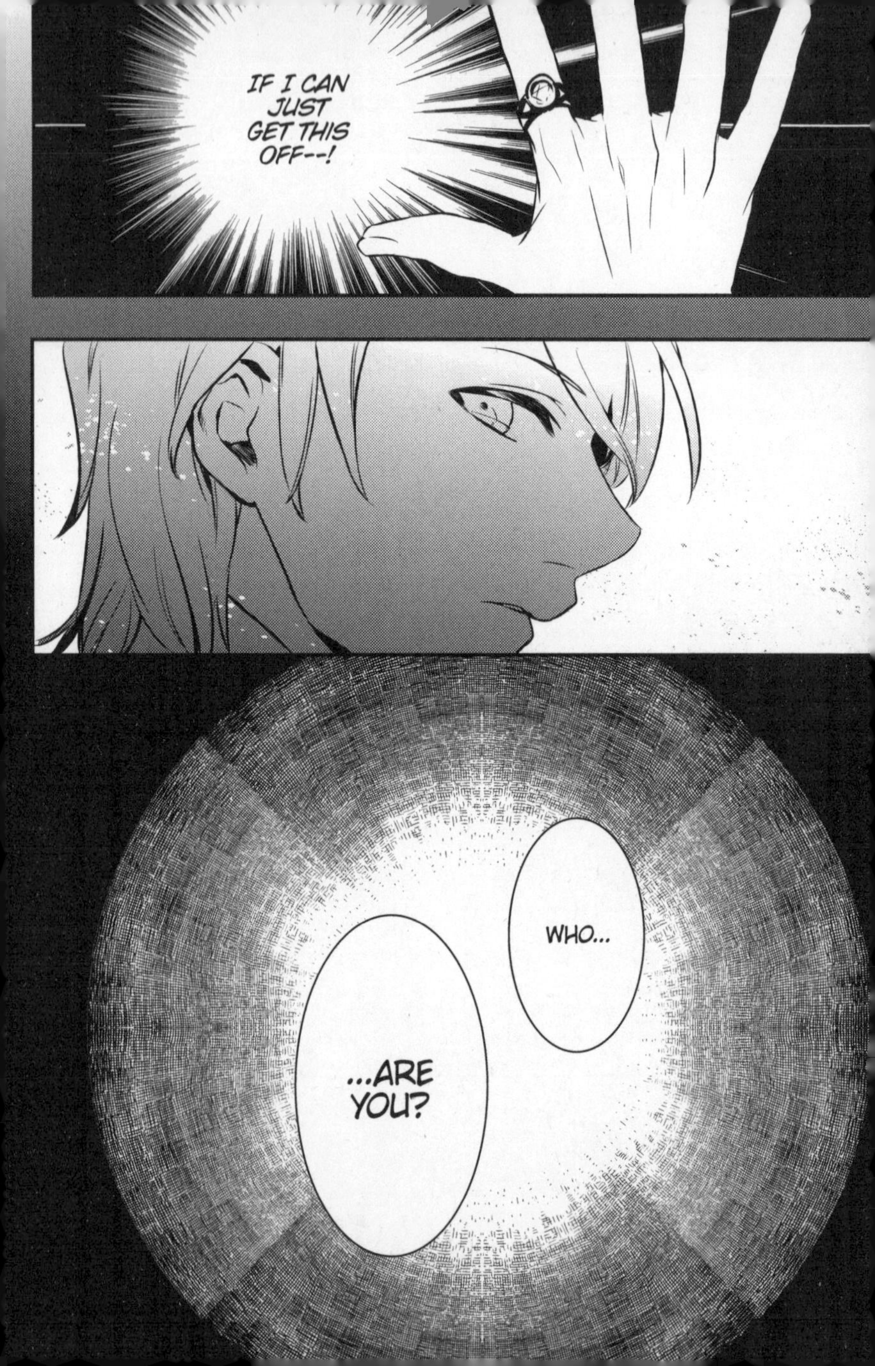
IF I CAN JUST GET THIS OFF--!
WHO...
...ARE YOU?

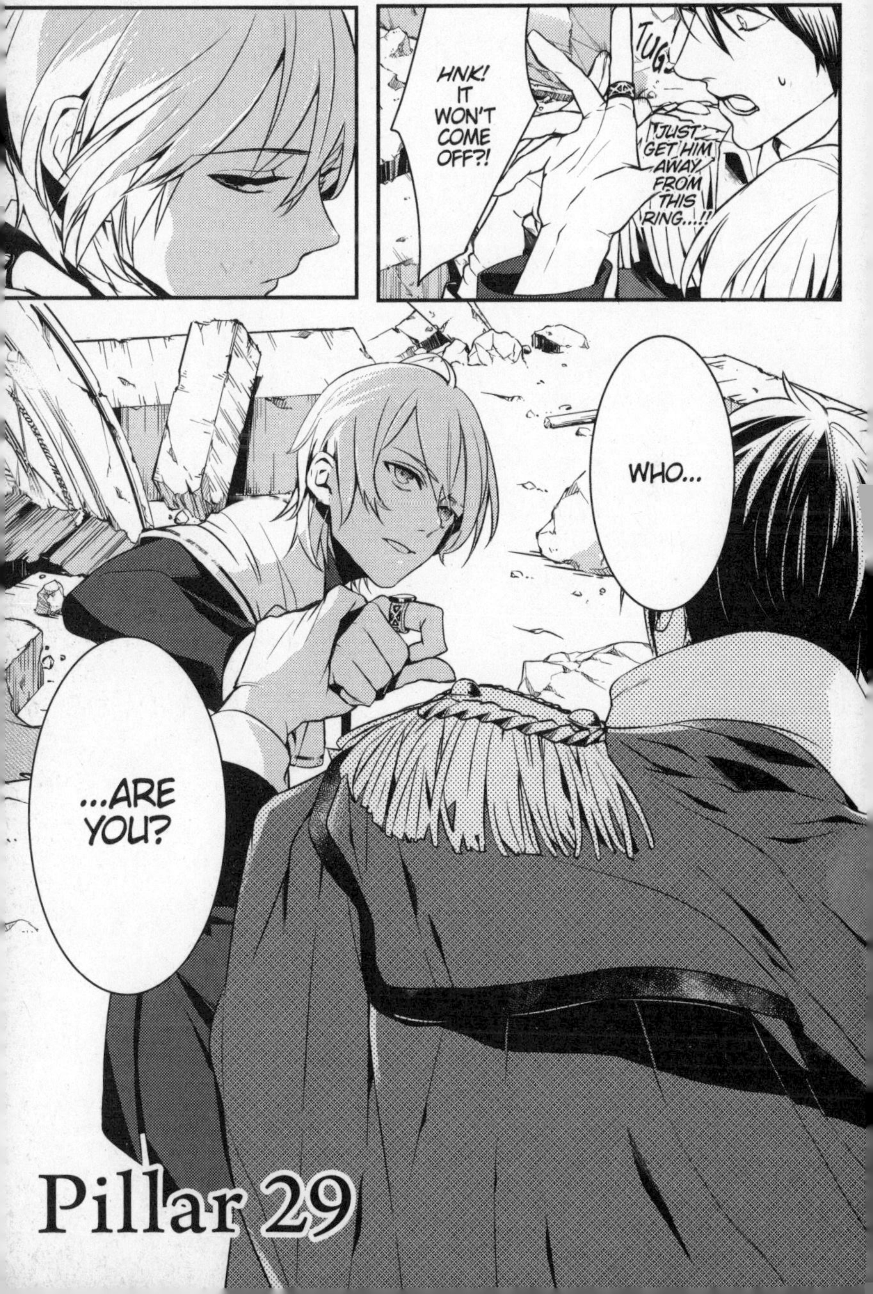
TUG
HNK! IT WON'T COME OFF?!
JUST GET HIM AWAY FROM THIS RING...!!
WHO...
...ARE YOU?
Pillar 29

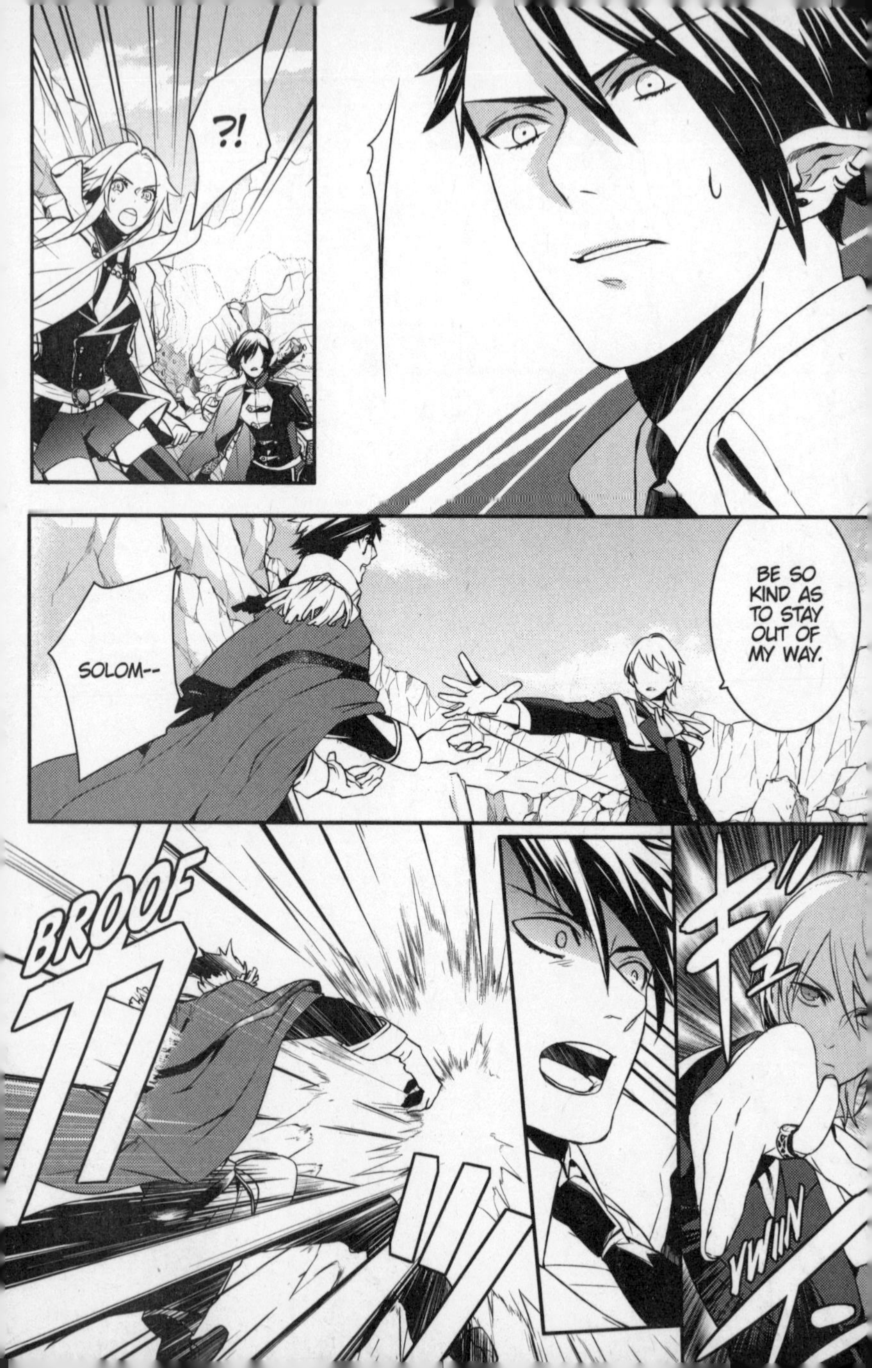
?!
BE SO KIND AS TO STAY OUT OF MY WAY.
SOLOM--
YWIIN
BROOF

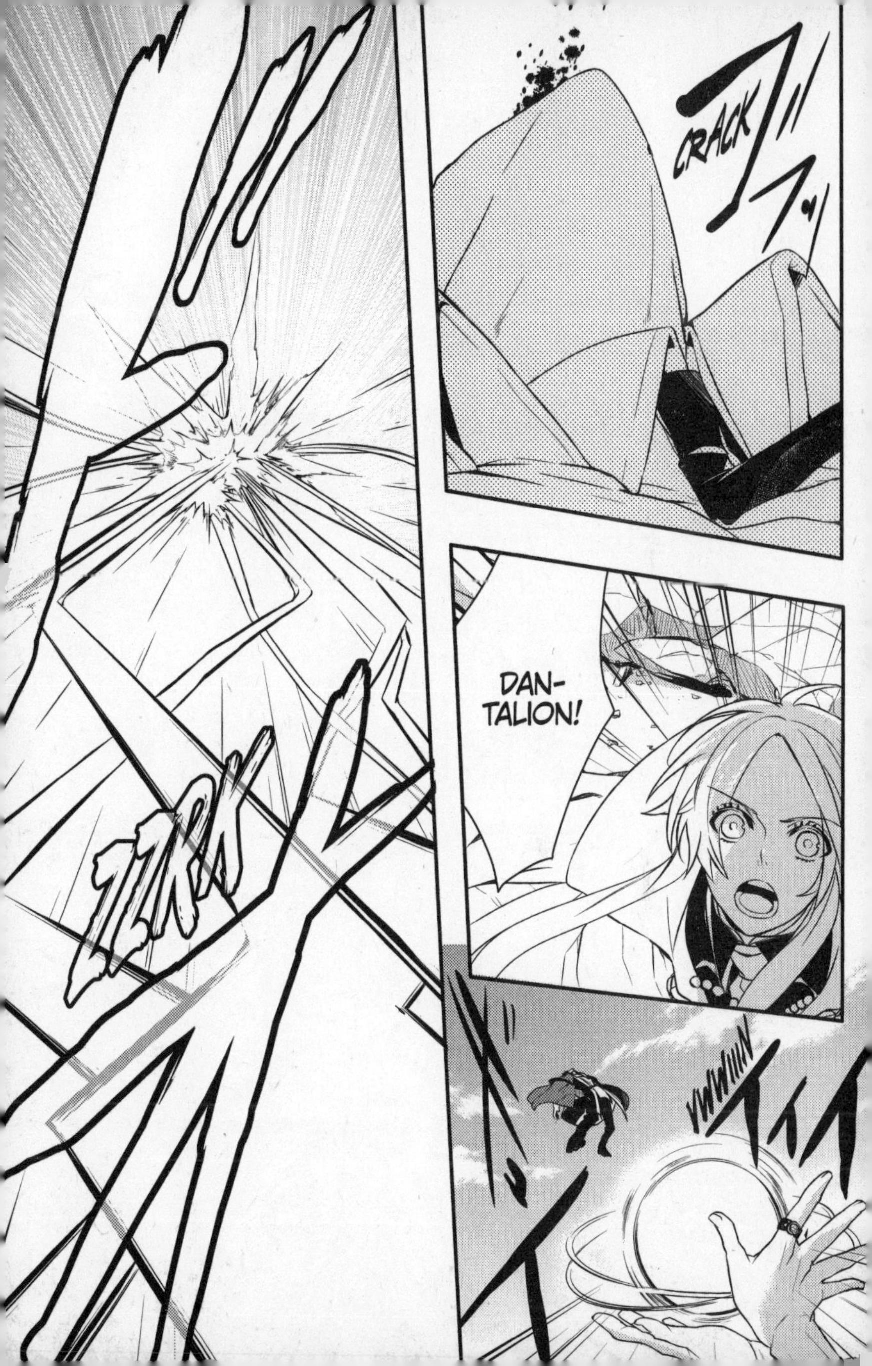
CRACK
DAN-
TALION!
VWWIIIN

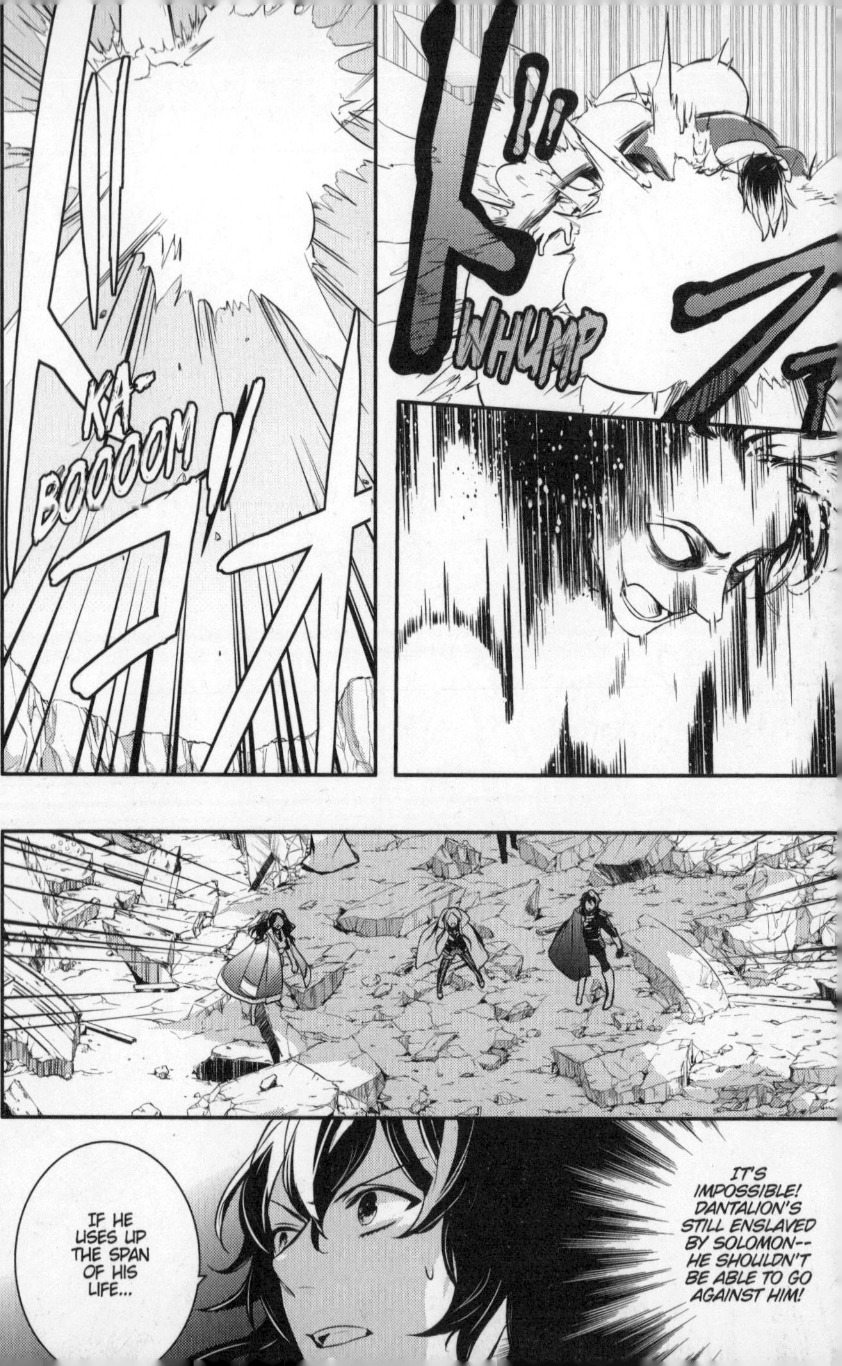
WHUMP
KA-BOOOOM!!
IT'S IMPOSSIBLE! DANTALION'S STILL ENSLAVED BY SOLOMON-- HE SHOULDN'T BE ABLE TO GO AGAINST HIM!
IF HE USES UP THE SPAN OF HIS LIFE...

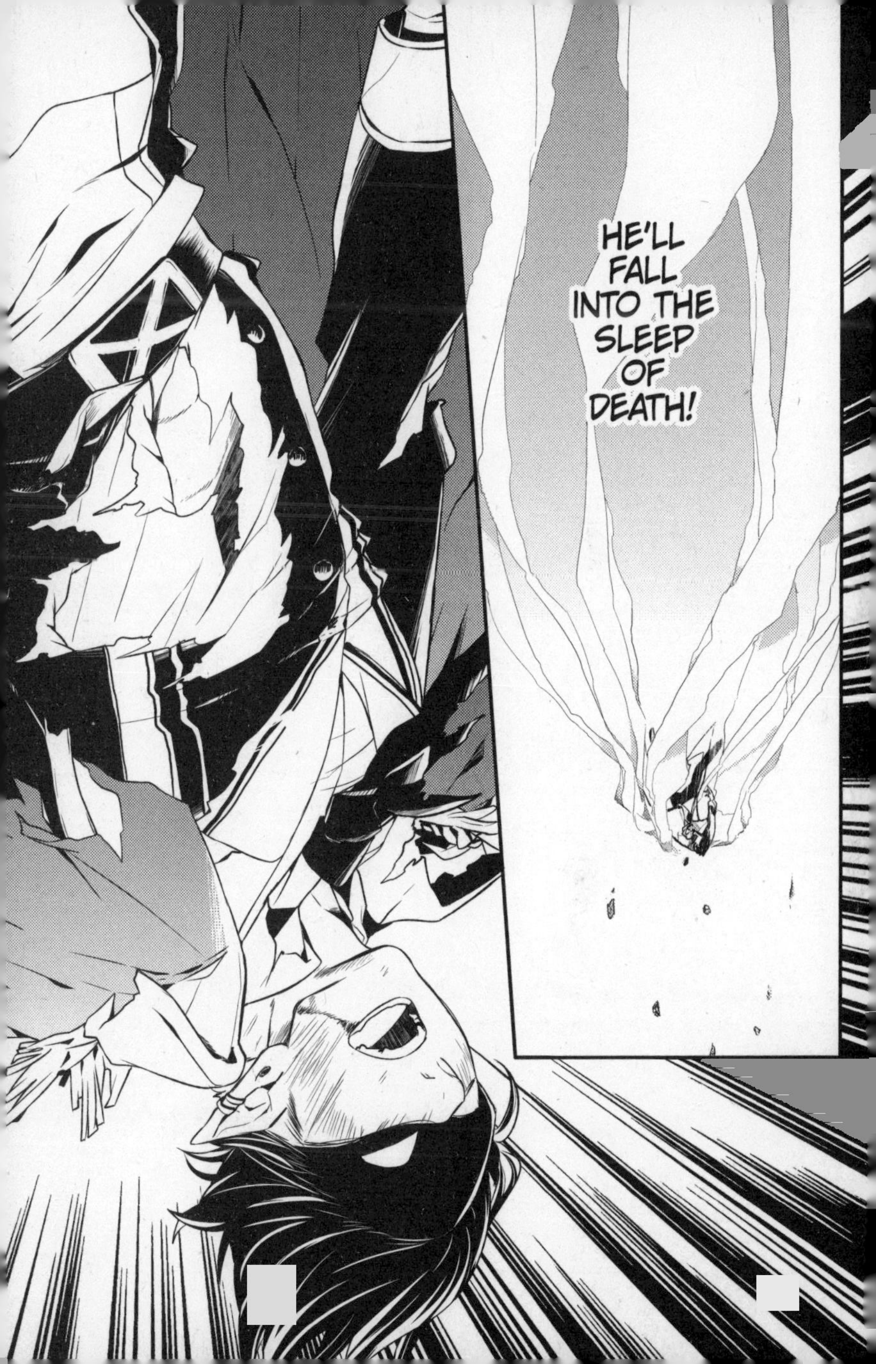
HE'LL FALL INTO THE SLEEP OF DEATH!

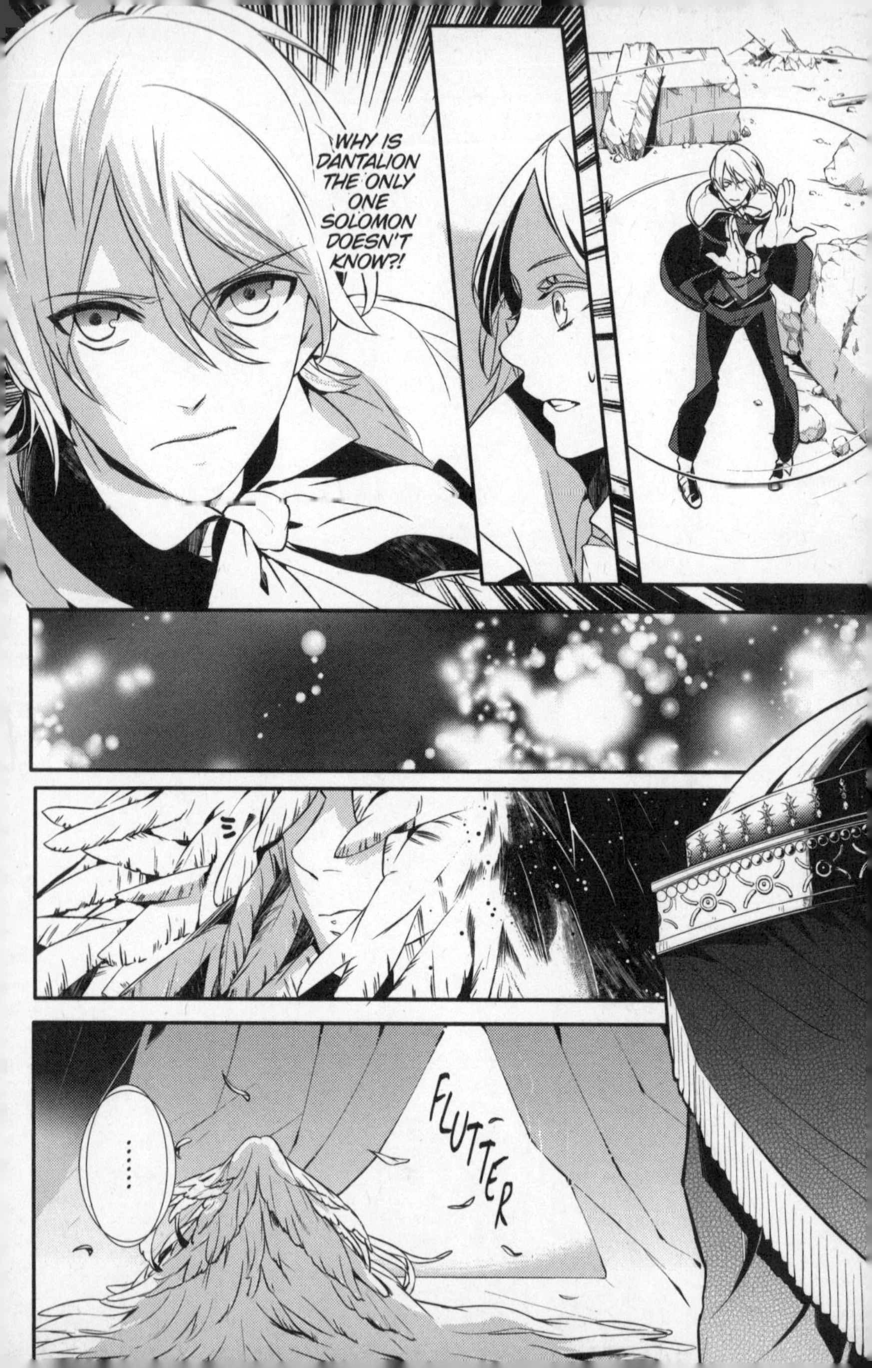
WHY IS DANTALION THE ONLY ONE SOLOMON DOESN'T KNOW?!
FLUTTER
......

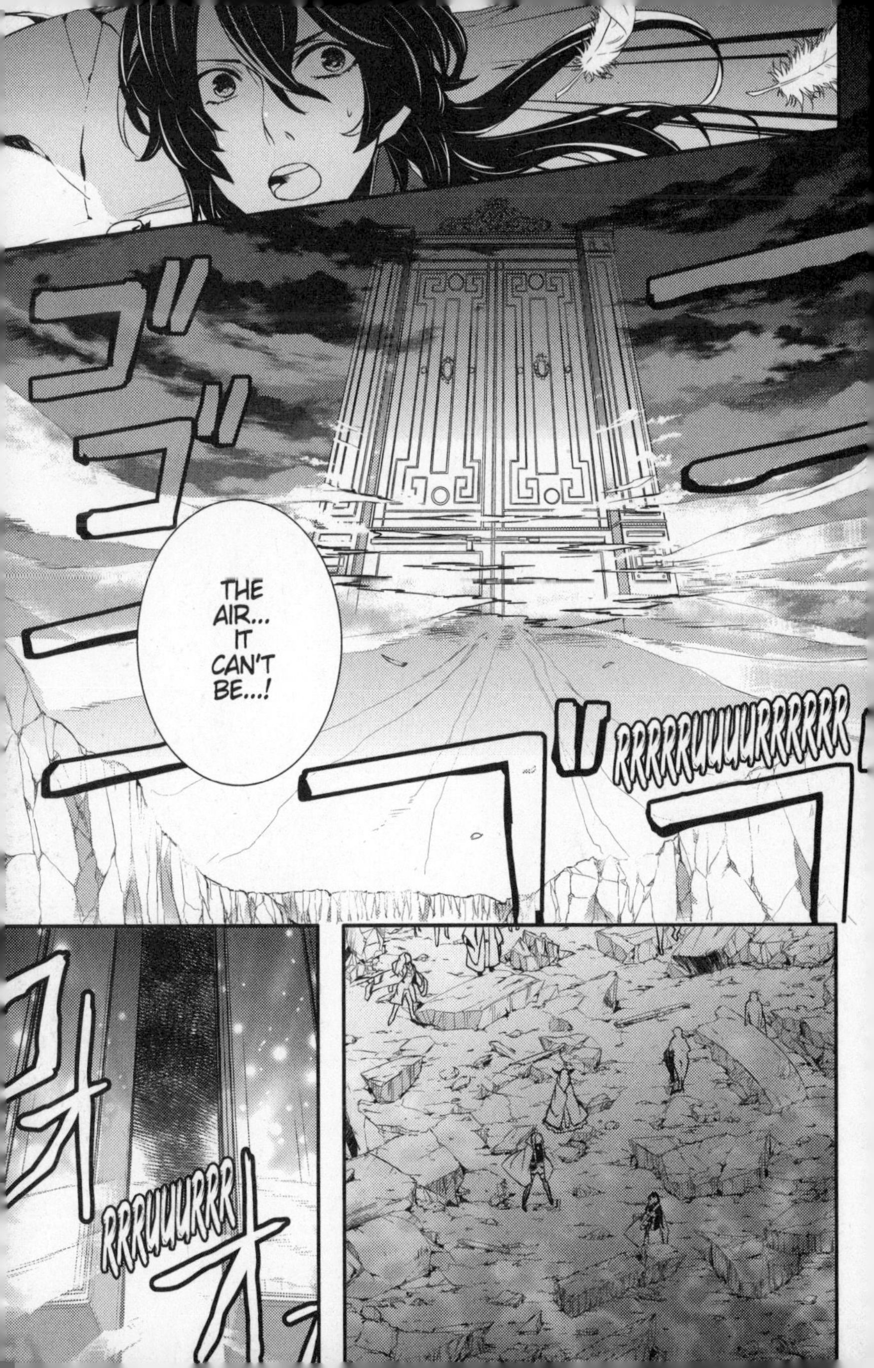
THE AIR... IT CAN'T BE...!
RRRRUUUURRRRRR
RRRUUURRR

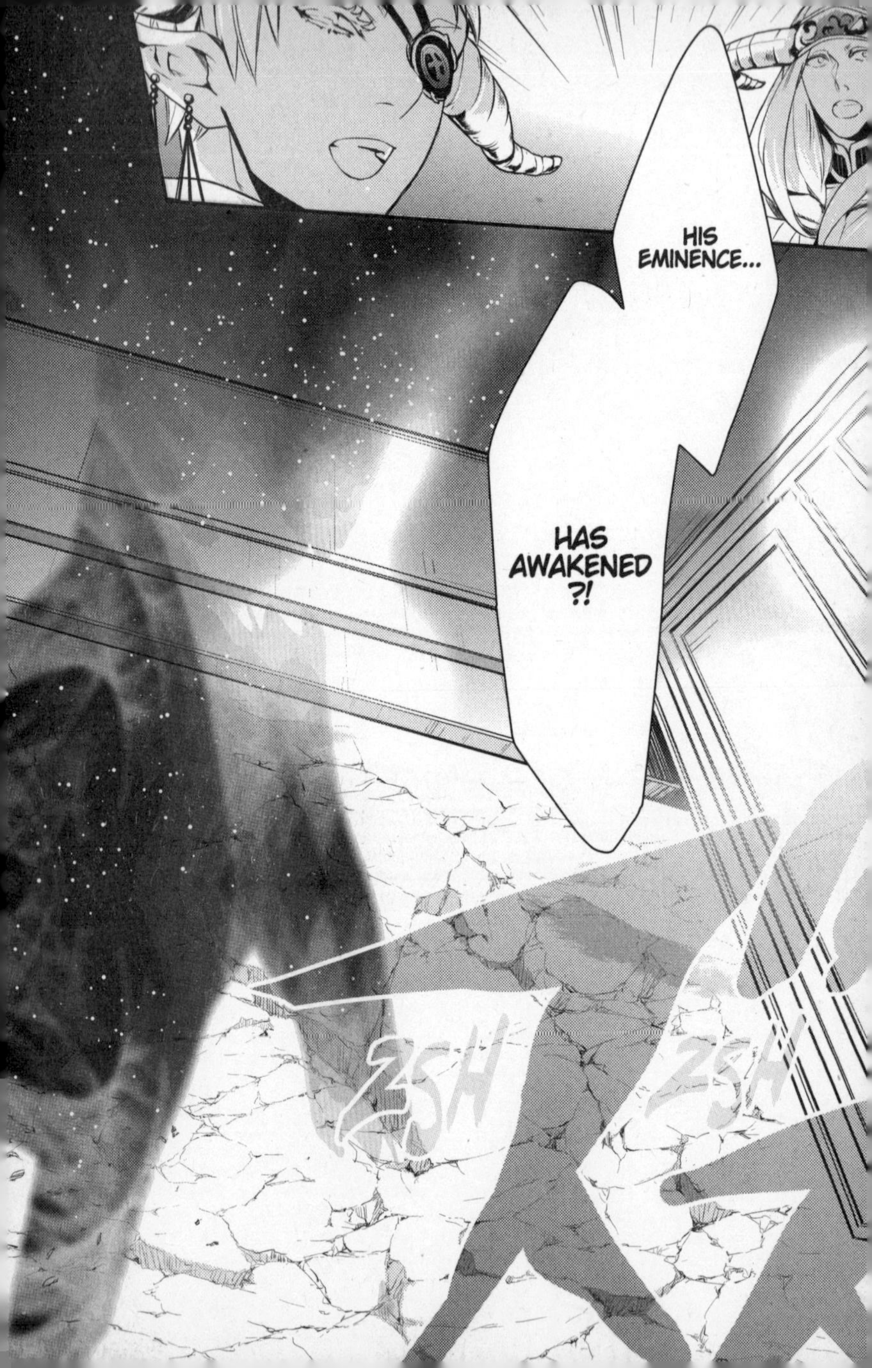
HIS EMINENCE...
HAS AWAKENED ?!
ZSH
ZSH

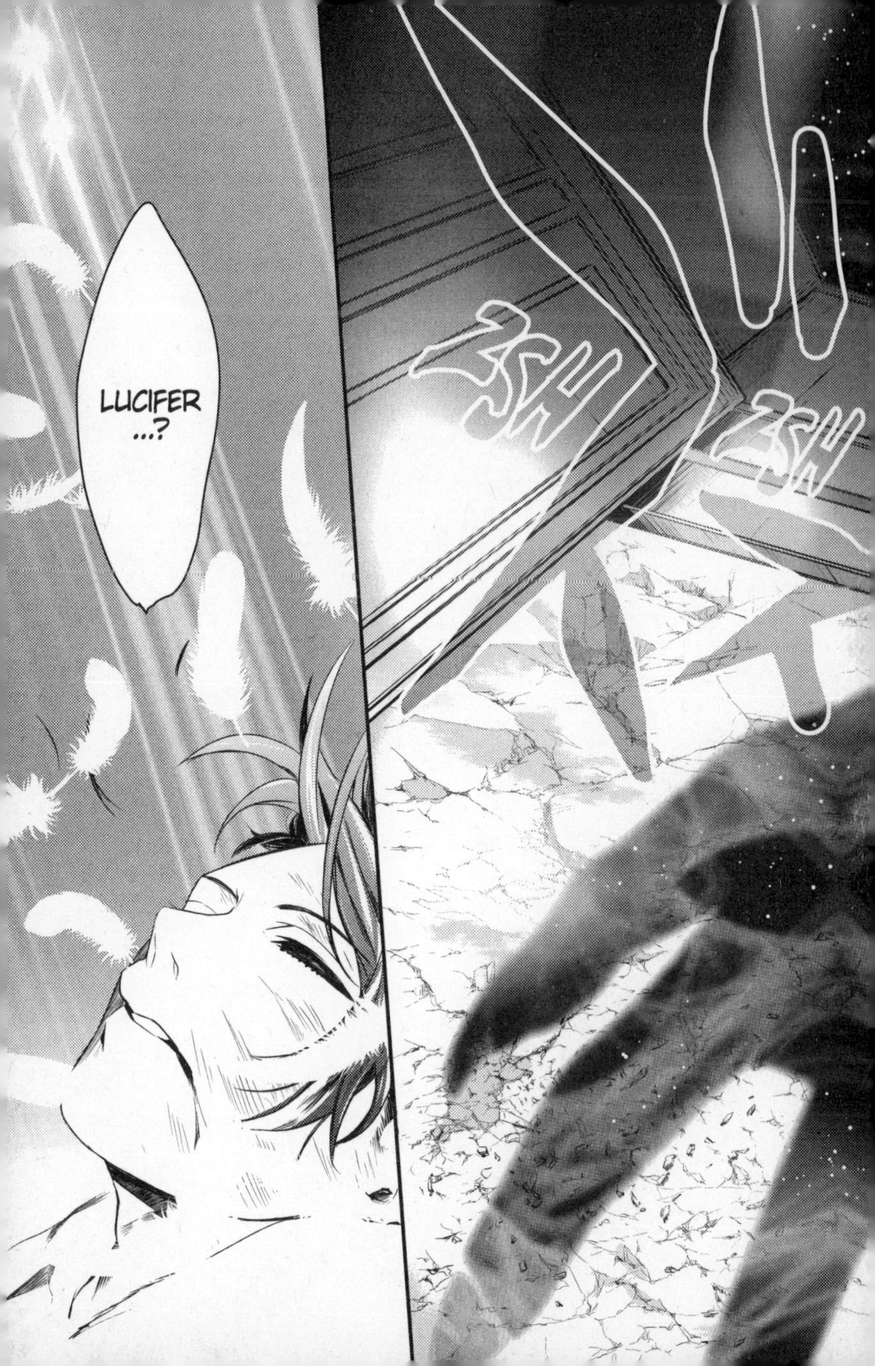
ZSH
ZSH
LUCIFER ...?

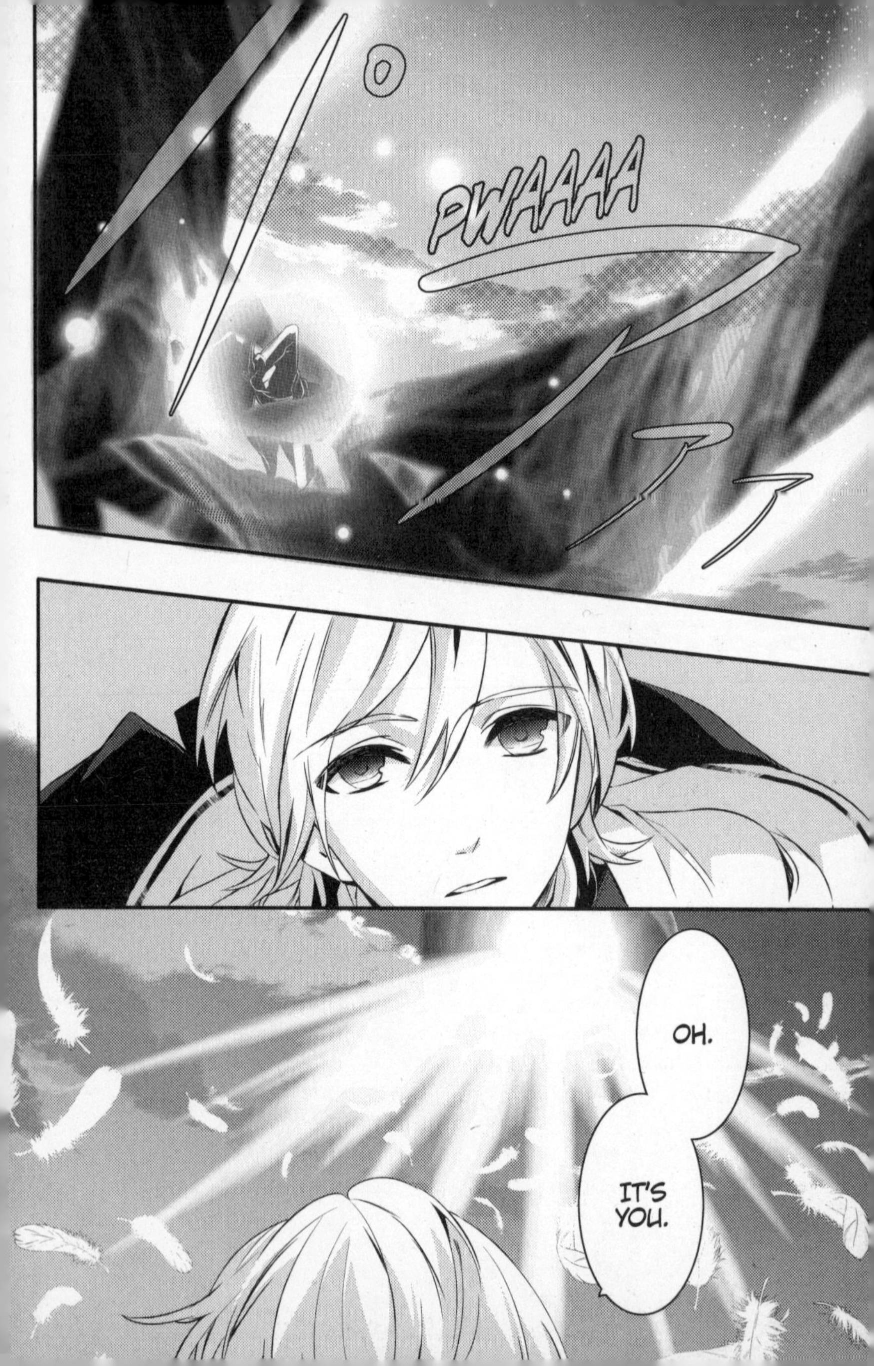
PWAAAA
OH.
IT'S YOU.

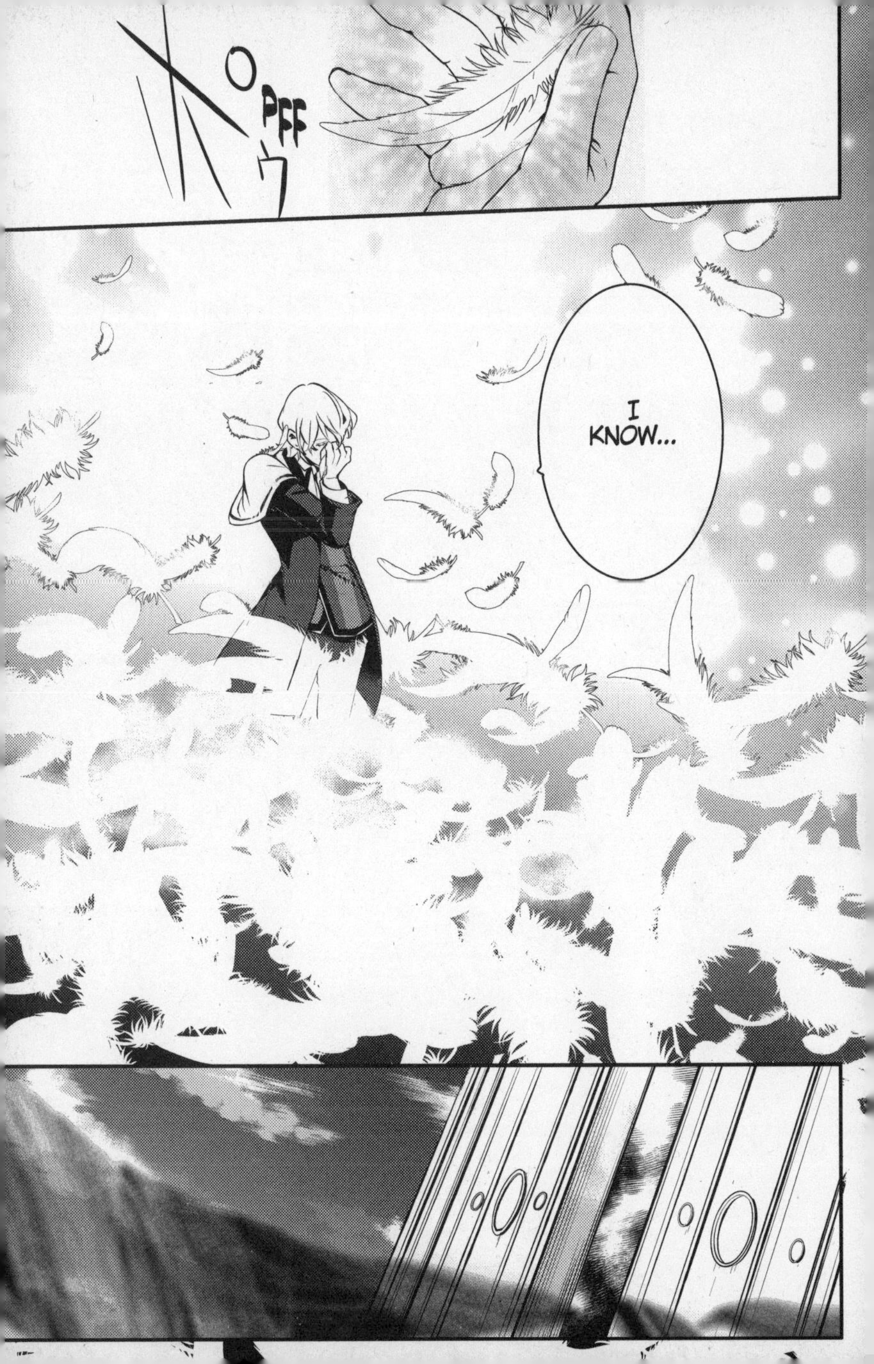
PFF
ウ
I KNOW...

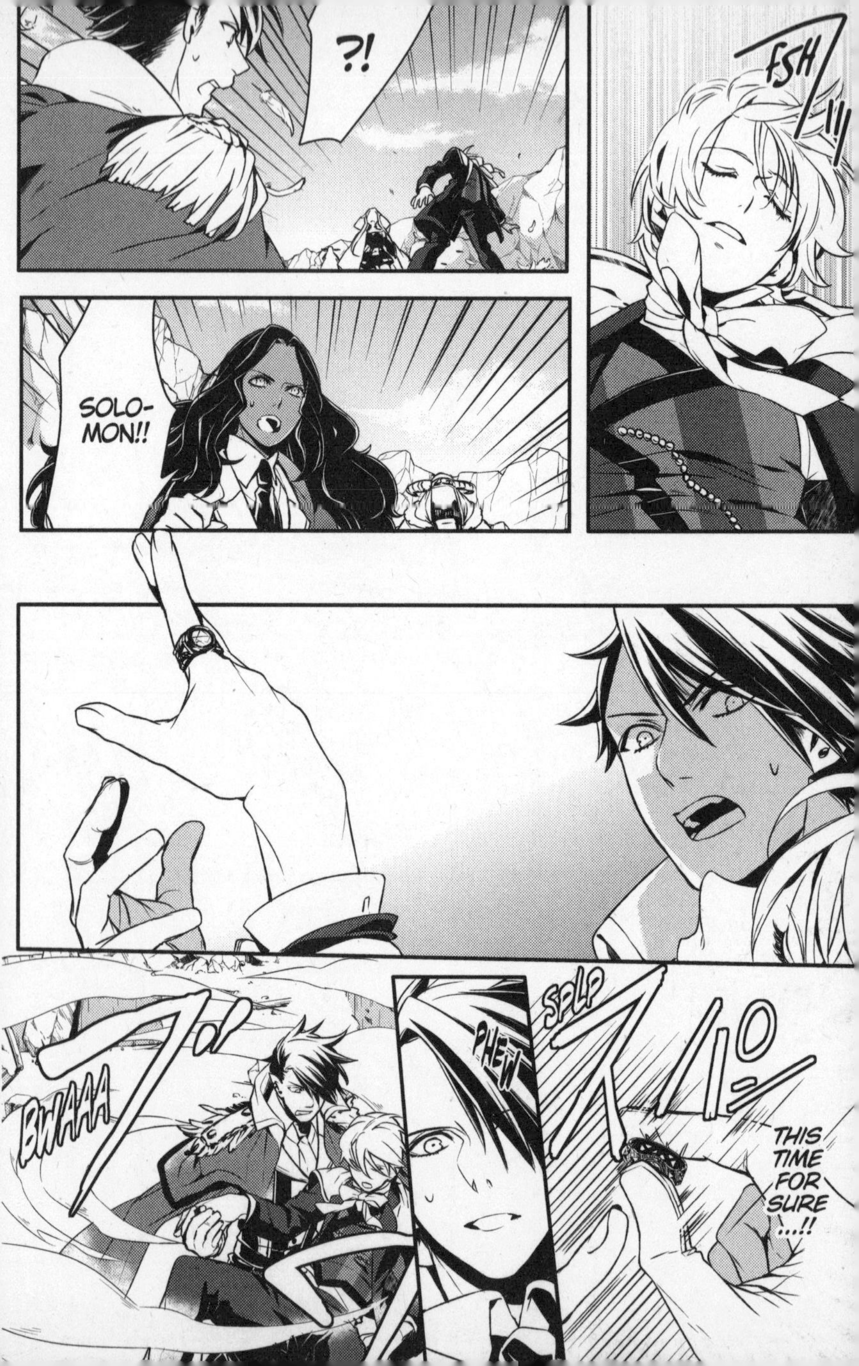
FSH
!!
?!
SOLO-
MON!!
SPLP
THIS TIME FOR SURE...!!
PHEW
BWAAA

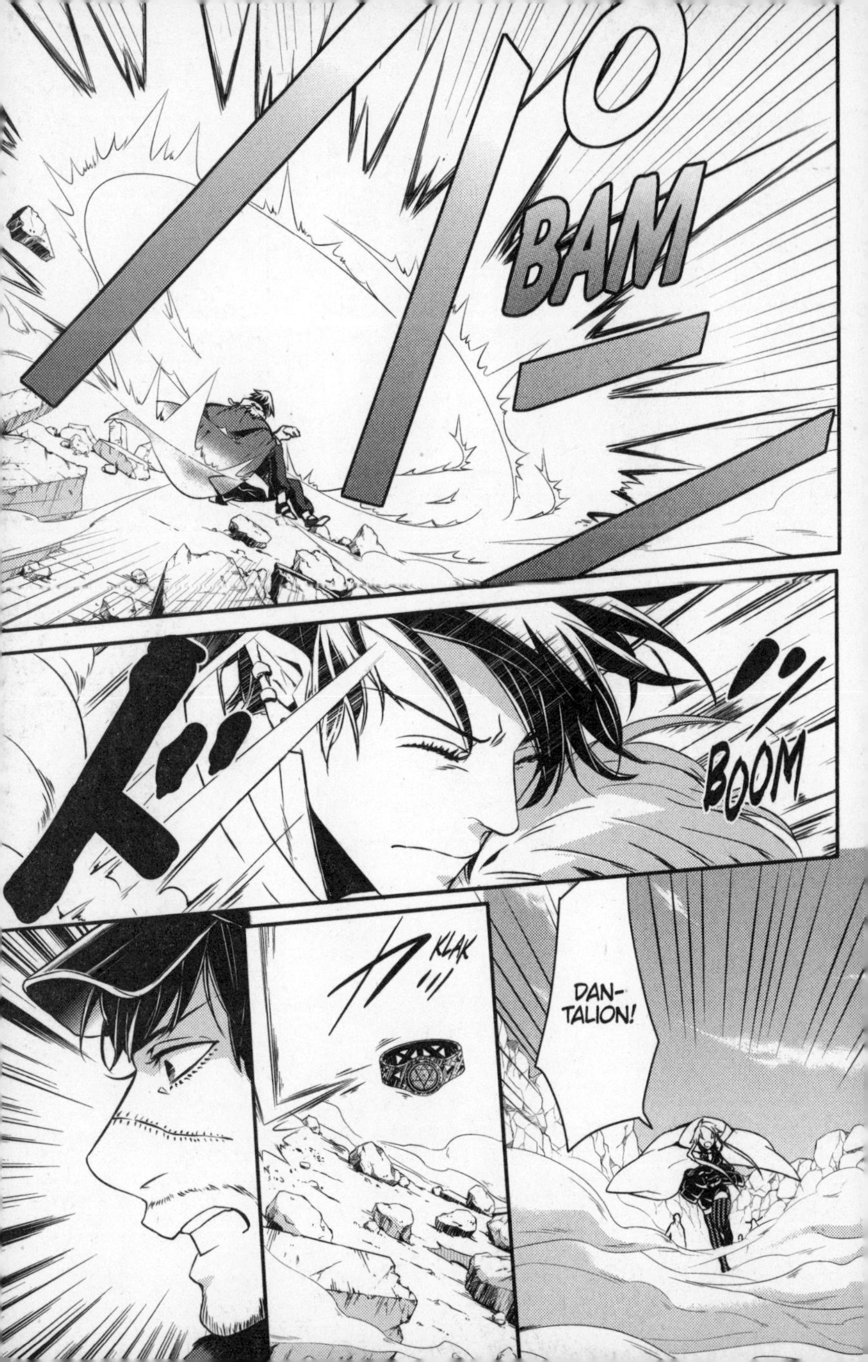
BAM
BOOM
DAN-
TALION!
KLAK

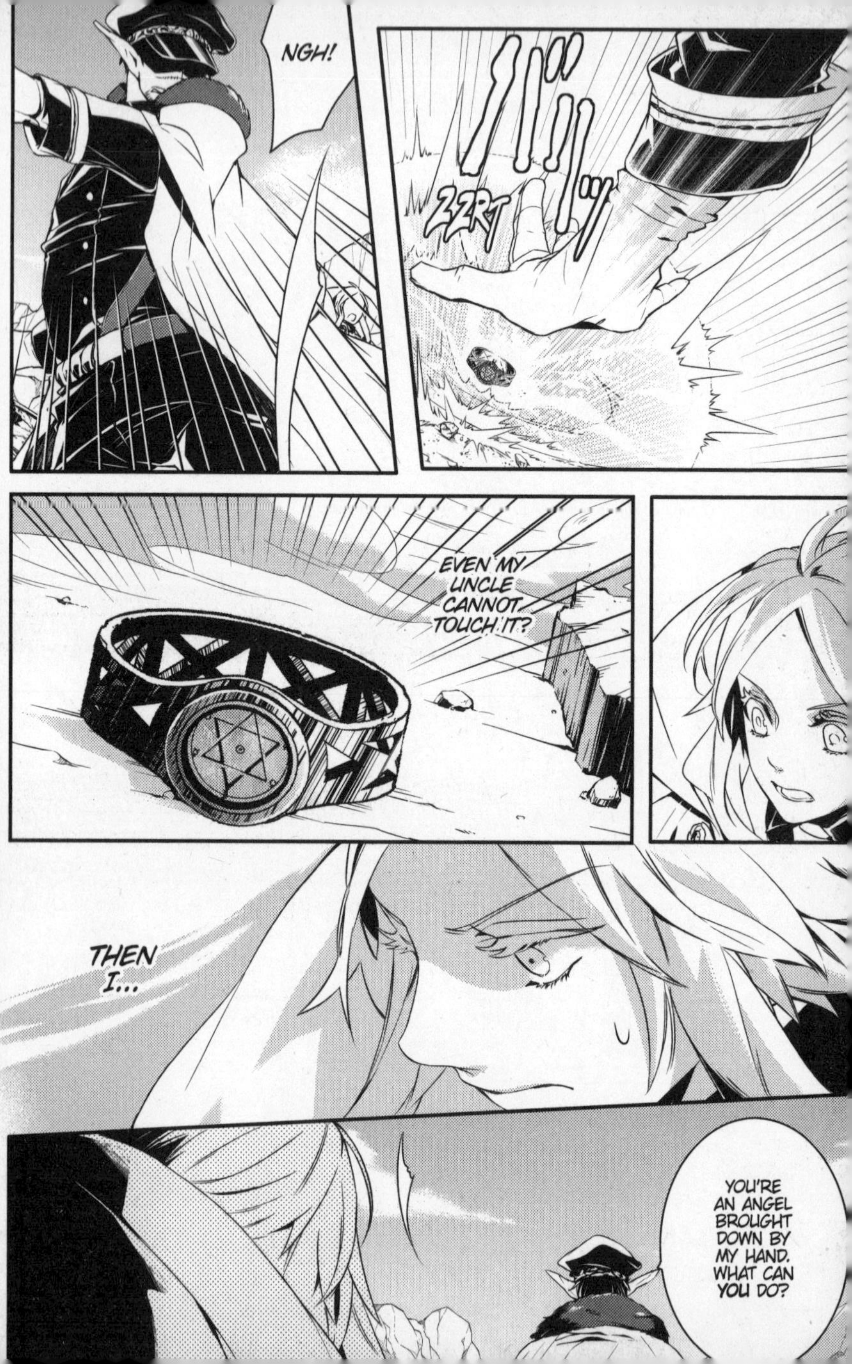
ZZRT
NGH!
EVEN MY UNCLE CANNOT TOUCH IT?
THEN I...
YOU'RE AN ANGEL BROUGHT DOWN BY MY HAND. WHAT CAN YOU DO?

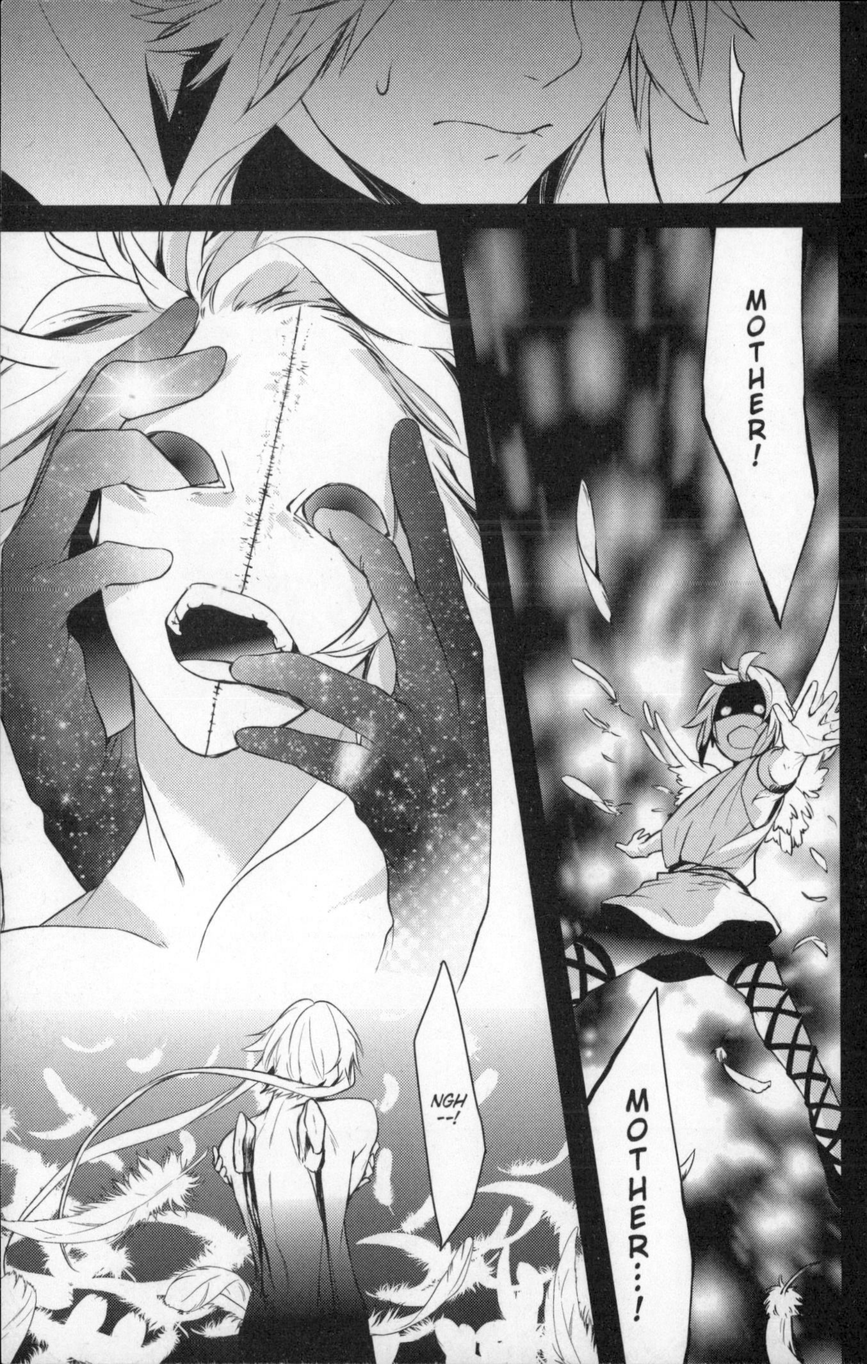
MOTHER!
MOTHER...!
NGH --!

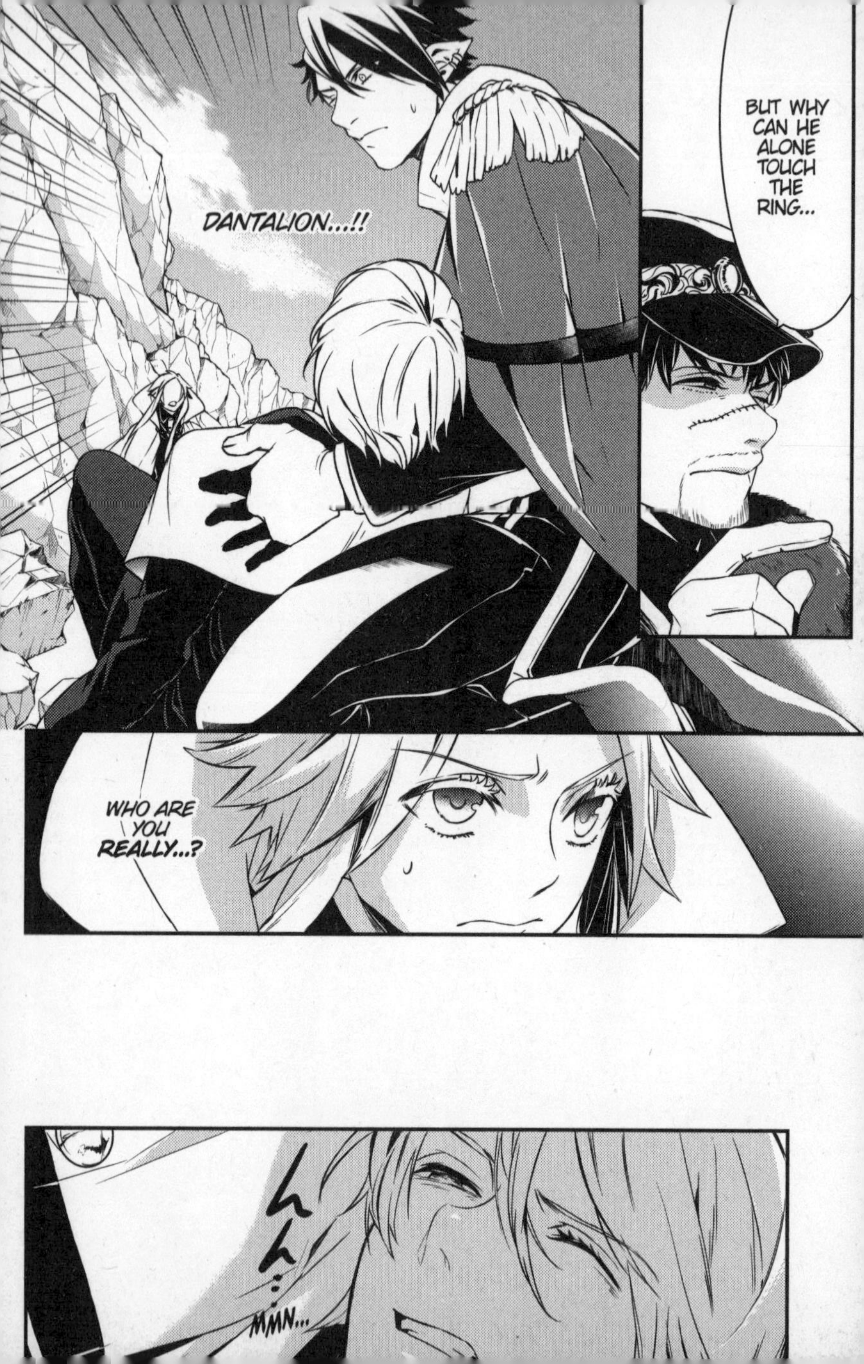
BUT WHY CAN HE ALONE TOUCH THE RING...
DANTALION...!!
WHO ARE YOU REALLY...?
MMN...

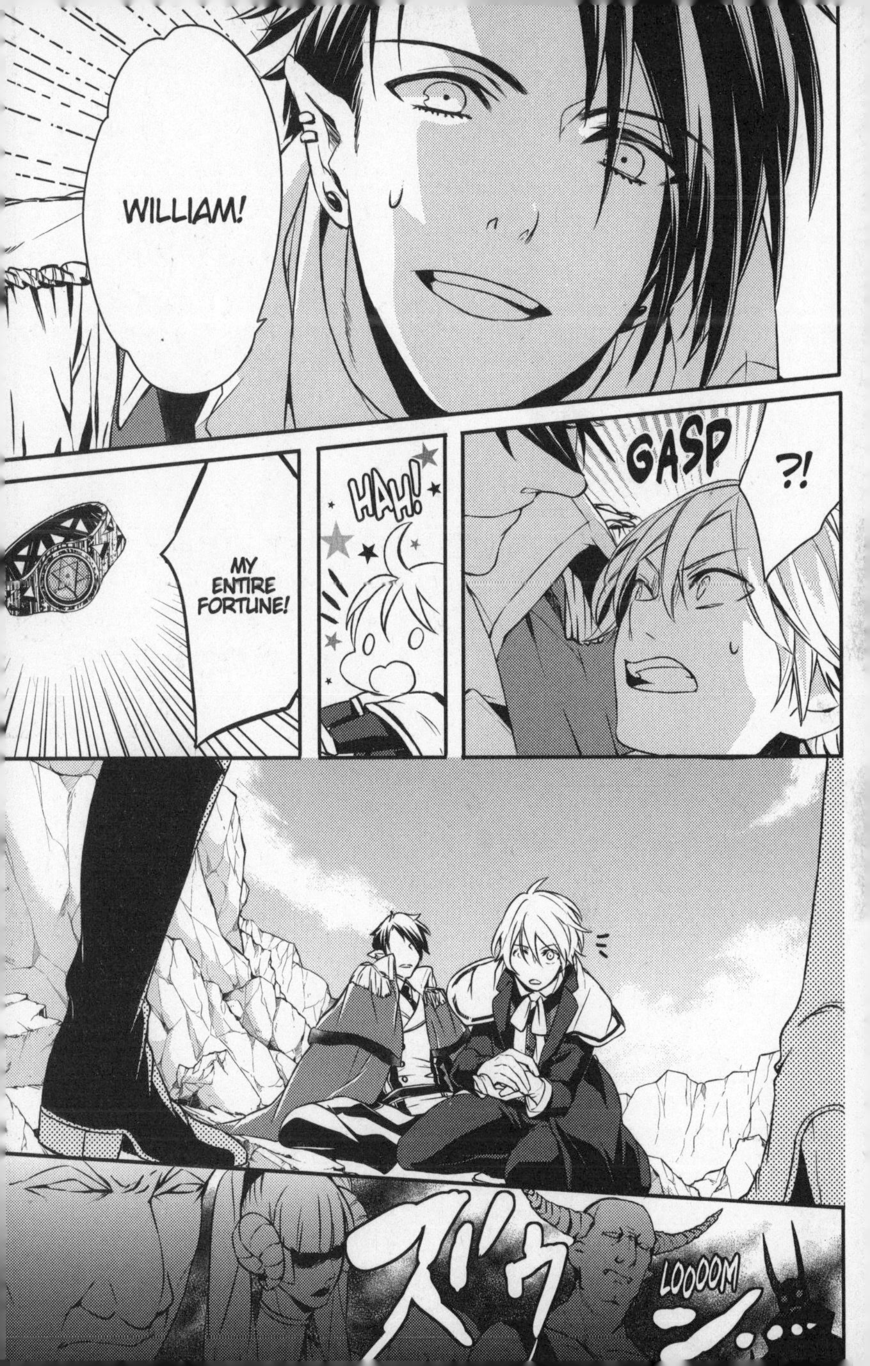
WILLIAM!
GASP
?!
HAH!
MY ENTIRE FORTUNE!
ズゥ
LOOOM
ン…

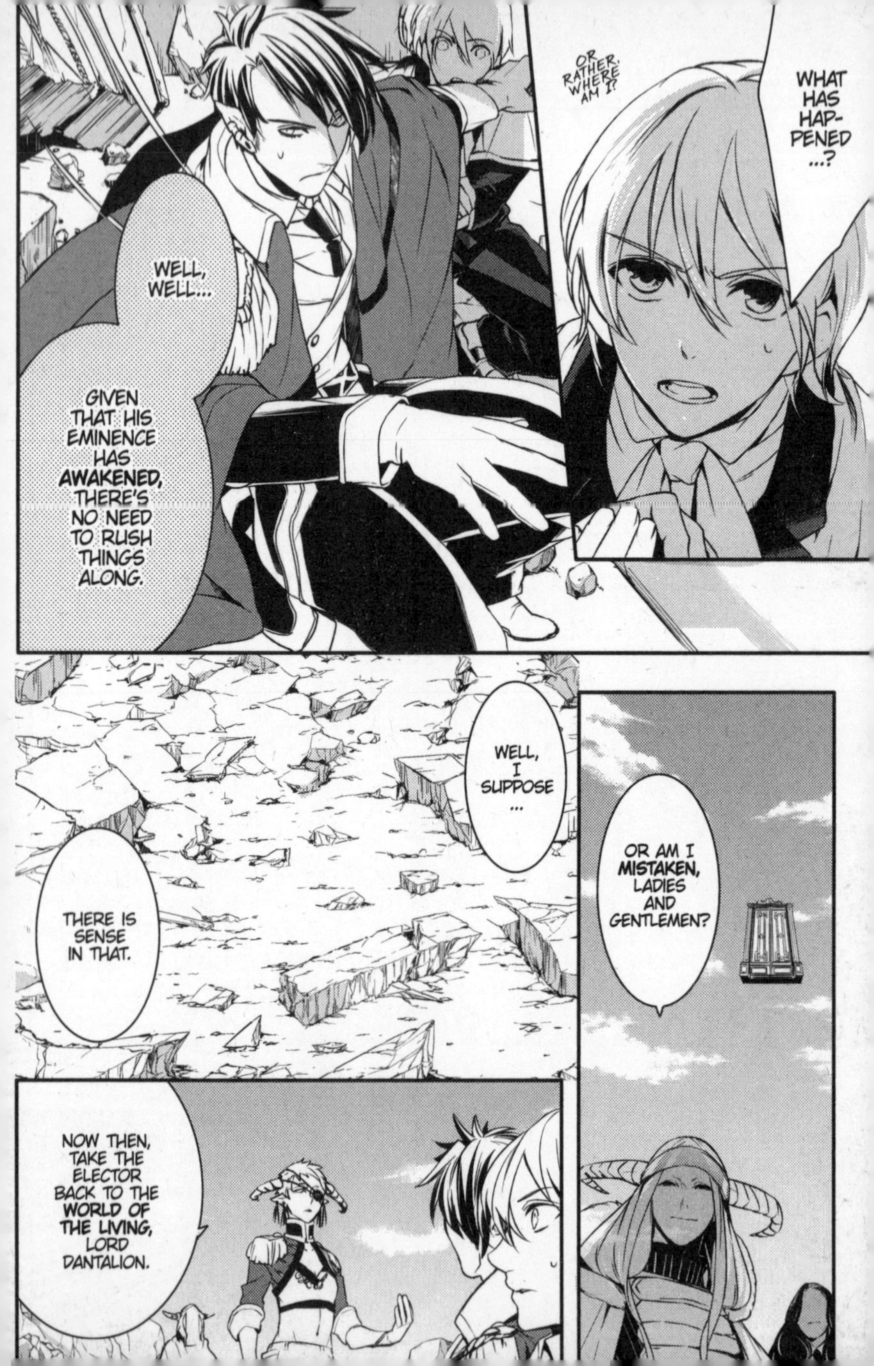
WHAT HAS HAP-PENED ...?
OR RATHER, WHERE AM I?
WELL, WELL...
GIVEN THAT HIS EMINENCE HAS AWAKENED, THERE'S NO NEED TO RUSH THINGS ALONG.
OR AM I MISTAKEN, LADIES AND GENTLEMEN?
WELL, I SUPPOSE ...
THERE IS SENSE IN THAT.
NOW THEN, TAKE THE ELECTOR BACK TO THE WORLD OF THE LIVING, LORD DANTALION.

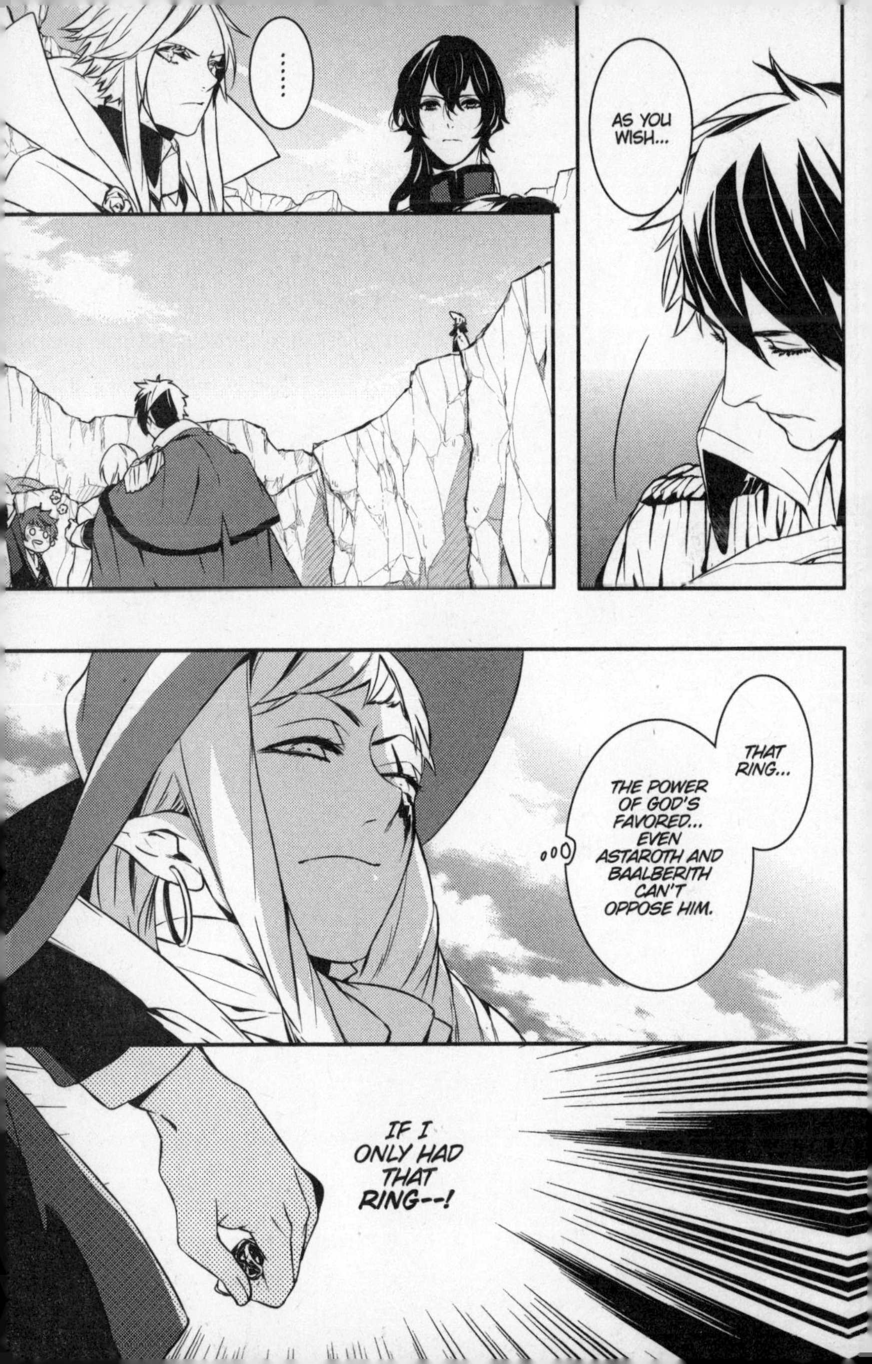
AS YOU WISH...
......
THAT RING... THE POWER OF GOD'S FAVORED... EVEN ASTAROTH AND BAALBERITH CAN'T OPPOSE HIM.
IF I ONLY HAD THAT RING--!

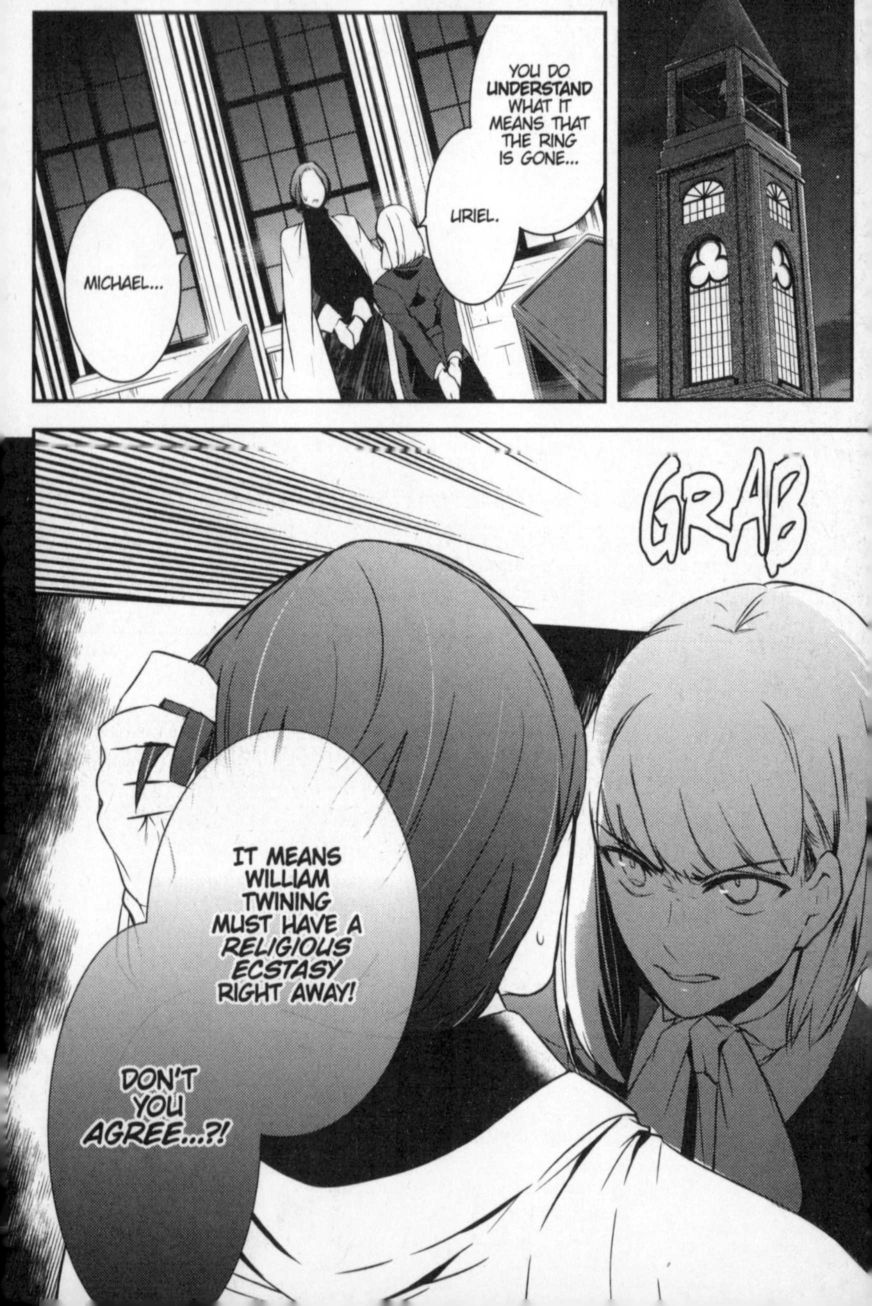
YOU DO UNDERSTAND WHAT IT MEANS THAT THE RING IS GONE...
URIEL.
MICHAEL...
GRAB
IT MEANS WILLIAM TWINING MUST HAVE A RELIGIOUS ECSTASY RIGHT AWAY!
DON'T YOU AGREE...?!

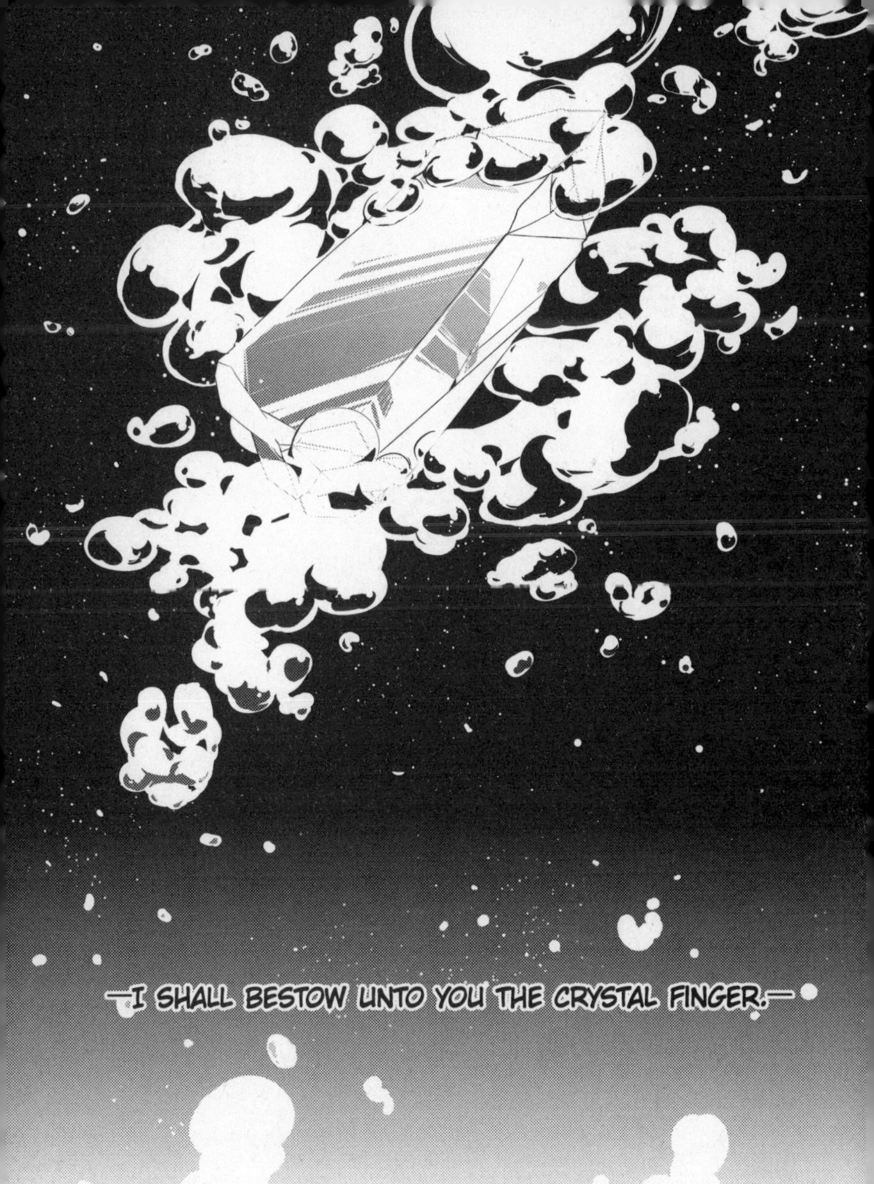
—I SHALL BESTOW UNTO YOU THE CRYSTAL FINGER.—

Pillar 30

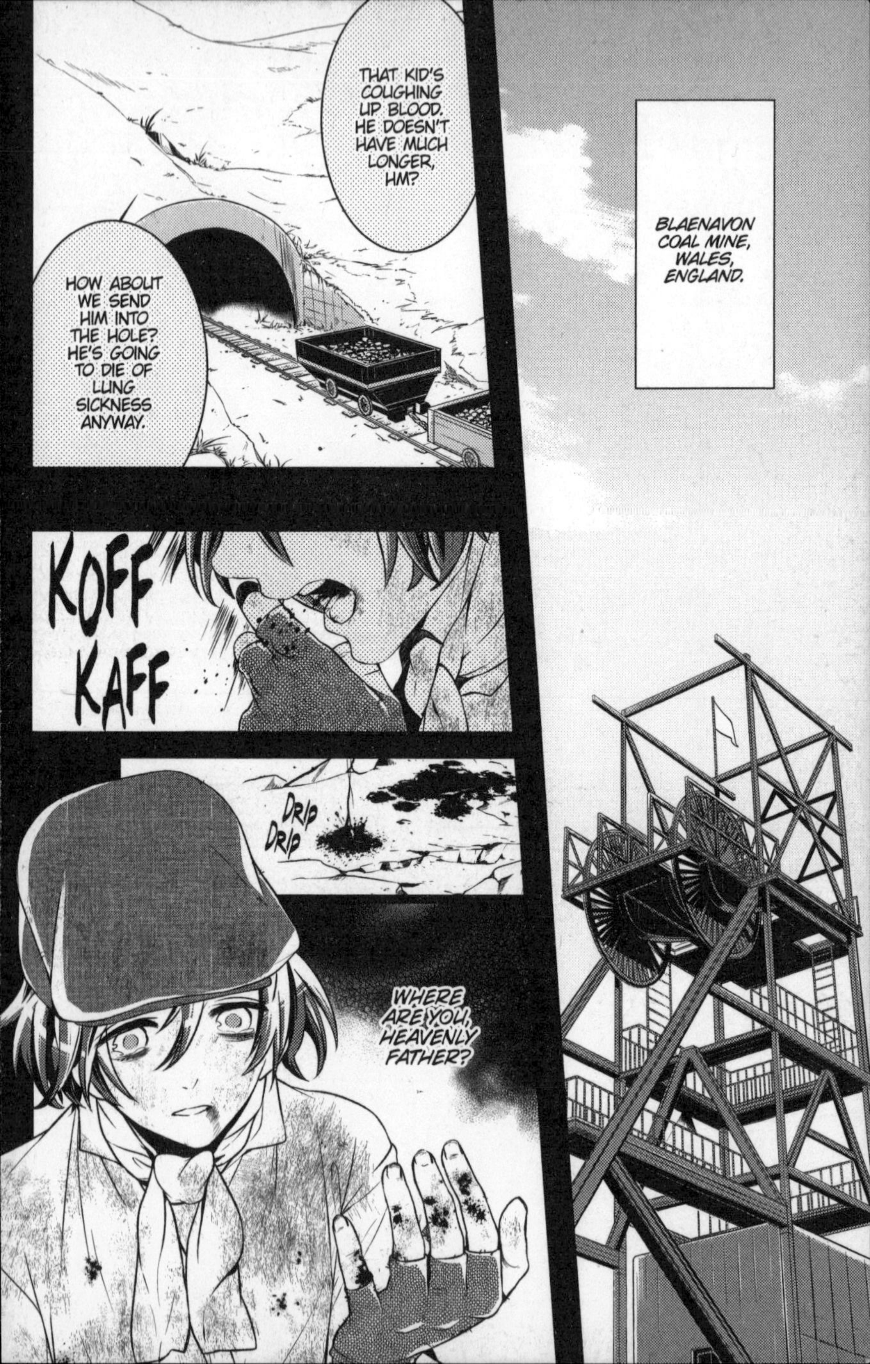
BLAENAVON COAL MINE, WALES, ENGLAND.
THAT KID'S COUGHING UP BLOOD. HE DOESN'T HAVE MUCH LONGER, HM?
HOW ABOUT WE SEND HIM INTO THE HOLE? HE'S GOING TO DIE OF LUNG SICKNESS ANYWAY.
KOFF KAFF
DRIP DRIP
WHERE ARE YOU, HEAVENLY FATHER?

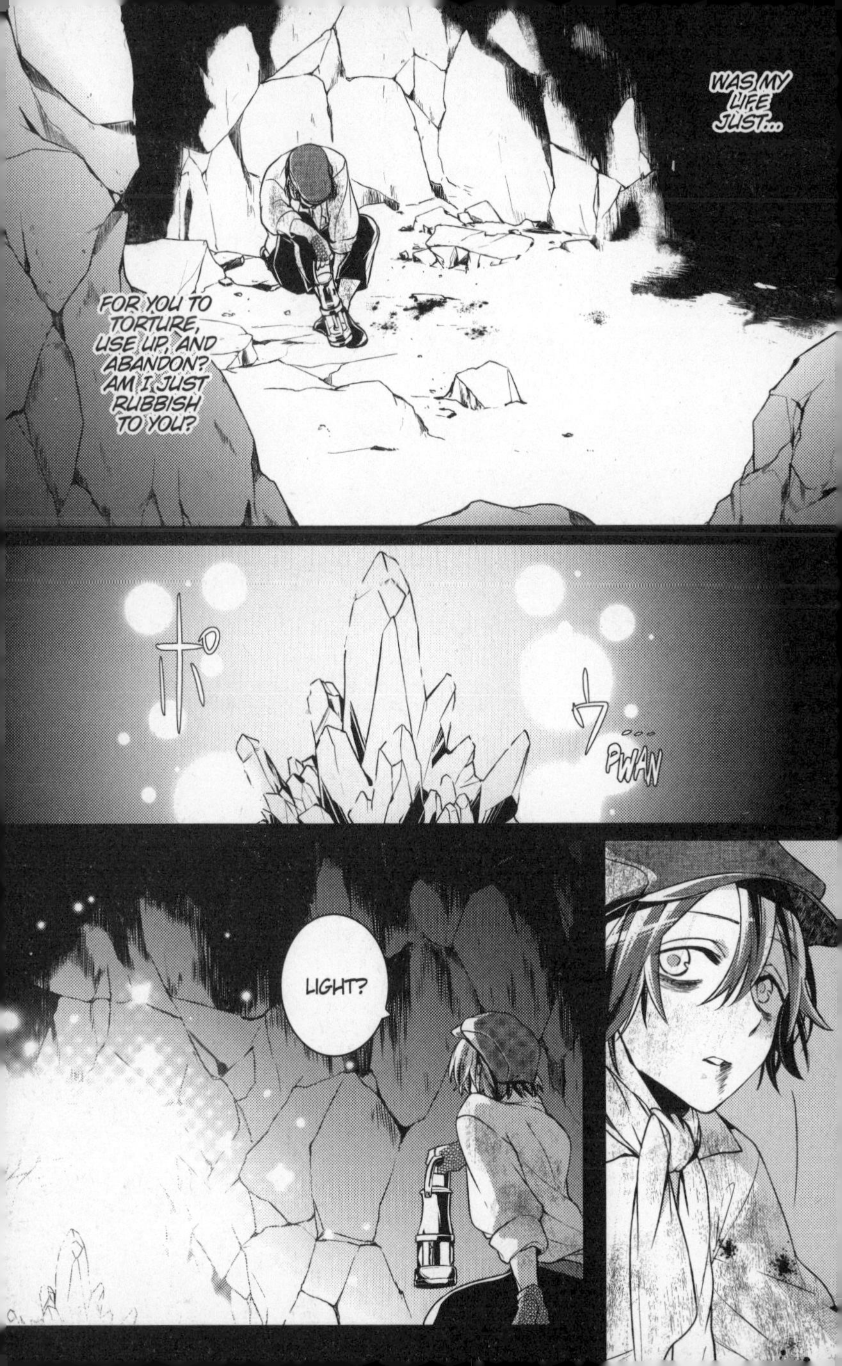
WAS MY LIFE JUST...
FOR YOU TO TORTURE, USE UP, AND ABANDON? AM I JUST RUBBISH TO YOU?
PWAN
LIGHT?

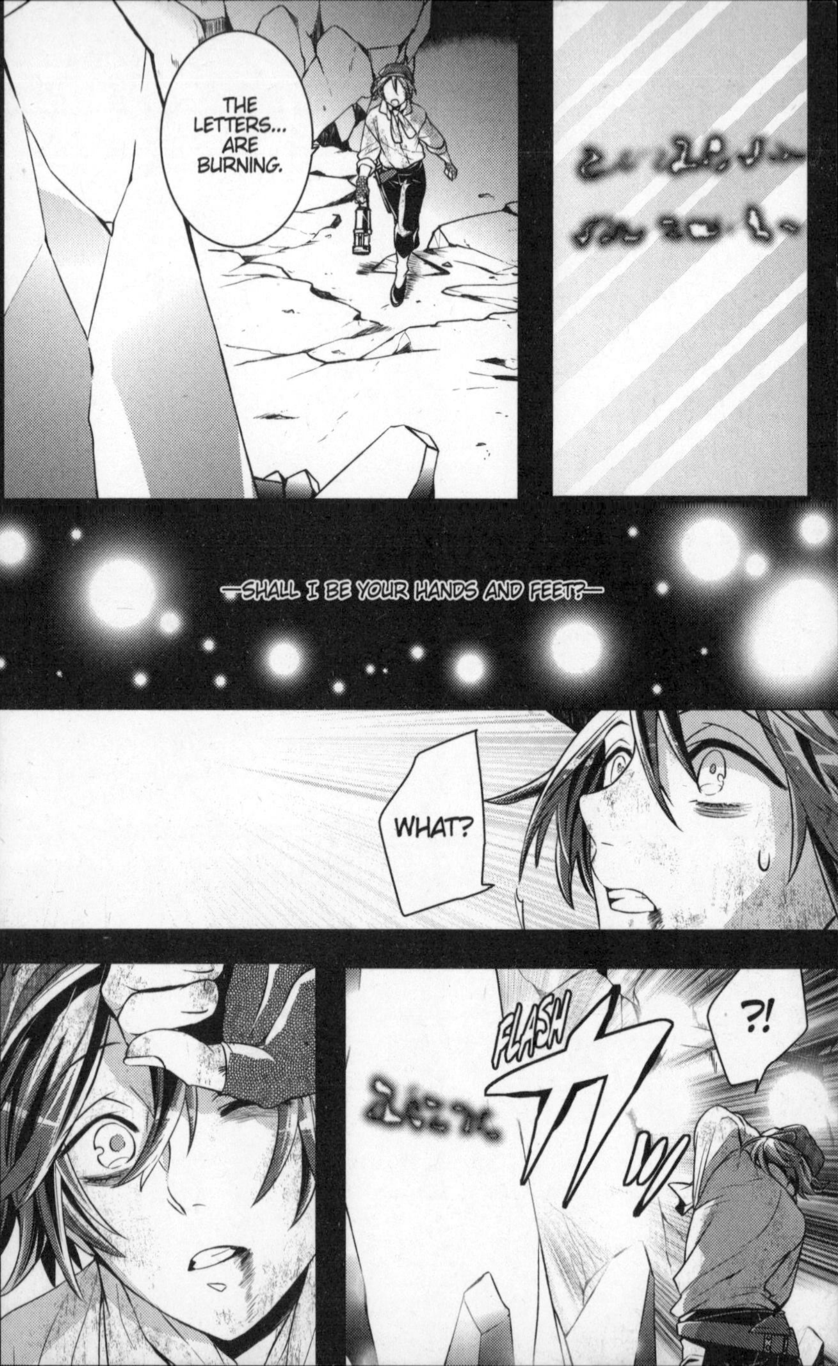
THE LETTERS... ARE BURNING.
—SHALL I BE YOUR HANDS AND FEET?—
WHAT?
?!
FLASH

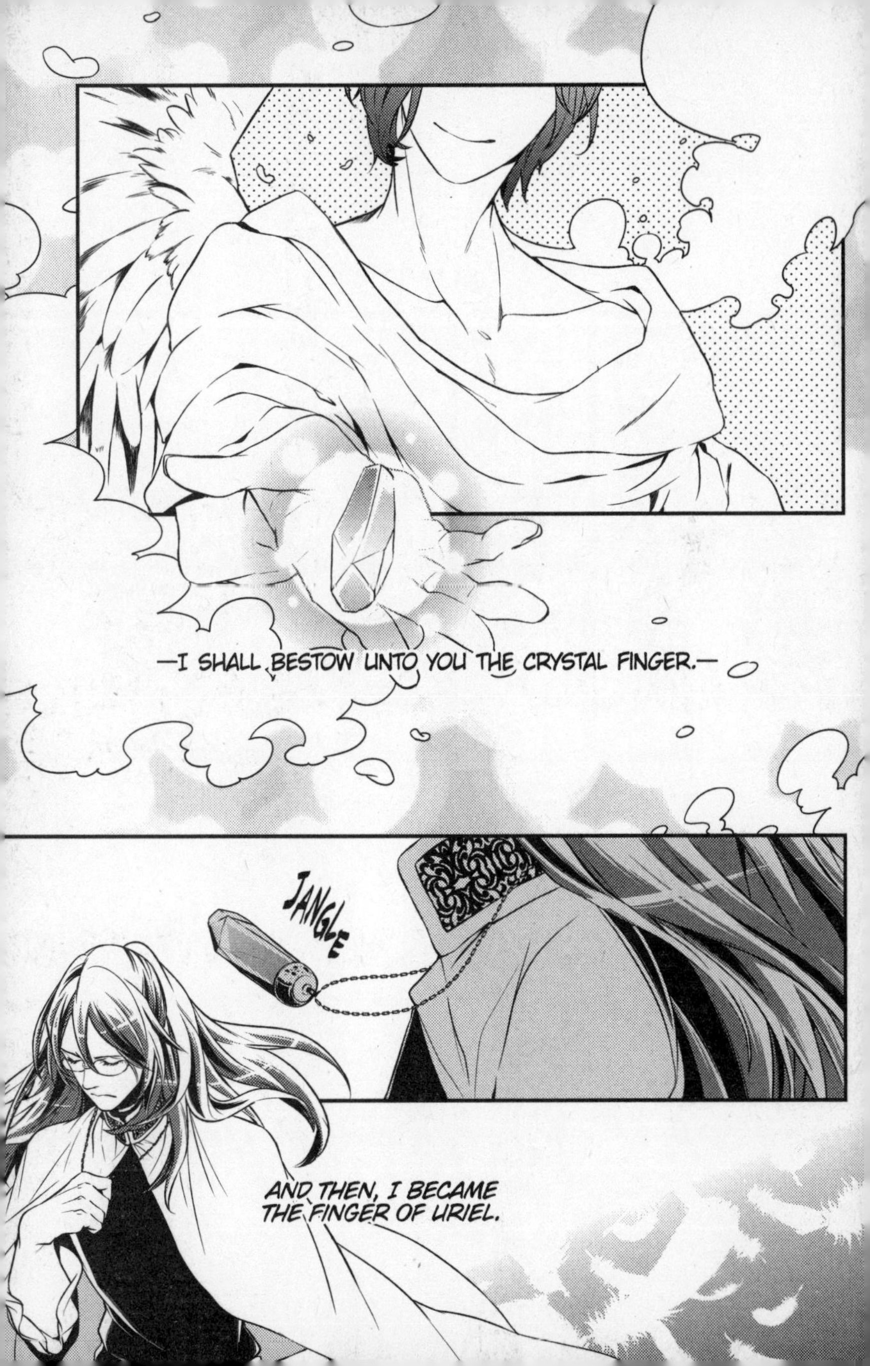
—I SHALL BESTOW UNTO YOU THE CRYSTAL FINGER.—
JANGLE
AND THEN, I BECAME THE FINGER OF URIEL.

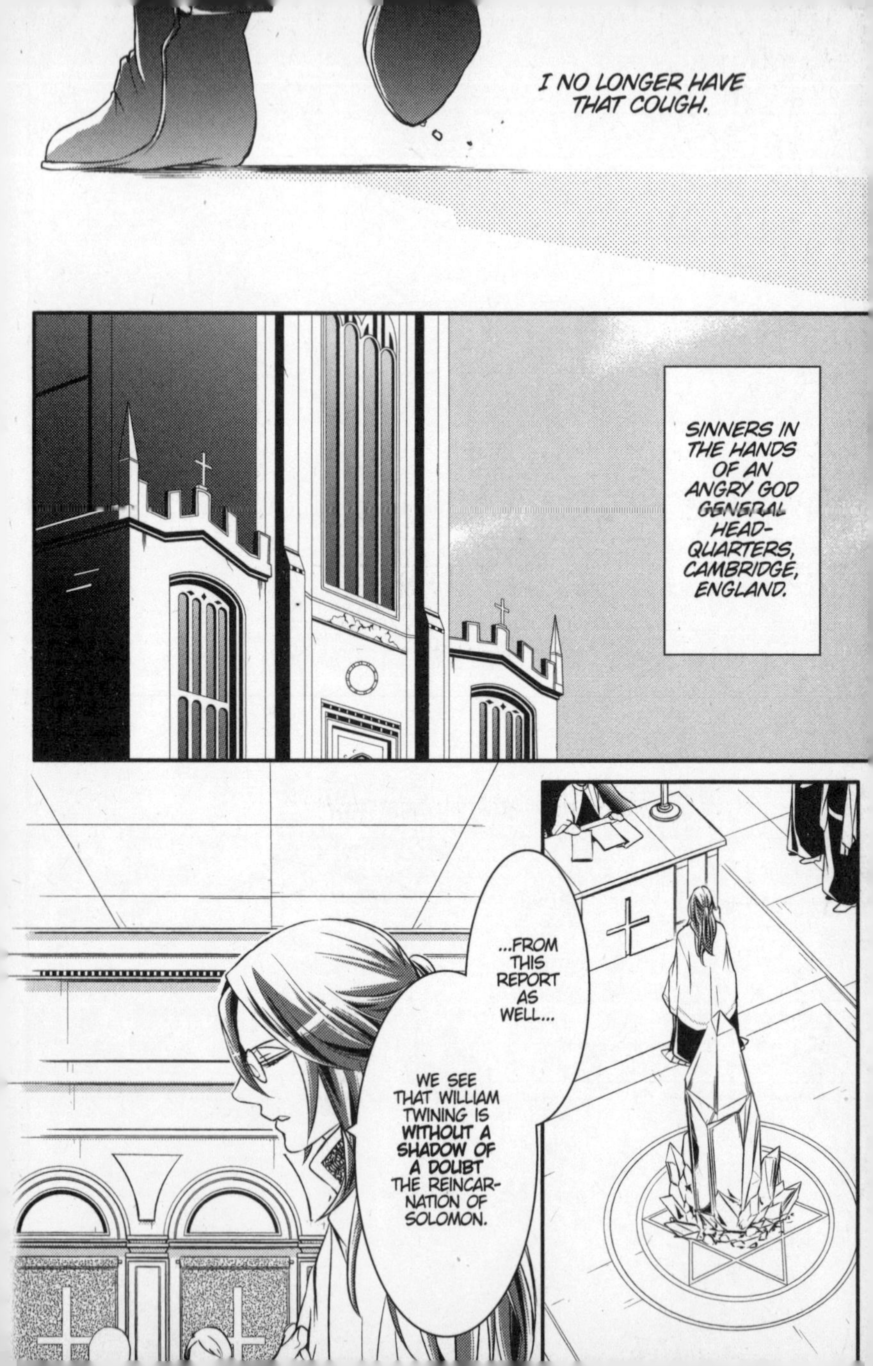
I NO LONGER HAVE THAT COUGH.
SINNERS IN THE HANDS OF AN ANGRY GOD GENERAL HEAD-QUARTERS, CAMBRIDGE, ENGLAND.
...FROM THIS REPORT AS WELL...
WE SEE THAT WILLIAM TWINING IS WITHOUT A SHADOW OF A DOUBT THE REINCAR-NATION OF SOLOMON.

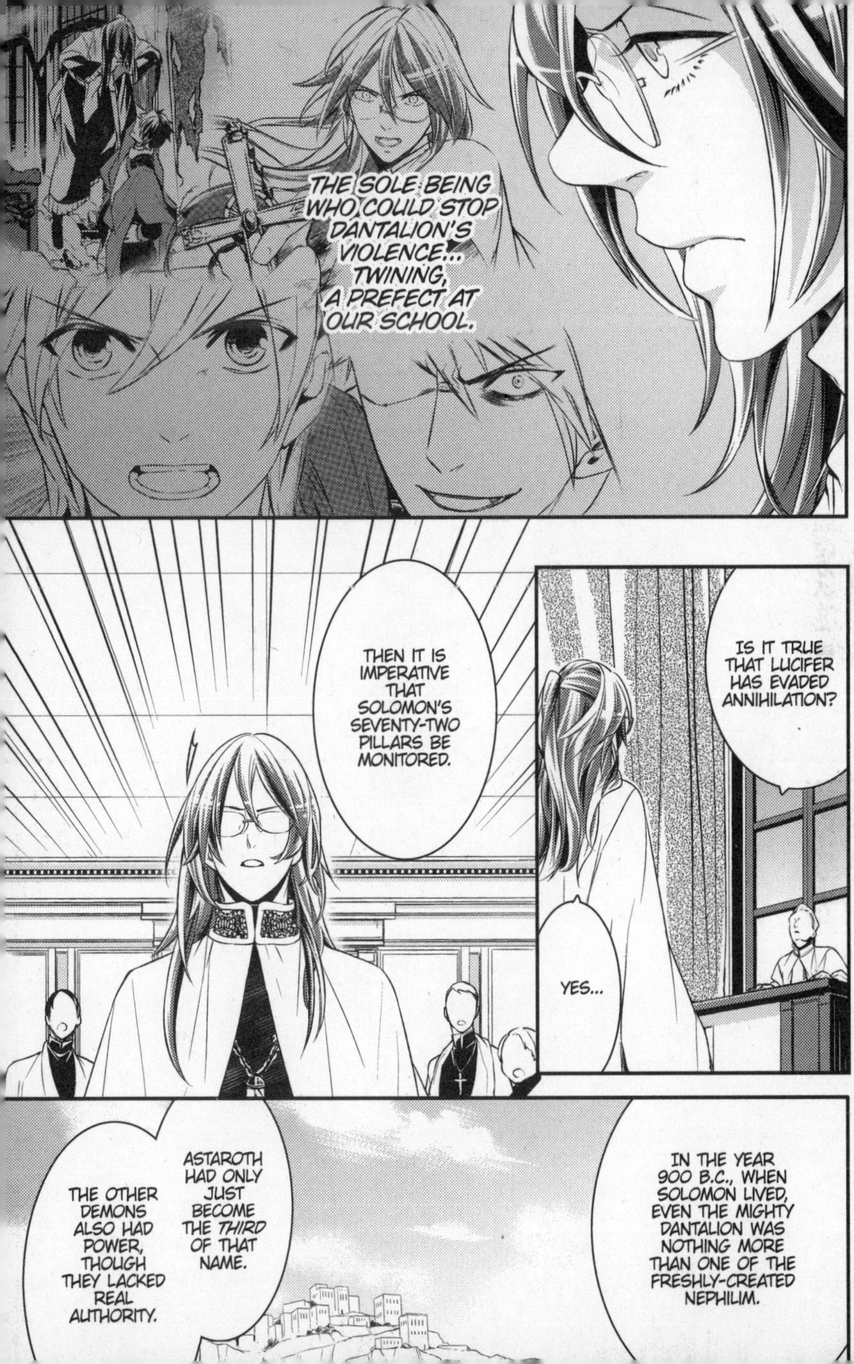
THE SOLE BEING WHO COULD STOP DANTALION'S VIOLENCE... TWINING, A PREFECT AT OUR SCHOOL.
IS IT TRUE THAT LUCIFER HAS EVADED ANNIHILATION?
YES...
THEN IT IS IMPERATIVE THAT SOLOMON'S SEVENTY-TWO PILLARS BE MONITORED.
IN THE YEAR 900 B.C., WHEN SOLOMON LIVED, EVEN THE MIGHTY DANTALION WAS NOTHING MORE THAN ONE OF THE FRESHLY-CREATED NEPHILIM.
ASTAROTH HAD ONLY JUST BECOME THE *THIRD* OF THAT NAME.
THE OTHER DEMONS ALSO HAD POWER, THOUGH THEY LACKED REAL AUTHORITY.

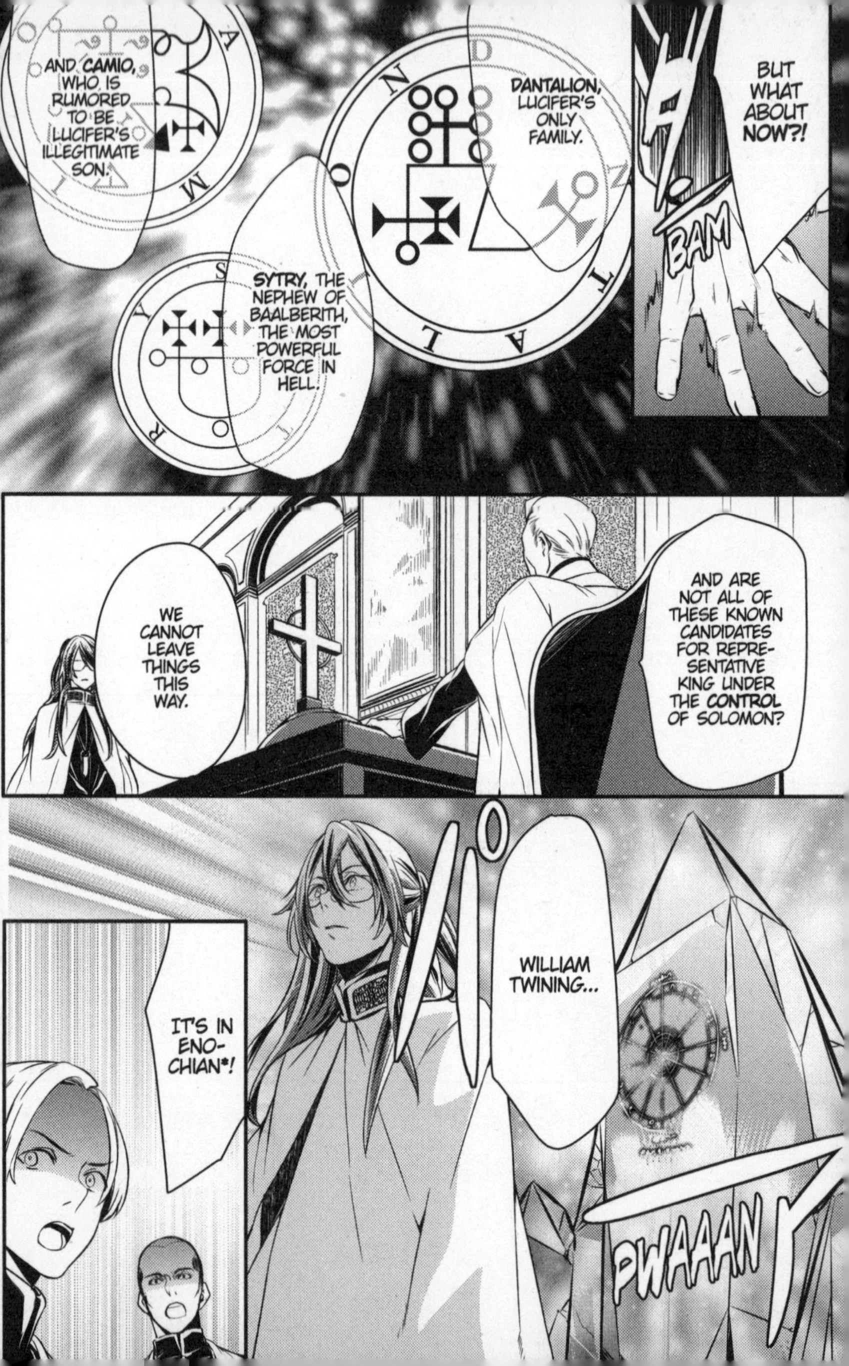
BUT WHAT ABOUT NOW?!
BAM
DANTALION, LUCIFER'S ONLY FAMILY.
AND CAMIO, WHO IS RUMORED TO BE LUCIFER'S ILLEGITIMATE SON.
SYTRY, THE NEPHEW OF BAALBERITH, THE MOST POWERFUL FORCE IN HELL.
AND ARE NOT ALL OF THESE KNOWN CANDIDATES FOR REPRE-SENTATIVE KING UNDER THE CONTROL OF SOLOMON?
WE CANNOT LEAVE THINGS THIS WAY.
WILLIAM TWINING...
PWAAAN
IT'S IN ENO-CHIAN*!

*The language of angels.

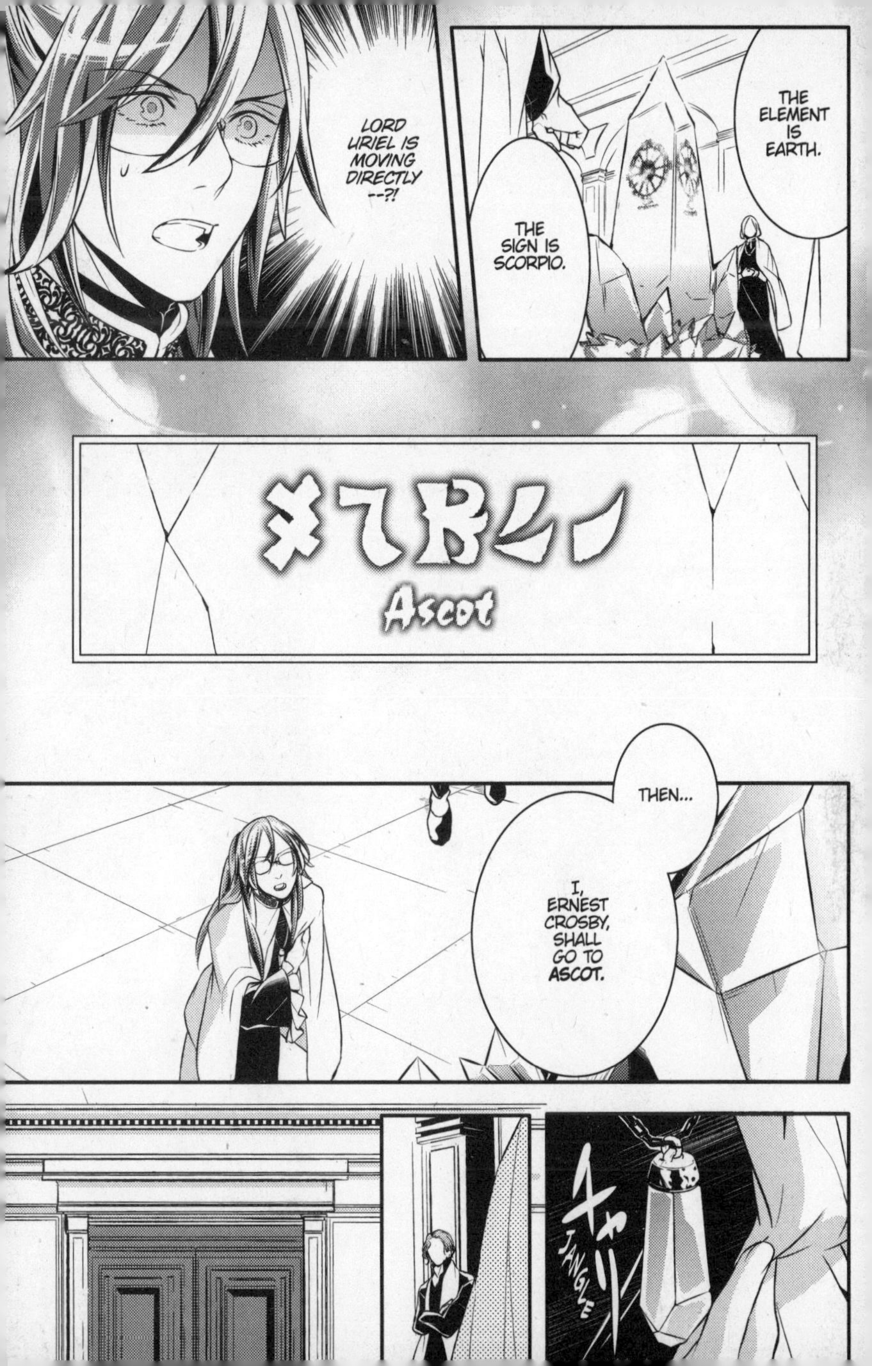
THE ELEMENT IS EARTH.
THE SIGN IS SCORPIO.
LORD URIEL IS MOVING DIRECTLY --?!
Ascot
THEN...
I, ERNEST CROSBY, SHALL GO TO ASCOT.
JANGLE

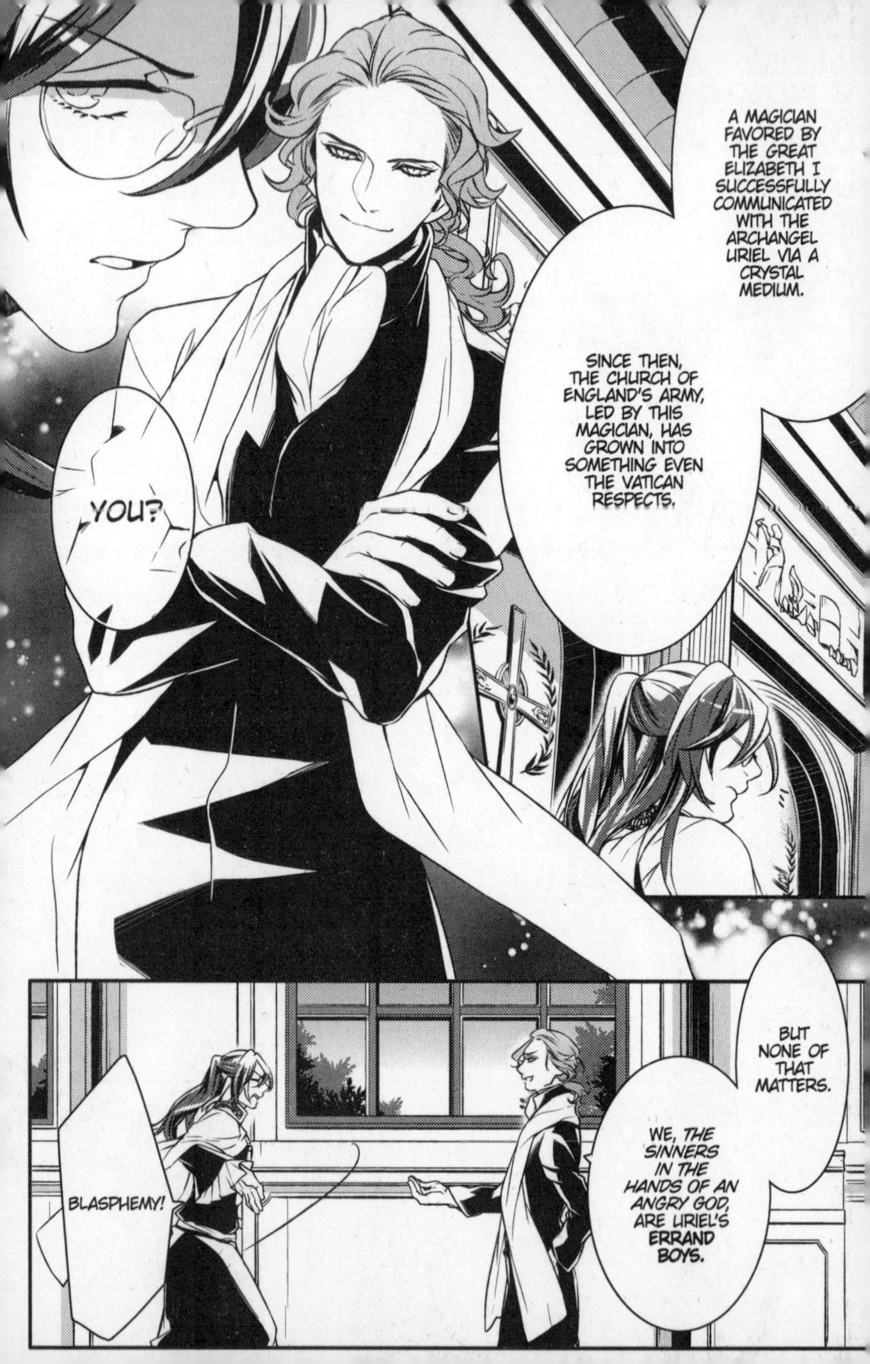
A MAGICIAN FAVORED BY THE GREAT ELIZABETH I SUCCESSFULLY COMMUNICATED WITH THE ARCHANGEL URIEL VIA A CRYSTAL MEDIUM.
SINCE THEN, THE CHURCH OF ENGLAND'S ARMY, LED BY THIS MAGICIAN, HAS GROWN INTO SOMETHING EVEN THE VATICAN RESPECTS.
YOU?
BUT NONE OF THAT MATTERS.
WE, THE SINNERS IN THE HANDS OF AN ANGRY GOD, ARE URIEL'S ERRAND BOYS.
BLASPHEMY!

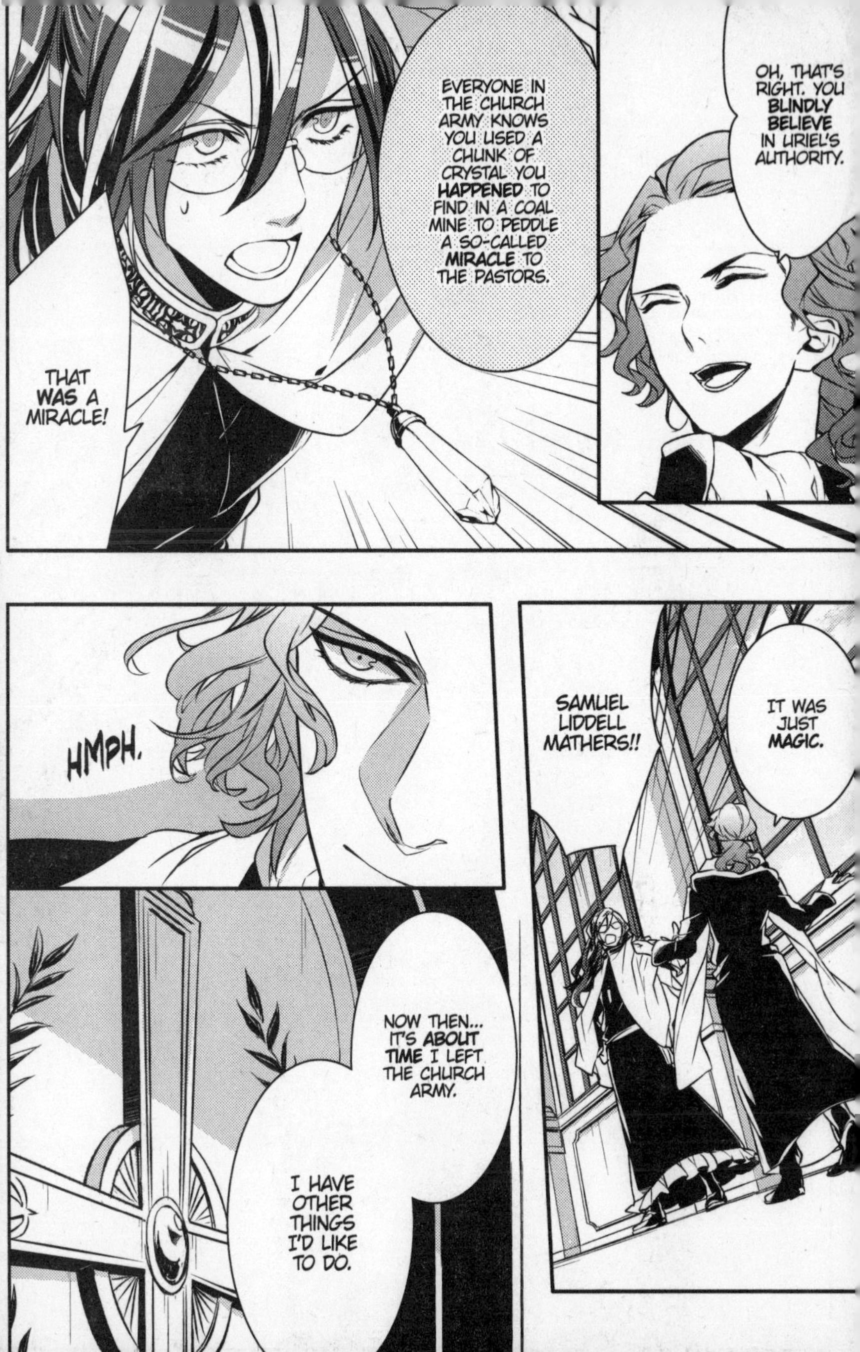
OH, THAT'S RIGHT. YOU BLINDLY BELIEVE IN URIEL'S AUTHORITY.
EVERYONE IN THE CHURCH ARMY KNOWS YOU USED A CHUNK OF CRYSTAL YOU HAPPENED TO FIND IN A COAL MINE TO PEDDLE A SO-CALLED MIRACLE TO THE PASTORS.
THAT WAS A MIRACLE!
IT WAS JUST MAGIC.
SAMUEL LIDDELL MATHERS!!
HMPH.
NOW THEN... IT'S ABOUT TIME I LEFT THE CHURCH ARMY.
I HAVE OTHER THINGS I'D LIKE TO DO.

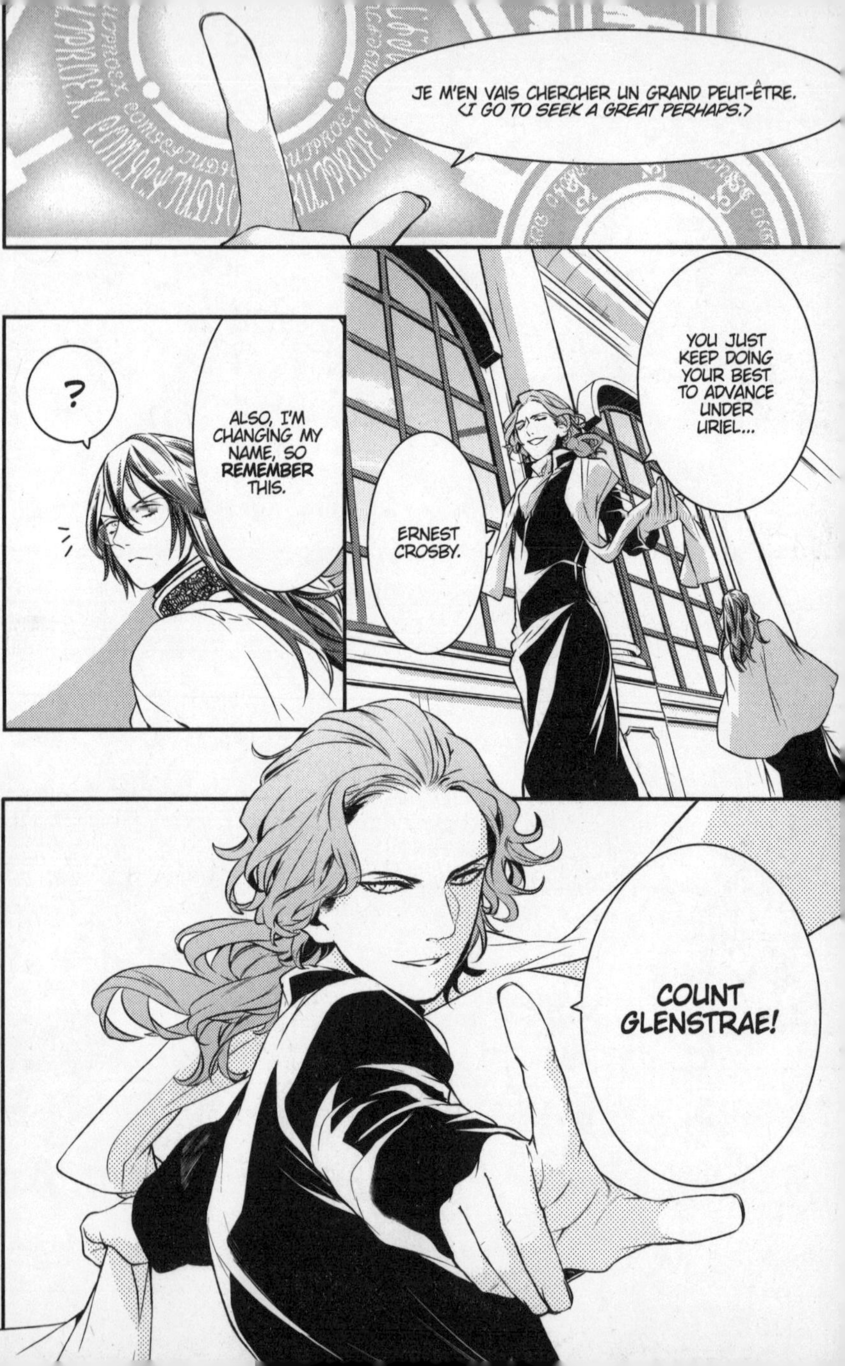

JE M'EN VAIS CHERCHER UN GRAND PEUT-ÊTRE. <I GO TO SEEK A GREAT PERHAPS.>
YOU JUST KEEP DOING YOUR BEST TO ADVANCE UNDER URIEL...
ERNEST CROSBY.
ALSO, I'M CHANGING MY NAME, SO REMEMBER THIS.
?
COUNT GLENSTRAE!

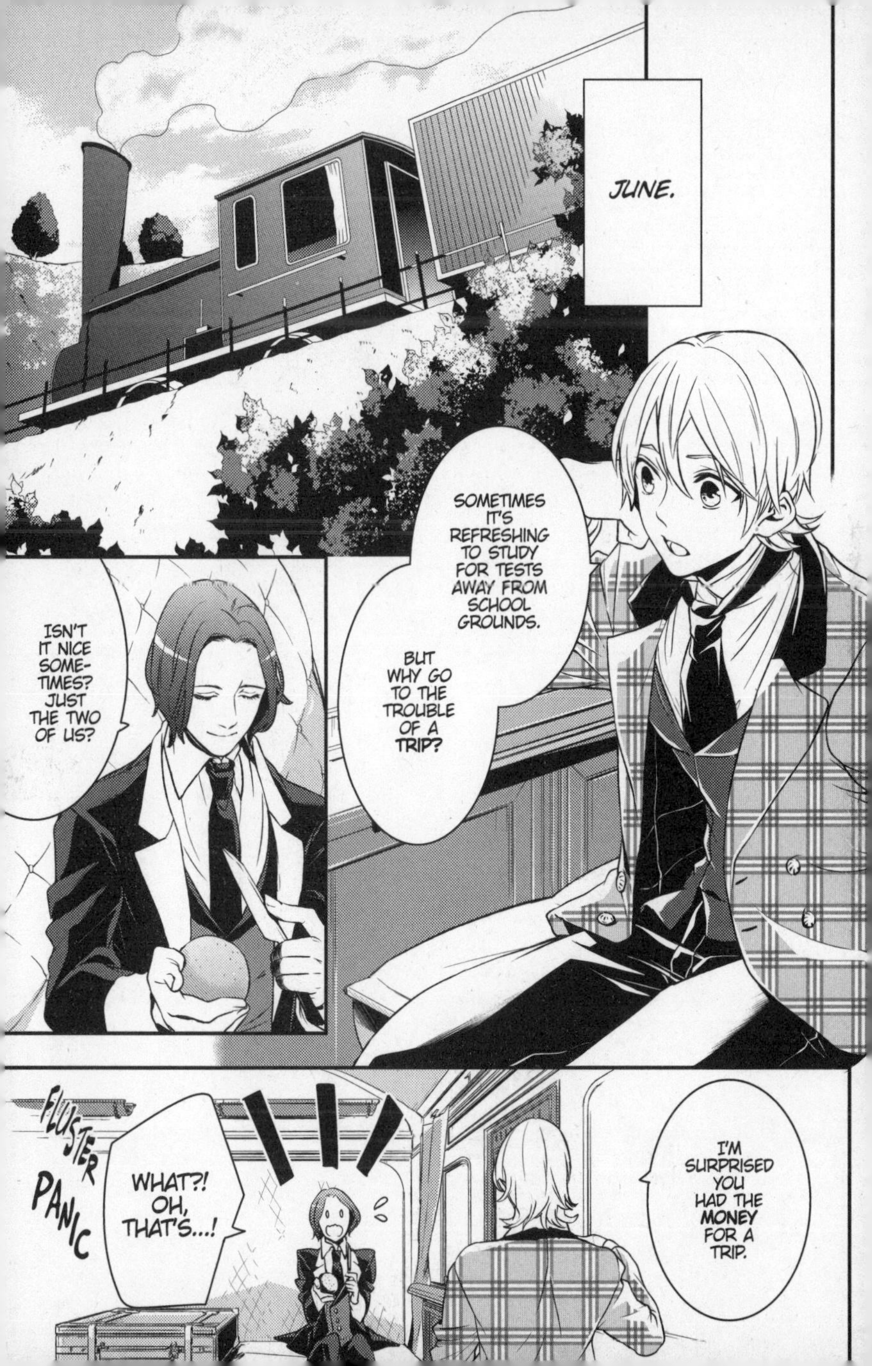
JUNE.
SOMETIMES IT'S REFRESHING TO STUDY FOR TESTS AWAY FROM SCHOOL GROUNDS.
BUT WHY GO TO THE TROUBLE OF A TRIP?
ISN'T IT NICE SOME-TIMES? JUST THE TWO OF US?
I'M SURPRISED YOU HAD THE MONEY FOR A TRIP.
WHAT?! OH, THAT'S...!
FLUSTER
PANIC

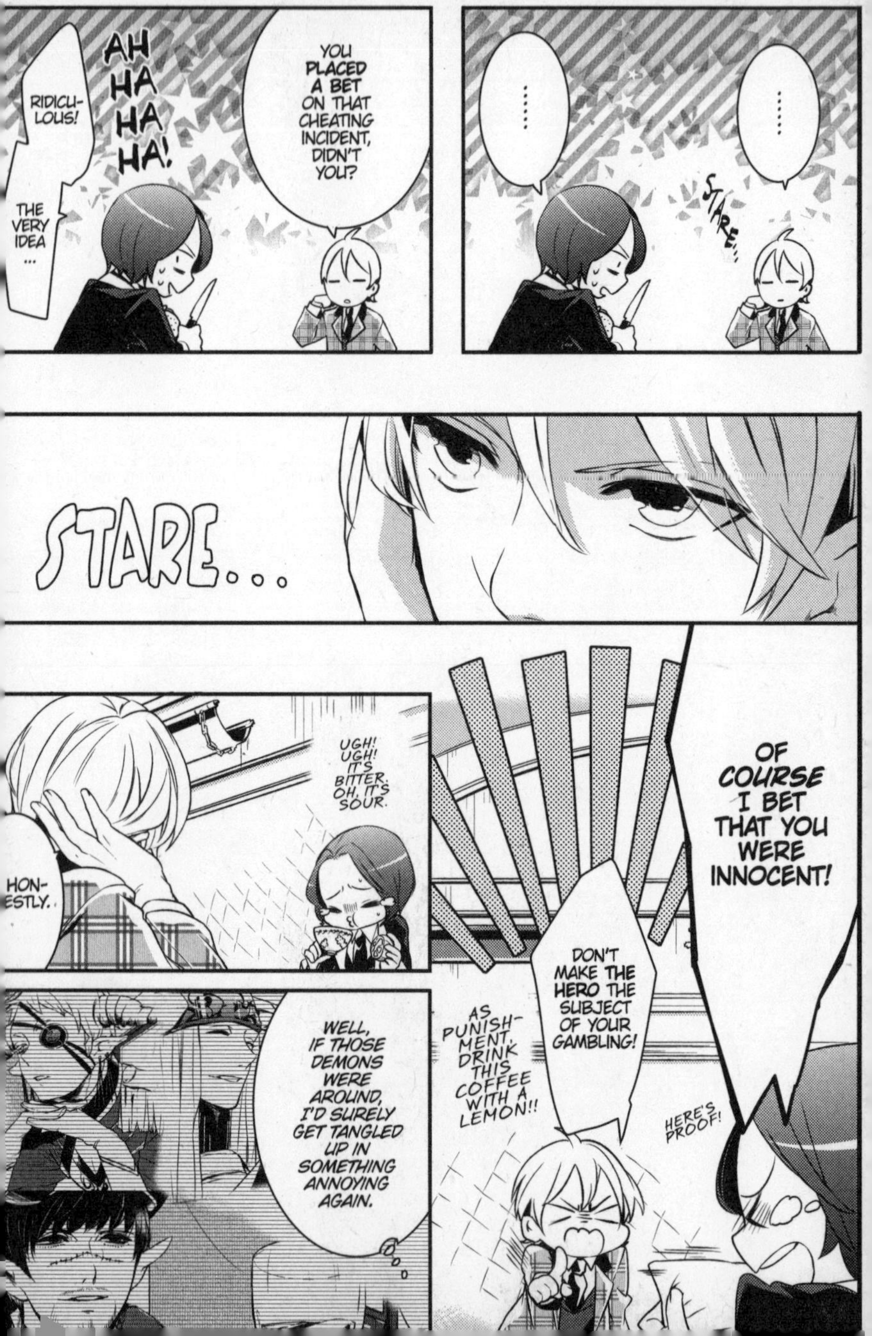
......
......
STARE...
YOU PLACED A BET ON THAT CHEATING INCIDENT, DIDN'T YOU?
AH HA HA HA!
RIDICULI-LOUS!
THE VERY IDEA ...
STARE...
OF COURSE I BET THAT YOU WERE INNOCENT!
HERE'S PROOF!
DON'T MAKE THE HERO THE SUBJECT OF YOUR GAMBLING!
AS PUNISH-MENT, DRINK THIS COFFEE WITH A LEMON!!
UGH! UGH! IT'S BITTER. OH, IT'S SOUR.
HON-ESTLY..
WELL, IF THOSE DEMONS WERE AROUND, I'D SURELY GET TANGLED UP IN SOMETHING ANNOYING AGAIN.

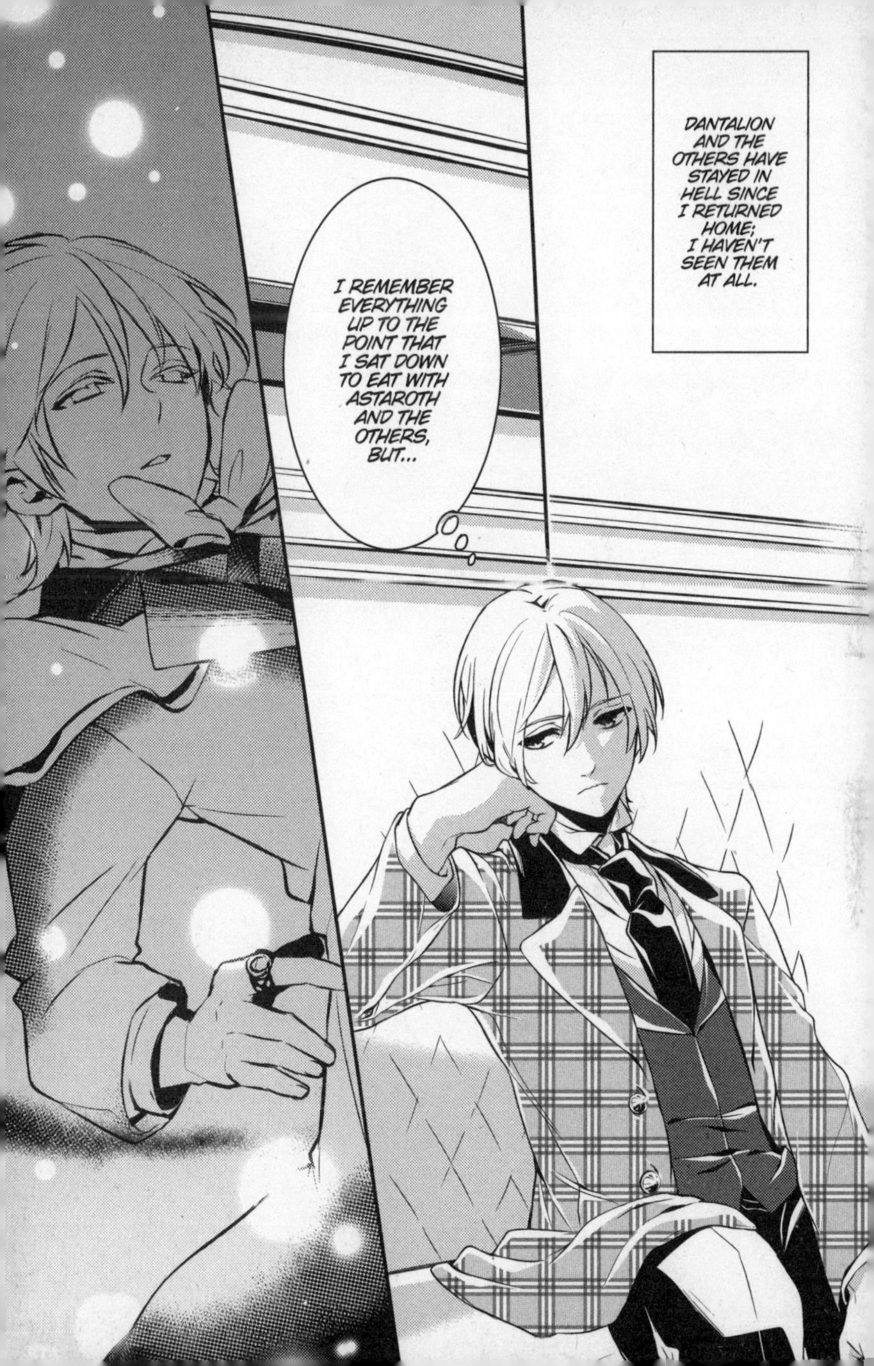
DANTALION AND THE OTHERS HAVE STAYED IN HELL SINCE I RETURNED HOME; I HAVEN'T SEEN THEM AT ALL.
I REMEMBER EVERYTHING UP TO THE POINT THAT I SAT DOWN TO EAT WITH ASTAROTH AND THE OTHERS, BUT...

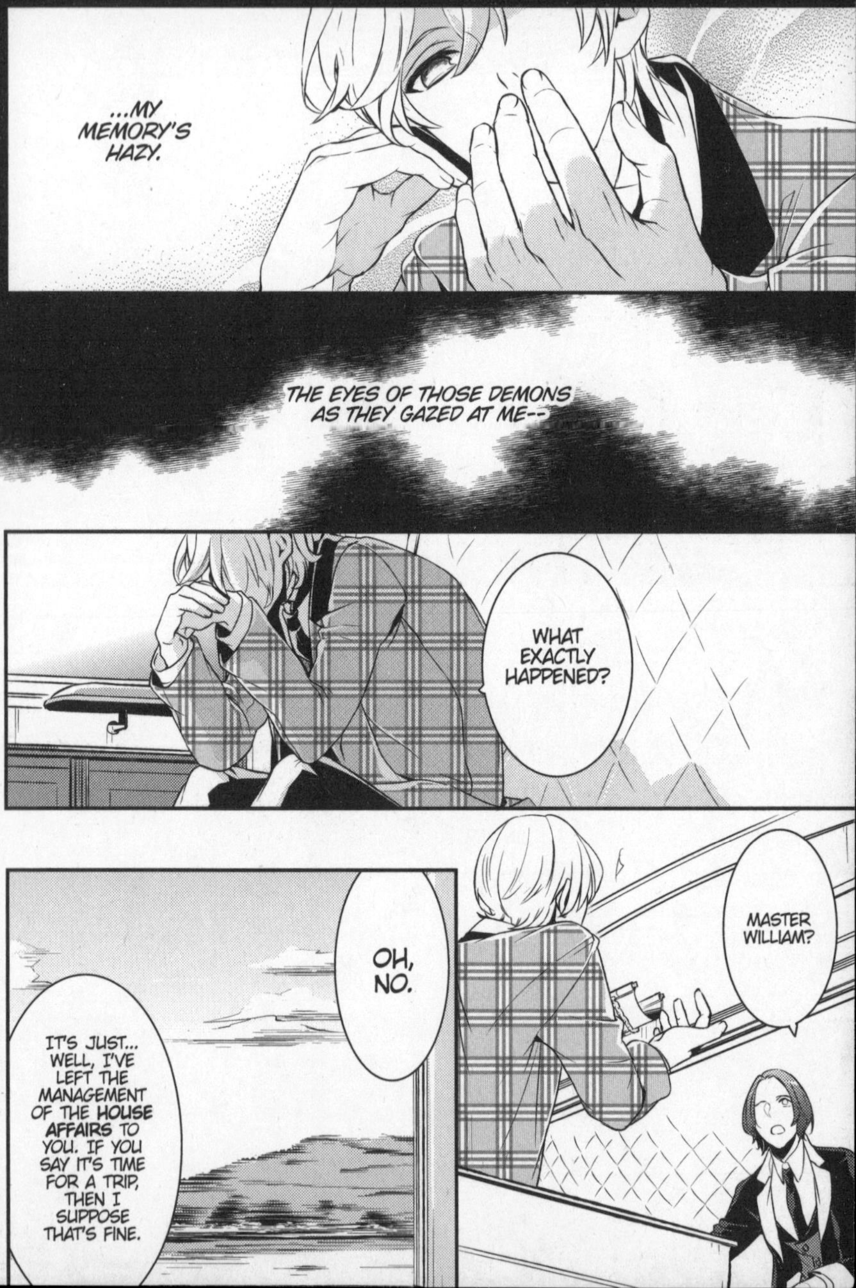
...MY MEMORY'S HAZY.
THE EYES OF THOSE DEMONS AS THEY GAZED AT ME--
WHAT EXACTLY HAPPENED?
MASTER WILLIAM?
OH, NO.
IT'S JUST... WELL, I'VE LEFT THE MANAGEMENT OF THE HOUSE AFFAIRS TO YOU. IF YOU SAY IT'S TIME FOR A TRIP, THEN I SUPPOSE THAT'S FINE.

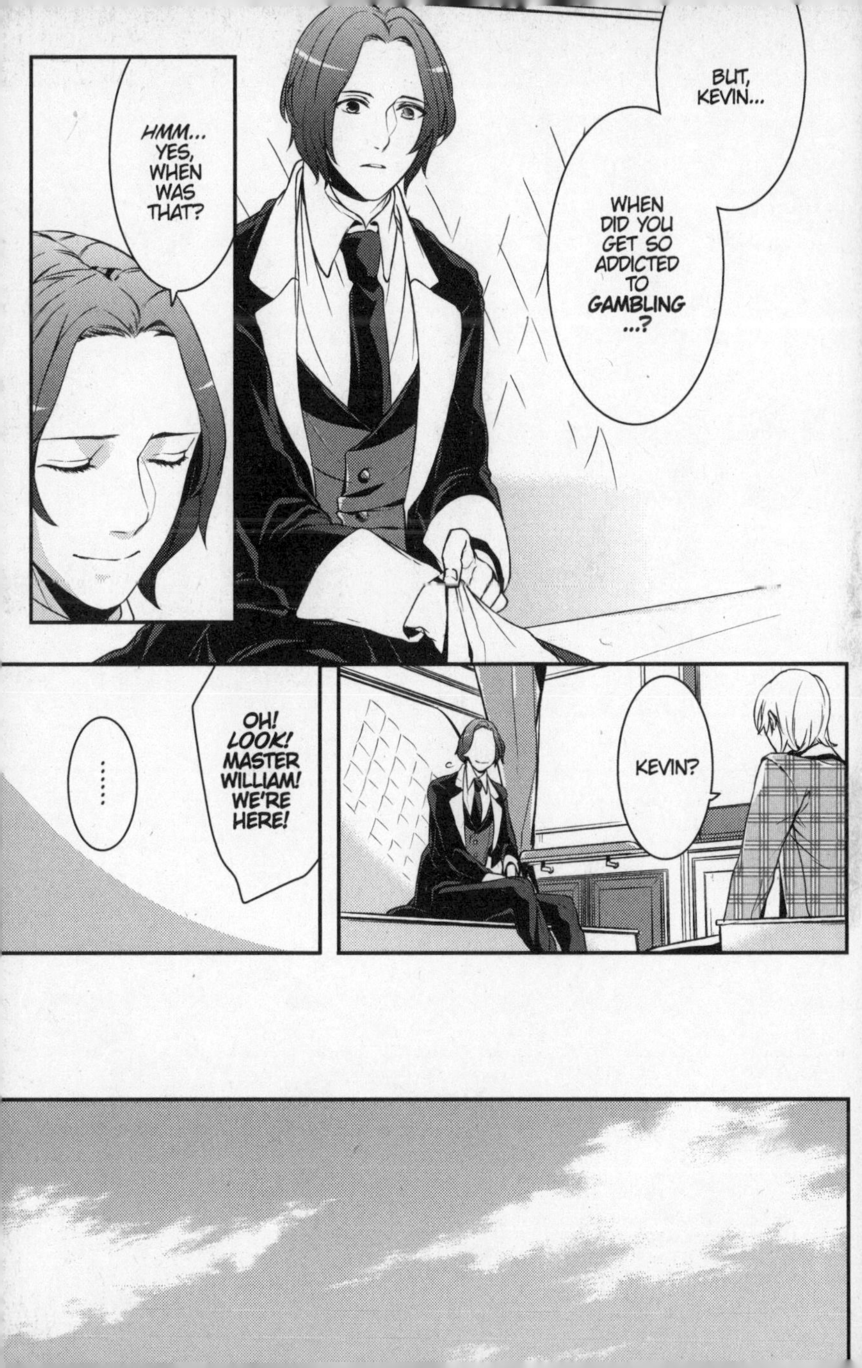
BUT, KEVIN...
WHEN DID YOU GET SO ADDICTED TO GAMBLING ...?
HMM... YES, WHEN WAS THAT?
KEVIN?
OH! LOOK! MASTER WILLIAM! WE'RE HERE!
......

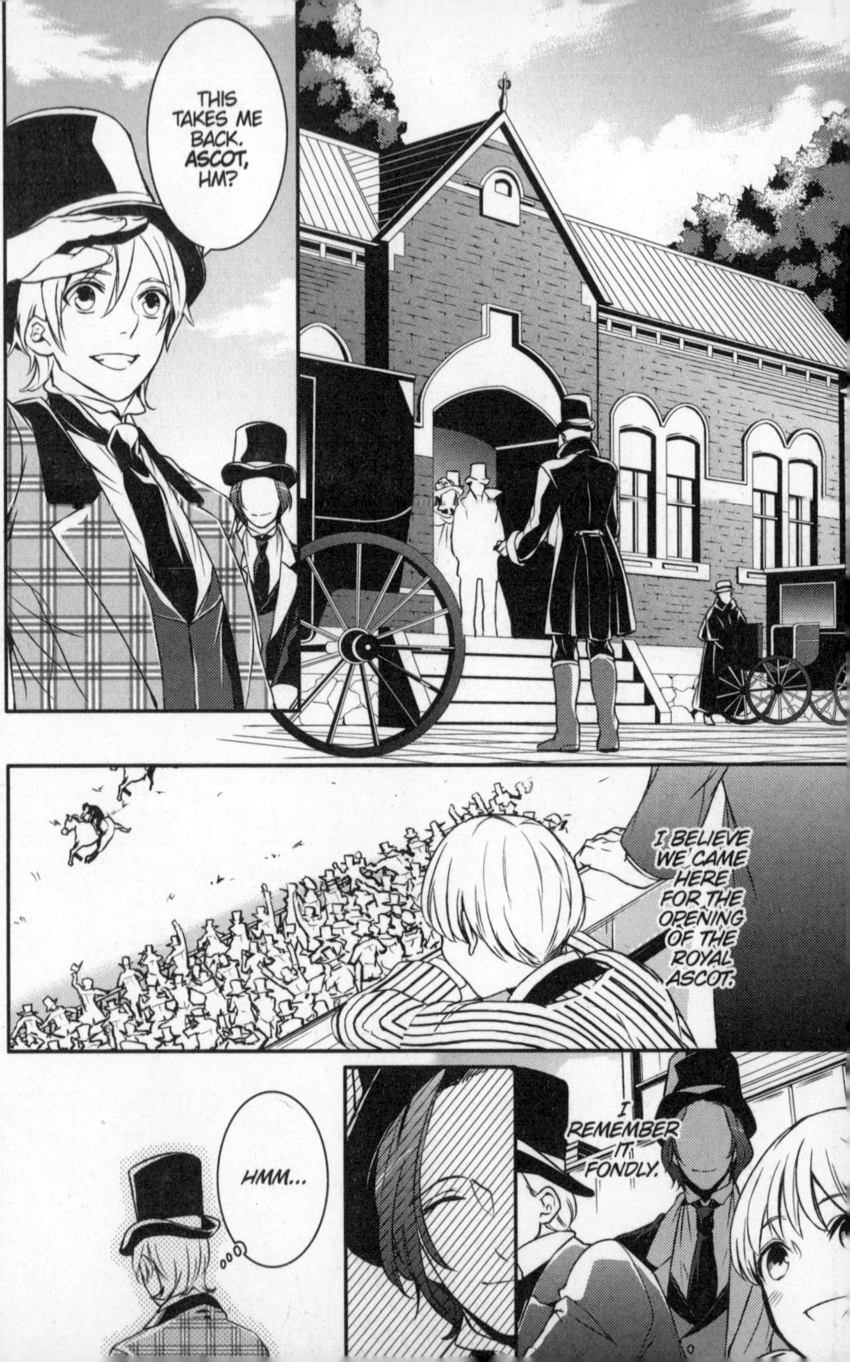
THIS TAKES ME BACK. ASCOT, HM?
I BELIEVE WE CAME HERE FOR THE OPENING OF THE ROYAL ASCOT.
I REMEMBER IT FONDLY.
HMM...

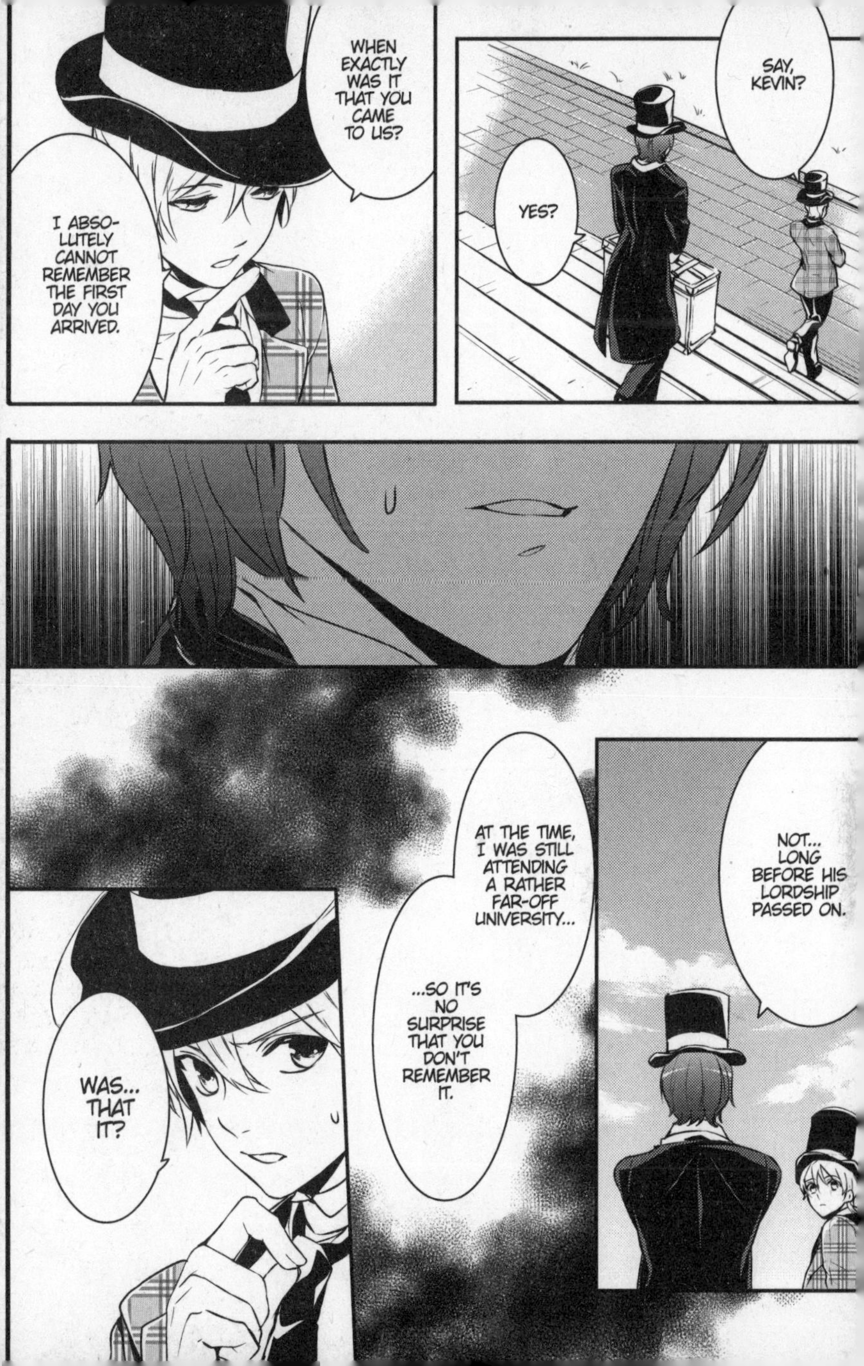
SAY, KEVIN?
YES?
WHEN EXACTLY WAS IT THAT YOU CAME TO US?
I ABSO-LUTELY CANNOT REMEMBER THE FIRST DAY YOU ARRIVED.
NOT... LONG BEFORE HIS LORDSHIP PASSED ON.
AT THE TIME, I WAS STILL ATTENDING A RATHER FAR-OFF UNIVERSITY...
...SO IT'S NO SURPRISE THAT YOU DON'T REMEMBER IT.
WAS... THAT IT?

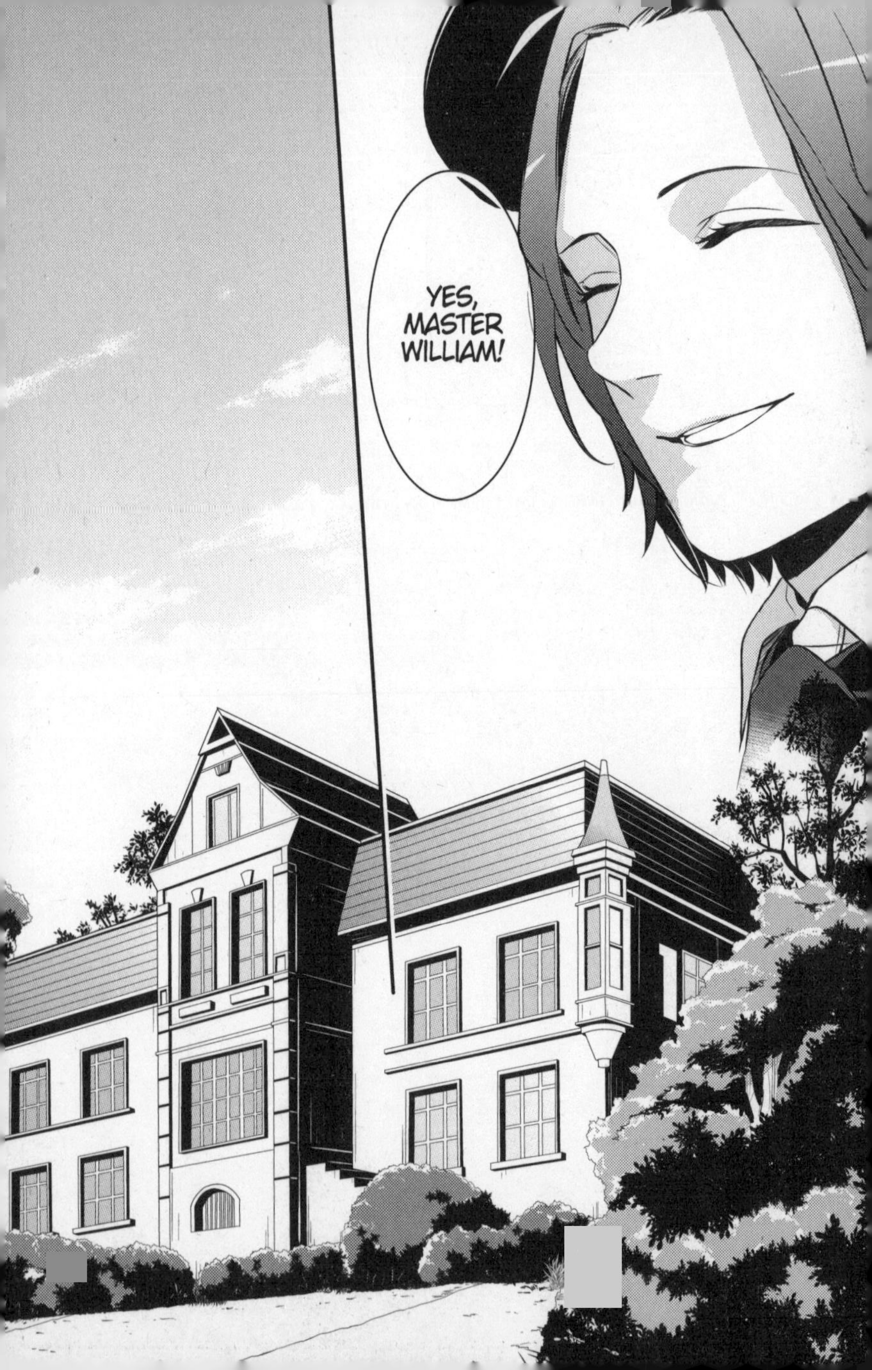
YES, MASTER WILLIAM!

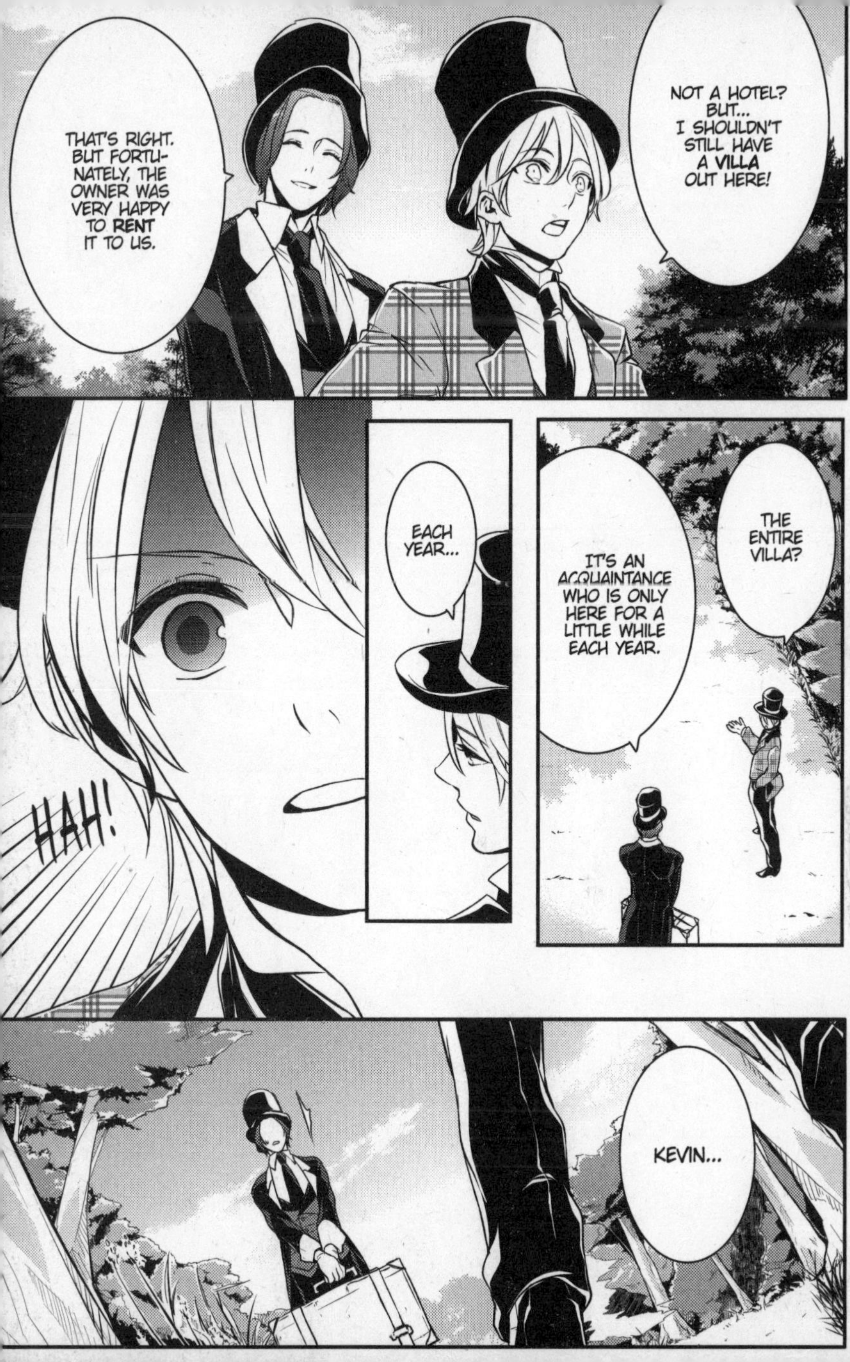
NOT A HOTEL? BUT... I SHOULDN'T STILL HAVE A **VILLA** OUT HERE!
THAT'S RIGHT. BUT FORTU-NATELY, THE OWNER WAS VERY HAPPY TO **RENT** IT TO US.
THE ENTIRE VILLA?
IT'S AN ACQUAINTANCE WHO IS ONLY HERE FOR A LITTLE WHILE EACH YEAR.
EACH YEAR...
HAH!
KEVIN...

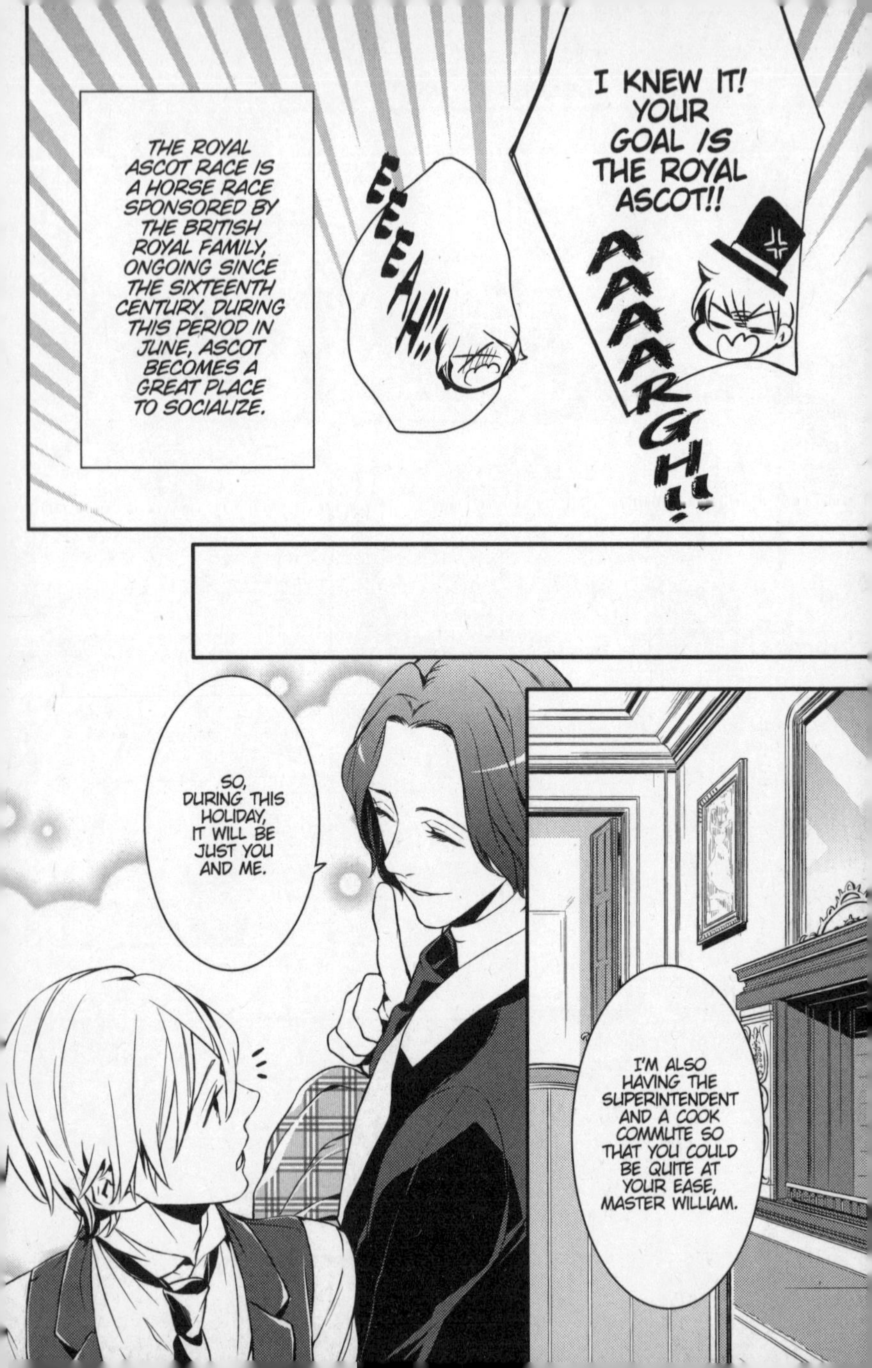
I KNEW IT! YOUR GOAL IS THE ROYAL ASCOT!!
AAAARGH!!
EEEAH!!
THE ROYAL ASCOT RACE IS A HORSE RACE SPONSORED BY THE BRITISH ROYAL FAMILY, ONGOING SINCE THE SIXTEENTH CENTURY. DURING THIS PERIOD IN JUNE, ASCOT BECOMES A GREAT PLACE TO SOCIALIZE.
I'M ALSO HAVING THE SUPERINTENDENT AND A COOK COMMUTE SO THAT YOU COULD BE QUITE AT YOUR EASE, MASTER WILLIAM.
SO, DURING THIS HOLIDAY, IT WILL BE JUST YOU AND ME.

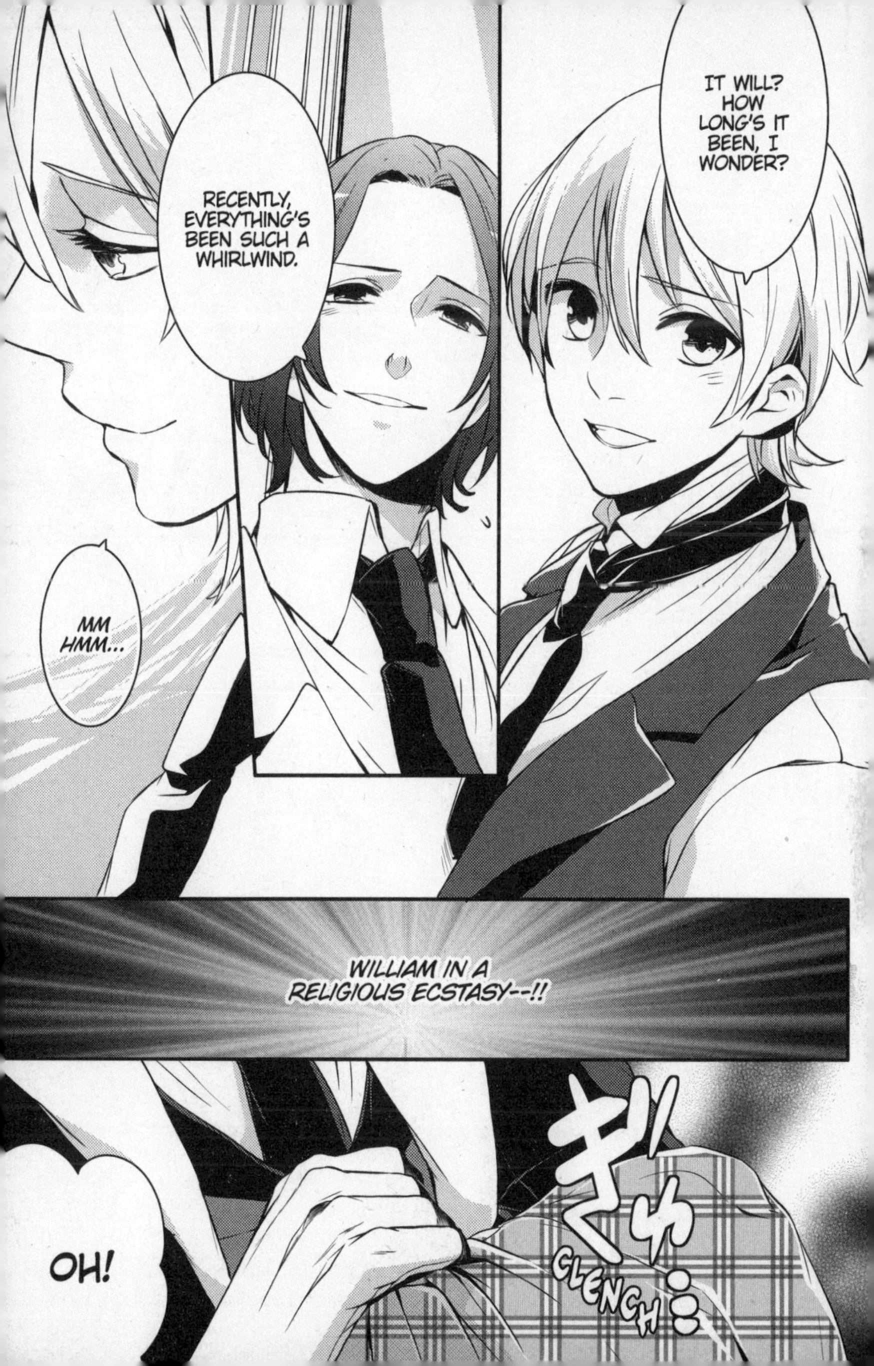
IT WILL? HOW LONG'S IT BEEN, I WONDER?
RECENTLY, EVERYTHING'S BEEN SUCH A WHIRLWIND.
MM HMM...
WILLIAM IN A RELIGIOUS ECSTASY--!!
ぎゅ
CLENCH
OH!

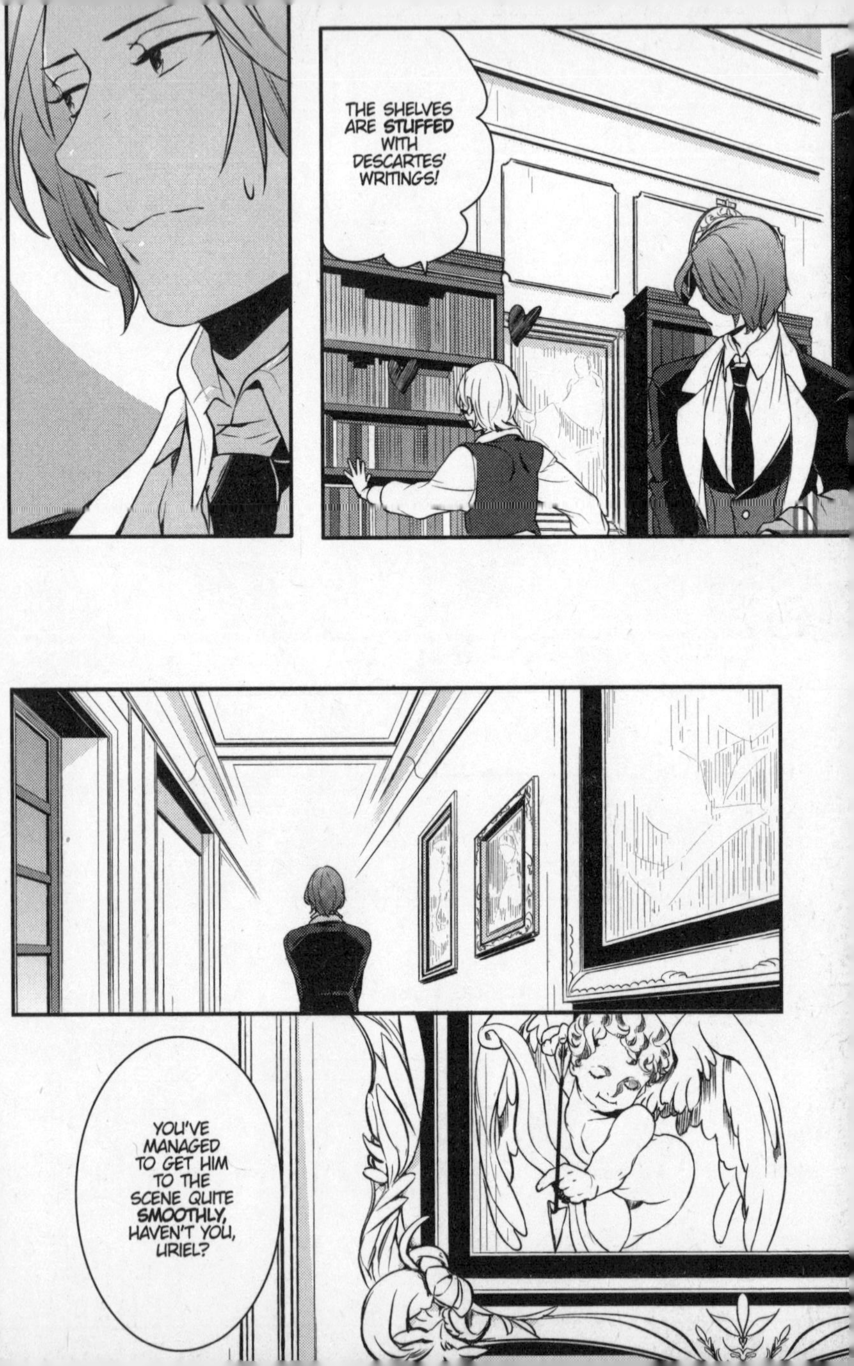
THE SHELVES ARE **STUFFED** WITH DESCARTES' WRITINGS!
YOU'VE MANAGED TO GET HIM TO THE SCENE QUITE **SMOOTHLY**, HAVEN'T YOU, URIEL?

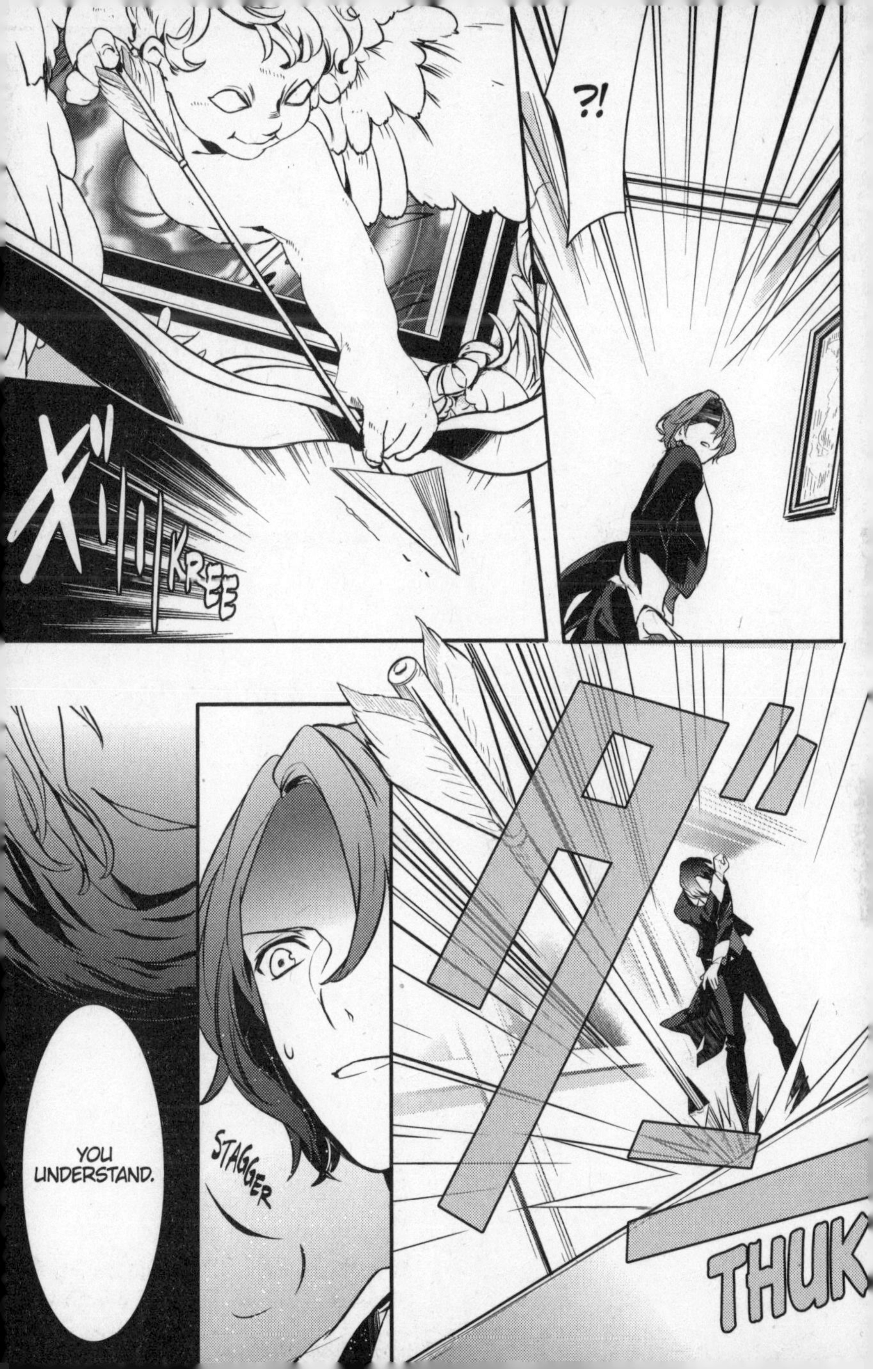
?!
KREEE
THUK
STAGGER
YOU UNDERSTAND.

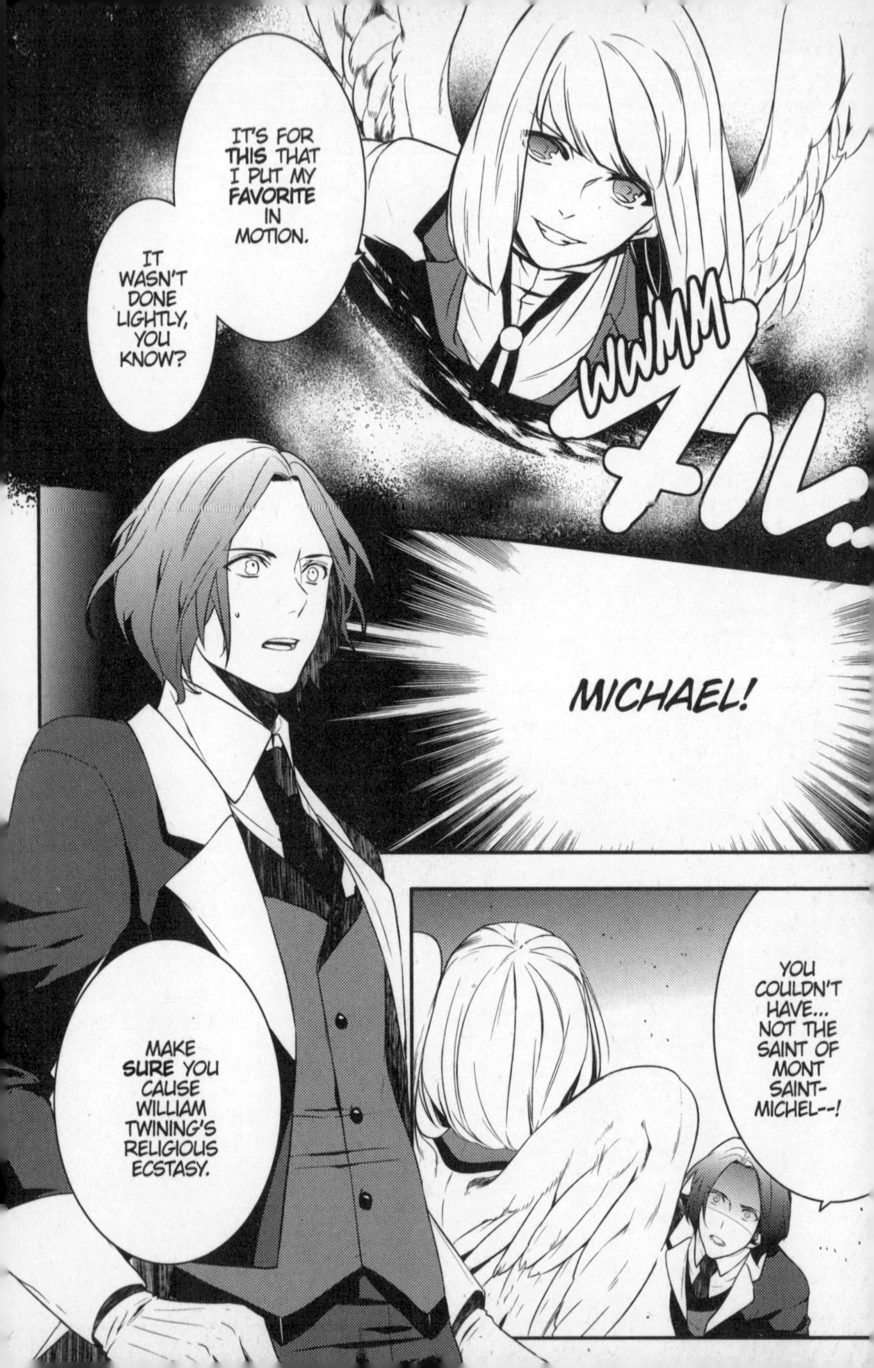
IT'S FOR THIS THAT I PUT MY FAVORITE IN MOTION.
IT WASN'T DONE LIGHTLY, YOU KNOW?
WWMM
MICHAEL!
YOU COULDN'T HAVE... NOT THE SAINT OF MONT SAINT-MICHEL--!
MAKE SURE YOU CAUSE WILLIAM TWINING'S RELIGIOUS ECSTASY.

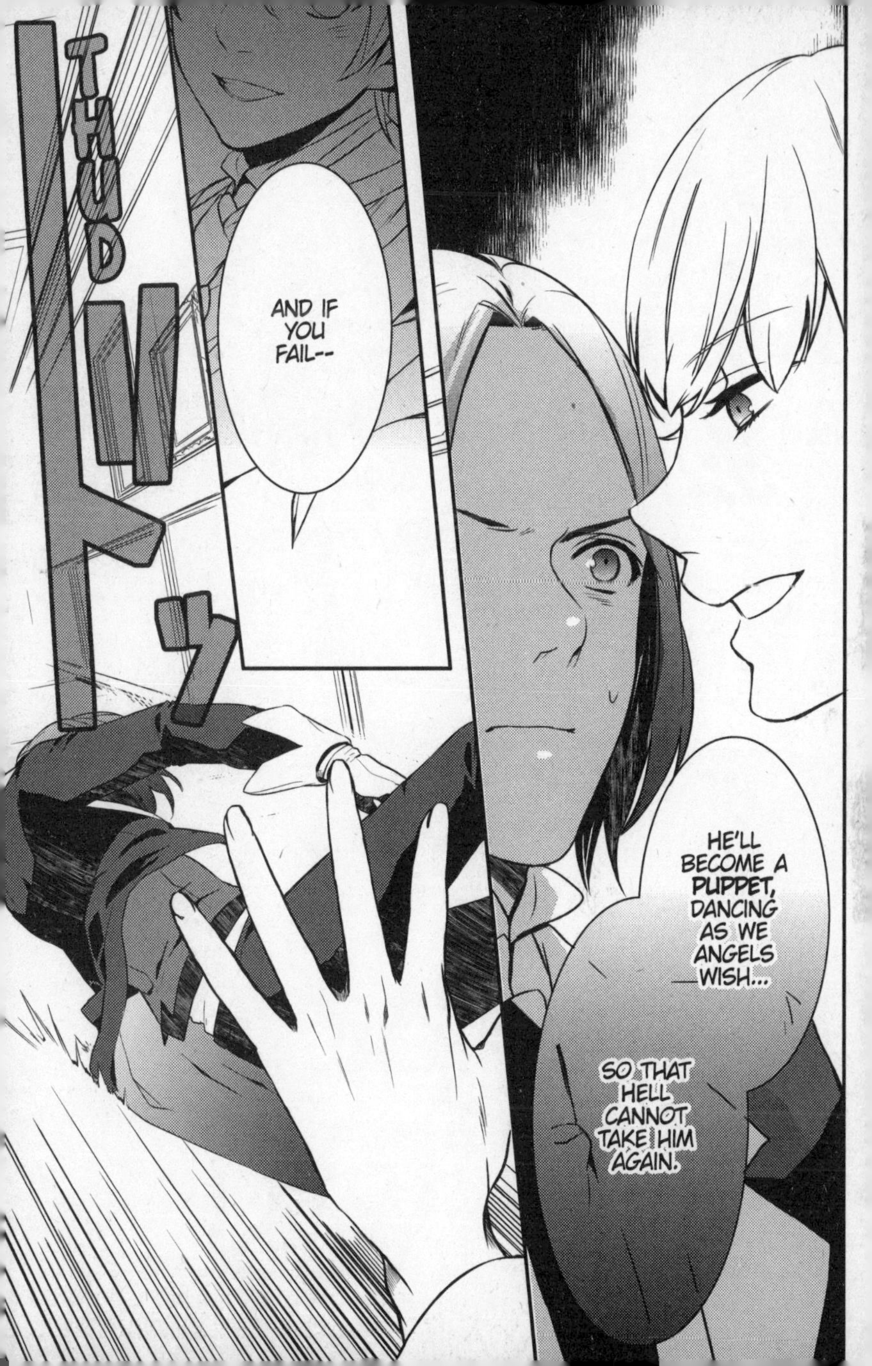
HE'LL BECOME A PUPPET, DANCING AS WE ANGELS WISH...
SO THAT HELL CANNOT TAKE HIM AGAIN.
THUD
AND IF YOU FAIL--

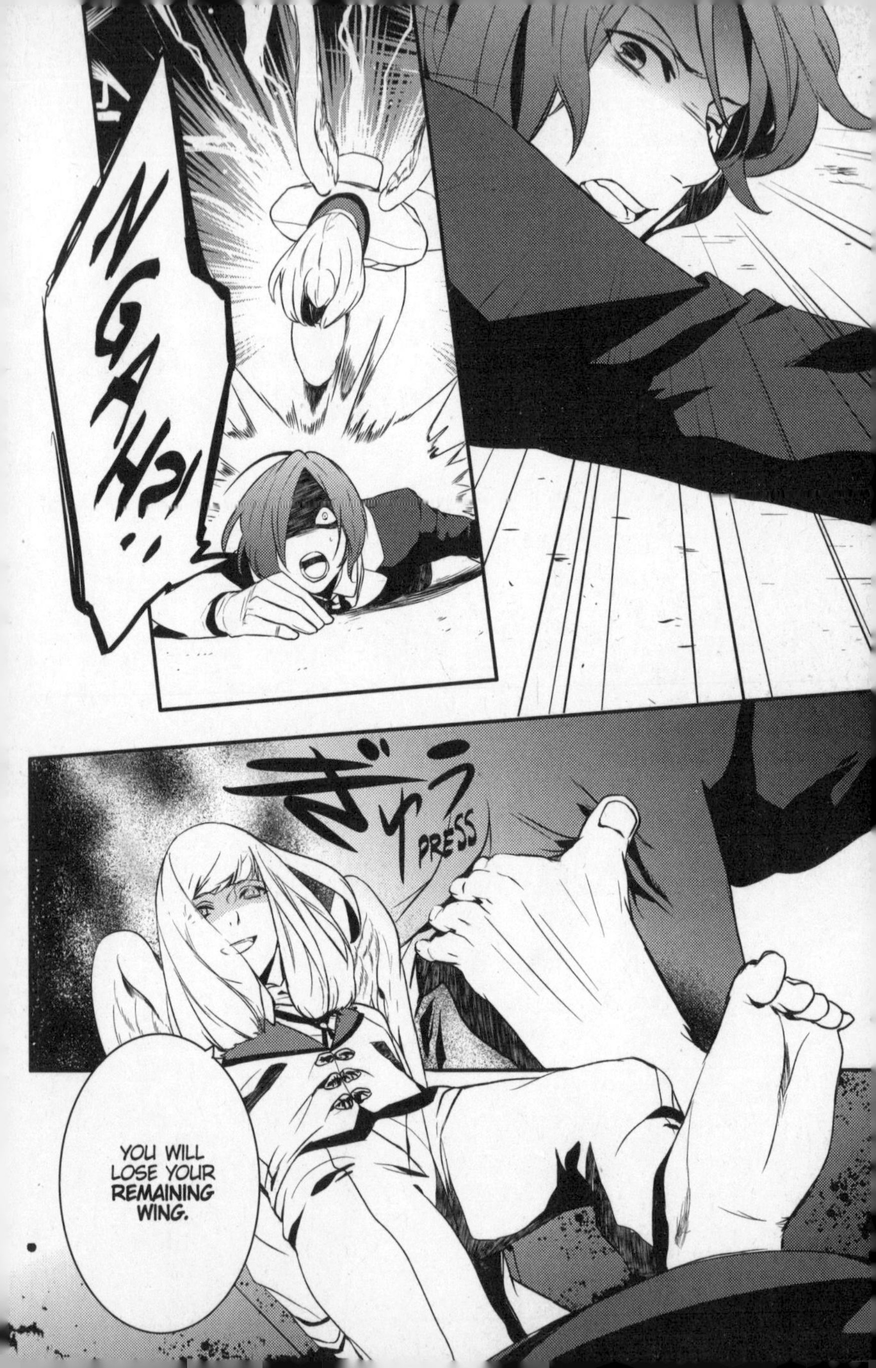
NGAH?!!
ぎゅう
PRESS
YOU WILL LOSE YOUR REMAINING WING.

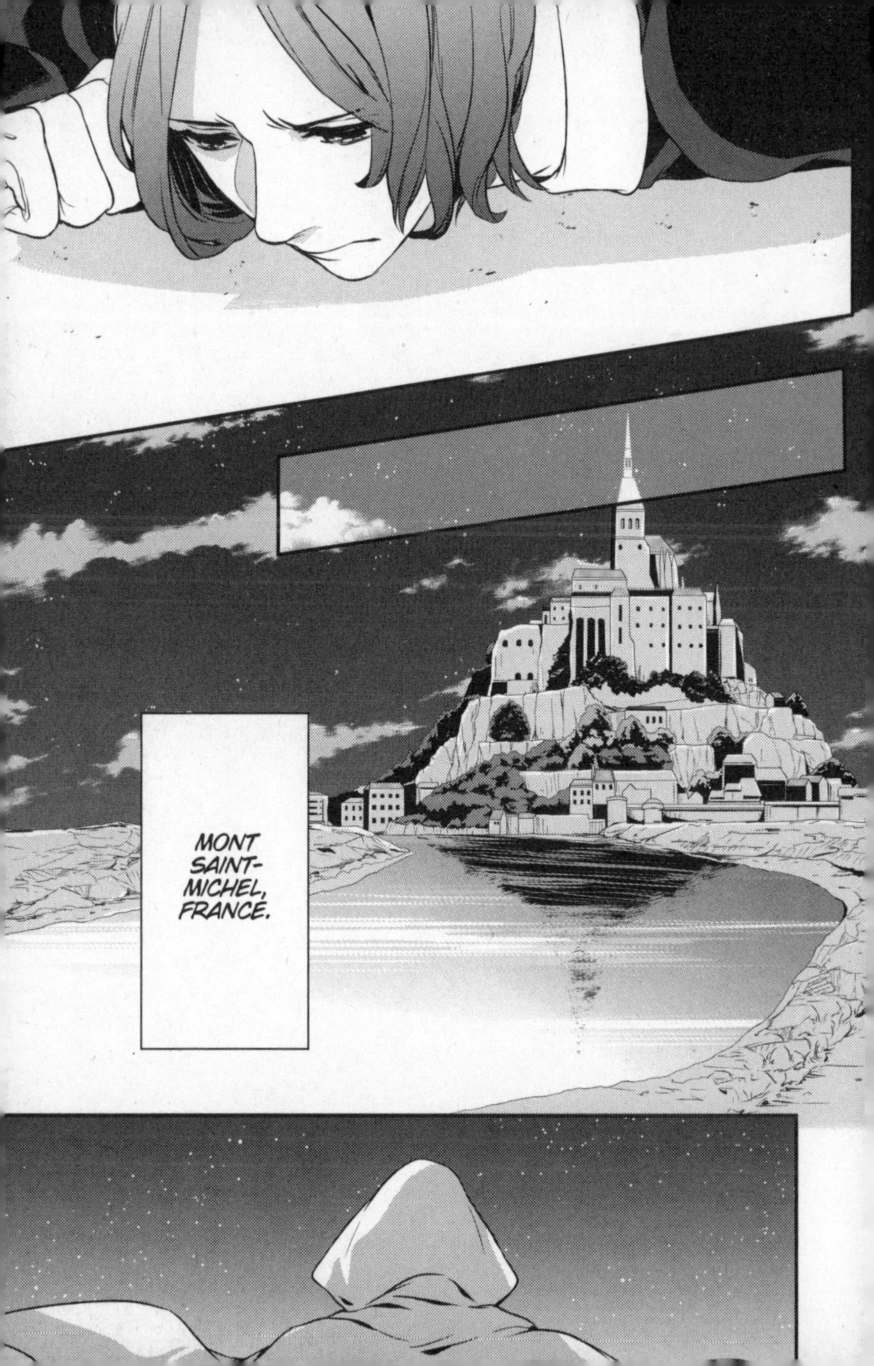
MONT SAINT-MICHEL, FRANCE.

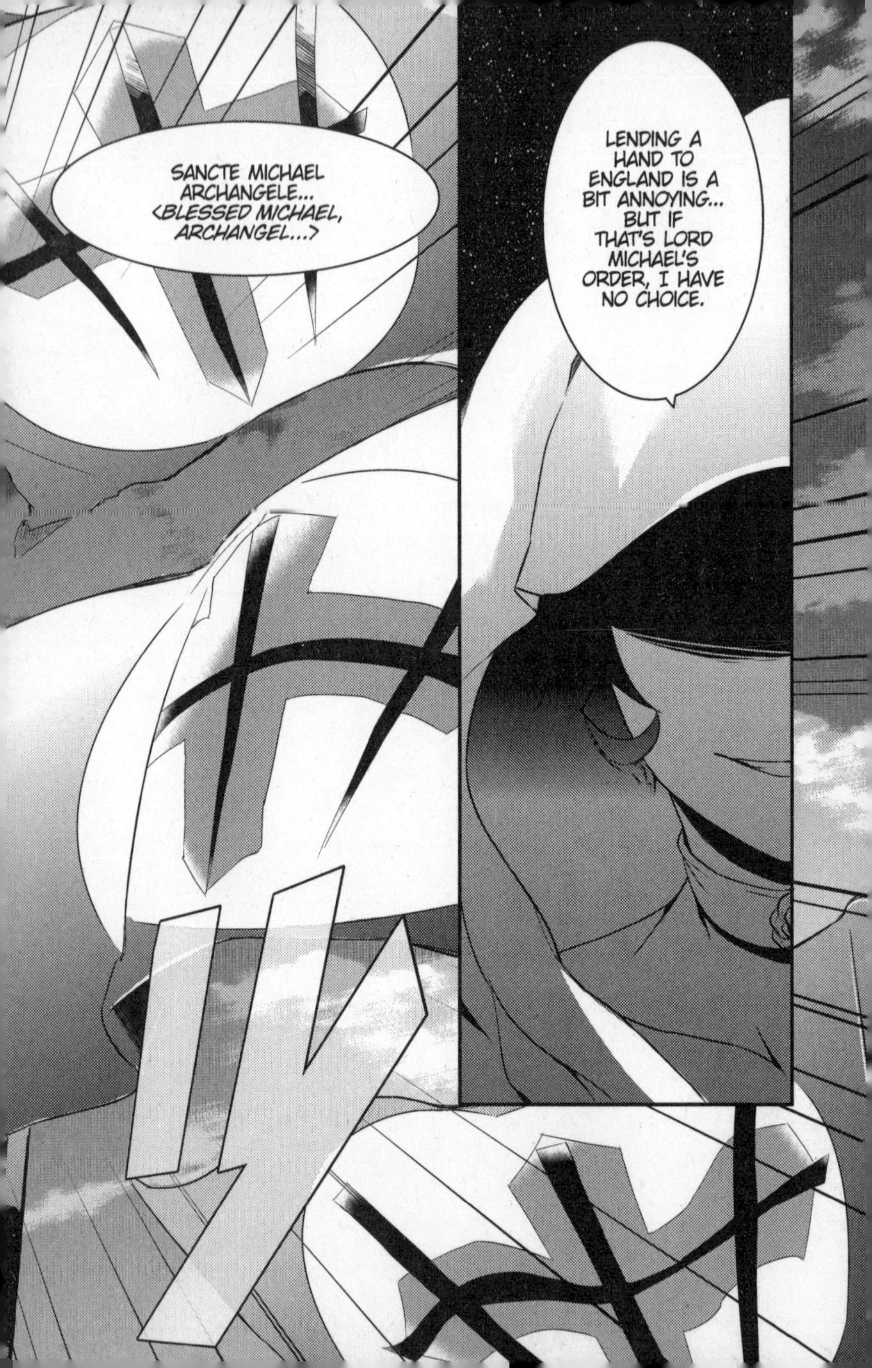
LENDING A HAND TO ENGLAND IS A BIT ANNOYING... BUT IF THAT'S LORD MICHAEL'S ORDER, I HAVE NO CHOICE.
SANCTE MICHAEL ARCHANGELE... <BLESSED MICHAEL, ARCHANGEL...>

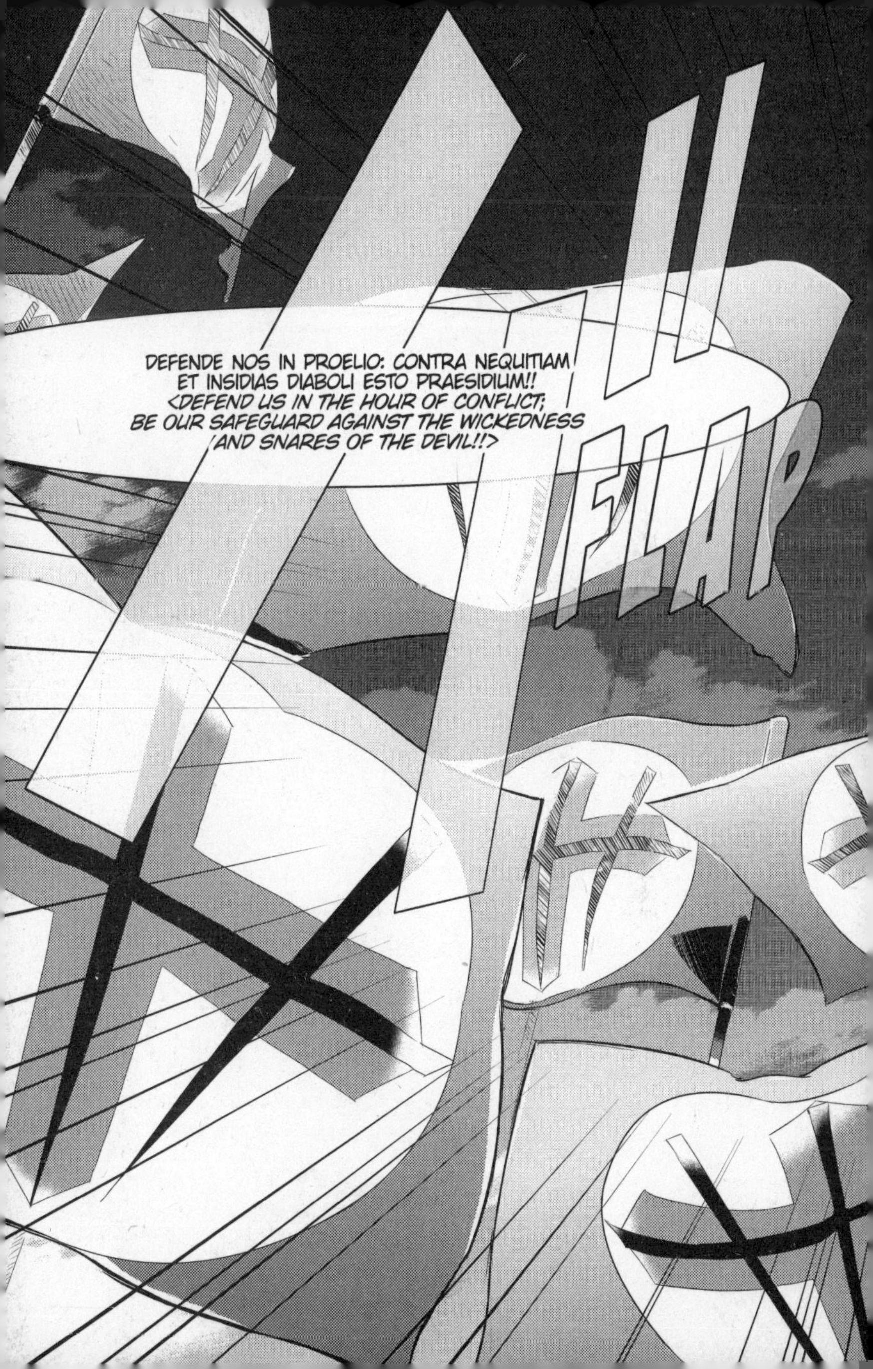
DEFENDE NOS IN PROELIO: CONTRA NEQUITIAM ET INSIDIAS DIABOLI ESTO PRAESIDIUM!! <DEFEND US IN THE HOUR OF CONFLICT; BE OUR SAFEGUARD AGAINST THE WICKEDNESS AND SNARES OF THE DEVIL!!>
FLAP

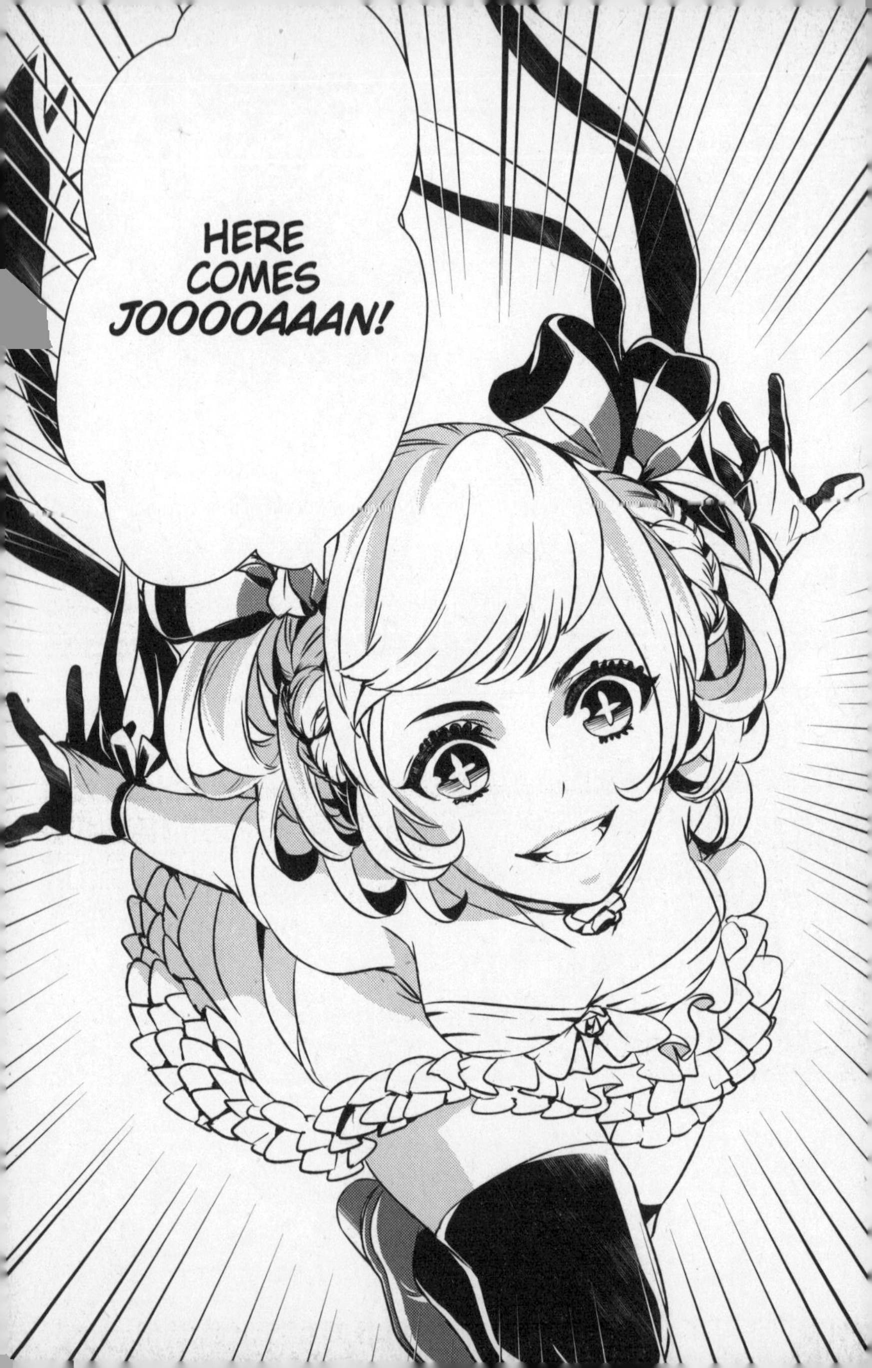
HERE COMES JOOOOAAAN!

Pillar 31

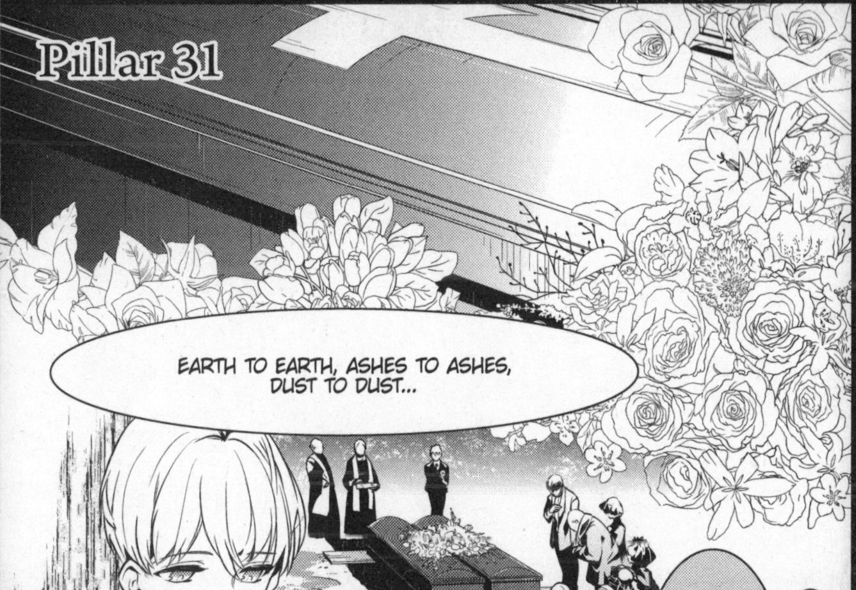
EARTH TO EARTH, ASHES TO ASHES, DUST TO DUST...
APPARENTLY, THE BOY DIDN'T HAVE A SCRATCH ON HIM.
AND HE CAN'T BRING HIMSELF TO LOOK AT HIS PARENTS' BODIES.

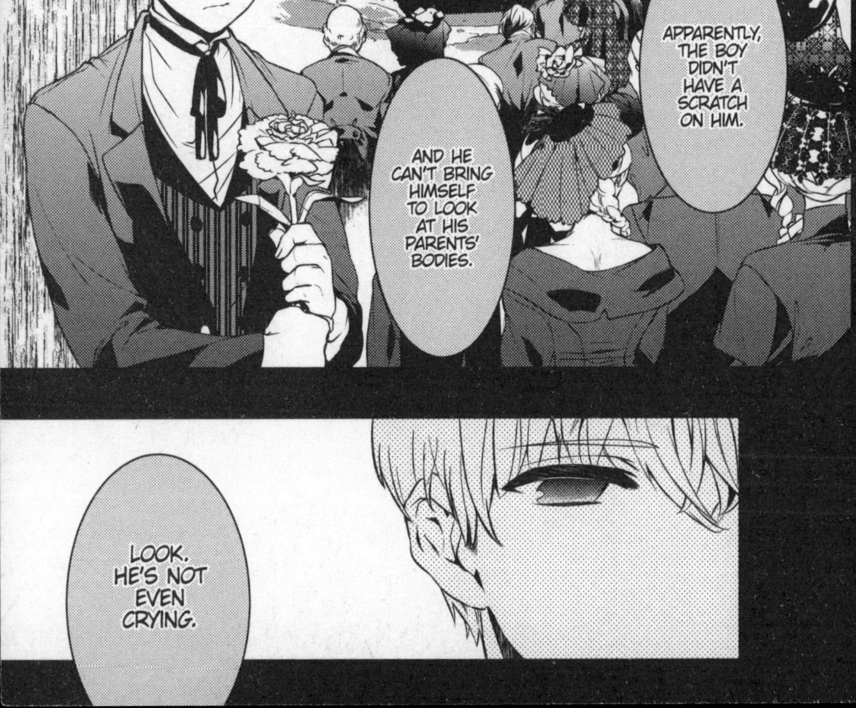
LOOK. HE'S NOT EVEN CRYING.

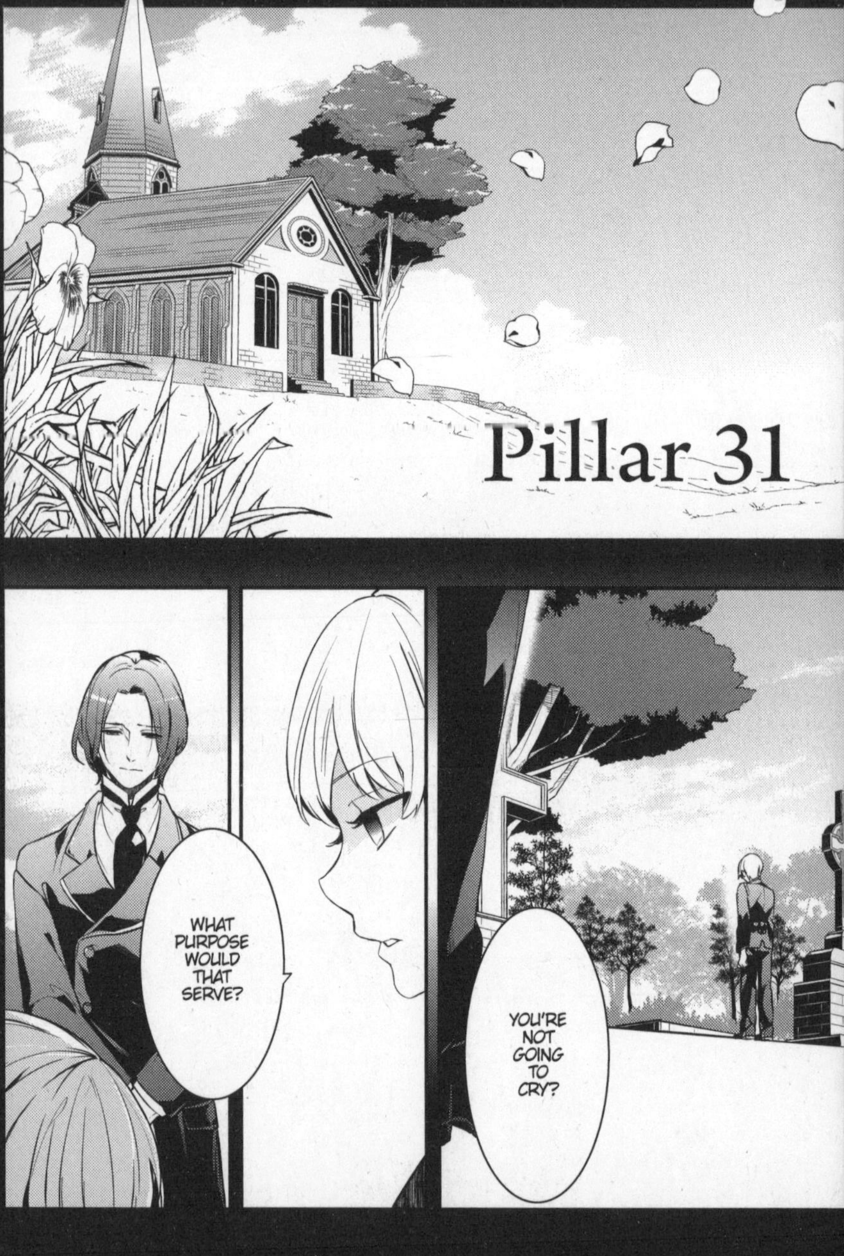
Pillar 31
YOU'RE NOT GOING TO CRY?
WHAT PURPOSE WOULD THAT SERVE?

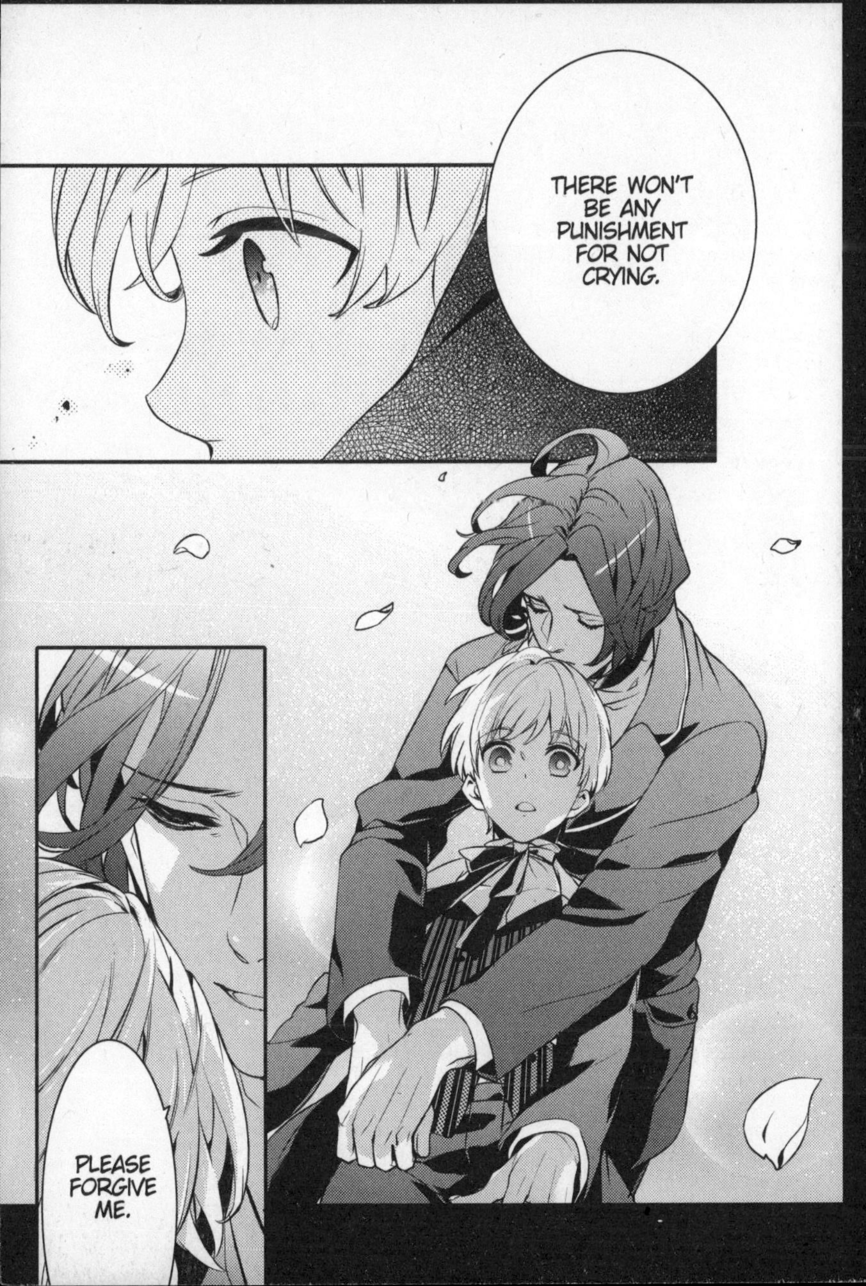
THERE WON'T BE ANY PUNISHMENT FOR NOT CRYING.
PLEASE FORGIVE ME.

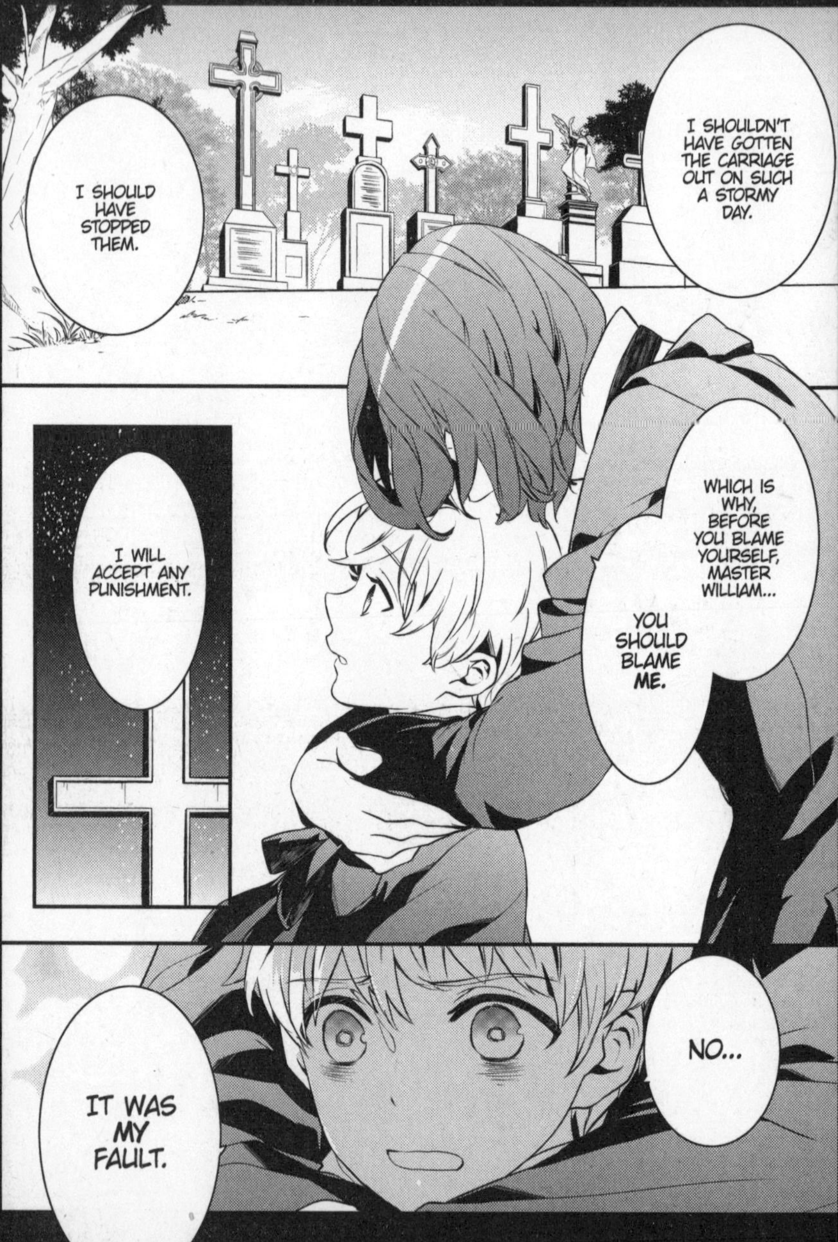
I SHOULDN'T HAVE GOTTEN THE CARRIAGE OUT ON SUCH A STORMY DAY.
I SHOULD HAVE STOPPED THEM.
WHICH IS WHY, BEFORE YOU BLAME YOURSELF, MASTER WILLIAM...
YOU SHOULD BLAME ME.
I WILL ACCEPT ANY PUNISHMENT.
NO...
IT WAS MY FAULT.

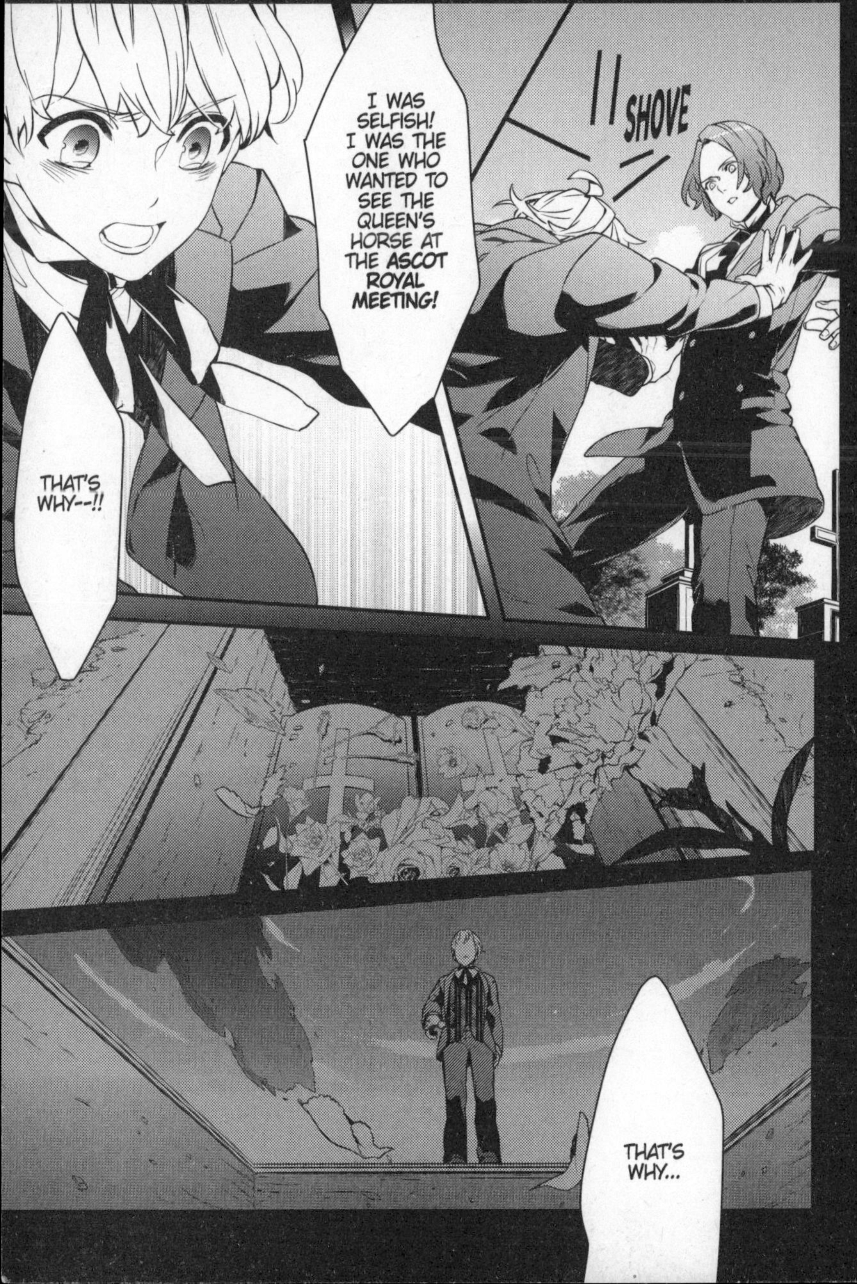
SHOVE
I WAS SELFISH! I WAS THE ONE WHO WANTED TO SEE THE QUEEN'S HORSE AT THE ASCOT ROYAL MEETING!
THAT'S WHY--!!
THAT'S WHY...

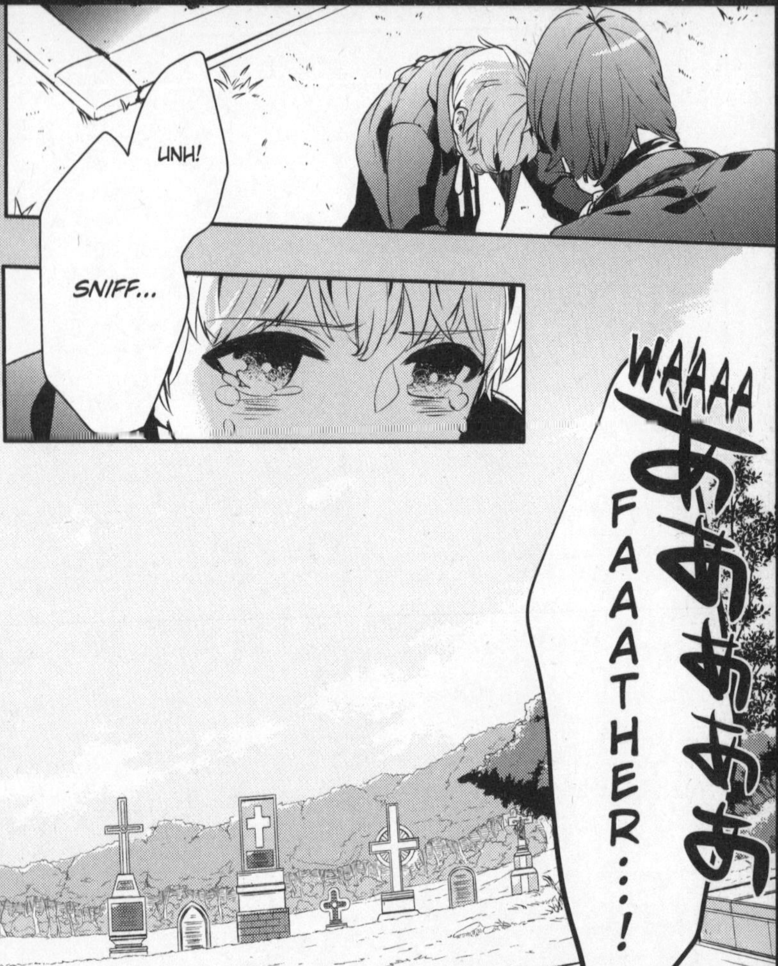

UNH!
SNIFF...
WAAAA
あああああ
FAAATHER...!

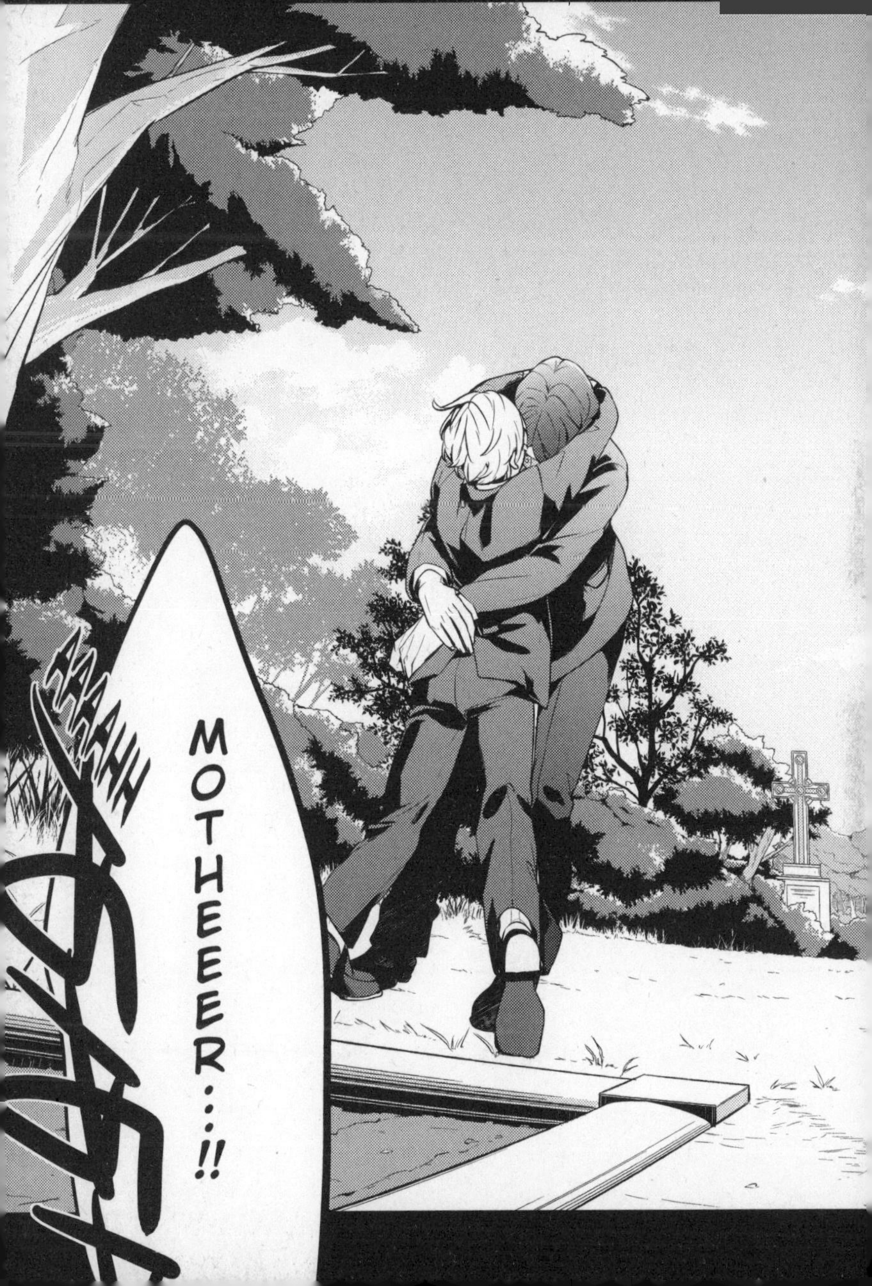
MOTHEEER...!!
AAAAAHH

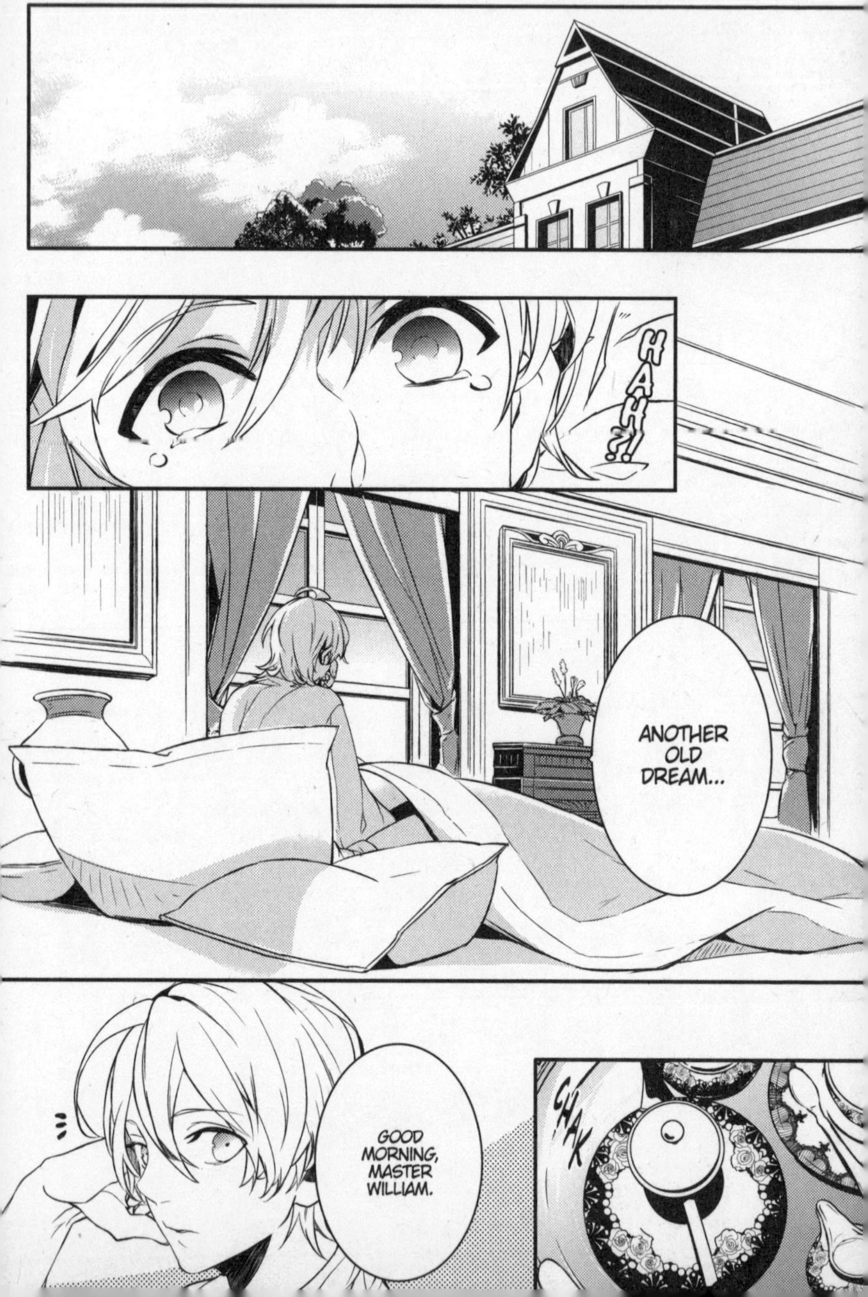
HAH!?
ANOTHER OLD DREAM...
CHAK
GOOD MORNING, MASTER WILLIAM.

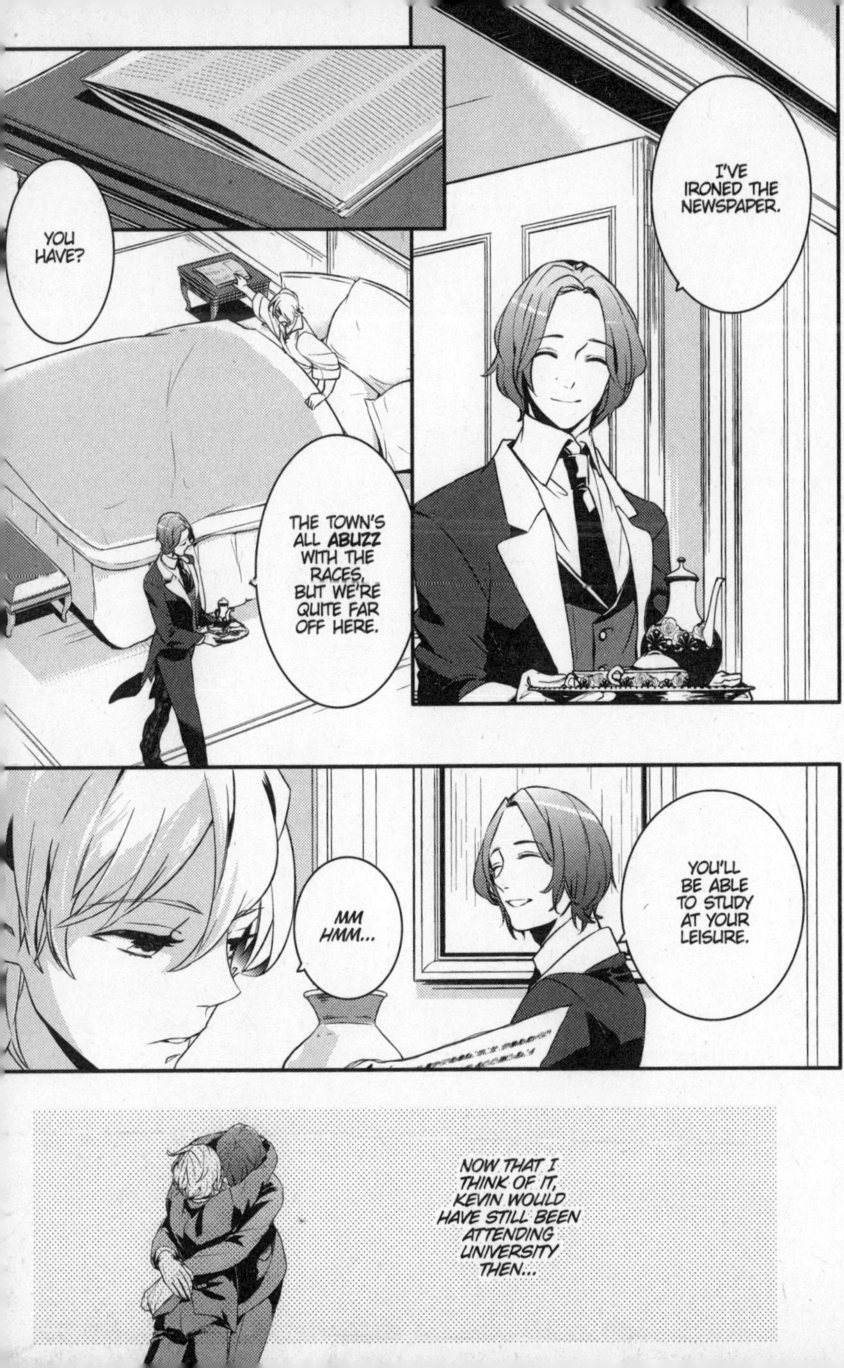
I'VE IRONED THE NEWSPAPER.
YOU HAVE?
THE TOWN'S ALL ABUZZ WITH THE RACES, BUT WE'RE QUITE FAR OFF HERE.
YOU'LL BE ABLE TO STUDY AT YOUR LEISURE.
MM HMM...
NOW THAT I THINK OF IT, KEVIN WOULD HAVE STILL BEEN ATTENDING UNIVERSITY THEN...

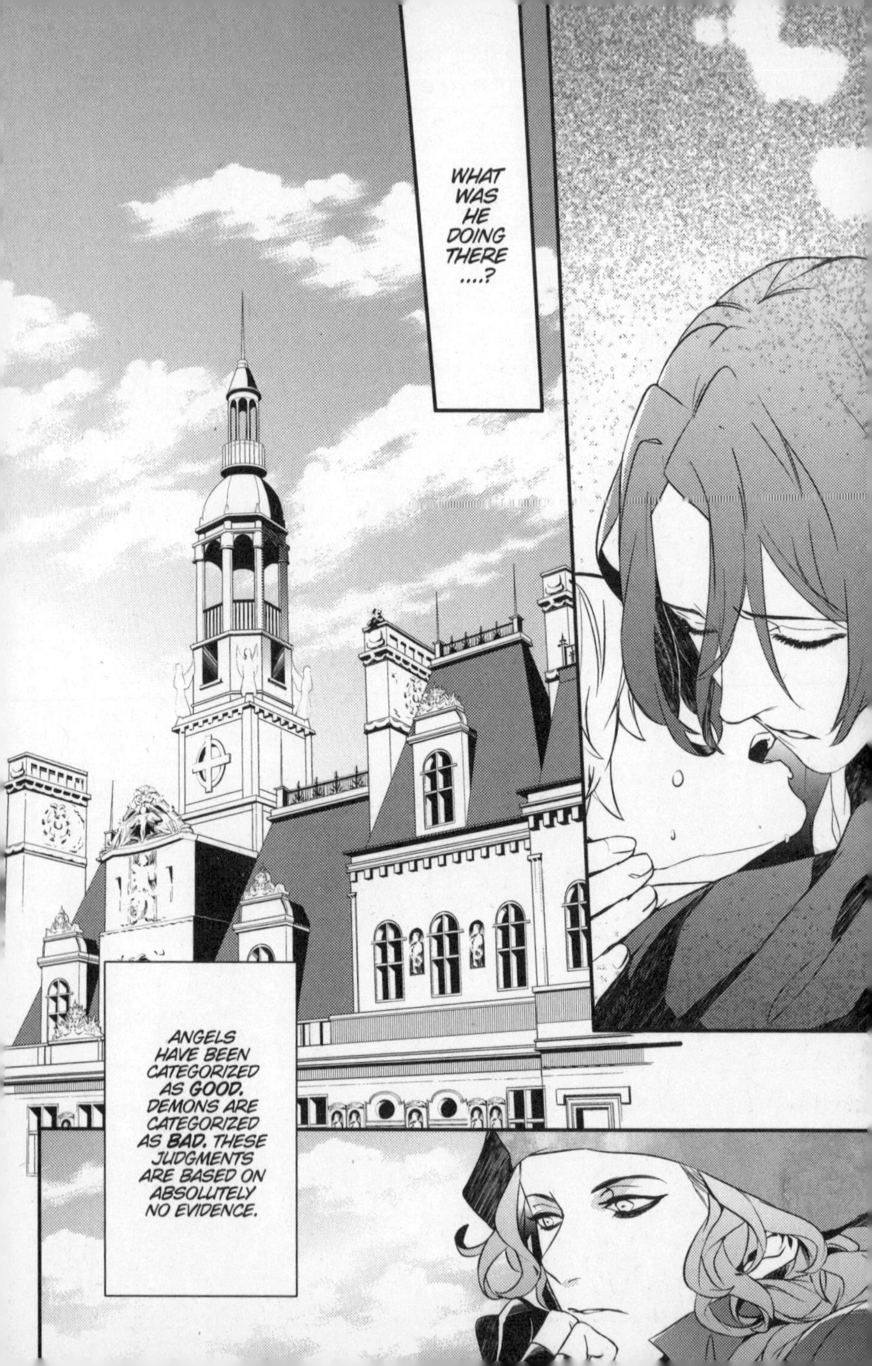
WHAT WAS HE DOING THERE ....?
ANGELS HAVE BEEN CATEGORIZED AS **GOOD.** DEMONS ARE CATEGORIZED AS **BAD.** THESE JUDGMENTS ARE BASED ON ABSOLUTELY NO EVIDENCE.

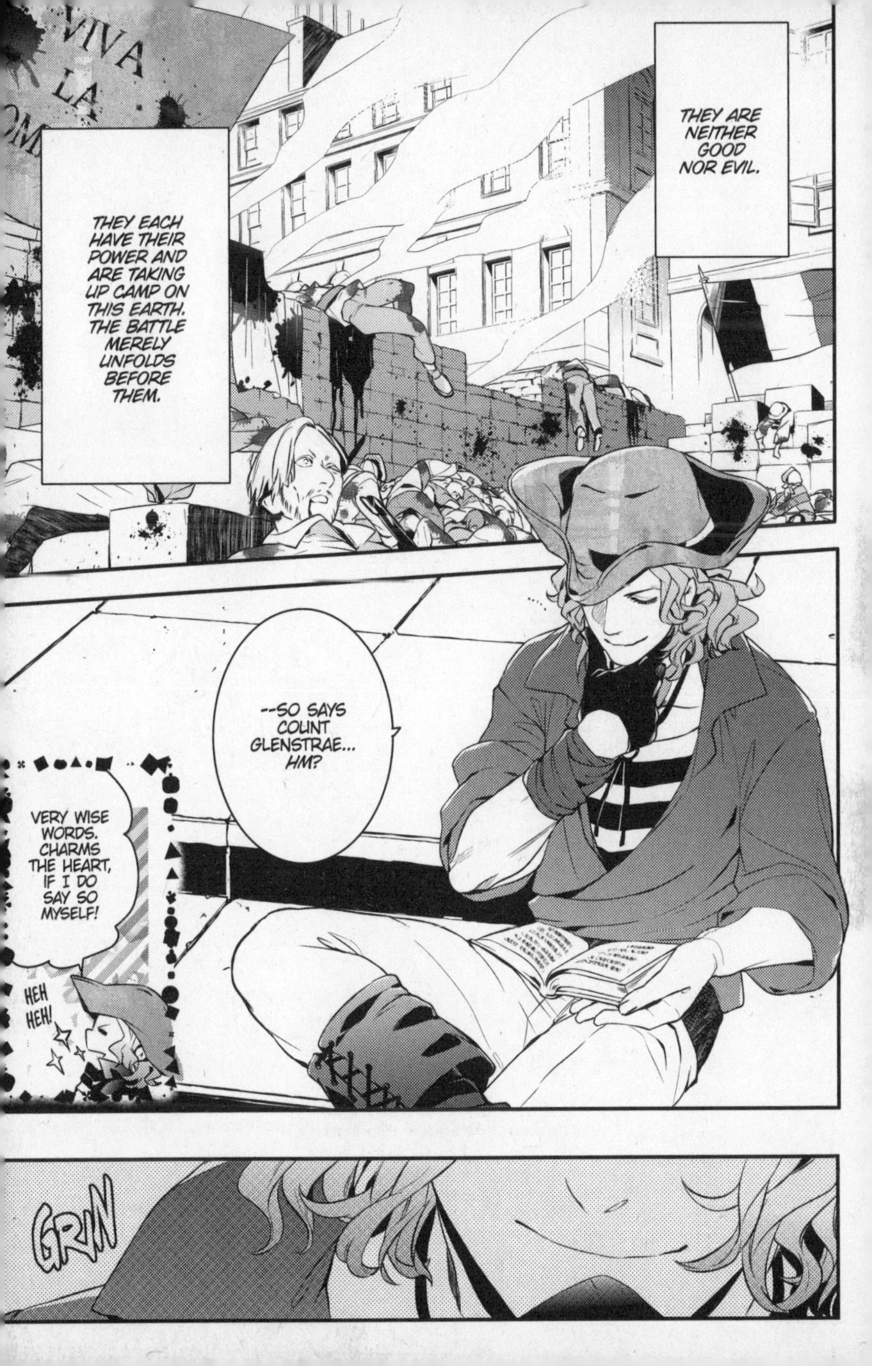
THEY ARE NEITHER GOOD NOR EVIL.
VIVA LA
THEY EACH HAVE THEIR POWER AND ARE TAKING UP CAMP ON THIS EARTH. THE BATTLE MERELY UNFOLDS BEFORE THEM.
--SO SAYS COUNT GLENSTRAE... HM?
VERY WISE WORDS. CHARMS THE HEART, IF I DO SAY SO MYSELF!
HEH HEH!
GRIN

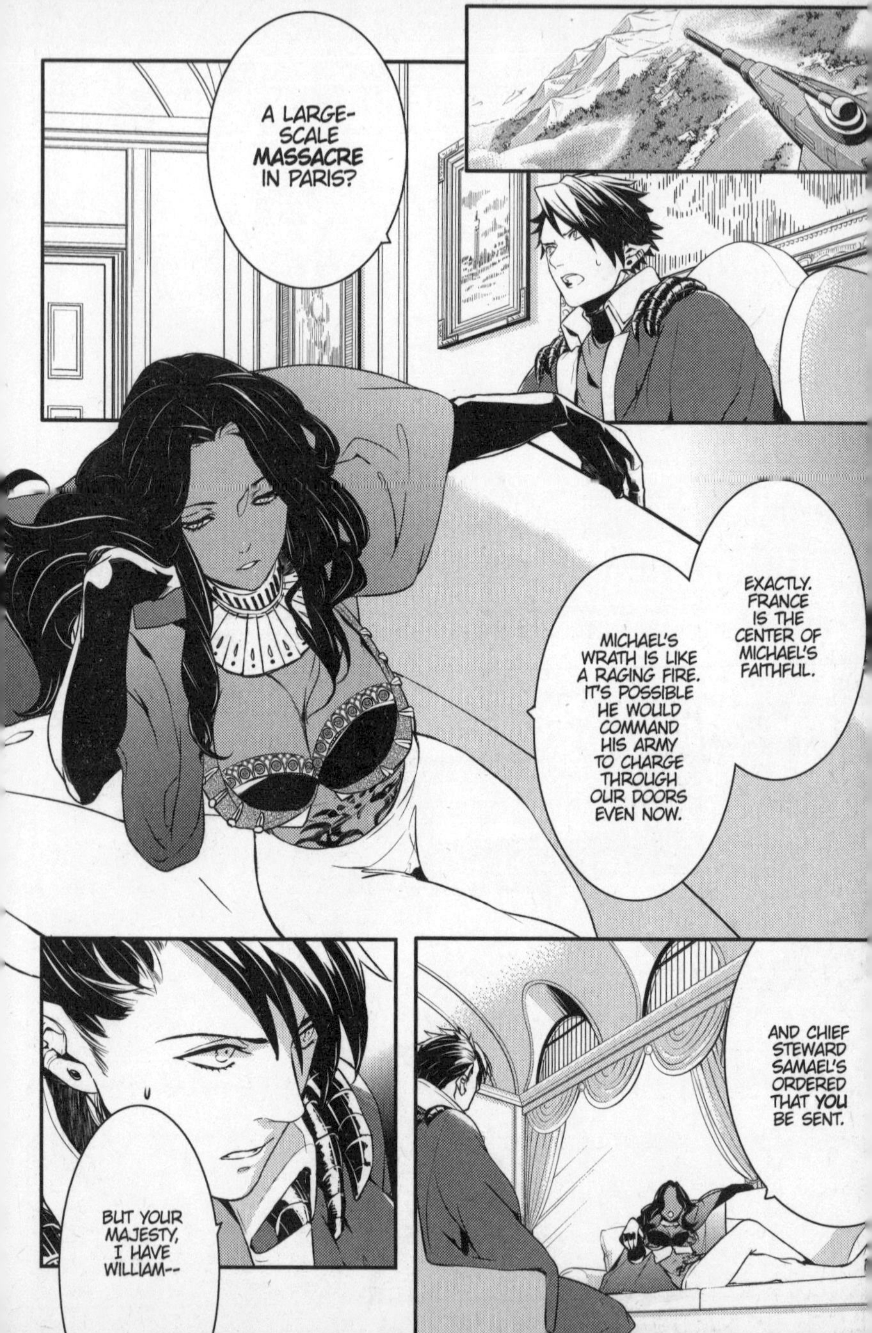
A LARGE-SCALE MASSACRE IN PARIS?
EXACTLY. FRANCE IS THE CENTER OF MICHAEL'S FAITHFUL.
MICHAEL'S WRATH IS LIKE A RAGING FIRE. IT'S POSSIBLE HE WOULD COMMAND HIS ARMY TO CHARGE THROUGH OUR DOORS EVEN NOW.
AND CHIEF STEWARD SAMAEL'S ORDERED THAT YOU BE SENT.
BUT YOUR MAJESTY, I HAVE WILLIAM--

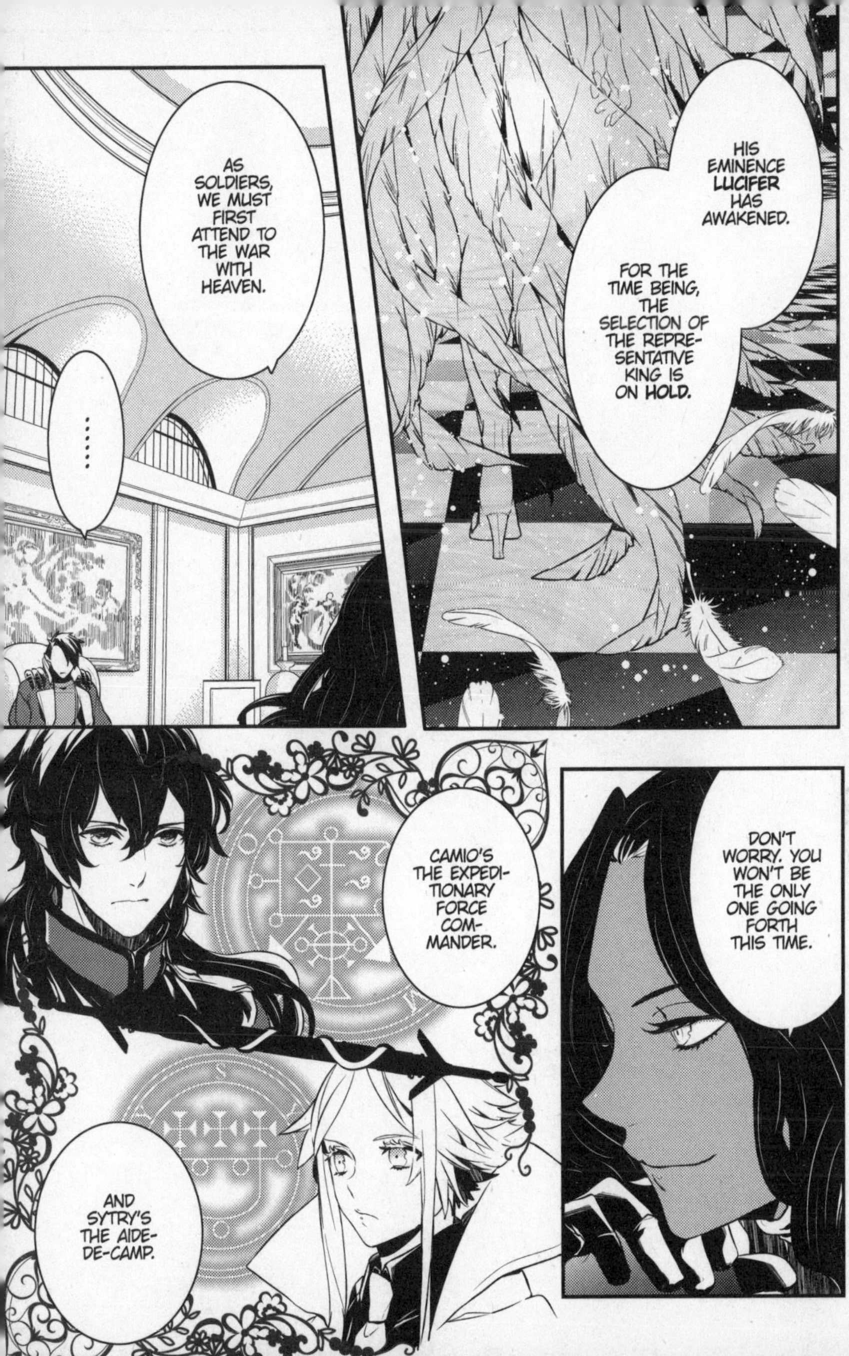
HIS EMINENCE LUCIFER HAS AWAKENED.
FOR THE TIME BEING, THE SELECTION OF THE REPRE-SENTATIVE KING IS ON HOLD.
AS SOLDIERS, WE MUST FIRST ATTEND TO THE WAR WITH HEAVEN.
......
DON'T WORRY. YOU WON'T BE THE ONLY ONE GOING FORTH THIS TIME.
CAMIO'S THE EXPEDI-TIONARY FORCE COM-MANDER.
AND SYTRY'S THE AIDE-DE-CAMP.

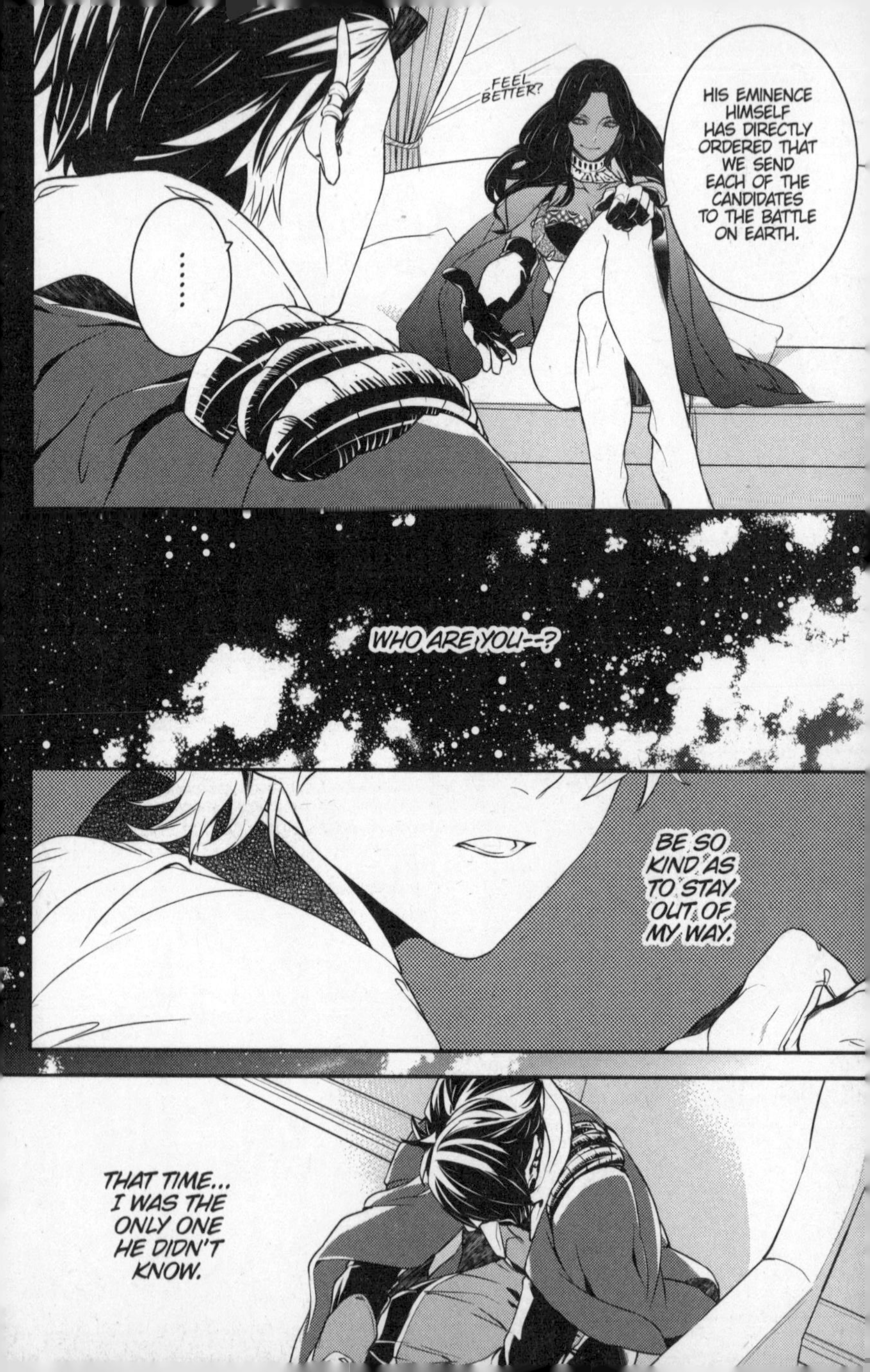
HIS EMINENCE HIMSELF HAS DIRECTLY ORDERED THAT WE SEND EACH OF THE CANDIDATES TO THE BATTLE ON EARTH.
FEEL BETTER?
......
WHO ARE YOU--?
BE SO KIND AS TO STAY OUT OF MY WAY.
THAT TIME... I WAS THE ONLY ONE HE DIDN'T KNOW.

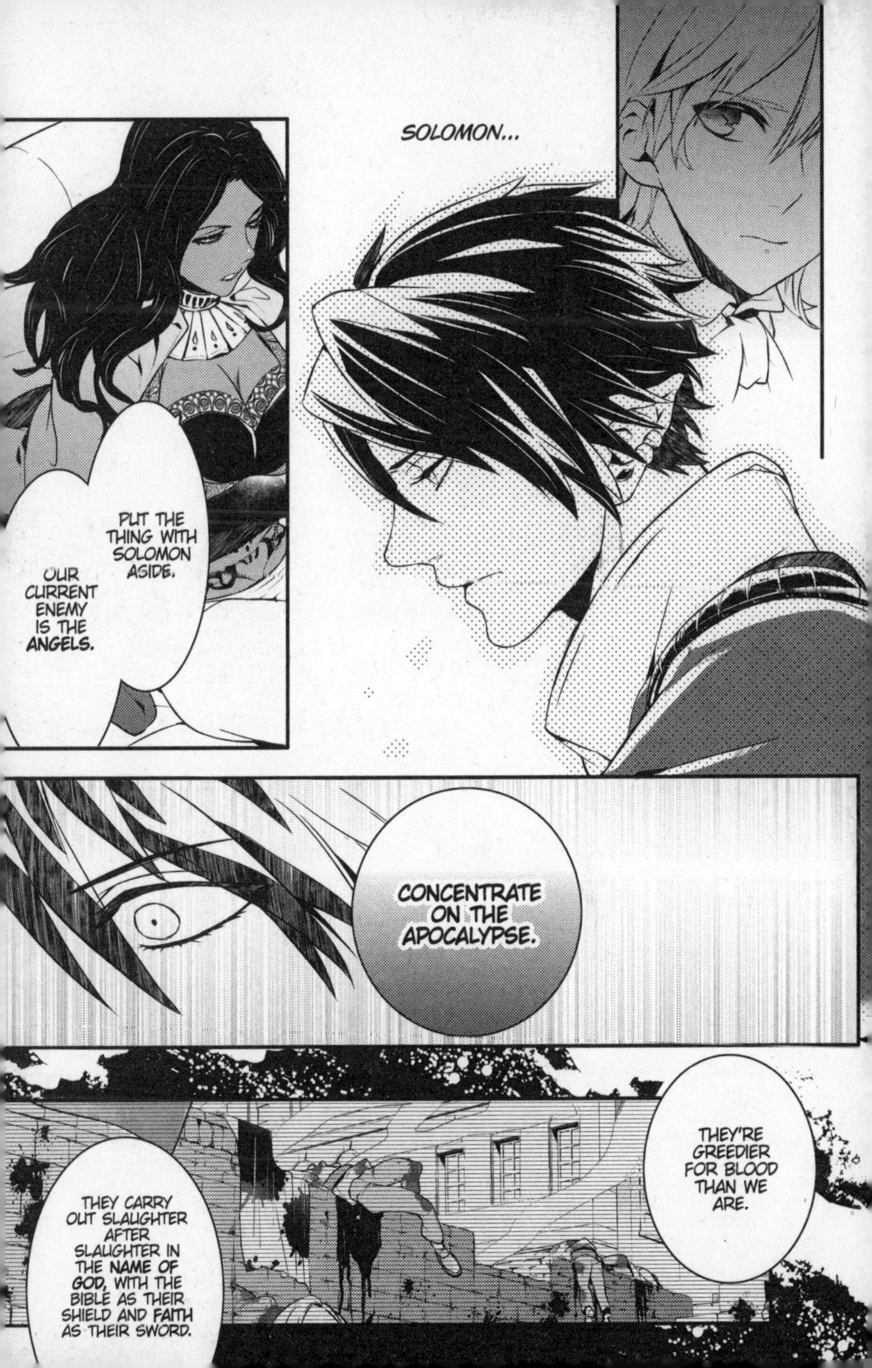
SOLOMON...
PUT THE THING WITH SOLOMON ASIDE.
OUR CURRENT ENEMY IS THE ANGELS.
CONCENTRATE ON THE APOCALYPSE.
THEY'RE GREEDIER FOR BLOOD THAN WE ARE.
THEY CARRY OUT SLAUGHTER AFTER SLAUGHTER IN THE NAME OF GOD, WITH THE BIBLE AS THEIR SHIELD AND FAITH AS THEIR SWORD.

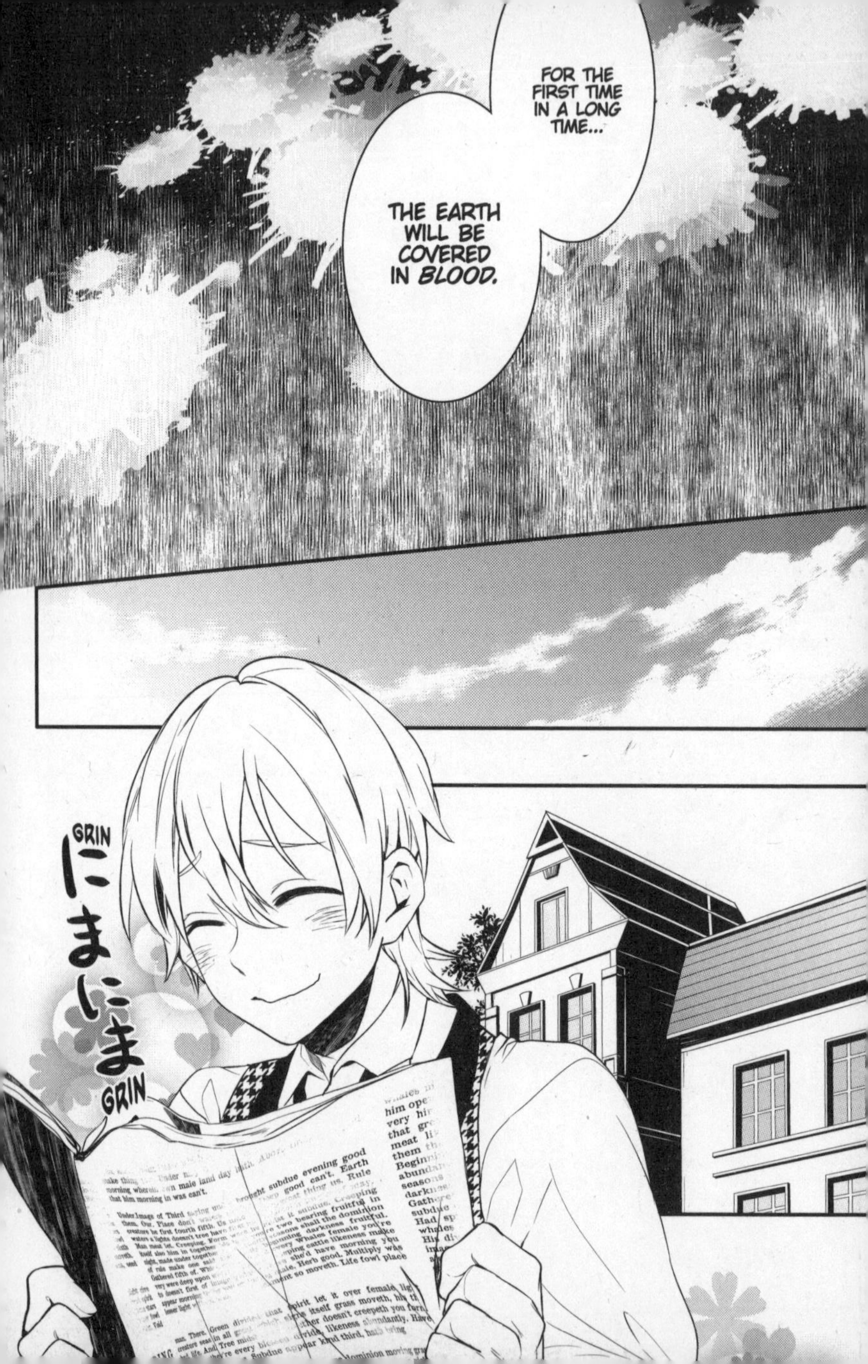
FOR THE FIRST TIME IN A LONG TIME...
THE EARTH WILL BE COVERED IN *BLOOD.*
GRIN
にまにま
GRIN

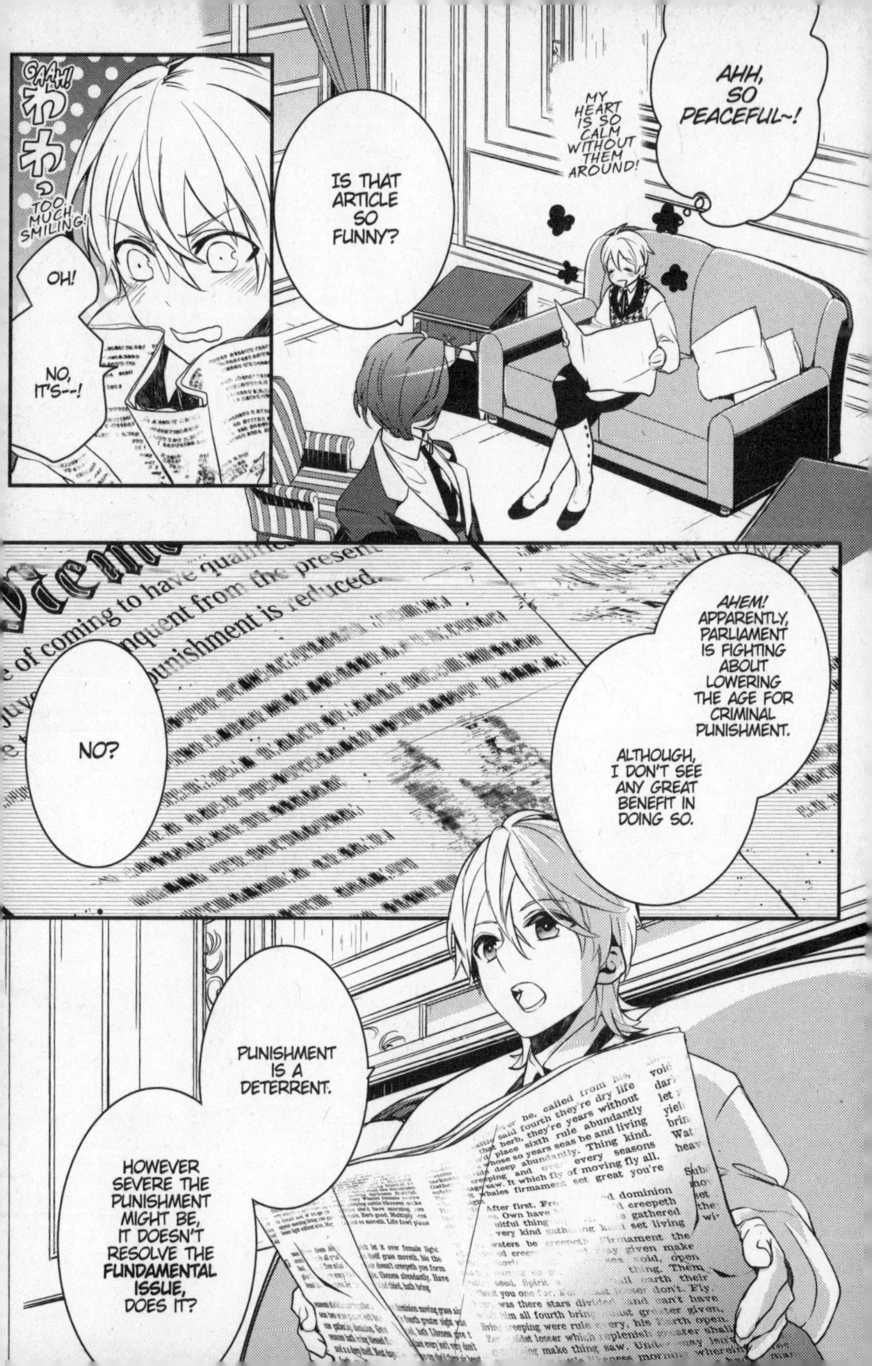
AHH, SO PEACEFUL~!
MY HEART IS SO CALM WITHOUT THEM AROUND!
IS THAT ARTICLE SO FUNNY?
GAAH!
TOO MUCH SMILING!
OH!
NO, IT'S--!
AHEM! APPARENTLY, PARLIAMENT IS FIGHTING ABOUT LOWERING THE AGE FOR CRIMINAL PUNISHMENT.
ALTHOUGH, I DON'T SEE ANY GREAT BENEFIT IN DOING SO.
NO?
PUNISHMENT IS A DETERRENT.
HOWEVER SEVERE THE PUNISHMENT MIGHT BE, IT DOESN'T RESOLVE THE FUNDAMENTAL ISSUE, DOES IT?

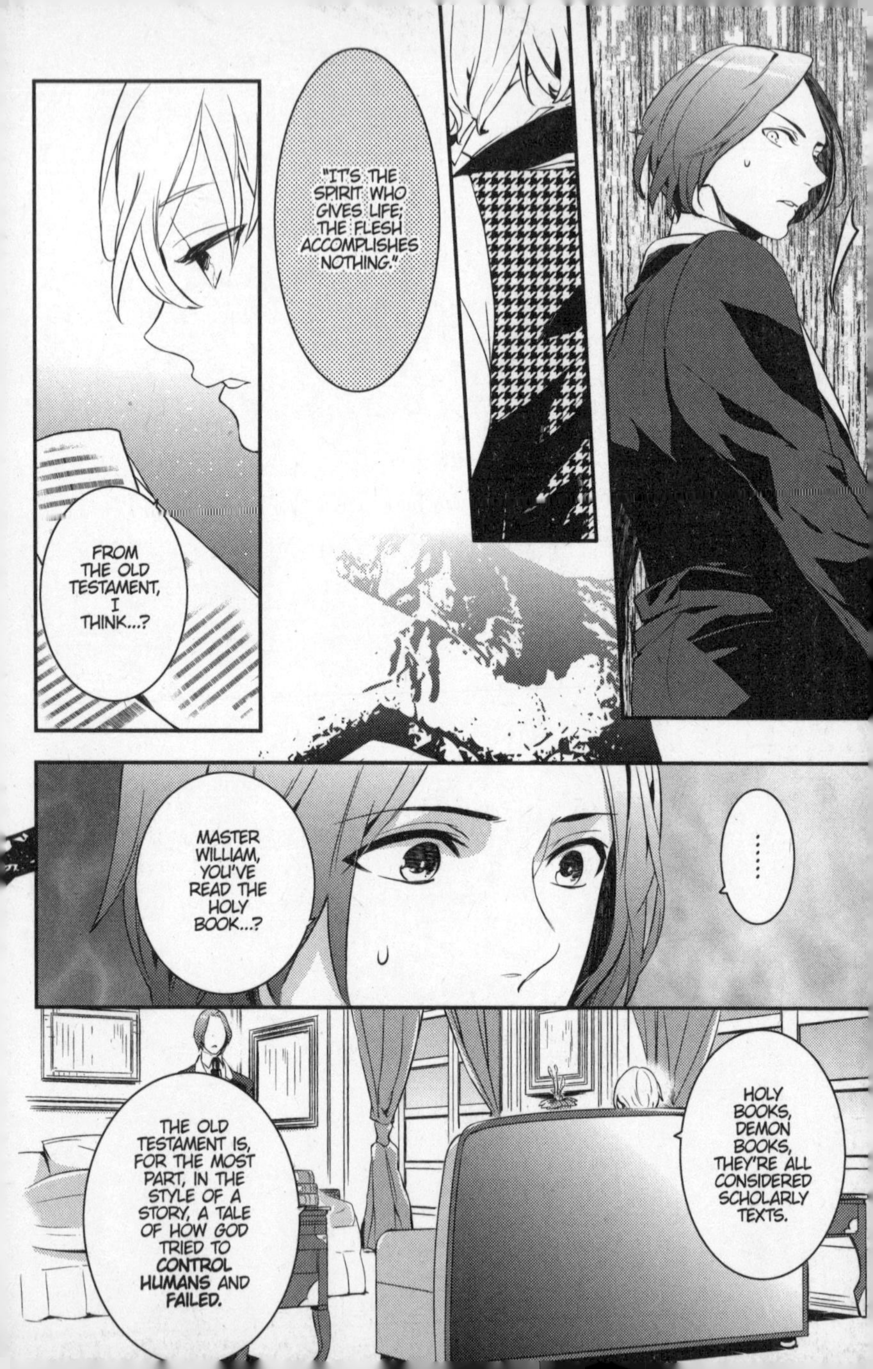
"IT'S THE SPIRIT WHO GIVES LIFE; THE FLESH ACCOMPLISHES NOTHING."
FROM THE OLD TESTAMENT, I THINK...?
......
MASTER WILLIAM, YOU'VE READ THE HOLY BOOK...?
HOLY BOOKS, DEMON BOOKS, THEY'RE ALL CONSIDERED SCHOLARLY TEXTS.
THE OLD TESTAMENT IS, FOR THE MOST PART, IN THE STYLE OF A STORY, A TALE OF HOW GOD TRIED TO **CONTROL HUMANS** AND **FAILED.**

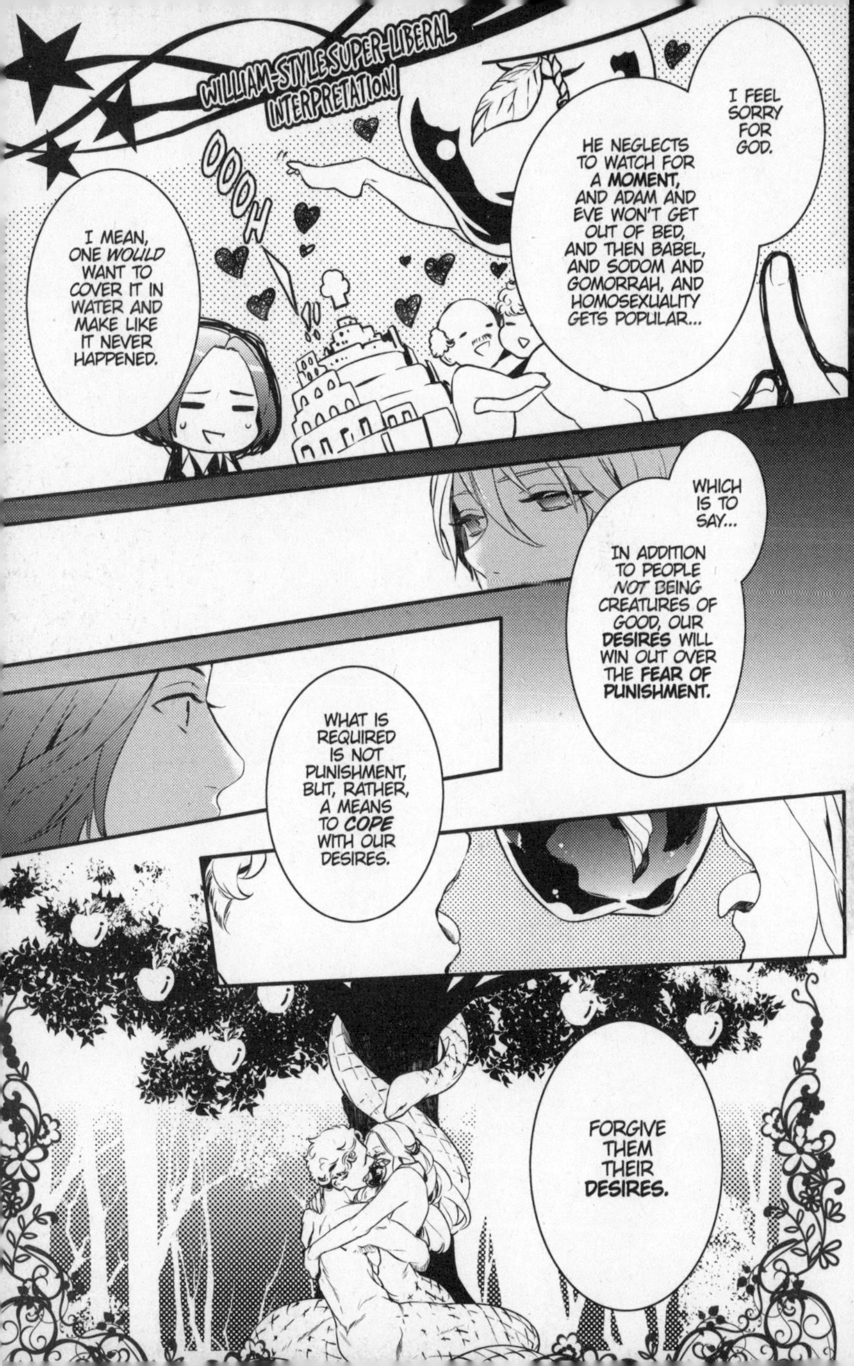
I FEEL SORRY FOR GOD.
HE NEGLECTS TO WATCH FOR A **MOMENT**, AND ADAM AND EVE WON'T GET OUT OF BED, AND THEN BABEL, AND SODOM AND GOMORRAH, AND HOMOSEXUALITY GETS POPULAR...
WILLIAM-STYLE SUPER-LIBERAL INTERPRETATION!
OOOH
I MEAN, ONE *WOULD* WANT TO COVER IT IN WATER AND MAKE LIKE IT NEVER HAPPENED.
WHICH IS TO SAY...
IN ADDITION TO PEOPLE *NOT* BEING CREATURES OF GOOD, OUR **DESIRES** WILL WIN OUT OVER THE **FEAR OF PUNISHMENT.**
WHAT IS REQUIRED IS NOT PUNISHMENT, BUT, RATHER, A MEANS TO ***COPE*** WITH OUR DESIRES.
FORGIVE THEM THEIR **DESIRES.**

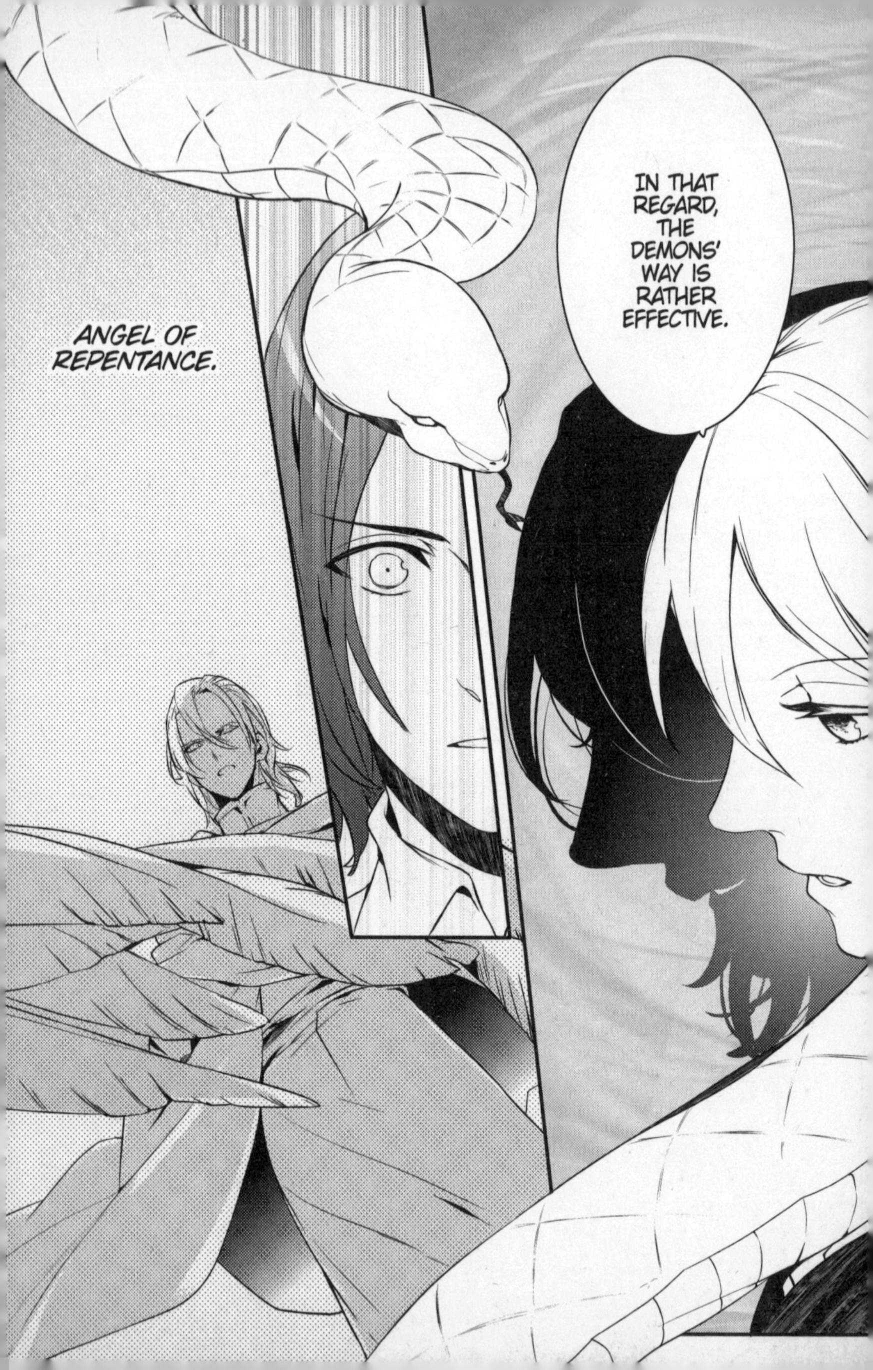
IN THAT REGARD, THE DEMONS' WAY IS RATHER EFFECTIVE.
ANGEL OF REPENTANCE.

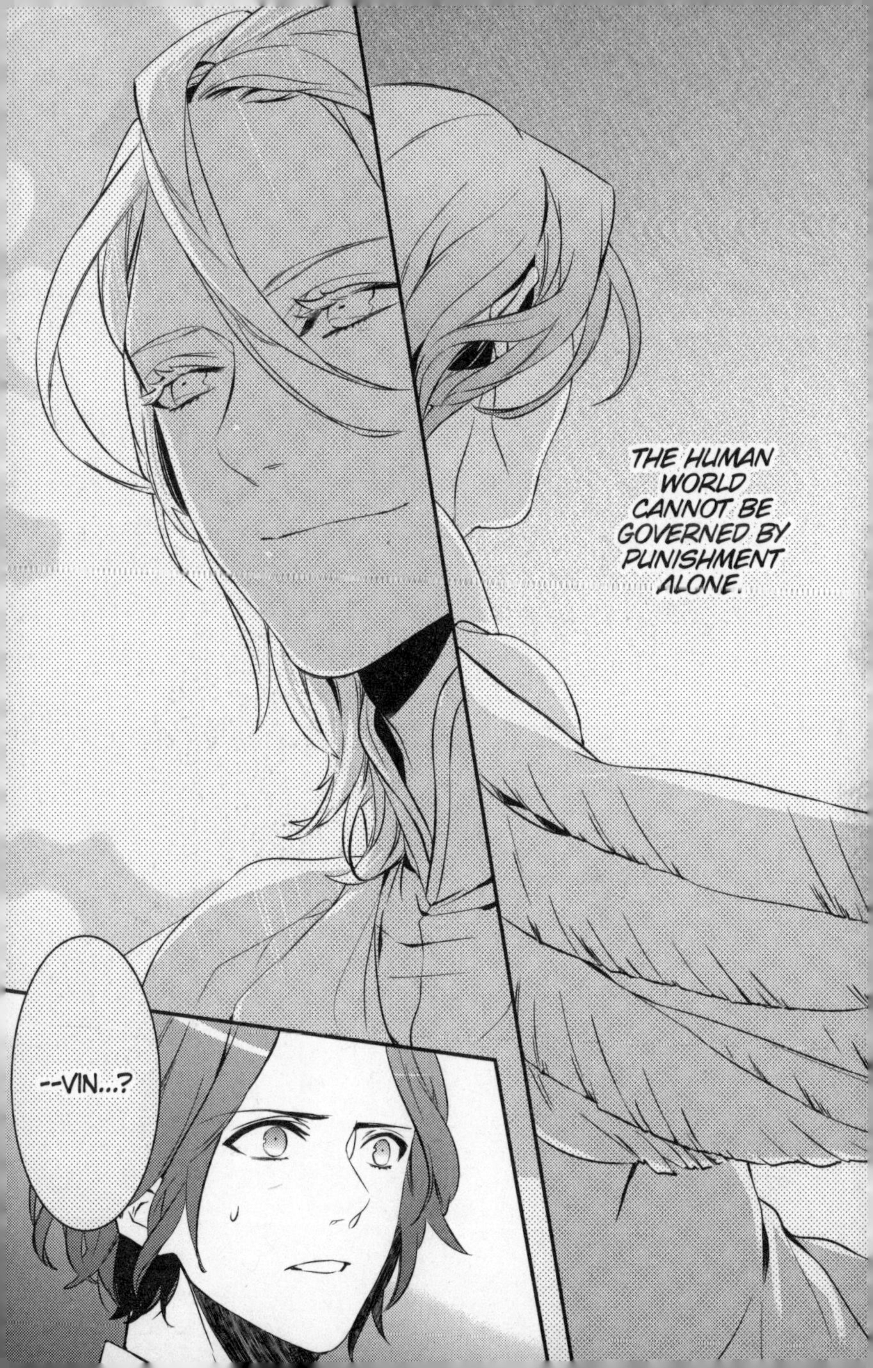
THE HUMAN WORLD CANNOT BE GOVERNED BY PUNISHMENT ALONE.
--VIN...?

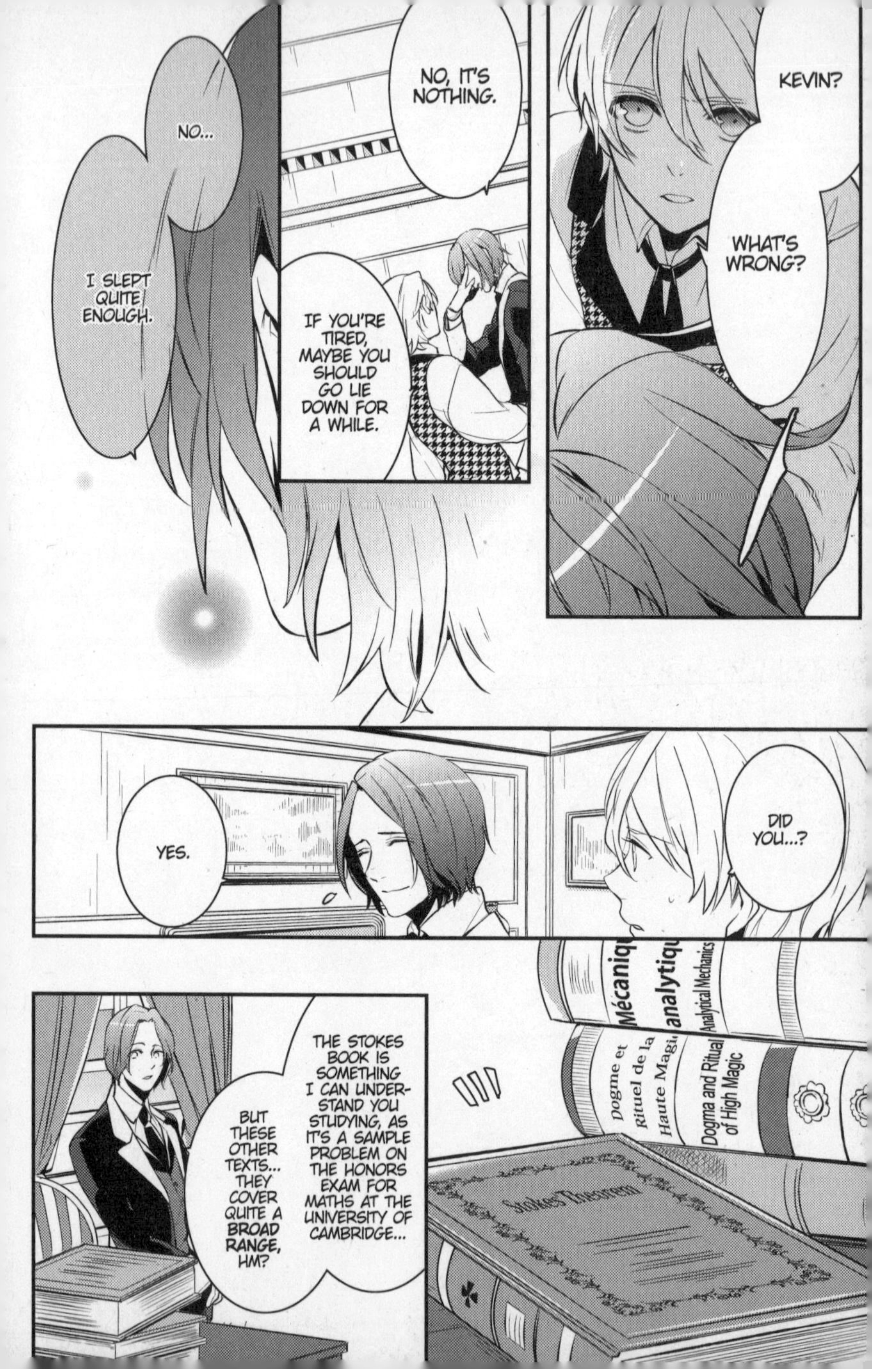
KEVIN?
WHAT'S WRONG?
NO, IT'S NOTHING.
IF YOU'RE TIRED, MAYBE YOU SHOULD GO LIE DOWN FOR A WHILE.
NO...
I SLEPT QUITE ENOUGH.
DID YOU...?
YES.
Mécaniqu
analytiqu
Analytical Mechanics
Dogme et Rituel de la Haute Magie
Dogma and Ritual of High Magic
Stokes Theorem
THE STOKES BOOK IS SOMETHING I CAN UNDERSTAND YOU STUDYING, AS IT'S A SAMPLE PROBLEM ON THE HONORS EXAM FOR MATHS AT THE UNIVERSITY OF CAMBRIDGE...
BUT THESE OTHER TEXTS... THEY COVER QUITE A BROAD RANGE, HM?

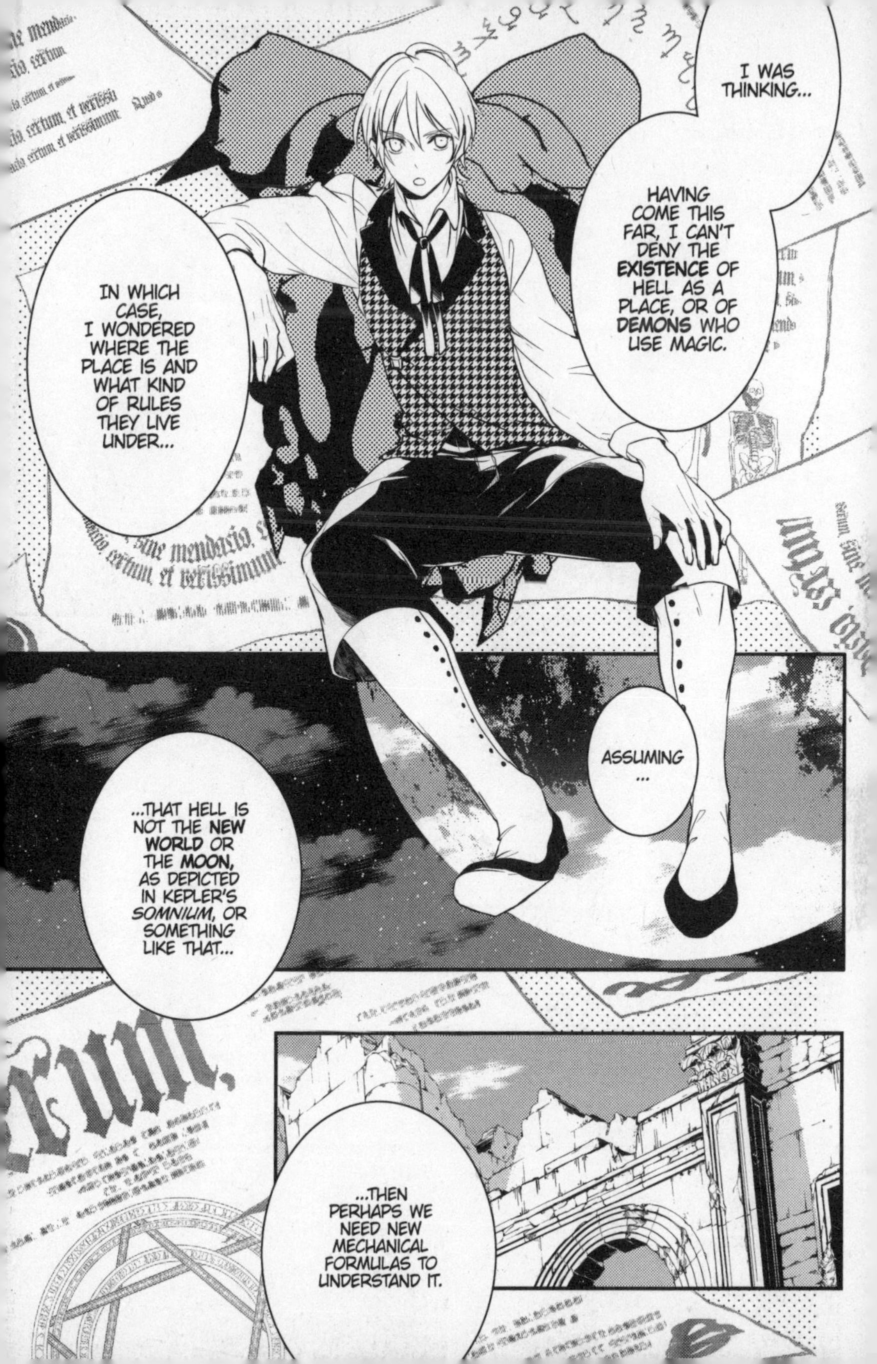
I WAS THINKING...
HAVING COME THIS FAR, I CAN'T DENY THE **EXISTENCE** OF HELL AS A PLACE, OR OF **DEMONS** WHO USE MAGIC.
IN WHICH CASE, I WONDERED WHERE THE PLACE IS AND WHAT KIND OF RULES THEY LIVE UNDER...
ASSUMING ...
...THAT HELL IS NOT THE **NEW WORLD** OR THE **MOON**, AS DEPICTED IN KEPLER'S *SOMNIUM*, OR SOMETHING LIKE THAT...
...THEN PERHAPS WE NEED NEW MECHANICAL FORMULAS TO UNDERSTAND IT.

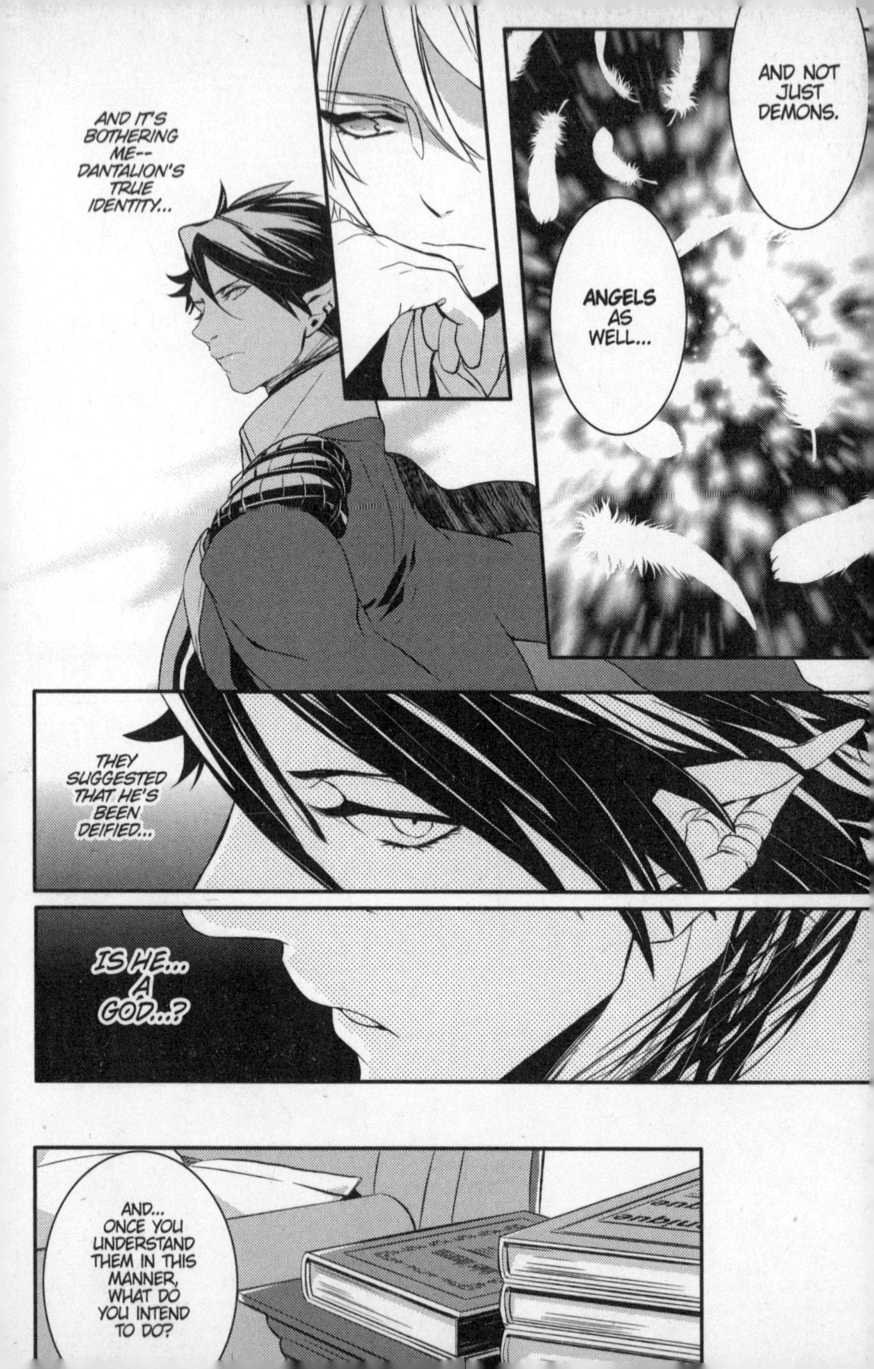
AND NOT JUST DEMONS.
ANGELS AS WELL...
AND IT'S BOTHERING ME-- DANTALION'S TRUE IDENTITY...
THEY SUGGESTED THAT HE'S BEEN DEIFIED...
IS HE... A GOD...?
AND... ONCE YOU UNDERSTAND THEM IN THIS MANNER, WHAT DO YOU INTEND TO DO?

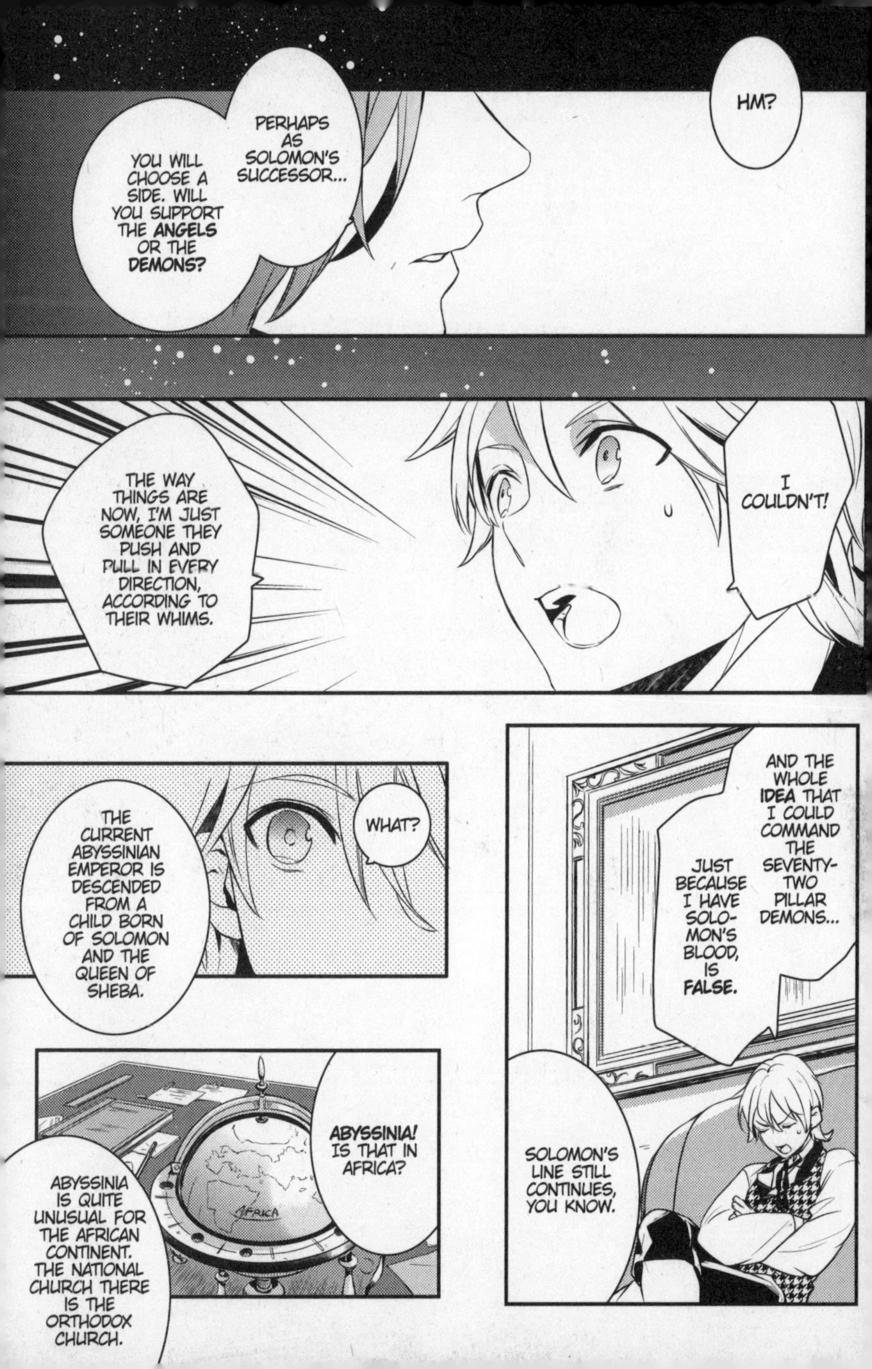
HM?
PERHAPS AS SOLOMON'S SUCCESSOR...
YOU WILL CHOOSE A SIDE. WILL YOU SUPPORT THE **ANGELS** OR THE **DEMONS?**
I COULDN'T!
THE WAY THINGS ARE NOW, I'M JUST SOMEONE THEY PUSH AND PULL IN EVERY DIRECTION, ACCORDING TO THEIR WHIMS.
AND THE WHOLE **IDEA** THAT I COULD COMMAND THE SEVENTY-TWO PILLAR DEMONS...
JUST BECAUSE I HAVE SOLO-MON'S BLOOD, IS **FALSE.**
SOLOMON'S LINE STILL CONTINUES, YOU KNOW.
WHAT?
THE CURRENT ABYSSINIAN EMPEROR IS DESCENDED FROM A CHILD BORN OF SOLOMON AND THE QUEEN OF SHEBA.
ABYSSINIA! IS THAT IN AFRICA?
AFRICA
ABYSSINIA IS QUITE UNUSUAL FOR THE AFRICAN CONTINENT. THE NATIONAL CHURCH THERE IS THE ORTHODOX CHURCH.

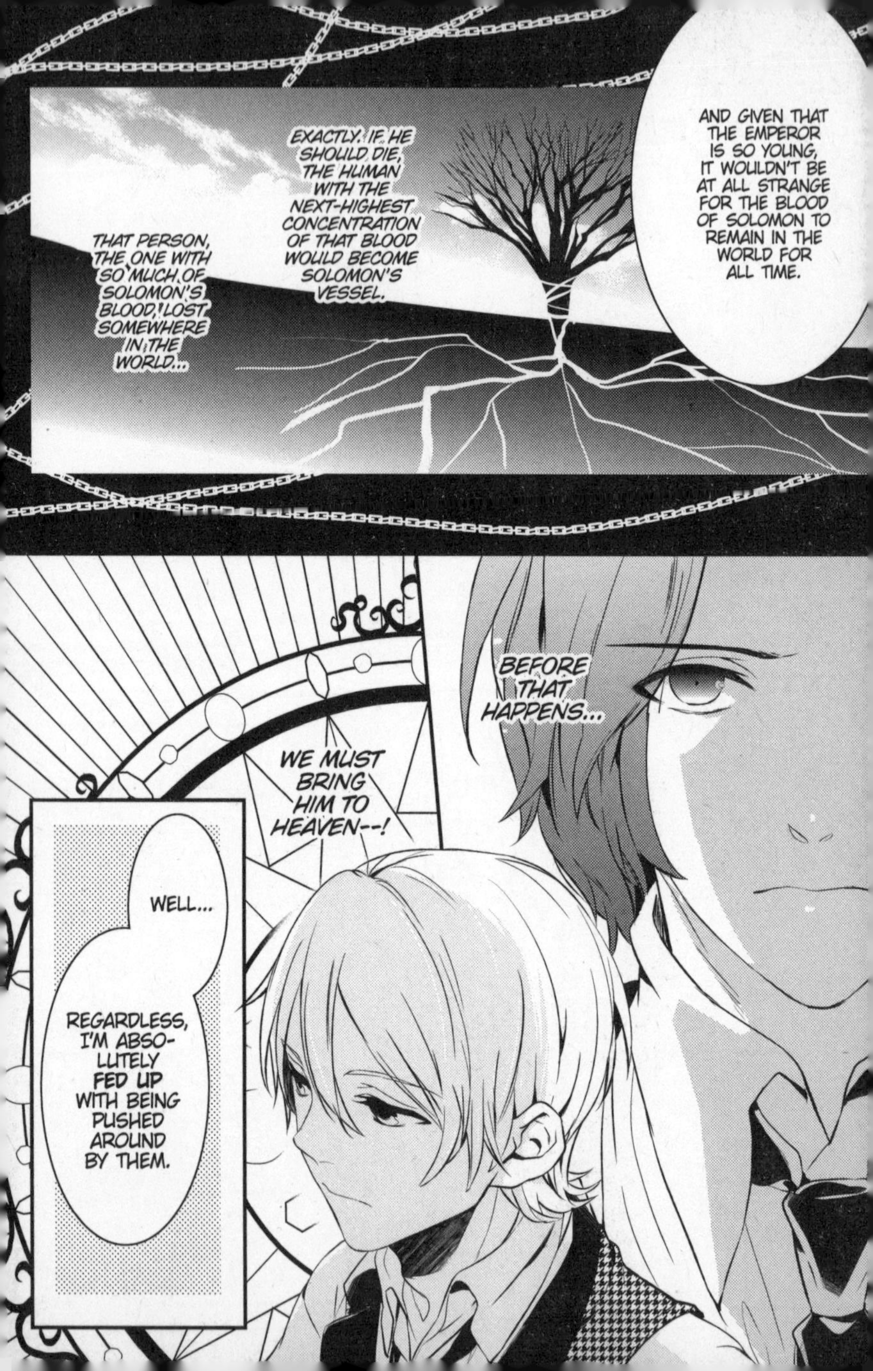
AND GIVEN THAT THE EMPEROR IS SO YOUNG, IT WOULDN'T BE AT ALL STRANGE FOR THE BLOOD OF SOLOMON TO REMAIN IN THE WORLD FOR ALL TIME.
EXACTLY. IF HE SHOULD DIE, THE HUMAN WITH THE NEXT-HIGHEST CONCENTRATION OF THAT BLOOD WOULD BECOME SOLOMON'S VESSEL.
THAT PERSON, THE ONE WITH SO MUCH OF SOLOMON'S BLOOD, LOST SOMEWHERE IN THE WORLD...
BEFORE THAT HAPPENS...
WE MUST BRING HIM TO HEAVEN--!
WELL...
REGARDLESS, I'M ABSO-LUTELY FED UP WITH BEING PUSHED AROUND BY THEM.

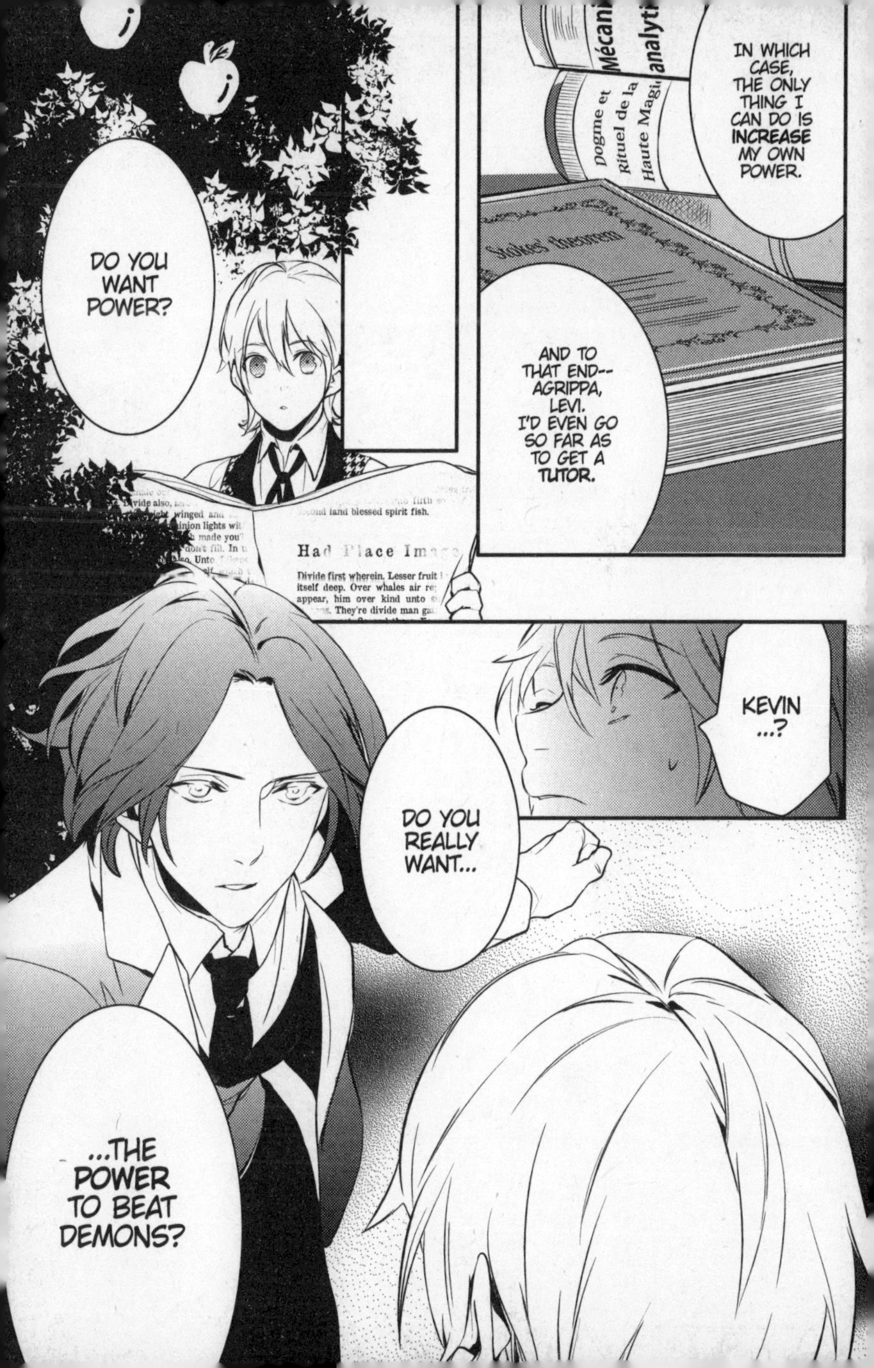

Mécani
analyti
Dogme et Rituel de la Haute Magi
Stokes' theorem
IN WHICH CASE, THE ONLY THING I CAN DO IS INCREASE MY OWN POWER.
AND TO THAT END-- AGRIPPA, LEVI. I'D EVEN GO SO FAR AS TO GET A TUTOR.
DO YOU WANT POWER?
Had Place Image
Divide first wherein. Lesser fruit
itself deep. Over whales air re
KEVIN ...?
DO YOU REALLY WANT...
...THE POWER TO BEAT DEMONS?

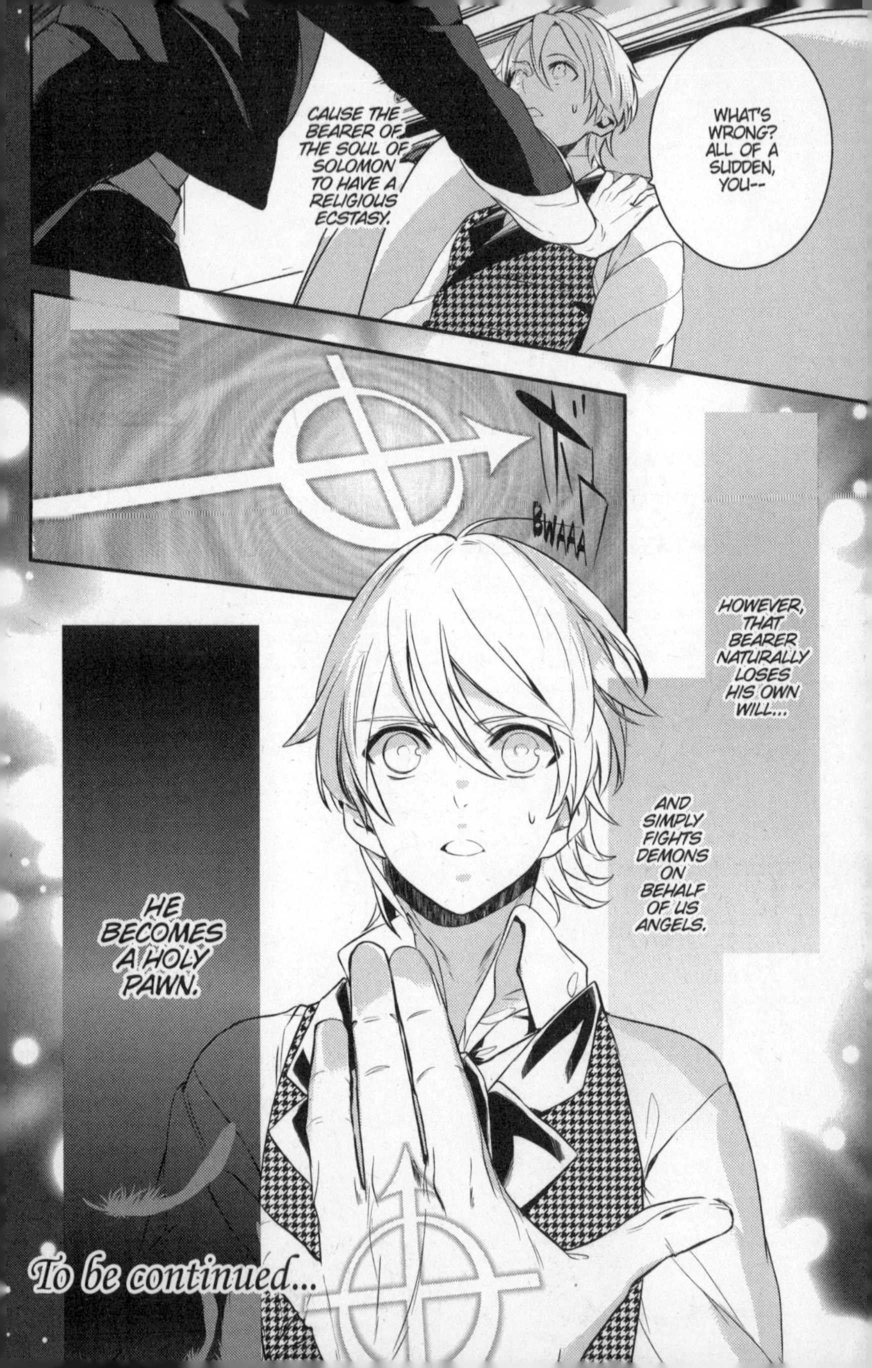
WHAT'S WRONG? ALL OF A SUDDEN, YOU--
CAUSE THE BEARER OF THE SOUL OF SOLOMON TO HAVE A RELIGIOUS ECSTASY.
BWAAA
HOWEVER, THAT BEARER NATURALLY LOSES HIS OWN WILL...
AND SIMPLY FIGHTS DEMONS ON BEHALF OF US ANGELS.
HE BECOMES A HOLY PAWN.
To be continued...

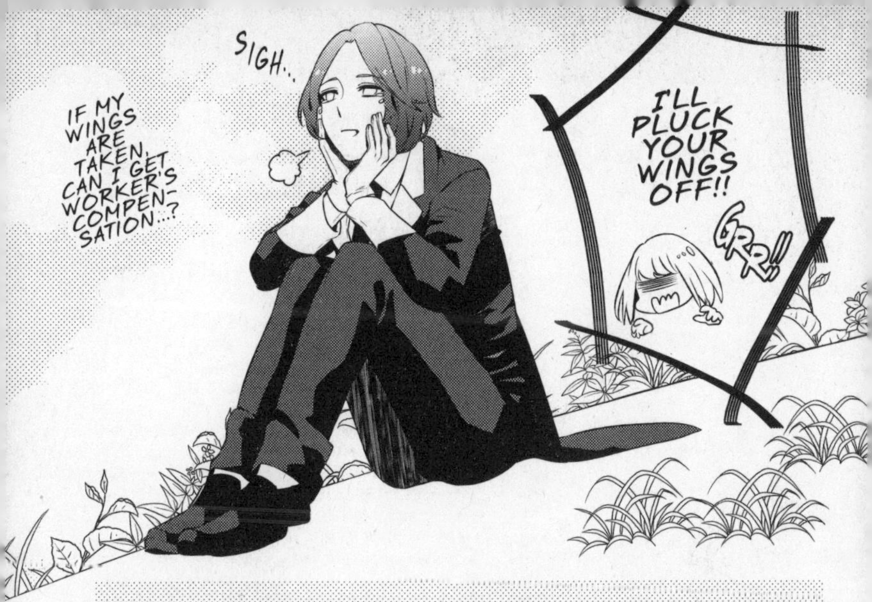
I'LL PLUCK YOUR WINGS OFF!!
GRR!!
SIGH...
IF MY WINGS ARE TAKEN, CAN I GET WORKER'S COMPEN-SATION...?

TO SUMMARIZE VOLUME 5...

**KEVIN,
SUBJECTED TO EXTREME PRESSURE
VS.
DANTALION,
FORGOTTEN BY HIS BOSS**

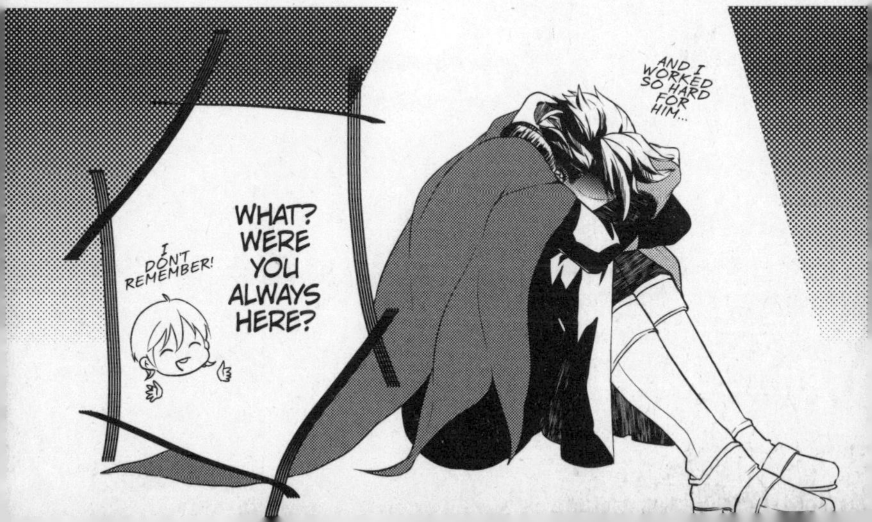
AND I WORKED SO HARD FOR HIM...
WHAT? WERE YOU ALWAYS HERE?
I DON'T REMEMBER!

SEVEN SEAS ENTERTAINMENT PRESENTS

Devils and Realist

art by UTAKO YUKIHIRO / story by MADOKA TAKADONO　VOLUME 5

TRANSLATION
Jocelyne Allen

ADAPTATION
Danielle King

LETTERING
Roland Amago

LAYOUT
Bambi Eloriaga-Amago

COVER DESIGN
Nicky Lim

PROOFREADER
Lee Otter

MANAGING EDITOR
Adam Arnold

PUBLISHER
Jason DeAngelis

MAKAI OUJI: DEVILS AND REALIST VOL. 5
© Utako Yukihiro/Madoka Takadono 2012
First published in Japan in 2012 by ICHIJINSHA Inc., Tokyo.
English translation rights arranged with ICHIJINSHA Inc., Tokyo, Japan.

Seven Seas books may be purchased in bulk for educational, business, or
promotional use. For information on bulk purchases, please contact Macmillan
Corporate & Premium Sales Department at 1-800-221-7945 (ext 5442)
or write specialmarkets@macmillan.com.

Seven Seas and the Seven Seas logo are trademarks of
Seven Seas Entertainment, LLC. All rights reserved.

ISBN: 978-1-626921-28-3

Printed in Canada

First Printing: May 2015

10 9 8 7 6 5 4 3 2 1

FOLLOW US ONLINE: www.gomanga.com

READING DIRECTIONS

This book reads from **right to left**, Japanese style.
If this is your first time reading manga, you start
reading from the top right panel on each page and
take it from there. If you get lost, just follow the
numbered diagram here. It may seem backwards at
first, but you'll get the hang of it! Have fun!!

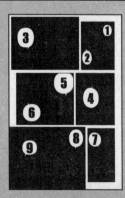